THE CONFLICT OF RELIGIONS IN
THE EARLY ROMAN EMPIRE

THE
CONFLICT OF RELIGIONS
IN THE
EARLY ROMAN EMPIRE

BY

T. R. GLOVER

COOPER SQUARE PUBLISHERS, INC.
NEW YORK
1975

Originally Published 1909
Published 1975 by Cooper Square Publishers, Inc.
59 Fourth Avenue, New York, New York 10003

Printed in the United States of America
by Sentry Press, Inc., New York, N. Y. 10013

Library of Congress Cataloging in Publication Data

Glover, Terrot Reaveley, 1869-1943.
   The conflict of religions in the early Roman Empire.
   Reprint of the 1932 ed. published by Methuen,
London.
    Includes index.
    1. Church history—Primitive and early church,
ca. 30-600. 2. Christianity and other religions.
3. Rome—Religion. I. Title.
BR170.G6   1975   200'.937   74-20182
ISBN 0-8154-0510-3

PREFACE

A LARGE part of this book formed the course of Dale Lectures delivered in Mansfield College, Oxford, in the Spring of 1907. For the lecture-room the chapters had to be considerably abridged; they are now restored to their full length, while revision and addition have further changed their character. They are published in accordance with the terms of the Dale foundation.

To see the Founder of the Christian movement and some of his followers as they appeared among their contemporaries; to represent Christian and pagan with equal goodwill and equal honesty, and in one perspective; to recapture something of the colour and movement of life, using imagination to interpret the data, and controlling it by them; to follow the conflict of ideals, not in the abstract, but as they show themselves in character and personality; and in this way to discover where lay the living force that changed the thoughts and lives of men, and what it was; these have been the aims of the writer,—impossible, but worth attempting. So far as they have been achieved, the book is relevant to the reader.

The work of others has made the task lighter. German scholars, such as Bousset, von Dobschütz, Harnack, Pfleiderer and Wernle; Professor F. C. Burkitt and others nearer home who have written of the beginnings of Christianity; Boissier, Martha and Professor Samuel Dill; Edward Caird, Lecky, and Zeller; with the authors of monographs, Croiset, de Faye, Gréard, Koziol, Oakesmith, Volkmann; these and others have been laid under contribution. In another way Dr Wilhelm Herrmann, of Marburg, and Thomas Carlyle have helped the

v

book. The references to ancient authorities are mostly of the writer's own gathering, and they have been verified.

Lastly, there are friends to thank, at Cambridge and at Woodbrooke, for the services that only friends can render—suggestion, criticism, approval, correction, and all the other kindly forms of encouragement and enlightenment.

ST JOHN'S COLLEGE,
CAMBRIDGE,
February 1909.

CONTENTS

THE CONFLICT OF RELIGIONS
IN THE EARLY ROMAN EMPIRE

CHAPTER I

ROMAN RELIGION

ON the Ides of March in the year 44 B.C. Julius Cæsar lay dead at the foot of Pompey's statue. His body had twenty three wounds. So far the conspirators had done their work thoroughly, and no farther. They had made no preparation for the government of the Roman world. They had not realized that they were removing the great organizing intelligence which stood between the world and chaos, and back into chaos the world swiftly rolled. They had hated personal government; they were to learn that the only alternative was no government at all. "Be your own Senate yourself"[1] wrote Cicero to Plancus in despair. There was war, there were faction fights, massacres, confiscations, conscriptions. The enemies of Rome came over her borders, and brigandage flourished within them.

At the end of his first *Georgic* Virgil prays for the triumph of the one hope which the world saw—for the preservation and the rule of the young Cæsar, and he sums up in a few lines the horror from which mankind seeks to be delivered. "Right and wrong are confounded; so many wars the world over, so many forms of wrong; no worthy honour is left to the plough; the husbandmen are marched away and the fields grow dirty; the hook has its curve straightened into the sword-blade. In the East, Euphrates is stirring up war, in the West, Germany: nay, close-neighbouring cities break their mutual league and draw the sword, and the war-god's unnatural fury rages over the whole world; even as when in the Circus the chariots burst

---

[1] Cic. *ad fam.* x, 16. 2, *Ipse tibi sis senatus.*

from their floodgates, they dash into the course, and pulling desperately at the reins the driver lets the horses drive him, and the car is deaf to the curb." [1]

Virgil's hope that Octavian might be spared to give peace to the world was realized. The foreign enemies were driven over their frontiers and thoroughly cowed; brigandage was crushed, and finally, with the fall of Antony and Cleopatra, the government of the whole world was once more, after thirteen years of suffering, disorder and death, safely gathered into the hands of one man. There was peace at last and Rome had leisure to think out the experience through which she had passed.

The thirteen years between the murder of Cæsar and the battle of Actium were only a part of that experience; for a century there had been continuous disintegration in the State. The empire had been increased, but the imperial people had declined. There had been civil war in Rome over and over again—murder employed as a common resource of politics, reckless disregard of the sacredness of life and property, and thorough carelessness of the State. The impression that England made upon Wordsworth in 1802 was precisely that left upon the mind of the serious Roman when he reflected upon his country. All was "rapine, avarice, expense."

> Plain living and high thinking are no more:
> The homely beauty of the good old cause
> Is gone; our peace, our fearful innocence,
> And pure religion breathing household laws.

Such complaints, real or conventional, are familiar to the readers of the literature of the last century before Christ. Everyone felt that a profound change had come over Rome. Attempts had been made in various ways to remedy this change; laws had been passed; citizens had been banished and murdered; armies had been called in to restore ancient principles; and all had resulted in failure. Finally a gleam of restoration was seen when Julius began to set things in order, when he "corrected the year by the Sun" and gave promise of as true and deep-going a correction of everything else. His murder put an end to all this at the time, and it took thirteen years to regain the lost opportunity—and the years were not

[1] *Georgic* i, 505-514 (Conington's translation, with alterations).

altogether loss for they proved conclusively that there was now
no alternative to the rule of the " Prince."

Accordingly the Prince set himself to discover what was to
be done to heal the hurt of his people, and to heal it thoroughly.
What was the real disease? was the question that men asked ;
where was the root of all the evil? why was it that in old days
men were honest, governed themselves firmly, knew how to
obey, and served the State? A famous line of Ennius, written
two centuries before, said that the Roman Commonwealth stood
on ancient character, and on men.—

Moribus antiquis stat res Romana virisque.

Both these bases of the national life seemed to be lost—
were they beyond recall? could they be restored? What was
it that had made the "ancient character"? What was the
ultimate difference between the old Roman and the Roman
of the days of Antony and Octavian? Ovid congratulated
himself on the perfect congruity of the age and his personal
character—

hæc ætas moribus apta meis—

and he was quite right. And precisely in the measure that
Ovid was right in finding the age and his character in agreement, the age and national character were demonstrably
degenerate. It was the great question before the nation, its
statesmen, patriots and poets, to find why two hundred years
had wrought such a change.

It was not long before an answer was suggested. A reason
was found, which had a history of its own. The decline had
been foreseen. We are fortunately in possession of a forecast
by a Greek thinker of the second century B.C., who knew Rome
well—Polybius, the intimate of the younger Scipio. In the
course of his great summary of the Rome he knew, when he is
explaining her actual and future greatness to the Greek world,
he says:—" The most important difference for the better, which
the Roman Commonwealth appears to me to display, is in their
religious beliefs, for I conceive that what in other nations is
looked upon as a reproach, I mean a scrupulous fear of the
gods, is the very thing which keeps the Roman Commonwealth together; (συνέχειν τὰ 'Ρωμαίων πράγματα). To such an
extraordinary height is this carried among them (ἐκτετραγῴδηται

καὶ παρεισῆκται) both in private and public business, that nothing could exceed it. Many people might think this unaccountable, but in my opinion their object is to use it as a check upon the common people. If it were possible to form a state wholly of philosophers, such a custom would perhaps be unnecessary. But seeing that every multitude is fickle and full of lawless desires, unreasoning anger and violent passion, the only resource is to keep them in check by mysterious terrors and scenic effects of this sort (τοῖς ἀδήλοις φόβοις καὶ τῇ τοιαύτῃ τραγῳδίᾳ). Wherefore, to my mind, the ancients were not acting without purpose or at random, when they brought in among the vulgar those opinions about the gods and the belief in the punishments in Hades : much rather do I think that men nowadays are acting rashly and foolishly in rejecting them. This is the reason why, apart from anything else, Greek statesmen, if entrusted with a single talent, though protected by ten checking-clerks, as many seals and twice as many witnesses, yet cannot be induced to keep faith ; whereas among the Romans, in their magistracies and embassies, men have the handling of a great amount of money, and yet from pure respect to their oath keep their faith intact."[1] Later on Polybius limits his assertion of Roman honesty to "the majority"—the habits and principles of Rome were beginning to be contaminated.[2]

This view of the value of religion is an old one among the Greeks. Critias, the friend of Socrates, embodied it in verses, which are preserved for us by Sextus Empiricus. In summary he holds that there was a time when men's life knew no order, but at last laws were ordained to punish ; and the laws kept men from open misdeeds, " but they did many things in secret ; and then, I think, some shrewd and wise man invented a terror for the evil in case secretly they should do or say or think aught. So he introduced the divine, alleging that there is a divinity (δαίμων), blest with eternal life, who with his mind sees and hears, thinks, and marks these things, and bears a divine nature, who will hear all that is said among men and can see all that is done, and though in silence thou plan some evil, yet this shall not escape the gods." This was a most pleasant

---

[1] Polybius, vi, 56, Shuckburgh's Translation.
[2] Polybius, xviii, 35.

lesson which he introduced, "with a false reason covering truth"; and he said the gods abode in that region whence thunder and lightning and rain come, and so "he quenched lawlessness with laws." [1]

This was a shallow judgement upon religion. That "it utterly abolished religion altogether" was the criticism of Cicero's Academic.[2] But most of the contemporary views of the origin of religion were shallow. Euhemerism with its deified men, and inspiration with its distraught votaries were perhaps nobler, a little nobler, but in reality there was little respect for religion among the philosophic. But the practical people of the day accepted the view of Critias as wise enough. "The myths that are told of affairs in Hades, though pure invention at bottom, contribute to make men pious and up-right," wrote the Sicilian Diodorus at this very time.[3] Varro [4] divided religion into three varieties, mythical, physical (on which the less said in public, he owned, the better) and "civil," and he pronounced the last the best adapted for national purposes, as it consisted in knowing what gods state and citizen should worship and with what rites. "It is the in-terest," he said, "of states to be deceived in religion."

So the great question narrowed itself to this:—Was it possible for another shrewd and wise man to do again for Rome what the original inventor of religion had done for man-kind? once more to establish effective gods to do the work of police? Augustus endeavoured to show that it was still possible.

On the famous monument of Ancyra, which preserves for us the Emperor's official autobiography, he enumerates the temples he built—temples in honour of Apollo, of Julius, of Quirinus, of Juppiter Feretrius, of Jove the Thunderer, of Minerva, of the Queen Juno, of Juppiter Liberalis, of the Lares, of the Penates, of Youth, of the Great Mother, and the shrine known as the Lupercal; he tells how he dedicated vast sums from his spoils, how he restored to the temples of Asia the ornaments of which they had been robbed, and how he be-

---

[1] Sextus Empiricus, *Adv. mathematicos*, ix, 54.   [2] Cicero, *N.D.* i, 42, 118.
[3] Diodorus Siculus, i, 2.
[4] Quoted by Augustine, *C.D.* iv, 27; vi, 5; also referred to by Tertullian, *ad Natt.* ii, 1.

came Pontifex Maximus, after patiently waiting for Lepidus
to vacate the office by a natural death. His biographer
Suetonius tells of his care for the Sibylline books, of his in-
creasing the numbers, dignities and allowances of the priests,
and his especial regard for the Vestal Virgins, of his restoration of ancient ceremonies, of his celebration of festivals and
holy days, and of his discrimination among foreign religions,
his regard for the Athenian mysteries and his contempt for
Egyptian Apis.[1] His private feelings and instincts had a tinge
of superstition. He used a sealskin as a protection against
thunder; he carefully studied his dreams, was "much moved
by portents," and "observed days." [2]

The most lasting monument (*ære perennius*) of the restoration of religion by Augustus consists of the odes which Horace
wrote to forward the plans of the Emperor. They were very
different men, but it is not unreasonable to hold that Horace
felt no less than Augustus that there was something wrong
with the state. His personal attitude to religion was his own
affair, and to it we shall have to return, but in grave and
dignified odes, which he gave to the world, he lent himself to
the cause of reformation. He deplored the reckless luxury of
the day with much appearance of earnestness, and, though in
his published collections, these poems of lament are interleaved
with others whose burden is *sparge rosas*, he was serious in
some degree; for his own taste, at least when he came within
sight of middle life, was all for moderation. He spoke gravely
of the effect upon the race of its disregard of all the virtues
necessary for the continuance of a society. Like other poets
of the day, he found Utopias in distant ages and remote lands.
His idealized picture of the blessedness of savage life is not
unlike Rousseau's, and in both cases the inspiration was the
same—discontent with an environment complicated, extravagant and corrupt.

> Better with nomad Scythians roam,
> Whose travelling cart is all their home,
> Or where the ruder Getæ spread
> From steppes unmeasured raise their bread.

[1] Suetonius, *Augustus*, 31, 75, 93 ; Warde Fowler, *Roman Festivals*, p. 344.
[2] Suet. *Aug.* 90, 92.

There with a single year content
The tiller shifts his tenement;
Another, when that labour ends,
To the self-same condition bends.

The simple step-dame there will bless
With care the children motherless:
No wife by wealth command procures,
None heeds the sleek adulterer's lures.[1]

Other poets also imagined Golden Ages of quiet ease and idleness, but the conclusion which Horace drew was more robust. He appealed to the Emperor for laws, and effective laws, to correct the "unreined license" of the day, and though his poem declines into declamation of a very idle kind about "useless gold," as his poems are apt to decline on the first hint of rhetoric, the practical suggestion was not rhetorical— it was perhaps the purpose of the piece. In another famous poem, the last of a sequence of six, all dedicated to the higher life of Rome and all reaching an elevation not often attained by his odes, he points more clearly to the decline of religion as the cause of Rome's misfortunes.[2]

The idea that Rome's Empire was the outcome of her piety was not first struck out by Horace. Cicero uses it in one of his public speeches with effect and puts it into the mouth of his Stoic in the work on the Nature of the Gods.[3] Later on, one after another of the Latin Apologists for Christianity, from Tertullian[4] to Prudentius, has to combat the same idea. It was evidently popular, and the appeal to the ruined shrine and the neglected image touched—or was supposed to touch—the popular imagination.

Mankind are apt to look twice at the piety of a ruler, and the old question of Satan comes easily, "Doth Job serve God for naught?" Why does an Emperor wish to be called "the eldest son of the church?" We may be fairly sure in the case of Augustus that, if popular sentiment had been strongly against

---

[1] Horace, *Odes*, iii, 24, 9-20, Gladstone's version.

[2] Horace, *Odes*, iii, 6, *Delicta maiorum*.

[3] *De Haruspicum Responsis*, 9, 19; *N.D.* ii, 3, 8.

[4] E.g. *Apol.* 25, with a serious criticism of the contrast between Roman character before and after the conquest of the world,—before and after the invasion of Rome by the images and idols of Etruscans and Greeks.

the restoration of religion, he would have said less about it. We have to go behind the Emperor and Horace to discover how the matter really stood between religion and the Roman people.

We may first of all remark that, just as the French Revolution was in some sense the parent of the Romantic movement, the disintegration of the old Roman life was accompanied by the rise of antiquarianism. Cicero's was the last generation that learnt the Twelve Tables by heart at school *ut carmen necessarium*; and Varro, Cicero's contemporary, was the first and perhaps the greatest of all Roman antiquaries. So at least St Augustine held. Sixteen of his forty-one books of Antiquities Varro gave to the gods, for " he says he was afraid they would perish, not by any hostile invasion, but by the neglect of the Roman citizens, and from this he says they were rescued by himself, as from a fallen house, and safely stored and preserved in the memory of good men by books like his ; and that his care for this was of more service than that which Metellus is said to have shown in rescuing the sacred emblems of Vesta from the fire or Æneas in saving the penates from the Fall of Troy." [1] He rescued a good deal more than a later and more pious age was grateful for ; Augustine found him invaluable, but Servius, the great commentator on Virgil, called him " everywhere the foe of religion." [2] The poets, too, felt to the full the charm of antiquity. Propertius [3] and Ovid both undertook to write of olden days—of sacred things (" rooted out of ancient annals " [4]), and of the names of long ago. Virgil himself was looked upon as a great antiquary. Livy wrote of Rome's early history and told how Numa " put the fear of the gods " upon his people " as the most effective thing for an ignorant and rough multitude " ; [5] his history abounds in portents and omens, but he is not altogether a believer. As early as a generation before Rome was burnt by the Gauls it was remarked, he says, that foreign religion had invaded the city, brought by prophets who made money out of the superstitions they roused and the alien and unusual means they employed to procure the peace of the gods. [6]

---

[1] *Augustine C.D.* vi, 2.
[2] On *Æneid*, xi, 785.
[3] Propertius, v, 1, 69.
[4] Ovid, *Fasti*, i, 7.
[5] Livy, i, 19.
[6] Livy, iv, 30.

Nowhere perhaps is antiquarianism more fascinating than in the sphere of religion. The *Lupercalia* had once a real meaning. The sacrifice of goats and young dogs, and of sacred cakes that the Vestals made of the first ears of the last year's harvest; the *Luperci*, with blood on their brows, naked but for the skins of the slaughtered goats; the *februa* of goatskin, the touch of which would take sterility from a woman—all this is intelligible to the student of primitive religion; but when Mark Antony, Consul though he was, was one of the runners at the Lupercalia, it was not in the spirit of the ancient Latin. It was an antiquarian revival of an old festival of the countryside, which had perhaps never died out. At all events it was celebrated as late as the fifth century A.D., and it was only then abolished by the substitution of a Christian feast by Pope Gelasius.[1] Augustus took pains to revive such ceremonies. Suetonius mentions the " augury of safety," the " flaminate of Juppiter," the " Lupercal rite," and various sacred games.[2] Varro in one of his books, speaks of the Arval Brothers; and Archæology and the spade have recovered for us the *acta* of ninety-six of the annual meetings which this curious old college held at the end of May in the grove of Dea Dia. It is significant that the oldest of these *acta* refer to the meeting in 14 A.D., the year of Augustus' death. The hymn which they sang runs as follows :—

> *Enos Lases iuvate*
> *Neve lue rue Marmar sins incurrere in pleores*
> *Satur fu fere Mars limen sali sta berber*
> *Semunis Alternis advocapit conctos*
> *Enos Marmor iuvato*
> *Triumpe.*

The first five lines were repeated thrice, and *Triumpe* five times.[3] Quintilian tells us that "the hymns of the Salii were hardly intelligible to the priests themselves,"[4] yet they found admirers who amused Horace with their zeal for mere age and obscurity.[5]

---

[1] Plutarch, *Romulus*, 21 ; *Cæsar*, 61, Warde Fowler, *Roman Festivals*, p. 310 f.

[2] Suetonius, *Aug.* 31, Warde Fowler, *op. cit.* p. 190.

[3] Mommsen, *History*, i, p. 231, who translates the hymn.

[4] Quintilian, i, 6, 40. See specimen in Varro, *L.L.* vii, 26.

[5] *Epp.* ii, 1, 20-27, 86.

But an antiquarian interest in ritual is not inconsistent with indifference to religion. Varro, as we have seen, was criticized as an actual enemy of religion in spite of the services he claimed to have rendered to the gods—and the very claim justifies the criticism. So far as the literature of the last century B.C. and the stories current about the leading men in Rome allow us to judge, it is hard to suppose there has ever been an age less interested in religion. Cicero, for example, wrote—or, perhaps, compiled—three books "On the Nature of the Gods." He casts his matter into the form of a dialogue, in which in turn an Epicurean and a Stoic give their grounds for rejecting and for accepting the gods, and an Academic points out the inadequacy of the reasoning in both cases. He has also written on the immortality of the soul. But Cicero's correspondence is a more reliable index to his own beliefs and those of the society in which he moved. No society could be more indifferent to what we call the religious life. In theory and practice, in character and instinct, they were thoroughly secular. One sentence will exhibit Cicero's own feeling. He wrote to his wife from Brundusium on 30th April 58 B.C., when he was on his way to foreign exile: " If these miseries are to be permanent, I only wish, my dearest (*mea vita*), to see you as soon as possible and to die in your arms, since neither gods, whom *you* have worshipped with such pure devotion, nor men, whom *I* have always served, have made us any return." [1] Even when his daughter Tullia died, no sign of any hope of re-union escaped him in his letters, nor did Servius Sulpicius, who wrote him a beautiful letter of consolation, do more than merely hint at such a thing. " If the dead have consciousness, would she wish you to be so overcome of sorrow?" Horace, whose odes, as we have seen, are now and then consecrated to the restoration of religion, was every whit as secular-minded. He laughed at superstition and ridiculed the idea of a divine interest in men, when he expressed his own feeling. No one was ever more thoroughly Epicurean in the truest sense of the word; no one ever urged more pleasantly the Epicurean theory *Carpe diem*; no one ever had more deeply ingrained in him the belief *Mors ultima linea rerum est.* His candour, his humour, his friendliness, combine to give him a very human charm, but in all that is associated with the

---

[1] Cicero, *ad fam.* xiv, 4, 1.

religious side of man's thought and experience, he is sterile and insufficient. And Horace, like Cicero, represents a group. Fuscus Aristius, it is true, declined to rescue the poet from the bore on the ground that "it was the thirtieth Sabbath—and Horace could not wish to offend the Jews?" but we realize that this scruple was dramatic. Fuscus is said to have been a writer of comedies.[1]

But the jest of Fuscus was the earnest of many. If men were conscious of decay in the sanction which religion had once given to morality, there was still a great deal of vague religious feeling among the uneducated and partially educated classes. Again and again we read complaints of the folly of grandmothers and nurses, and it was from them that the first impressions of childhood came. Four centuries later than the period now under discussion it was still the same. "When once vain superstition obsessed the heathen hearts of our fathers, unchecked was its course through a thousand generations. The tender hope of the house shuddered, and worshipped whatever venerable thing his hoary grandsires showed him. Infancy drank in error with its mother's milk. Amid his cries the sacred meal was put between the baby's lips. He saw the wax dripping upon the stones, the black *Lares* trickling with unguent. A little child he saw the image of Fortune with her horn of wealth, and the sacred stone that stood by the house, and his mother pale at her prayers before it. Soon himself too, raised high on his nurse's shoulders, he pressed his lips to the stone, poured forth his childish prayers, and asked riches for himself from the blind rock, and was sure that, whatever one wished, that was where to ask. Never did he lift his eyes and his mind to turn to the citadel of reason, but he believed, and held to the foolish custom, honouring with blood of lambs the gods of his family. And then when he went forth from his home, how he marvelled at the public festivals, the holy days and the games, and gazed at the towering Capitol, and saw the laurelled servants of the gods at the temples while the Sacred Way echoed to the lowing of the victims." So wrote Prudentius.[2] So too wrote Tibullus —"Keep me, *Lares* of my fathers; for ye bred me to manhood when a tender child I played at your feet."[3]

---

[1] Hor. *Sat.* i, 9, 69 : Porphyrion is the authority for the comedies.

[2] Prudentius, *contra Symmachum*, i, 197-218.   [3] Tibullus, i, 10, 15.

How crowded the whole of life was with cult and ritual and usage, how full of divinities, petty, pleasing or terrible, but generally vague and ill-defined, no one will readily realize without special study, but some idea of the complexity of the Roman's divine environment can be gained from even a cursory survey of Ovid's *Fasti*, for example, or Tertullian's *Apology*, or some of the chapters of the fourth book of Augustine's *City of God.* "When," asks Augustine, "can I ever mention in one passage of this book all the names of gods and goddesses, which they have scarcely been able to compass in great volumes, seeing that they allot to every individual thing the special function of some divinity?" He names a few of the gods of agriculture —Segetia, Tutilina, Proserpina, Nodutus, Volutina, Patelana, Lacturnus, Matuta, etc. "I do not mention all."[1] "Satan and his angels have filled the whole world," said Tertullian.[2]

Gods of this type naturally make little figure in literature though Proserpina, in consequence of her identification with the Greek Persephone, achieved a great place and is indeed the subject of the last great poem written under the Roman Empire. But there were other gods of countryside and woodland, whom we know better in art and poetry. "Faunus lover of fugitive Nymphs" is charming enough in Horace's ode, and Fauns, Pans and Satyrs lend themselves readily to grotesque treatment in statue and gem and picture. But the country people took them seriously. Lucretius, speaking of echoes among the hills, says:—"These spots the people round about fancy that goat-footed Satyrs and nymphs inhabit; they say that they are the Fauns, whose noise and sportive play breaks the still silence of the night as they move from place to place. . . . They tell us that the country people far and wide full oft hear Pan, when, nodding the pine-cap on his half-bestial head, he runs over the gaping reeds with curved lip. . . . And of other like monsters and marvels they tell us, that they may not be thought to inhabit lonely places, abandoned even by the gods."[3] Cicero

---

[1] *C.D.* iv, 8. "To an early Greek," says Mr Gilbert Murray, "the earth, water and air were full of living eyes : of *theoi*, of *daimones*, of *Kēres*. One early poet says emphatically that the air is so crowded full of them that there is no room to put in the spike of an ear of corn without touching one."—*Rise of Greek Epic*, p. 82.

[2] *de Spect.* 5 ; cf. *de Idol.* 16 ; *de cor. mil.* 13, gods of the door ; *de Anima*, 39, goddesses of child-birth.

[3] Lucr. iv, 580 f. Virg. *Æn.* viii, 314.

makes his Stoic say their voices are often to be heard.[1] Pliny, in his *Natural History*, says that certain dogs can actually see Fauns ; he quotes a prescription, concocted of a dragon's tongue, eyes and gall, which the Magi recommend for those who are "harassed by gods of the night and by Fauns" ;[2] for they did not confine themselves to running after nymphs, but would chase human women in the dark.

Plutarch has a story of King Numa drugging a spring from which "two dæmons, Picus and Faunus," drank—"creatures who must be compared to Satyrs or Pans in some respects and in others to the Idæan Dactyli," beings of great miraculous power.[3] A countryside haunted by inhabitants of more or less than human nature, part beasts and part fairies or devils, is one thing to an unbeliever who is interested in art or folk-lore, but quite another thing to the uneducated man or woman who has heard their mysterious voices in the night solitude and has suffered in crop, or house, or herd from their ill-will.[4] What the Greek called "Panic" fears were attributed in Italy to Fauns.[5]

"Trees," says Pliny, "were temples of divinities, and in the old way the simple country folk to this day dedicate any remarkable tree to a god. Nor have we more worship for images glittering with gold and ivory than for groves and the very silence that is in them."[6] The country people hung rags and other offerings on holy trees—the hedge round the sacred grove at Aricia is specially mentioned by Ovid as thus honoured.[7] The river-god of the Tiber had his sacred oak hung with spoils of fallen foes.[8]

Holy wells too were common, which were honoured with models of the limbs their waters healed, and other curious gifts, thrown into them—as they are still in every part of the Old World. Horace's fount of Bandusia is the most famous of these in literature.[9] It was an old usage to throw garlands into springs and to crown wells on October 13th.[10] Streams and

---

[1] Cic. *N.D.* ii, 2, 6 : cf. *De Div.* i, 45, 101. Warde Fowler, *Roman Festivals*, pp. 256 ff. on the Fauni.

[2] Pliny, *N.H.* viii, 151 ; xxx, 84.

[3] Plutarch, *Numa*, 15 ; *de facie in orbe lunæ*, 30 ; Ovid, *Fasti*, iii, 291.

[4] Horace's ode attests the power of the Fauns over crops and herds.

[5] Dionys. Hal. v, 16.   [6] Pliny, *N.H.* xii, 3.

[7] Ovid, *Fasti*, iii, 267. *Licia dependent longas velantia sæpes, et posita est meritæ multa tabella deæ.*

[8] Virgil, *Æn.* x, 423.   [9] Horace, *Odes*, iii, 13.

[10] W. Warde Fowler, *Roman Festivals*, p. 240.

wells alike were haunted by mysterious powers, too often malevolent.[1]

Ovid describes old charms to keep off vampires, *striges*, from the cradles of children.[2]

In fact the whole of Nature teemed with beings whom we find it hard to name. They were not pleasant enough, and did not appeal enough to the fancy, to merit the name "fairies"—at least since *The Midsummer Night's Dream* was written. Perhaps they are nearer "The little People"—the nameless "thim ones."[3] They were neither gods nor demons in our sense of the words, though Greek thinkers used the old Homeric word δαίμων to describe them or the diminutive of it, which allowed them to suppose that Socrates' δαιμόνιον was something of the kind.

But these Nature-spirits, whatever we may call them, were far from being the only superhuman beings that encompassed man. Every house had its *Lares* in a little shrine (*lararium*) on the hearth, little twin guardian gods with a dog at their feet, who watched over the family, and to whom something was given at every meal, and garlands on great days. Legend said that Servius Tullius was the son of the family *Lar*.[4] The *Lares* may have been spirits of ancestors. The Emperor Alexander Severus set images of Apollonius, Christ, Abraham and Orpheus, "and others of that sort" in his *lararium*.[5] Not only houses but streets and cross-roads had *Lares*; the city had a thousand, Ovid said, besides the *genius* of the Prince who gave them;[6] for Augustus restored two yearly festivals in their honour in Spring and Autumn. There were also the *Penates* in every home, whom it would perhaps be hard to distinguish very clearly from the *Lares*. Horace has a graceful ode to "Phidyle" on the sufficiency of the simplest sacrifices to these little gods of home and hearth.[7] The worship of these family gods was almost the only

---

[1] Cf. Tertullian, *de Baptismo*, 5. *Annon et alias sine ullo sacramento immundi spiritus aquis incubant, adfectantes illam in primordio divini spiritus gestationem? Sciunt opaci quique fontes, et avii quique rivi, et in balneis piscinæ et euripi in domibus, vel cisternæ et putei, qui rapere dicuntur, scilicet per vim spiritus nocentis. Nympholeptos et lymphaticos et hydrophobos vocant quos aquæ necaverunt aut amentia vel formidine exercuerunt. Quorsum ista retulimus? Ne quis durius credat angelum dei sanctum aquis in salutem hominis temperandis adesse.*

[2] Ovid, *Fasti*, vi, 155 f.

[3] Cf. (Lucian) *Asinus*, 24. ποῖ βαδίζεις ἀωρίᾳ ταλαίπωρε ; οὐδὲ τὰ δαιμόνια δέδοικας.

[4] Pliny, *N.H.* xxxvi, 204.   [5] Lampridius, *Alex. Sev.* 29. 2.

[6] *Fasti*, v. 145. Cf. Prudentius, *adv. Symm.* ii, 445 f.

[7] *Odes*, iii, 23. *Farre pio.*

part of Roman religion that was not flooded and obscured by
the inrush of Oriental cults.

"The Ancients," said Servius, "used the name *Genius* for
the natural god of each individual place or thing or man,"[1] and
another antiquary thought that the *genius* and the *Lar* might be
the same thing. For some reason men of letters laid hold upon
the *genius*, and we find it everywhere. Why there should be
such difference even between twin brothers,

> *He* only knows whose influence at our birth
> O'errules each mortal's planet upon earth,
> The attendant genius, temper-moulding pow'r,
> That stamps the colour of man's natal hour.[2]

The idea of this spiritual counterpart pervades the ancient world.
It appears in Persia as the *fravashi*.[3] It is in the Syrian
Gnostic's Hymn of the Soul, as a robe in the form and likeness
of a man.—

> It was myself that I saw before me as in a mirror ;
> Two in number we stood, but only one in appearance.[4]

It is also probable that the "Angel" of Peter and the "Angels
of the little children" in the New Testament represent the same
idea. The reader of Horace hardly needs to be reminded of
the birthday feast in honour of the *genius,—indulge genio*.
December, as the month of Larentalia and Saturnalia, is the
month welcome to every *genius*, Ovid says.[5]

The worship of all or most of these spirits of the country and
of the home was joyful, an affair of meat and drink. The
primitive sacrifice brought man and god near one another in the
blood and flesh of the victim, which was of one race with them
both.[6] It was on some such ground that the Jews would not
"eat with blood," lest the soul of the beast should pass into the

---

[1] On *Georgic* i, 302, See Varro, *ap.* Aug. *C.D.* vii, 13.   Also Tert. *de Anima*, 39,
*Sic et omnibus genii deputantur, quod dæmonum nomen est.   Adeo nulla ferme
nativitas munda, utique ethnicorum.*

[2] Hor. *Ep.* ii. 2, 187 f. Howes' translation.   Cf. *Faerie Queene*, II, xii, 47.

[3] See J. H. Moulton in *Journal of Theological Studies*, III, 514.

[4] Burkitt, *Early Eastern Christianity*, p. 222.

[5] *Fasti*, iii, 57 ; Seneca,*Ep.* 18. 1, *December est mensis : cum maxime civitas sudat,
ius luxuriæ publicæ datum est . . . ut non videatur mihi errasse qui dixit: olim
mensem Decembrem fuisse nunc annum.*

[6] Cf. Robertson Smith, *Religion of the Semites*, lect. xi.

man. There were feasts in honour of the dead, too, which the church found so dear to the people that it only got rid of them by turning them into festivals of the Martyrs. It was not idly that St Paul spoke of "meat offered to idols" and said that the Kingdom of God was not eating or drinking.

In addition to all these spirits of living beings, of actions and of places, we have to reckon the dead. There were *Manes*—a name supposed to mean "the kindly ones," a caressing name given with a purpose and betraying a real fear. There were also ghosts, *larvæ* and *lemures*.[1] It was the thought of these that made burial so serious a thing, and all the ritual for averting the displeasure of the dead. The *Parentalia* were celebrated on the 13th of February in their honour,[2] and in May the *Lemuria*. It is, we are told, for this reason that none will marry in May.[3] Closely connected with this fear of ghosts and of the dead is that terror of death which Lucretius spends so much labour in trying to dissipate.

"I see no race of men," wrote Cicero, "however polished and educated, however brutal and barbarous, which does not believe that warnings of future events are given and may be understood and announced by certain persons,"[4] and he goes on to remark that Xenophanes and Epicurus were alone among philosophers in believing in no kind of Divination.[5] "Are we to wait till beasts speak? Are we not content with the unanimous authority of mankind?"[6] The Stoics, he says, summed up the matter as follows:—

"If there are gods and they do not declare the future to men; then *either* they do not love men; *or* they are ignorant of what is to happen; *or* they think it of no importance to men to know it; *or* they do not think it consistent with their majesty to tell men; *or* the gods themselves are unable to indicate it. But *neither* do they not love men, for they are benefactors and friends to mankind; *nor* are they ignorant of what they themselves appoint and ordain; *nor* is it of no importance to us to know the future—for we shall be more careful if we do; *nor* do they count it alien to their majesty, for there is nothing nobler than kindness; *nor* are they unable to foreknow. *Therefore* no

---

[1] Warde Fowler, *Roman Festivals*, pp. 106 f.
[2] Ovid, *Fasti*, ii, 409 f. Warde Fowler, *op. cit.* pp. 306 f.   [3] Ovid, *Fasti*, v, 490.
[4] *De Divinatione*, i, 1, 2.   [5] *ib.* i, 3, 5.   [6] *ib.* i, 39, 84.

gods, no foretelling ; but there are gods; therefore they foretell. Nor, if they foretell, do they fail to give us ways to learn what they foretell ; nor, if they give us such ways, is there no divination ; therefore, there is divination." [1]

All this reasoning comes after the fact. The whole world believed in divination, and the Stoics found a reason for it.[2] The flight of birds, the entrails of beasts, rain, thunder, lightning, dreams, everything was a means of Divination. Another passage from the same Dialogue of Cicero will suffice. Superstition, says the speaker, "follows you up, is hard upon you, pursues you wherever you turn. If you hear a prophet, or an omen ; if you sacrifice; if you catch sight of a bird ; if you see a Chaldean or a *haruspex*; if it lightens, if it thunders, if anything is struck by lightning ; if anything like a portent is born or occurs in any way—something or other of the kind is bound to happen, so that you can never be at ease and have a quiet mind. The refuge from all our toils and anxieties would seem to be sleep. Yet from sleep itself the most of our cares and terrors come." [3] How true all this is will be seen by a moment's reflexion on the abundance of signs, omens and dreams that historians so different as Livy and Plutarch record. Horace uses them pleasantly enough in his Odes—like much else such things are charming, if one does not believe in them.[4] But it is abundantly clear that it took an effort to be rid of such belief. A speaker in Cicero's *Tusculans* remarks on the effrontery of philosophers, who *boast* that by Epicurus' aid "they are freed from those most cruel of tyrants, eternal terror and fear by day and by night." [5] When a man boasts of moral progress, of his freedom from avarice, what, asks Horace, of other like matters?

> You're not a miser. Good—but prithee say,
> Is every vice with avarice flown away? . . .
> Does Superstition ne'er your heart assail
> Nor bid your soul with fancied horrors quail?

---

[1] *De Divinatione*, i, 38, 82, 83. Cf. Tertullian, *de Anima*, 46. *Sed et Stoici deum malunt providentissimum humanæ institutioni inter cetera præsidia divinatricum artium et disciplinarum somnia quoque nobis indidisse, peculiare solatium naturalis oraculi.*

[2] Panaetius and Seneca should be excepted from this charge.

[3] Cic. *de Div.* ii, 72, 149, 150. Cf. *de Legg.* ii, 13, 32. Plutarch also has the same remark about sleep and superstition.

[4] Cf. *Odes*, iii, 27.   [5] *Tusculans*, i, 21, 48.

Or can you smile at magic's strange alarms,
Dreams, witchcraft, ghosts, Thessalian spells and charms?[1]

Horace's "conversion" is recorded in one of his odes, but it may be taken too seriously.

That superstition so gross was accompanied by paralysing belief in magic, enchantment, miracle, astrology[2] and witchcraft generally, is not surprising. The historians of the Early Empire have plenty to say on this. It should be remembered that the step between magic and poisoning is a very short one. Magic, says Pliny, embraces the three arts that most rule the human mind, medicine, religion and mathematics—a triple chain which enslaves mankind.[3]

We have thus in Roman society a political life of a highly developed type, which has run through a long course of evolution and is now degenerating ; we have a literature based upon that of Greece and implying a good deal of philosophy and of intellectual freedom ; and, side by side with all this, a religious atmosphere in which the grossest and most primitive of savage conceptions and usages thrive in the neighbourhood of a scepticism as cool and detached as that of Horace. It is hard to realize that a people's experience can be so uneven, that development and retardation can exist at once in so remarkable a degree in the mind of a nation. The explanation is that we judge peoples and ages too much by their literature, and by their literature only after it has survived the test of centuries. In all immortal literature there is a common note ; it deals with the deathless and the vital ; and superstition, though long enough and tenacious enough of life, is outlived and outgrown by "man's unconquerable mind." But the period before us is one in which, under a rule that robbed men of every liberating interest in life, and left society politically, intellectually and morally sterile and empty, literature declined, and as it declined, it sank below the level of that flood of vulgar superstition, which rose higher and higher, as in each generation men were less wishful to think and less capable of thought.

---

[1] Hor. *Ep.* ii, 2, 208 ; Howes.
[2] Tertullian, *de Idol.* 9, *scimus magiæ et astrologiæ inter se societatem.*
[3] Pliny the elder on Magic, *N.H.* xxx, opening sections ; *N.H.* xxviii, 10, on incantations, *polleantne aliquid verba et incantamenta carminum.*

But our theme is religion, and so far we have discussed nothing but what we may call superstition—and even Plutarch would hardly quarrel with the name. That to people possessed by such beliefs in non-human powers, in beings which beset human life with malignity, the restoration of ancient cult and ritual would commend itself, is only natural. To such minds the purpose of all worship is to induce the superhuman being to go peaceably away, and sacrifice implies not human sin, but divine irritation, which may be irrational. To the religious temperament, the essential thing is some kind of union, some communion, with the Divine; and sacrifice becomes the means to effect the relation of life to a higher will,—to a holier will, we might say, if we allow to the word "holy" a width of significance more congenial to ancient than to modern thought. And this higher will implies a divinity of wider reach than the little gods of primitive superstition, a power which may even be less personal if only it is great. Religion asks for the simplification of man's relations with his divine environment, for escape from the thousand and one petty marauders of the spirit-world into the empire of some strong and central authority, harsh, perhaps, or even cruel, but at least a controlling force in man's experience. If this power is moral, religion is at once fused with morality; if it is merely physical, religion remains non-moral, and has a constant tendency to decline into superstition, or at least to make terms with it.

In the hereditary religion of Rome, the only power that could possibly have been invested with any such character was Jupiter Capitolinus, but he had too great a likeness to the other gods of Italy—the gods with names, that is, for some of the more significant had none—Bona Dea and Dea Dia for example. Jupiter had his functions, but on the whole they were local, and there was very little or nothing in him to quicken thought or imagination. It was not till the Stoics made him more or less the embodiment of monotheism, that he had a chance of becoming the centre of a religion in the higher sense of the word, and even then it was impossible; for first, he was at best little more than an impersonal dogma, and, secondly, the place was filled by foreign goddesses of far greater warmth and colour and activity. *Stat magni nominis umbra.*

It was during the second Punic War that Cybele was brought from Asia Minor to Rome and definitely established as one of the divinities of the City.[1] The Great Mother of the gods, she represented the principle of life and its repro-duction, and her worship appealed to every male and female being in the world. It inspired awe, and it prompted to joy and merriment; it was imposing and it was mysterious. Lucretius has a famous description of her pageant :—

"Adorned with this emblem (the mural crown), the image of the divine Mother is carried nowadays through wide lands in awe-inspiring state. Different nations after old-established ritual name her Idæan Mother, and give for escort Phrygian bands. . . . Tight-stretched tambourines and hollow cymbals thunder all round to the stroke of their open hands, and horns menace with hoarse-sounding music, and the hollow pipe stirs their minds with its Phrygian strain. They carry weapons before them, emblems of furious rage, meet to fill the thank-less souls and godless breasts of the rabble with terror for the Divinity of the Goddess. So, when first she rides in pro-cession through great cities and mutely enriches mortals with a blessing not expressed in words, they straw all her path with brass and silver, presenting her with bounteous alms, and scatter over her a snow-shower of roses, over-shadowing the mother and her troops of attendants. Here an armed band, to which the Greeks give the names of Phrygian Curetes, join in the game of arms and leap in measure, all dripping with blood, and the awful crests upon their heads quiver and shake."[2]

The invariable features of the worship of Cybele are men-tioned here, the eunuch priests, the tambourines, the shouting and leaping and cutting with knives, and the collection of money.[3] There is no indication of any control being exercised over these priests of Cybele by a central authority, and little bands of them strolled through the Mediterranean lands, mak-ing their living by exhibiting themselves and their goddess and gathering petty offerings. They had a bad name and they seem to have deserved it. In the book called *The Ass*,

---

[1] Livy, xxix, 11, 14 ; Ovid, *Fasti*, iv, 179 f. The goddess was embodied in a big stone.

[2] Lucretius, ii, 608 f.   [3] Cf. Strabo, c. 470 ; Juvenal, vi, 511 f.

once ascribed to Lucian, is a short account of such a band. The ass, who is really a man transformed, is the speaker. "The next day they packed up the goddess and set her on my back. Then we drove out of the city and went round the country. When we entered any village, I, the god-bearer (a famous word, θεοφόρητος [1]) stood still, and the crowd of flutists blew like mad, and the others threw off their caps and rolled their heads about, and cut their arms with the swords and each stuck his tongue out beyond his teeth and cut it too, so that in a moment everything was full of fresh blood. And, I, when I saw this for the first time, stood trembling in case the goddess might need an ass' blood too. When they had cut themselves about in this way, they collected from the bystanders obols and drachmas; and one or another would give them figs and cheeses and a jar of wine, and a medimnus of wheat and barley for the ass. So they lived upon these and did service to the goddess who rode on my back." [2]

The *Attis* of Catullus gives a vivid picture of the frenzy which this worship could excite. Juvenal complains of the bad influence which the priests of Cybele, among others, had upon the minds of Roman ladies. St Augustine long afterwards says that "till yesterday" they were to be seen in the streets of Carthage "with wet hair, whitened face and mincing walk." It is interesting to note in passing that the land which introduced the Mother of the Gods to the Roman world, also gave the name Θεοτόκος (Mother of God) to the church.

Egypt also contributed gods to Rome, who forced themselves upon the state. The Senate forbade them the Capitol and had their statues thrown down, but the people set them up again with violence.[3] Gabinius, the Consul of 58 B.C., stopped the erection of altars to them, but eight years later the Senate had to pass a decree for the destruction of their shrines. **No**

---

[1] See Ramsay, *Church in the Roman Empire*, p. 397. The Latins used the word *divinus* in this way—Seneca, *de beata vita*, 26, 8.

[2] (Lucian) Asinus, 37. The same tale is amplified in Apuleius' *Golden Ass*, where the episode of these priests is given with more detail, in the eighth book. Seneca hints that a little blood might make a fair show; see his picture of the same, *de beata vita*, 26, 8.

[3] Tertullian, *ad Natt.* i, 10 ; *Apol.* 6. He has the strange fancy that Serapis was originally the Joseph of the book of Genesis, *ad Natt.* ii, 8.

workman dared lay hand to the work, so the consul Paullus stripped off his consular toga, took an axe and dealt the first blow at the doors.[1] Another eight years passed, and the Triumvirs, after the death of Cæsar, built a temple to Isis and Serapis to win the goodwill of the masses.[2] The large foreign and Eastern element in the city populace must be remembered. When Octavian captured Alexandria, he forgave the guilty city "in honour of Serapis," but on his return to Rome he destroyed all the shrines of the god within the city walls. In time Isis laid hold of the month of November, which had otherwise no festivals of importance.

Isis seems to have appealed to women. Tibullus complains of Delia's devotion to her, and her ritual. There were baths and purifications ; the worshippers wore linen garments and slept alone. Whole nights were spent sitting in the temple amid the rattling of the sistrum. Morning and evening the votary with flowing hair recited the praises of the goddess.[3] Isis could make her voice heard on occasion, or her snake of silver would be seen to move its head, and penance was required to avert her anger. She might bid her worshippers to stand in the Tiber in the winter, or to crawl, naked and trembling, with blood-stained knees, round the Campus Martius—the Iseum stood in the Campus as it was forbidden within the City Walls ; or to fetch water from Egypt to sprinkle in the Roman shrine. They were high honours indeed that Anubis claimed, as, surrounded by shaven priests in linen garments, he scoured the city and laughed at the people who beat their breasts as he passed.[4] The "barking" Anubis might be despised by Virgil and others, but the vulgar feared him as the attendant of Isis and Serapis.[5] Isis began to usurp the functions of Juno Lucina, and women in childbed called upon her to deliver them.[6] She gave oracles, which were familiar perhaps even so early as Ennius' day,[7] and men and women slept in the temples of Isis and Serapis, as they did in those of Æsculapius, to obtain in dreams the knowledge they needed to appease the god, or to

---

[1] Valerius Maximus, i, 3, 4.   [2] Dio C. xlvii, 15.

[3] Tibullus, i, 3, 23 f. Cf. Propertius, ii, 28, 45 ; Ovid, *A.A.* iii, 635.

[4] Juvenal, vi, 522 f.

[5] Lucan, viii, 831, *Isin semideosque canes.*

[6] Ovid, *Am.* ii, 13, 7.

[7] Unless *Isiaci coniectores* is Cicero's own phrase, *de Div.* i, 58, 132.

recover their health, or what not.[1] It is not surprising that the shrines of Isis are mentioned by Ovid and Juvenal as the resorts of loose women.[2]

The devotion of the women is proved by the inscriptions which are found recording their offerings to Isis. One woman, a Spaniard, may be taken as an illustration. In honour of her daughter she dedicated a silver statue to Isis, and she set forth how the goddess wore a diadem composed of one big pearl, six little pearls, emeralds, rubies, and jacinths ; earrings of emeralds and pearls ; a necklace of thirty-six pearls and eighteen emeralds (with two for clasps) ; bracelets on her arms and legs ; rings on her fingers ; and emeralds on her sandals.[3] There is evidence to show that the Madonna in Southern Italy is really Isis re-named. Isis, like the Madonna, was painted and sculptured with a child in her arms (Horus, Harpocrates). Their functions coincide as closely as this inscription proves that their offerings do.[4]

> Die Mutter Gottes zu Kevlaar
> Trägt heut' ihr bestes Kleid.

At first, it is possible that Egyptian religion, as it spread all over the world, was little better than Phrygian, but it had a better future. With Plutarch's work upon it we shall have to deal later on. Apuleius, at the end of the second century worshipped an Isis, who identified all the Divinities with herself and was approached through the most imposing sacraments. She was the power underlying all nature, but there was a spiritual side to her worship. Two centuries or so later, Julian "the Apostate" looks upon Serapis as Catholics have done upon St Peter—he is "the kindly and gentle god, who set souls utterly free from becoming or birth ($\gamma\epsilon\nu\epsilon\sigma\epsilon\omega\varsigma$) and does not, when once they are free, nail them down to other bodies in punishment, but conveys them upward and brings them into the

---

[1] Cicero, *Div.* ii, 59, 121. For ἐγκοίμησις or *incubatio* see Mary Hamilton, *Incubation* (1906)

[2] Clem. Alex. *Pædag.* iii, 28, to the same effect. Tertullian on the temples, *de Pud.* c. 5. Reference may be made to the hierodules of the temples in ancient Asia and in modern India.

[3] *Corp. Inscr. Lat.* ii, 3386. The enumeration of the jewels was a safeguard against theft.

[4] Flinders Petrie, *Religion of Ancient Egypt*, p. 44 ; Hamilton, *Incubation*, pp. 174, 182 f.

ideal world." [1] It is possible that some hint of this lurked in the religion from the first, and, if it did, we need not be surprised that it escaped Juvenal's notice.

It was not merely gods that came from the East, but a new series of religious ideas. Here were religions that claimed the whole of life, that taught of moral pollution and of reconciliation, that gave anew the old sacramental value to rituals,—religions of priest and devotee, equalizing rich and poor, save for the cost of holy rites, and giving to women the consciousness of life in touch with the divine. The eunuch priests of Cybele and the monks of Serapis introduced a new abstinence to Western thought. It is significant that Christian monasticism and the coenobite life began in Egypt, where, as we learn from papyri found in recent years, great monasteries of Serapis existed long before our era. Side by side with celibacy came vegetarianism.

No polytheistic religion can exclude gods from its pantheon ; all divinities that man can devise have a right there. Thus Cybele and Isis made peace with each other and with all the gods and goddesses whom they met in their travels—and with all the *dæmonia* too. Their cults were steeped in superstition, and swung to and fro between continence and sensuality. They orientalized every religion of the West and developed every superstitious and romantic tendency. In the long run, they brought Philosophy to its knees, abasing it to be the apologist of everything they taught and did, and dignifying themselves by giving a philosophic colouring to their mysticism. But this is no strange thing. A religion begins in magic with rites and symbols that belong to the crudest Nature-worship—to agriculture, for instance, and the reproductive organs—and gradually develops or absorbs higher ideas, till it may reach the unity of the godhead and the immortality of the soul ; but the ultimate question is, will it cut itself clear of its past? And this the religions of Cybele and Isis never satisfactorily achieved.

In the meantime they promised little towards a moral regeneration of society. They offered men and women emotions, but they scarcely touched morality. To the terrors of life, already many enough, they added crowning fears, and cramped and dwarfed the minds of men.

[1] Julian, *Or.* iv, 136 B.

"O hapless race of men!" cried Lucretius, "when they attributed such deeds to the gods and added cruel anger thereto! what groanings did they then beget for themselves, what wounds for us, what tears for our children's children! No act of piety is it to be often seen with veiled head turning toward a stone, to haunt every altar, to lie prostrate on the ground with hands outspread before the shrines of gods, to sprinkle the altars with much blood of beasts and link vow to vow—no! rather to be able to look on all things with a mind at peace."[1] And a mind at peace was the last thing that contemporary religion could offer to any one. "Human life," he says, "lay visibly before men's eyes foully crushed to earth under the weight of Religion, who showed her head from the quarters of heaven with hideous aspect lowering upon men," till Epicurus "dared first to uplift mortal eyes against her face and first to withstand her. . . . The living force of his soul gained the day; on he passed far beyond the flaming walls of the world and traversed in mind and spirit the immeasurable universe. And thence he returns again a conqueror, to tell us what can and what cannot come into being; in short on what principle each thing has its powers defined, its deep-set boundary mark. So Religion is put under our feet and trampled upon in its turn; while as for us, his victory sets us on a level with heaven."[2]

It was the establishment of law which brought peace to Lucretius. In the ease of mind which we see he gained from the contemplation of the fixity of cause and effect, in the enthusiasm with which he emphasizes such words as *rationes*, *fœdera*, *leges*, with which he celebrates *Natura gubernans*, we can read the horrible weight upon a feeling soul of a world distracted by the incalculable caprices of a myriad of divine or dæmonic beings.[3] The force with which he flings himself against the doctrine of a future life shows that it is a fight for freedom. If men would rid themselves of "the dread of something after death"—and they could if they would, for reason will do it—they could live in "the serene temples of the wise"; the gods would pass from their minds; bereavement would lose its sting, and life would no longer be brutalized by the cruelties of terror. Avarice, treachery, murder, civil war, suicide—all these things are the fruit of this fear of death.[4]

[1] Lucr. v, 1194.　[2] Lucr. i, 62-79.　[3] See Patin. *La Poésie Latine*, i. 120.
[4] Lucr. iii, 60 f.

Religion, similarly, "often and often has given birth to sinful and unholy deeds." The illustration, which he uses, is the sacrifice of Iphigenia, and it seems a little remote. Yet Pliny says that in 97 B.C. in the consulship of Lentulus and Crassus, a decree of the Senate forbade human sacrifice—*ne homo immolaretur.* "It cannot be estimated," he goes on, "what a debt is owed to the Romans who have done away (in Gaul and Britain) with monstrous rites, in which it was counted the height of religion to kill a man, and a most healthful thing to eat him."[1] Elsewhere he hints darkly at his own age having seen something of the kind, and there is an obscure allusion in Plutarch's life of Marcellus to "unspeakable rites, that none may see, which are performed (?) upon Greeks and Gauls."[2] "At the temple of Aricia," says Strabo, "there is a barbarian and Scythian practice. For there is there established a priest, a runaway slave, who has killed with his own hand his predecessor. There he is, then, ever sword in hand, peering round about, lest he should be attacked, ready to defend himself." Strabo's description of the temple on the lake and the precipice overhanging it adds to the impressiveness of the scene he thus pictures.[3] If human sacrifice was rare in practice, none the less it was in the minds of men.

Tantum religio potuit suadere malorum

concludes Lucretius, and yet it was not perhaps his last thought.

M. Patin has a fine study of the poet in which he deals with "the anti-Lucretius in Lucretius." Even in the matter of religion, his keen observation of Nature frequently suggests difficulties which are more powerfully expressed and more convincing than the arguments with which he himself tries to refute them. "When we look up to the heavenly regions of the great universe, the æther set on high above the glittering stars, and the

---

[1] Pliny, *N.H.* xxx, 12, 13. Warde Fowler, *Roman Festivals*, pp. 111 f. on the *Argei* and the whole question of human sacrifice. For Plutarch's explanation of it as due not to gods but to evil demons who enforced it, see p. 107.

[2] Pliny, *N.H.* xxviii, 12; Plutarch, *Marcellus*, 3, where, however, the meaning may only be that the rites are done in symbol; he refers to the actual sacrifice of human beings in the past. See Tertullian, *Apol.* 9 on sacrifice of children in Africa in the reign of Tiberius.

[3] Strabo, c. 239. Strabo was a contemporary of Augustus. Cf. J. G. Frazer, *Adonis Attis Osiris*, p. 63, for another instance in this period.

thought comes into our mind of the sun and moon and their courses ; then indeed in hearts laden with other woes that doubt too begins to wake and raise its head—can it be perchance after all, that we have to do with some vast Divine power that wheels those bright stars each in his orbit ? Again who is there whose mind does not shrink into itself with fear of the gods, whose limbs do not creep with terror, when the parched earth rocks under horrible blow of the thunderbolt, and the roar sweeps over the vast sky ? . . . When too the utmost fury of the wild wind scours the sea and sweeps over its waters the admiral with his stout legions and his elephants, does he not in prayer seek peace with the gods ? . . . but all in vain, since, full oft, caught in the whirlwind, he is driven, for all his prayers, on, on to the shoals of death. Thus does some hidden power trample on mankind. . . . Again, when the whole earth rocks under their feet, and towns fall at the shock or hang ready to collapse, what wonder if men despise themselves, and make over to the gods high prerogative and marvellous powers to govern all things ? " [1]

That Lucretius should be so open to impressions of this kind, in spite of his philosophy, is a measure of his greatness as a poet. It adds weight and worth to all that he says—to his hatred of the polytheism and superstition round about him, and to his judgment upon their effect in darkening and benumbing the minds of men. He understands the feelings which he dislikes—he has felt them. The spectacle of the unguessed power that tramples on mankind has moved him ; and he has suffered the distress of all delicate spirits in times of bloodshed and disorder. He knows the effect of such times upon those who still worship. " Much more keenly in evil days do they turn their minds to religion." [2]

[1] Lucr. v, 1204-1240. We may compare Browning's *Bp. Blougram* on the instability of unbelief :—

> Just when we are safest, there's a sunset-touch,
> A fancy from a flower-bell, some one's death,
> A chorus-ending from Euripides—
> And that's enough for fifty hopes and fears
> As old and new at once as nature's self,
> To rap and knock and enter in our soul,
> Take hands and dance there, a fantastic ring,
> Round the ancient idol, on his base again,—
> The grand Perhaps ! We look on helplessly.

[2] Lucr. iii, 53.

We have now to consider another poet, a disciple of
Lucretius in his early years, who, under the influence of Nature
and human experience, moved away from Epicureanism, and
sought reconciliation with the gods, though he was too honest
with himself to find peace in the systems and ideas that were
yet available.

Virgil was born in the year 70 B.C.—the son of a little self-
made man in a village North of the Po. He grew up in the
country, with a spirit that year by year grew more sensitive to
every aspect of the world around him. No Roman poet had a
more gentle and sympathetic love of Nature ; none ever entered
so deeply and so tenderly into the sorrows of men. He lived
through forty years of Civil War, veiled and open. He saw its
effects in broken homes and aching hearts, in coarsened minds
and reckless lives. He was driven from his own farm, and had,
like Æneas, to rescue an aged and blind father. Under such
experience his early Epicureanism dissolved—it had always
been too genial to be the true kind. The Epicurean should
never go beyond friendship, and Virgil loved. His love of the
land in which he was born showed it to him more worthy to be
loved than men had yet realized. Virgil was the pioneer who discovered the beauty, the charm and the romance of Italy. He
loved the Italians and saw poetry in their hardy lives and quiet
virtues, though they were not Greeks. His love of his father
and of his land opened to him the significance of all love, and
the deepening and widening of his experience is to be read in
the music, stronger and profounder, that time reveals in his
poetry.

Here was a poet who loved Rome more than ever did
Augustus or Horace, and he had no such speedy cure as they
for "the woes of sorrowful Hesperia." The loss of faith in the
old gods meant more to him than to them, so his tone in speaking of them is quieter, a great deal, than that of Horace. He
took the decline of morals more seriously and more inwardly,
and he saw more deeply into the springs of action ; he could
never lightly use the talk of rapid and sweeping reformation, as
his friend did in the odes which the Emperor inspired. He had
every belief in Augustus, who was dearer to him personally than
to Horace, and he hoped for much outcome from the new
movement in the State. But with all his absorbing interest in

his own times—and how deep that interest was, only long and minute study of his poems will reveal—he was without scheme or policy. He came before his countrymen, as prophets and poets do in all ages—a child in affairs, but a man in inward experience ; he had little or nothing to offer but the impressions left upon his soul by human life. He had the advantage over most prophets in being a "lord of language"; he drew more music from Latin words than had ever been achieved before or was ever reached again.

He told men of a new experience of Nature. It is hardly exaggeration to say that he stands nearer Wordsworth in this feeling than any other poet. He had the same "impulses of deeper birth"; he had seen new gleams and heard new voices ; he had enjoyed what no Italian had before, and he spoke in a new way, unintelligible then, and unintelligible still, to those who have not seen and heard the same things. The gist of it all he tried to give in the language of Pantheism, which the Stoics had borrowed from Pythagoras :—" The Deity, they tell us, pervades all, earth and the expanse of sea, and the deep vault of heaven ; from Him flocks, herds, men, wild beasts of every sort, each creature at its birth draws the bright thread of life ; further, to Him all things return, are restored and reduced—death has no place among them ; but they fly up alive into the ranks of the stars and take their seats aloft in the sky." So John Conington did the passage into English. But in such cases it may be said with no disrespect to the commentator who has done so much for his poet, the original words stand to the translation, as Virgil's thought did to the same thought in a Stoic's brain.

> *Deum namque ire per omnis*
> *Terrasque tractusque maris cælumque profundum ;*
> *Hinc pecudes, armenta, viros, genus omne ferarum,*
> *Quemque sibi tenues nascentem arcessere vitas ;*
> *Scilicet huc reddi deinde ac resoluta referri*
> *Omnia, nec morti esse locum, sed viva volare*
> *Sideris in numerum atque alto succedere cælo.*
>
> (Georgics, iv, 221.)

The words might represent a fancy, or a dogma of the schools and many no doubt so read them, because they had no experience to help them. But to others it is clear that the passage is one of the deepest import, for it is the key to Virgil's mind and the thought is an expression of what we can call by no other name than religion. Around him men and women were seeking communion with gods; he had had communion with what he could not name—he had experienced religion in a very deep, abiding and true way. There is nothing for it—at least for Englishmen—but to quote the "lines composed a few miles above Tintern Abbey"—

> I have felt
> A presence that disturbs me with the joy
> Of elevated thoughts; a sense sublime
> Of something far more deeply interfused,
> Whose dwelling is the light of setting suns,
> And the round ocean, and the living air,
> And the blue sky, and in the mind of man;
> A motion and a spirit, that impels
> All thinking things, all objects of all thought,
> And rolls through all things.

Virgil's experience did not stop here; like Wordsworth, he found

> Nature's self
> By all varieties of human love
> Assisted.

He had been a son and a brother; and such relations of men to men impressed him—they took him into the deepest and most beautiful regions of life; and one of the charms of Italy was that it was written all over with the records of human love and helpfulness. The clearing, the orchard, the hilltop town, the bed of flowers, all spoke to him "words that could not be uttered." His long acquaintance with such scripts brought it about that he found

> in man an object of delight,
> Of pure imagination and of love—

and he came to the Roman people with a deep impression of human worth—something unknown altogether in Roman poetry before or after. Lucretius was impressed with man's insignificance in the universe; Horace, with man's folly. Virgil's poetry throbbed with the sense of man's grandeur and his sanctity.

This human greatness, which his poetry brought home to the sympathetic reader, was not altogether foreign to the thought of the day. *Homo sacra res homini*[1] was the teaching of the Stoics, but man was a more sacred thing to the poet than to the philosopher, for what the philosopher conceived to be a flaw and a weakness in man, the poet found to be man's chief significance. The Stoic loudly proclaimed man to be a member of the universe. The poet found man knit to man by a myriad ties, the strength of which he realized through that pain against which the Stoic sought to safeguard him. Man revealed to the poet his inner greatness in the haunting sense of his limitations —he could not be self-sufficient (αὐτάρκης) as the Stoic urged ; he depended on men, on women and children, on the beauty of grass and living creature, of the sea and sky. And even all these things could not satisfy his craving for love and fellowship ; he felt a "hunger for the infinite." Here perhaps is the greatest contribution of Virgil to the life of the age.

He, the poet to whom man and the world were most various and meant most, came to his people, and, without any articulate expression of it in direct words, made it clear to them that he had felt a gap in the heart of things, which philosophy could never fill. Philosophy could remove this sense of incompleteness, but only at the cost of love ; and love was to Virgil, as his poetry shows, the very essence of life. Yet he gave, and not altogether unconsciously, the impression that in proportion as love is apprehended, its demands extend beyond the present. The sixth book of the *Æneid* settles nothing and proves nothing, but it expresses an instinct, strong in Virgil, as the result of experience, that love must reach beyond the grave. Further, the whole story of Æneas is an utterance of man's craving for God, of the sense of man's incompleteness without a divine complement. These are the records of Virgil's life, intensely individual, but not peculiar to himself. In the literature of his century, there is little indication of such instincts, but the history of four hundred years shows that they were deep in the general heart of man.

These impressions Virgil brought before the Roman world.

---

[1] Seneca, *Ep.* 95, 33.

As such things are, they were a criticism, and they meant a change of values. In the light of them, the restoration of religion by Augustus became a little thing; the popular superstition of the day was stamped as vulgar and trivial in itself, while it became the sign of deep and unsatisfied craving in the human heart; and lastly the current philosophies, in the face of Virgil's poetry, were felt to be shallow and cold, talk of the lip and trick of the brain. Of course this is not just to the philosophers who did much for the world, and without whom Virgil would not have been what he was. None the less, it was written in Virgil's poetry that the religions and philosophies of mankind must be thought over anew.

This is no light contribution to an age or to mankind. In this case it carries with it the whole story that lies before us. Such an expression of a common instinct gave new force to that instinct; it added a powerful impulse to the deepest passion that man knows; and, in spite of the uncertainties which beset the poet himself, it gave new hope to mankind that the cry of the human heart for God was one that should receive an answer.

CHAPTER II

THE STOICS

" I AM entering," writes Tacitus,[1] " upon the history of a period, rich in disasters, gloomy with wars, rent with seditions, nay, savage in its very hours of peace. Four Emperors perished by the sword; there were three civil wars; there were more with foreigners — and some had both characters at once. . . . Rome was wasted by fires, its oldest temples burnt, the very Capitol set in flames by Roman hands. There was defilement of sacred rites; adulteries in high places; the sea crowded with exiles; island rocks drenched with murder. Yet wilder was the frenzy in Rome; nobility, wealth, the refusal of office, its acceptance—everything was a crime, and virtue the surest ruin. Nor were the rewards of informers less odious than their deeds; one found his spoils in a priesthood or a consulate; another in a provincial governorship; another behind the throne; and all was one delirium of hate and terror; slaves were bribed to betray their masters, freedmen their patrons. He who had no foe was destroyed by his friend."

It was to this that Virgil's hope of a new Golden Age had come—*Redeunt Saturnia regna.* Augustus had restored the Republic; he had restored religion; and after a hundred years here is the outcome. Tacitus himself admits that the age was not "barren of virtues," that it "could show fine illustrations" of family love and friendship, and of heroic death. It must also be owned that the Provinces at large were better governed than under the Republic; and, further, that, when he wrote Tacitus thought of a particular period of civil disorder and that not a long one. Yet the reader of his *Annals* will feel that the description will cover more than the year 69; it is essentially true of the reigns of Tiberius, Gaius, Claudius and Nero, and it was to be true again of the reign of Domitian—of perhaps eighty years of the first century of our era. If it was not true

[1] *Hist.* i, 2.

of the whole Mediterranean world, or even of the whole of
Rome, it was true at least of that half-Rome which gave its
colour to the thinking of the world.

Through all the elaborate pretences devised by Augustus to
obscure the truth, through all the names and phrases and
formalities, the Roman world had realized the central fact of
despotism.[1] The Emperors themselves had grasped it with
pride and terror.   One at least was insane, and the position
was enough to turn almost any brain.   " Monarchy," in
Herodotus' quaint sentence,[2] " would set the best man outside
the ordinary thoughts."   Plato's myth of Gyges was fulfilled—
of the shepherd, who found a ring that made him invisible, and
in its strength seduced a queen, murdered a king and became a
tyrant.   Gaius banished his own sisters, reminding them that
he owned not only islands but swords ; and he bade his grand-
mother remember that he could " do anything he liked and do
it to anybody."[3]   Oriental princes had been kept at Rome as
hostages and had given the weaker-minded members of the
Imperial family new ideas of royalty.   The very word was
spoken freely—in his treatise " On Clemency " Seneca uses again
and again the word *regnum* without apology.

But what gave Despotism its sting was its uncertainty.
Augustus had held a curiously complicated set of special powers
severally conferred on him for specified periods, and technically
they could be taken from him.   The Senate was the Emperor's
partner in the government of the world, and it was always conceivable that the partnership might cease, for it was not a
definite institution—prince followed prince, it is true, but there
was an element of accident about it all.   The situation was
difficult ; Senate and Emperor eyed each other with suspicion
—neither knew how far the other could go, or would go ; neither
knew the terms of the partnership.   Tiberius wrote despatches
to the Senate and he was an artist in concealing his meaning.
The Senate had to guess what he wished ; if it guessed wrong,
he would resent the liberty ; if it guessed right, he resented the
appearance of servility.   The solitude of the throne grew more
and more uneasy.

[1] Tac. *Ann.* iv, 33, *sic converso statu neque alia re Romana quam si unus
imperitet.*
[2] Hdt. iii, 80.   Cf. Tac. *A.* vi, 48, 4, *vi dominationis convulsus et mutatus.*
[3] Suetonius, *Gaius*, 29.

Again, the republican government had been in the hands of free men, who ruled as magistrates, and the imperial government had no means of replacing them, for one free-born Roman could not take service with another. The Emperor had to fall back upon his own household. His Secretaries of State were slaves and freedmen—men very often of great ability, but their past was against them. If it had not depraved them, none the less it left upon them a social taint, which nothing could remove. They were despised by the men who courted them, and they knew it. It was almost impossible for such men not to be the gangrene of court and state. And as a fact we find that the freedman was throughout the readiest agent for all evil that Rome knew, and into the hands of such men the government of the world drifted. Under a weak, or a careless, or even an absent, Emperor Rome was governed by such men and such methods as we suppose to be peculiar to Sultanates and the East.

The honour, the property, the life of every Roman lay in the hands of eunuchs and valets, and, as these quarrelled or made friends, the fortunes of an old nobility changed with the hour. It had not been so under Augustus, nor was it so under Vespasian, nor under Trajan or his successors; but for the greater part of the first century A.D. Rome was governed by weak or vicious Emperors, and they by their servants. The spy and the informer were everywhere.

To this confusion fresh elements of uncertainty were added by the astrologer and mathematician, and it became treason to be interested in "the health of the prince." Superstition ruled the weakling—superstition, perpetually re-inforced by fresh hordes of Orientals, obsequious and unscrupulous. Seneca called the imperial court, which he knew, "a gloomy slave-gaol" (*triste ergastulum*).[1]

Reduced to merely registering the wishes of their rulers, the Roman nobility sought their own safety in frivolity and extravagance. To be thoughtful was to be suspected of independence and to invite danger. We naturally suppose moralists and satirists to exaggerate the vices of their contemporaries, but a sober survey of Roman morals in the first century—at any rate before 70 A.D.—reveals a great deal that

---

[1] Sen. *de ira*, iii, 15, 3.

is horrible. (Petronius is not exactly a moralist or a satirist,
and there is plenty of other evidence.) Marriage does not thrive
alongside of terror, nor yet where domestic slavery prevails, and
in Rome both militated against purity of life. The Greek girl's
beauty, her charm and wit, were everywhere available. For
amusements, there were the gladiatorial shows,—brutal, we
understand, but their horrible fascination we fortunately cannot
know. The reader of St Augustine's *Confessions* will remember
a famous passage on these games. The gladiators were the
popular favourites of the day. They toured the country, they
were modelled and painted. Their names survive scratched by
loafers on the walls of Pompeii. The very children played
at being gladiators, Epictetus said—"sometimes athletes, now
monomachi, now trumpeters." The Colosseum had seats for
80,000 spectators of the games, "and is even now at once the
most imposing and the most characteristic relic of pagan
Rome."[1]

Life was terrible in its fears and in its pleasures. If the
poets drew Ages of Gold in the latter days of the Republic,
now the philosophers and historians looked away to a "State of
Nature," to times and places where greed and civilization were
unknown. In those happy days, says Seneca, they enjoyed
Nature in common; the stronger had not laid his hand upon
the weaker; weapons lay unused, and human hands, unstained
by human blood, turned all the hatred they felt upon the wild
beasts; they knew quiet nights without a sigh, while the stars
moved onward above them and the splendid pageant of Night;
they drank from the stream and knew no water-pipes, and their
meadows were beautiful without art; their home was Nature
and not terrible; while our abodes form the greatest part of our
terror.[2] In Germany, writes Tacitus, the marriage-bond is
strict; there are no shows to tempt virtue; adultery is rare;
none there makes a jest of vice, *nec corrumpere et corrumpi
seculum vocatur*; none but virgins marry and they marry to bear
big children and to suckle them, *sera iuvenum venus eoque
inexhausta pubertas*; and the children inherit the sturdy frames
of their parents.[3]

But whatever their dreams of the ideal, the actual was

---

[1] Lecky, *European Morals*, i, 275; Epictetus, *D*. iii, 15.
[2] Seneca, *Ep*. 90. 36-43.   [3] Tacitus, *Germany*, cc. 18-20.

around them, and men had to accommodate themselves to it.
In France before the Revolution, men spoke of the government
as "despotism tempered by epigrams," and the happy phrase is
as true of Imperial Rome. "Verses of unknown authorship
reached the public and provoked " Tiberius,[1] who complained
of the " circles and dinner-parties." Now and again the authors
were discovered and were punished sufficiently. The tone of
the society that produced them lives for ever in the *Annals* of
Tacitus. It is worth noting how men and women turned to
Tacitus and Seneca during the French Revolution and found
their own experience written in their books.[2]

Others unpacked their hearts with words in tyrannicide
declamations and imitations of Greek tragedy. Juvenal laughs
at the crowded class-room busy killing tyrants,—waiting himself till they were dead. The tragedies got nearer the mark.
Here are a few lines from some of Seneca's own :—

> Who bids all pay one penalty of death
> Knows not a tyrant's trade. Nay, vary it—
> Forbid the wretch to die, and slay the happy. (*H.F.* 515.)

> And is there none to teach them stealth and sin ?
> Why! then the throne will! (*Thyestes* 313.)

> Let him who serves a king, fling justice forth,
> Send every scruple packing from his heart ;
> Shame is no minister to wait on kings. (*Phædra* 436.)

But bitterness and epigram could not heal ; and for healing
and inward peace men longed more and more,[3] as they felt
their own weakness, the power of evil and the terror of life ; and
they found both in a philosophy that had originally come into
being under circumstances somewhat similar. They needed
some foundation for life, some means of linking the individual
to something that could not be shaken, and this they found in
Stoicism. The Stoic philosopher saw a unity in this world of
confusion—it was the " Generative Reason "—the σπερματικὸς
λόγος, the Divine Word, or Reason, that is the seed and vital
principle, whence all things come and in virtue of which they

---

[1] Tac. *A.* i, 72. Suetonius (*Tib.* 59) quotes specimens.
[2] See Boissier, *Tacite*, 188 f. ; *l'opposition sous les Cesars*, 208-215.
[3] Persius, v, 73, *libertate opus est.*

live. All things came from fiery breath, πνεῦμα διάπυρον, and
returned to it. The whole universe was one polity—πολιτεία
τοῦ κόσμου—in virtue of the spirit that was its origin and its
life, of the common end to which it tended, of the absolute and
universal scope of the laws it obeyed—mind, matter, God, man,
formed one community. The soul of the individual Roman
partook of the very nature of God—*divinæ particula auræ*[1]—
and in a way stood nearer to the divine than did anything else
in the world, every detail of which, however, was some manifestation of the same divine essence. All men were in truth of
one blood, of one family,—all and each, as Seneca says, sacred
to each and all.[2] (*Unum me donavit* [*sc. Natura rerum*] *omnibus,
uni mihi omnes.*)

Taught by the Stoic, the troubled Roman looked upon himself at once as a fragment of divinity,[3] an entity self-conscious
and individual, and as a member of a divine system expressive
of one divine idea, which his individuality subserved. These
thoughts gave him ground and strength. If he seemed to be
the slave and plaything of an Emperor or an imperial freedman, none the less a divine life pulsed within him, and he was an
essential part of "the world." He had two havens of refuge—
the universe and his own soul—both quite beyond the reach of
the oppressor. Over and over we find both notes sounded in
the writings of the Stoics and their followers—God within you
and God without you. "Jupiter is all that you see, and all that
lives within you."[4] There is a Providence that rules human and
all other affairs; nothing happens that is not appointed; and
to this Providence every man is related. "He who has once
observed with understanding the administration of the world,
and learnt that the greatest and supreme and most comprehensive community is the system (σύστημα) of men and God, and
that from God come the seeds whence all things, and especially
rational beings, spring, why should not that man call himself a
citizen of the world [Socrates' word κόσμιος], why not a son of
God?"[5] And when we consider the individual, we find that God

---

[1] Horace, *Sat.* ii, 2, 79.

[2] See Edward Caird, *Evolution of Theology in the Greek Philosophers*, vol. ii,
lectures xvii to xx, and Zeller, *Eclectics*, pp. 235-245.   Seneca, *B. V.* 20, 3.

[3] Epictetus, *D.* ii, 8, σὺ ἀπόσπασμα εἶ τοῦ θεοῦ.

[4] Lucan, ix, 564-586, contains a short summary of Stoicism, supposed to be spoken
by Cato.   [5] Epictetus, *D.* i, 9 (some lines omitted).

has put in his power " the best thing of all, the master thing "—
the rational faculty. What is not in our power is the entire
external world, of which we can alter nothing, but the use we
make of it and its "appearances"[1] is our own. Confine yourself
to "what is in your power" (τὰ ἐπί σοι), and no man can hurt
you. If you can no longer endure life, leave it; but remember
in doing so to withdraw quietly, not at a run; yet, says the
sage, " Men ! wait for God ; when He shall give you the signal
and release you from this service, then go to Him ; but for the
present endure to dwell in this place where He has set you."[2]

To sum up ; the end of man's being and his true happiness is
what Zeno expressed as "living harmoniously," a statement
which Cleanthes developed by adding the words "with Nature."
Harmony with Nature and with oneself is the ideal life; and
this the outside world of Emperors, freedmen, bereavements and
accidents generally, can neither give nor take away. "The
end," says Diogenes Laertius, "is to act in conformity with
nature, that is, at once with the nature which is in us and with
the nature of the universe, doing nothing forbidden by that
common law which is the right reason that pervades all things,
and which is, indeed, the same in the Divine Being who
administers the universal system of things. Thus the life
according to nature is that virtuous and blessed flow of existence, which is enjoyed only by one who always acts so as to
maintain the harmony between the dæmon (δαίμων) within the
individual and the will of the power that orders the universe." [3]

This was indeed a ·philosophy for men, and it was also
congenial to Roman character, as history had already shown.
It appealed to manhood, and whatever else has to be said of
Stoics and Stoicism, it remains the fact that Stoicism inspired
nearly all the great characters of the early Roman Empire, and
nerved almost every attempt that was made to maintain the
freedom and dignity of the human soul.[4] The government was
not slow to realise the danger of men with such a trust in themselves and so free from fear.

On paper, perhaps, all religions and philosophies may at first
glance seem equally good, and it is not till we test them in life

---

[1] φαντασίαι, impressions left on the mind by things or events.
[2] Epictetus, *D.* i, 9.
[3] Diogenes Laertius, vii, 1, 53 ; see Caird, *op. cit.* vol. ii, p. 124.
[4] See Lecky, *European Morals*, i, 128, 129.

that we can value them aright. And even here there is a wide field for error. Every religion has its saints—men recognizable to everyone as saints in the beauty, manhood and tenderness of their character—and it is perhaps humiliating to have to acknowledge that very often they seem to be so through some happy gift of Nature, quite independently of any effort they make, or of the religion to which they themselves generally attribute anything that redeems them from being base. We have to take, if possible, large masses of men, and to see how they are affected by the religion which we wish to study—average men, as we call them—for in this way we shall escape being led to hasty conclusions by happy instances of natural endowment, or of virtues carefully acquired in favourable circumstances of retirement or helpful environment. Side by side with such results as we may reach from wider study, we have to set our saints and heroes, for while St Francis would have been tender and Thrasea brave under any system of thought, it remains that the one was Christian and the other Stoic. We need the individual, if we are to avoid mere rough generalities; but we must be sure that he is representative in some way of the class and the system under review.

As representatives of the Stoicism of the early Roman Empire, two men stand out conspicuous—men whose characters may be known with a high degree of intimacy. The one was a Roman statesman, famous above all others in his age, and a man of letters—one of those writers who reveal themselves in every sentence they write and seem to leave records of every mood they have known. The other was an emancipated slave, who lived at Nicopolis in Epirus, away from the main channels of life, who wrote nothing, but whose conversations or monologues were faithfully recorded by a disciple.

"Notable Seneca," writes Carlyle, "so wistfully desirous to stand well with Truth and yet not ill with Nero, is and remains only our perhaps niceliest proportioned half-and-half, the plausiblest Plausible on record; no great man, no true man, no man at all . . . 'the father of all such as wear shovel-hats.'" This was in the essay on Diderot written in 1833; and we find in his diary for 10th August 1832, when Carlyle was fresh from reading Seneca, an earlier judgment to much the same effect—"He is father of all that work in sentimentality, and, by fine speaking

and decent behaviour, study to serve God and mammon, to
stand well with philosophy and not ill with Nero. His *force*
had mostly oozed out of him, or corrupted itself into *benevolence*,
virtue, sensibility. Oh! the everlasting clatter about virtue!
virtue!! In the Devil's name be virtuous and no more about it."

Even in his most one-sided judgments Carlyle is apt to
speak truth, though it is well to remember that he himself said
that little is to be learnt of a man by dwelling only or mainly
on his faults. That what he says in these passages is in some
degree true, every candid reader must admit; but if he had
written an essay instead of a paragraph we should have seen that
a great deal more is true of Seneca. As it is, we must take what
Carlyle says as representing a judgment which has often been
passed upon Seneca, though seldom in such picturesque terms.
It is in any case truer than Mommsen's description of Cicero.

Seneca was born at Cordova in Spain about the Christian
era—certainly not long before it. His father was a rich man of
equestrian rank, a rhetorician, who has left several volumes of
rhetorical compositions on imaginary cases. He hated philosophy, his son tells us.[1] Seneca's mother seems to have been
a good woman, and not the only one in the family; for his
youth was delicate and owed much to the care of a good aunt
at Rome; and his later years were spent with a good wife
Pompeia Paulina, who bore him two little short-lived boys.

In one of his letters (108) Seneca tells us of his early life in
Rome. He went to the lectures of Attalus, a Stoic teacher,
who laid great stress on simplicity of life and independence of
character and was also interested in superstition and soothsaying.
The pupil was a high-minded and sensitive youth, quick then,
as he remained through life, to take fire at an idea.[2] " I used to
be the first to come and the last to go; and as he walked I
would lead him on to further discussions, for he was not only
ready for those who would learn, but he would meet them."
" When I heard Attalus declaim against the vices, errors and
evils of life, I would often pity mankind; and as for him I
thought of him as one on high, far above human nature's
highest. He himself used to say he was a king [a Stoic

[1] *Ep.* 108, 22, *philosophiam oderat.*
[2] With these passages compare the fine account which Persius gives (*Sat.* v) of
his early studies with the Stoic Cornutus.

paradox at which Horace had laughed]; but he seemed to me more than king,—the judge of kings. When he began to commend poverty, and to show that whatever is more than need requires, is a useless burden to him that has it, I often longed to leave the room a poor man. When he attacked our pleasures and praised the chaste body, the sober table, the pure mind, I delighted to refrain, not merely from unlawful pleasures, but from needless ones too. Some of it has stuck by me, Lucilius, for I made a good beginning." All his life long, in fact, he avoided the luxuries of table and bath, and drank water. He continues, "Since I have begun to tell you how much more keenly I began philosophy in my youth than I persevere with it in my old age, I am not ashamed to own what love of Pythagoras Sotion waked in me." Sotion recommended vegetarianism on the grounds which Pythagoras had laid down. "But you do not believe," he said, "that souls are allotted to one body after another, and that what we call death is transmigration? You don't believe that in beasts and fishes dwells the mind (*animum*) that was once a man's? . . . Great men have believed it; so maintain your own opinion, but keep the matter open. If it is true, then to have abstained from animal food will be innocence; if it is false, it will still be frugality."[1] So for a year Seneca was a vegetarian with some satisfaction and he fancied that his mind was livelier than when he was "an eater of beef."[2] It is as well not to quote some contemporary methods of preparing meat.[3] However, after a while some scandal arose about foreign religions, and vegetarianism was counted a "proof of superstition," and the old rhetorician, more from dislike of philosophy than from fear of calumny, made it an excuse to put a little pressure on his philosophic son, who obediently gave up the practice. Such is the ardour of youth, he concludes,—a good teacher finds idealists ready to his hand. The fault is partly in the teachers, who train us to argue and not to live, and partly in the pupils too, whose aim is to have the wits trained and not the mind. "So what was philosophy becomes philology—the love of words."[4]

There is a certain gaiety and good humour about these

---

[1] Plutarch, *de esu carnium*, ii, 5.

[2] Plutarch, *de esu carnium*, i, 6, on clogging the soul by eating flesh. Clem. Alex. *Pæd.* ii, 16, says St Matthew lived on seeds, nuts and vegetables, and without meat.

[3] Plutarch, *de esu carnium*, ii, 1.   [4] Sen. *Ep.* 108, 3, 13-23.

confessions, which is closely bound up with that air of tolerance and that sense of buoyant ease[1] which pervade all his work. Here the tone is in keeping with the matter in hand, but it is not always. Everything seems so easy to him that the reader begins to doubt him and to wonder whether he is not after all "The plausiblest Plausible on record." We associate experience with a style more plain, more tense, more inevitable; and the extraordinary buoyancy of Seneca's writing suggests that he can hardly have known the agony and bloody sweat of the true teacher. Yet under the easy phrases there lay a real sincerity. From his youth onward he took life seriously, and, so far as is possible for a man of easy good nature, he was in earnest with himself.

Like other youths of genius, he had had thoughts of suicide, but on reflexion, he tells us, he decided to live, and his reason was characteristic. While for himself he felt equal to dying bravely, he was not so sure that his "kind old father" would be quite so brave in doing without him. It was to philosophy, he says, that he owed his resolution.[2]

Apart from philosophy, he went through the ordinary course of Roman education. He "wasted time on the grammarians,"[3] whom he never forgave, and at whom, as "guardians of Latin speech"[4] he loved to jest,—and the greatest of all Roman Grammarians paid him back in the familiar style of the pedagogue. Rhetoric came to him no doubt by nature, certainly by environment; it conspicuously haunted his family for three generations.[5] He duly made his appearance at the bar—making more speeches there than Virgil did, and perhaps not disliking it so much. But he did not like it, and, when his father died, he ceased to appear, and by and by found that he had lost the power to plead as he had long before lost the wish.[6]

On the accession of Claudius to the Imperial throne in 41 A.D., Seneca, now in middle life, was for some reason banished to Corsica, and there for eight weary years he remained, till the Empress Messalina fell. A little treatise, which he wrote

---

[1] This is a quality that Quintilian notes in his style for praise or blame. Others (Gellius, *N.A.* xii, 2) found in him *levis et quasi dicax argutia.*

[2] *Ep.* 78, 2, 3, *patris me indulgentissimi senectus retinuit.*

[3] *Ep.* 58, 5. [4] *Ep.* 95, 65.

[5] His nephew Lucan, Quintilian severely says, was "perhaps a better model for orators than for poets." [6] *Ep.* 49, 2. Virgil made one speech.

to console his mother, survives—couched in the rhetoric she knew so well. If the language is more magnificent than sons usually address to their mothers, it must be remembered that he wrote to console her for misfortunes which he was himself enduring. The familiar maxim that the mind can make itself happy and at home anywhere is rather like a platitude, but it loses something of that character when it comes from the lips of a man actually in exile. Another little work on the subject, which he addressed later on to Polybius, the freedman of Claudius, stands on a different footing, and his admirers could wish he had not written it. There is flattery in it of a painfully cringing tone. "The Emperor did not hurl him down so utterly as never to raise him again; rather he supported him when evil fortune smote him and he tottered; he gently used his godlike hand to sustain him and pleaded with the Senate to spare his life. . . . He will see to his cause. . . . He best knows the time at which to show favour. . . . Under the clemency of Claudius, exiles live more peacefully than princes did under Gaius." [1] But a little is enough of this.

It is clear that Seneca was not what we call a strong man. A fragile youth, a spirit of great delicacy and sensibility, were no outfit for exile. Nor is it very easy to understand what exile was to the educated Roman. Some were confined to mere rocks, to go round and round them for ever and never leave them. Seneca had of course more space, but what he endured, we may in some measure divine from the diaries and narratives that tell of Napoleon's life on St Helena. The seclusion from the world, the narrow range, the limited number of faces, the red coats, the abhorred monotony, told heavily on every temper, on gaoler and prisoner alike, even on Napoleon; and Seneca's temperament was not of stuff so stern. We may wish he had not broken down, but we cannot be surprised that he did. It was human of him. Perhaps the memory of his own weakness and failure contributed to make him the most sympathetic and the least arrogant of all Stoics.

At last Messalina reached her end, and the new Empress, Agrippina, recalled the exile in 49 A.D., and made him tutor of her son, Nero; and from now till within two years of his death Seneca lived in the circle of the young prince. When Claudius died in 54, Seneca and Burrus became the guardians of the

[1] ad Polybium, 13, 2, 3.

Emperor and virtually ruled the Empire. It was a position of great difficulty. Seneca grew to be immensely rich, and his wealth and his palaces and gardens[1] weakened his influence, while they intensified the jealousy felt for a minister so powerful. Yet perhaps none of his detractors guessed the limits of his power as surely as he came to feel them himself. Some measure of the situation may be taken from what befell when the freedwoman Claudia Acte became the mistress of Nero. "His older friends did not thwart him," says Tacitus, "for here was a girl, who, without harm to anyone, gratified his desires, since he was utterly estranged from his wife Octavia."[2] Later on, we learn, Seneca had to avail himself of Acte's aid to prevent worse scandals.

In February 55 A.D. the young prince Britannicus was poisoned at Nero's table. He was the son of Claudius and the brother of Octavia—a possible claimant therefore to the Imperial throne. Nero, not more than eighteen years old, told the company quite coolly that it was an epileptic seizure, and the feast went on, while the dead boy was carried out and buried there and then in the rain—in a grave prepared before he had entered the dining-hall.[3] Ten months later Seneca wrote his tractate on Clemency. Nero should ask himself "Am I the elected of the gods to be their vice-gerent on earth? The arbiter of life and death to the nations?" and so forth. He is gently reminded of the great light that fronts the throne; that his anger would be as disastrous as war; that "Kings gain from kindness a greater security, while their cruelty swells the number of their enemies." Seneca wanders a good deal, but his drift is clear— and the wretchedness of his position.

That Burrus and he had no knowledge of Nero's design to do away with his mother, is the verdict of Nero's latest historian, but to Seneca fell the horrible task of writing the explanatory letter which Nero sent to the Senate when the murder was done. Perhaps to judge him fairly, one would need to have been a Prime Minister. It may have been a necessary thing to do, in order to maintain the world's government, but the letter imposed on nobody, and Thrasea Pætus at once rose from his seat and walked conspicuously out.

From the year 59 Nero was more than ever his own master

---

[1] Juvenal, x, 16, *magnos Senecæ prædivitis hortos.*
[2] *Ann.* xiii, 12, 2.   [3] Tac. *Ann.* xiii, 15·17.

His guardians' repeated condonations had set him free, and the lad, who had "wished he had never learned writing" when he had to sign his first death-warrant, began from now to build up that evil fame for which the murders of his brother and his mother were only the foundation. For three years Seneca and Burrus kept their places—miserably enough. Then Burrus found a happy release in death, and with him died the last of Seneca's influence.[1] Seneca begged the Emperor's leave to retire from the Court, offering him the greater part of his wealth, and it was refused. It had long been upon his mind that he was too rich. In 58 a furious attack was made upon him by "one who had earned the hate of many," Publius Suillius; this man asked in the Senate "by what kind of wisdom or maxims of philosophy" Seneca had amassed in four years a fortune equal to two and a half millions sterling; and he went on to accuse him of intrigue with princesses, of hunting for legacies, and of "draining Italy and the provinces by boundless usury."[2] There was probably a good deal of inference in these charges, if one may judge by the carelessness of evidence which such men show in all ages. Still Seneca felt the taunt, and in a book "On the Happy Life," addressed to his brother Gallio, he dealt with the charge. He did not claim to be a sage (17, 3); his only hope was day by day to lessen his vices—he was still in the thick of them; perhaps he might not reach wisdom, but he would at least live for mankind "as one born for others,"[3] would do nothing for glory, and all for conscience, would be gentle and accessible even to his foes; as for wealth, it gave a wise man more opportunity, but if his riches deserted him, they would take nothing else with them; a philosopher might have wealth, "if it be taken forcibly from no man, stained with no man's blood, won by no wrong done to any, gained without dishonour; if its spending be as honest as its getting, if it wake no envy but in the envious."[4] The treatise has a suggestion of excitement, and there is a good deal of rhetoric in it. Now he proposed to the Emperor to put his words into action, and Nero would not permit him—he was not ready for the odium of despoiling his guardian, and the old man's name might still be of use to cover deeds in which he had no share. Seneca was not to resign his

---

[1] Tac. *Ann.* xiv, 51.   [2] Tac. *Ann.* xiii, 42.
[3] *B.V.* 20, 3.   [4] *B.V.* 23, 1.

wealth nor to leave Rome. Nero's words as given by Tacitus are pleasant enough, but we hardly need to be told their value.[1]

It was merely a reservation of the death sentence, and Seneca must have known it. The only thing now was to wait till he should receive the order to die, and Seneca occupied the time in writing. If what he wrote has a flushed and excited air, it is not surprising. The uncertainity of his position had preyed upon him while he was still Minister—"there are many," he had written, "who must hold fast to their dizzy height; it is only by falling that they can leave it."[2] He had fallen, and still he had to live in uncertainty; he had always been a nervous man.

The end came in 65, in connexion with the conspiracy of Piso. Tacitus is not altogether distinct as to the implication of Seneca in this plot, but modern historians have inclined to believe in his guilt—if guilt it was.[3] Mr Henderson, in particular, is very severe on him for this want of "gratitude" to his benefactor and pupil, but it is difficult to see what Nero had done for him that he would not have preferred undone.[4] Perhaps at the time, and certainly later on, Seneca was regarded as a possible substitute for Nero upon the throne;[5] but he was well over sixty and frail, nor is it clear that the world had yet decided that a man could be Emperor without being a member of the Julian or Claudian house. Seneca, in fact any man, must have felt that any one would be better than Nero, but he had himself conspicuously left the world, and, with his wife, was living the philosophic life—a vegetarian again, and still a water-drinker.[6] Seneca was ready for the death-summons and at once opened his veins. Death came slowly, but it came; and he died, eloquent to the last—*novissimo quoque momento suppeditante eloquentia.*

Such is the story of Seneca. Even in bare outline it shows something of his character—his kindliness and sensibility, his weakness and vanity; but there are other features revealed in his books and his many long letters to Lucilius. No Roman, perhaps, ever laid more stress on the duty of gentleness and forgiveness.[7] "Look at the City of Rome," he says, "and the

---

[1] Tac. *Ann.* xiv, 52-56. [2] *de tranqu. animi,* 10, 6.
[3] Tac. *Ann.* xiv, 65; xv, 45-65. [4] B. W. Henderson, *Nero,* pp. 280-3.
[5] Tac. *Ann.* xv, 65; Juvenal, viii, 212. [6] Tac. *Ann.* xv, 45, 6.
[7] This is emphasized by Zeller, *Eclectics,* 240, and by Dill, *Roman Society from Nero to Marcus,* 324, 326.

crowds unceasingly pouring through its broad streets—what a solitude, what a wilderness it would be, were none left but whom a strict judge would acquit. We have all done wrong (*peccavimus*), some in greater measure, some in less, some on purpose, some by accident, some by the fault of others; we have not stood bravely enough by our good resolutions ; despite our will and our resistance, we have lost our innocence. Nor is it only that we have acted amiss ; we shall do so to the end."[1] He is anxious to make Stoicism available for his friends; he tones down its gratuitous harshness, accommodates, conciliates. He knows what conscience is ; he is recognized as a master in dealing with the mind at variance with itself, so skilfully does he analyse and lay bare its mischiefs. Perhaps he analyses too much—the angel, who bade Hermas cease to ask concerning sins and ask of righteousness, might well have given him a word. But he is always tender with the man to whom he is writing. If he was, as Quintilian suggests, a " splendid assailant of the faults of men," it is the faults of the unnamed that he assails; his friends' faults suggest his own, and he pleads and sympathizes. His style corresponds with the spirit in which he thinks. "You complain," he writes to Lucilius, " that my letters are not very finished in style. Who talks in a finished style unless he wishes to be affected ? What my talk would be, if we were sitting or walking together, unlaboured and easy, that is what I wish my letters to be, without anything precious or artificial in them."[2] And he has in measure succeeded in giving the air of talk to his writing—its ease, its gaiety, even its rambling and discursiveness. He always sees the friend to whom he writes, and talks to him—sometimes at him—and not without some suggestion of gesticulation. He must have talked well—though one imagines that, like Coleridge on Highgate Hill, he probably preferred the listener who sat "like a passive bucket to be pumped into." Happily the reader is not obliged to be quite so passive.

But we shall not do him justice if we do not recognize his high character. In an age when it was usual to charge every one with foulness, natural and unnatural, Dio Cassius alone among writers suggests it of Seneca; and, quite apart from his particular bias in this case, Dio is not a high authority,—

[1] *ae Clem.* i, 6.

more especially as he belonged to a much later generation. If his talk is of "virtue! virtue!" Seneca's life was deliberately directed to virtue. In the midst of Roman society, and set in the highest place but one in the world, he still cherished ideals, and practised self-discipline, daily self-examination. "This is the one goal of my days and of my nights: this is my task, my thought—to put an end to my old faults."[1] His whole philosophy is practical, and directed to the reformation of morals. The Stoic paradoxes, and with them every part of philosophy which has no immediate bearing upon conduct, he threw aside. His language on the accumulation of books recalls the amusement of St Francis at the idea of possessing a breviary. And further, we may note that whatever be charged against him as a statesman, not his own master, and as a writer, not always quite in control of his rhetoric, Seneca was fundamentally truthful with himself. He never hid his own weakness; he never concealed from himself the difficulty of his ideals; he never tried to delude himself with what he could not believe. The Stoics had begun long since to make terms with popular religion, but Seneca is entirely free from delusions as to the gods of popular belief. He saw clearly enough that there was no truth in them, and he never sought help from anything but the real. He is a man, trained in the world,[2] in touch with its problems of government, with the individual and his questions of character, death and eternity,—a man tender, pure and true—too great a man to take the purely negative stand of Thrasea, or to practise the virtue of the schools in "arrogant indolence." But he has hardly reached the inner peace which he sought.

The story of Epictetus can be more briefly told, for there is very little to tell.[3] He was born at Hierapolis in Phrygia:— he was the slave of Nero's freedman Epaphroditus, and somehow managed to hear the lectures of the Stoic Musonius. Eventually he was set free, and when Domitian expelled the philosophers from Rome, he went to Nicopolis in Epirus,[4] where he lived and taught—lame, neat, poor and old. How

---

[1] *Ep.* 61, 1.

[2] Lucian, *Nigrinus*, 19, says there is no better school for virtue, no truer test of moral strength, than life in the city of Rome.

[3] Gellius, *N.A.* ii, 18, 10. [4] Gell. *N.A.* xv, 11, 5.

he taught is to be seen in the discourses which Arrian took down in the reign of Trajan,—" Whatever I heard him say, I tried to write down exactly, and in his very words as far as I could—to keep them as memorials for myself of his mind and of his outspokenness. So they are, as you would expect, very much what a man would say to another on the spur of the moment—not what he would write for others to read afterwards. . . . . His sole aim in speaking was to move the minds of his hearers to the best things. If then these discourses should achieve this, they would have the effect which I think a philosopher's words should have. But if they do not, let my readers know that, when he spoke them, the hearer could not avoid being affected as Epictetus wished him to be. If the discourses do not achieve this, perhaps it will be my fault, or perhaps it may be inevitable. Farewell."

Such, save for a sentence or two omitted, is Arrian's preface,—thereafter no voice is heard but that of Epictetus. To place, time or persons present the barest allusions only are made. " Someone said . . . And Epictetus spoke." The four books of Arrian give a strong impression of fidelity. We hear the tones of the old man, and can recognize "the mind and the outspokenness," which Arrian cherished in memory— we understand why, as we read. The high moral sense of the teacher, his bursts of eloquence, his shrewdness, his abrupt turns of speech, his apostrophes—"Slave!" he cries, as he addresses the weakling—his diminutives of derision, produce the most lively sense of a personality. There is wit, too, but like Stoic wit in general it is hard and not very sympathetic ; it has nothing of the charm and delicacy of Plato's humour, nor of its kindliness.

Here and there are words and thoughts which tell of his life. More than once he alludes to his age and his lameness— " A lame old man like me." But perhaps nowhere in literature are there words that speak so loud of a man without experience of woman or child. " On a voyage," he says, " when the ship calls at a port and you go ashore for water, it amuses you to pick up a shell or a plant by the way ; but your thoughts ought to be directed to the ship, and you must watch lest the captain call, and then you must throw away all those things, that you may not be flung aboard, tied like the sheep. So in life, suppose that instead of some little shell or plant, you are given some-thing in the way of wife or child (ἀντὶ βολβαρίου καὶ κοχλιδίου γυναικάριον καὶ παιδίον) nothing need hinder. *But*, if the captain call, run to the ship letting them all go and never looking round. If you are old, do not even go far from the ship, lest you fail to come when called."[1] He bids a man endure hunger; he can only die of it. " But my wife and children also suffer hunger, (οἱ ἐμοὶ πεινήσουσι). What then? does their hunger lead to any other place? Is there not for them the same descent, wherever it lead? Below, is it not the same for them as for you?"[2] "If you are kissing your child, or brother, or friend, never give full licence to the appearance (τὴν φαντασίαν); check your pleasure ... remind yourself that you love a mortal thing, a thing that is not your own (οὐδὲν τῶν σαυτοῦ). . . . What harm does it do to whisper, as you kiss the child, ' To-morrow you will die'?" This is a thought he uses more than once,[3] though he knows the attractiveness of lively children.[4] He recommends us to practise resignation—beginning on a broken jug or cup, then on a coat or puppy, and so up to oneself and one's limbs, children, wife or brothers.[5] "If a man wishes his son or his wife not to do wrong, he really wishes what is another's not to be another's."[6]

As to women, a few quotations will show his detachment. He seems hardly to have known a good woman. " Do not admire your wife's beauty, and you are not angry with the adulterer. Learn that a thief and an adulterer have no place among the things that are yours, but among those which are not yours and not in your power,"[7] and he illustrates his philosophy with an anecdote of an iron lamp stolen from him, which he replaced with an earthenware one. From fourteen years old, he says, women think of nothing and aim at nothing

---

[1] *Manual*, 7. I have constantly used Long's translation, but often altered it. It is a fine piece of work, well worth the English reader's study.

[2] *D*. iii, 26. Compare and contrast Tertullian, *de Idol*, 12, *fides famem non timet. Scit enim famem non minus sibi contemnendam propter Deum quam omne mortis genus*. The practical point is the same, perhaps ; the motive, how different !

[3] *D*. iii, 24 ; iv, 1 ; *M*. 11, 26.

[4] *D*. ii, 24. He maintains, too, against Epicurus the naturalness of love for children ; once born, we cannot help loving them, *D*. i, 23.

[5] *D*. iv, 1.   [6] *D*. iv, 5, θέλει τὰ ἀλλότρια μὴ εἶναι ἀλλότρια.

[7] *D*. i, 18. This does not stop his condemning the adulterer, *D*. ii, 4 (man, he said, is formed for fidelity), 10. Seneca on outward goods, *ad Marciam*, 10.

but lying with men.[1]   Roman women liked Plato's Republic for the licence they wrongly supposed it gave.[2]   He constantly speaks of women as a temptation, nearly always using a diminutive κοράσιον, κορασίδιον—little girls—and as a temptation hardly to be resisted by young men.   He speaks of their "softer voices."[3]   A young philosopher is no match for a "pretty girl"; let him fly temptation.[4]   "As to pleasure with women, abstain as far as you can, before marriage; but if you do indulge in it, do it in the way conformable to custom.   Do not, however, be disagreeable to those who take such pleasures, nor apt to rebuke them or to say often that you do not."[5]   All this may be taken as the impression left by Rome and the household of Epaphroditus upon a slave's mind.   It may be observed that he makes nothing like Dio Chrysostom's condemnation of prostitution—an utterance unexampled in pagan antiquity.

It is pleasanter to turn to other features of Epictetus.   He has a very striking lecture on personal cleanliness.[6]   In proportion as men draw near the gods by reason, they cling to purity of soul and body.   Nature has given men hands and nostrils; so, if a man does not use a handkerchief, "I say, he is not fulfilling the function of a man."   Nature has provided water.   "It is impossible that some impurity should not remain in the teeth after eating. 'So wash your teeth,' says Nature.   Why? 'That you may be a man and not a beast—a pig.'"   If a man would not bathe and use the strigil and have his clothes washed —"either go into a desert where you deserve to go, or live alone and smell yourself."   He cannot bear a dirty man,— "who does not get out of his way?"   It gives philosophy a bad name, he says; but it is quite clear that that was not his chief reason.   He would sooner a young man came to him with his hair carefully trimmed than with it dirty and rough; such care implied "some conception of the beautiful," which it was only necessary to direct towards the things of the mind; "but if a man comes to me filthy and dirty, with a moustache down to his knees—what *can* I say to him?"   "But whence am I to get a fine cloak?   Man! you have water; wash it!"

---

[1] *M.* 40.
[2] Fragment, 53.
[3] *D.* i, 16.
[4] *D.* iii, 12, classing the κορασίδιον with wine and cake.
[5] *M.* 33.
[6] *D.* iv, 11.

Pupils gathered round him and he became famous, as we can see in the reminiscences of Aulus Gellius.[1] Sixty or seventy years after his death a man bought his old earthenware lamp for three thousand drachmas.[2] Even in his lifetime men began to come about "the wonderful old man" who were hardly serious students. They wished, he says, to occupy the time while waiting to engage a passage on a ship—they happened to be passing (πάροδός ἐστιν) and looked in to see him as if he were a statue. "We can go and see Epictetus too.—Then you go away and say; Oh! Epictetus was nothing! he talked bad Greek—oh! barbarous Greek!"[3] Others came to pick up a little philosophic language for use in public. Why could they not philosophize and say nothing? he asked. "Sheep do not vomit up their grass to show the shepherd how much they have eaten—no! they digest it inside, and then produce wool and milk outside."[4] He took his teaching seriously as a matter of life, and he looked upon it as a service done to mankind—quite equivalent to the production of "two or three ugly-nosed children."[5] He has a warm admiration for the Cynic philosopher's independence of encumberments—how can he who has to teach mankind go looking after a wife's confinement—or "something to heat the water in to give the baby a bath?"[6]

These then are the two great teachers of Stoicism, the outstanding figures, whose words and tones survive, whose characters are familiar to us. They are clearly preachers, both of them, intent on the practical reformation of their listeners or correspondents. For them conduct is nine-tenths of life. Much of their teaching is of course the common property of all moral teachers —the deprecation of anger, of quarrelsomeness, of self-indulgence, of grumbling, of impurity, is peculiar to no school. Others have emphasized that life is a campaign with a general to be obeyed, if you can by some instinct divine what he is signalling.[7] But

---

[1] Gell. *N.A.* i, 2, 6 ; xvii, 19, 1.   [2] Lucian, *adv. Indoct.* 13.

[3] *D.* iii, 9.   [4] *M.* 46.

[5] *D.* iii, 22, κακόρυγκα παιδία.

[6] *D.* iii, 22. Lucian says Epictetus urged Demonax to take a wife and leave some one to represent him in posterity. "Very well, Epictetus," said Demonax, "give me one of your own daughters" (*v. Demon.* 55).

[7] Epict. *D.* iii, 24. στρατεία τίς ἐστιν ὁ βίος ἑκάστου, καὶ αὕτη μακρὰ καὶ ποικίλη. τηρεῖν σε δεῖ τὸ τοῦ στρατηγοῦ πρόσνευμα καὶ τοῦ στρατιώτου πράσσειν ἕκαστα, εἰ οἷόν τε μαντευόμενος ὃ θέλει.

perhaps it was a new thing in the Western World, when so much accent was laid on conduct. The terror of contemporary life, with its repulsiveness, its brutality and its fascination, drove men in search of the moral guide. The philosopher's school was an infirmary, not for the glad but for the sorry.[1] "That man," says Seneca, "is looking for salvation—*ad salutem spectat.*"

Men sought the help of the philosopher, and relapsed. "He thinks he wishes reason. He has fallen out with luxury, but he will soon make friends with her. But he says he is offended with his own life! I do not deny it; who is not? Men love their vices and hate them at the same time."[2] So writes Seneca of a friend of Lucilius and his fugitive thoughts of amendment, and Epictetus is no less emphatic on the crying need for earnestness. The Roman world was so full of glaring vice that every serious man from Augustus onward had insisted on some kind of reformation, and now men were beginning to feel that the reformation must begin within themselves. The habit of daily self-examination became general among the Stoics, and they recommended it warmly to their pupils. Here is Seneca's account of himself.

"When the day was over and Sextius had gone to his night's rest, he used to ask his mind (*animum*): 'what bad habit of yours have you cured to-day? what vice have you resisted? in what respect are you better?' Anger will cease and will be more moderate, when it knows it must daily face the judge. Could anything be more beautiful than this habit of examining the whole day? What a sleep is that which follows self-scrutiny! How calm, how deep and free, when the mind is either praised or admonished, when it has looked into itself, and like a secret censor makes a report upon its own moral state. I avail myself of this power and daily try my own case. When the light is removed from my sight, and my wife, who knows my habit, is silent, I survey my whole day and I measure my words again. I hide nothing from myself; I pass over nothing. For why should I be afraid of any of my errors, when I can say: 'See that you do it no more, now I forgive you. In that discussion, you spoke too pugnaciously; after this do not engage with the ignorant; they will not learn who have never

---

[1] Epict. *D.* iii, 23.   [2] Sen. *Ep.* 112, 3.

learned. That man you admonished too freely, so you did him no good; you offended him. For the future, see not only whether what you say is true, but whether he to whom it is said will bear the truth.'"[1]

Similar passages might be multiplied. "Live with yourself and see how ill-furnished you are," wrote Persius (iv, 52) the pupil of Cornutus. "From heaven comes that word 'know thyself,'" said Juvenal. A rather remarkable illustration is the letter of Serenus, a friend of Seneca's, of whose life things are recorded by Tacitus that do not suggest self-scrutiny. In summary it is as follows :—

"I find myself not quite free, nor yet quite in bondage to faults which I feared and hated. I am in a state, not the worst indeed, but very querulous and uncomfortable, neither well nor ill. It is a weakness of the mind that sways between the two, that will neither bravely turn to right nor to wrong. Things disturb me, though they do not alter my principles. I think of public life; something worries me, and I fall back into the life of leisure, to be pricked to the will to act by reading some brave words or seeing some fine example. I beg you, if you have any remedy to stay my fluctuation of mind, count me worthy to owe you peace. To put what I endure into a simile, it is not the tempest that troubles me, but sea-sickness."[2]

Epictetus quotes lines which he attributes to Pythagoras—

> Let sleep not come upon thy languid eyes
> Ere thou has scanned the actions of the day—
> Where have I sinned ? What done or left undone ?
> From first to last examine all, and then
> Blame what is wrong, in what is right, rejoice.[3]

These verses, he adds, are for use, not for quotation. Elsewhere he gives us a parody of self-examination—the reflections of one who would prosper in the world—"Where have I failed in flattery ? Can I have done anything like a free man, or a noble-minded ? Why did I say that ? Was it not in my power to lie ? Even the philosophers say nothing hinders a man from telling a lie."[4]

[1] de ira, iii, 36, 1-4.   [2] Sen. de tranqu. animi, 1.
[3] Epict. D. iii, 10. I have here slightly altered Mr Long's rendering.
[4] D. iv, 6.

But self-examination may take us further.[1] We come into the world, he says, with some innate idea (ἔμφυτος ἔννοια) of good and evil, as if Nature had taught us; but we find other men with different ideas,—Syrians and Egyptians, for instance. It is by a comparison of our ideas with those of other men that philosophy comes into being for us. "The beginning of philosophy—with those at least who enter upon it aright—by the door—is a consciousness of one's own weakness and insufficiency in necessary things (ἀσθενείας καὶ ἀδυναμίας)." We need rules or canons, and philosophy determines these for us by criticism.[2]

This reference to Syrians and Egyptians is probably not idle. The prevalence of Syrian and Egyptian religions, inculcating ecstatic communion with a god and the soul's need of preparation for the next world, contributed to the change that is witnessed in Stoic philosophy. The Eastern mind is affecting the Greek, and later Stoicism like later Platonism has thoughts and ideals not familiar to the Greeks of earlier days. It was with religions, as opposed to city cults, that Stoicism had now to compete for the souls of men; and while it retains its Greek characteristics in its intellectualism and its slightly-veiled contempt for the fool and the barbarian, it has taken on other features. It was avowedly a rule of life rather than a system of speculation and it was more, for the doctrine of the Spermaticos Logos (the Generative Reason) gave a new meaning to conduct and opened up a new and rational way to God. Thus Stoicism, while still a philosophy was pre-eminently a religion, and even a gospel—Good News of emancipation from the evil in the world and of union with the Divine.

Stoicism gave its convert a new conception of the relation of God and man. One Divine Word was the essence of both—Reason was shared by men and gods, and by pure thought men came into contact with the divine mind. Others sought communion in trance and ritual—the Stoic when he was awake, at his highest and best level, with his mind and not his hand, in thoughts, which he could understand and assimilate, rather than in magical formulæ, which lost their value when they became

---

[1] Cf. Persius, iii, 66-72, *causas cognoscite rerum, quid sumus aut quidnam victuri gignimur . . . quem te deus esse iussit et humana qua parte locatus es in re.*

[2] *D.* ii, 11. See Davidson, *Stoic Creed*, pp. 69, 81, on innate ideas. Plutarch, *de coh. ira*, 15, on Zeno's doctrine, τὸ σπέρμα σύμμιγμα καὶ κέρασμα τῶν τῆς ψυχῆς δυνάμεων ὑπάρχειν ἀπεσπασμένον.

intelligible. God and men formed a polity, and the Stoic was the fellow-citizen of the gods, obeying, understanding and adoring, as they did, one divine law, one order—a partaker of the divine nature, a citizen of the universe, a free man as no one else was free, because he knew his freedom and knew who shared it with him. He stood on a new footing with the gods, and for him the old cults passed away, superseded by a new worship which was divine service indeed.

"How the gods are to be worshipped, men often tell us. Let us not permit a man to light lamps on the Sabbath, for the gods need not the light, and even men find no pleasure in the smoke. Let us forbid to pay the morning salutation and to sit at the doors of the temples; it is human interest that is courted by such attentions: God, he worships who knows Him. Let us forbid to take napkins and strigils to Jove, to hold the mirror to Juno. God seeks none to minister to him; nay! himself he ministers to mankind; everywhere he is, at the side of every man. Let a man hear what mode to keep in sacrifices, how far to avoid wearisomeness and superstition: never will enough be done, unless in his mind he shall have conceived God as he ought, as in possession of all things, as giving all things freely. What cause is there that the gods should do good? Nature. He errs, who thinks they *can* not do harm; they *will* not. They cannot receive an injury nor do one. To hurt and to be hurt are one thing. Nature, supreme and above all most beautiful, has exempted them from danger and from being dangerous. The beginning of worship of the gods is to believe gods are; then to attribute to them their own majesty, to attribute to them goodness, without which majesty is not, to know it is they who preside over the universe, who rule all things by their might, who are guardians of mankind, at times [1] thoughtful of individuals. They neither give nor have evil; but they chastise, they check, they assign penalties and sometimes punish in the form of blessing. Would you propitiate the gods? Be good! He has worshipped them enough who has imitated them." [2]

---

[1] The qualification may be illustrated from Cicero's Stoic, *de Nat. Deor.* ii, 66, 167, *Magna di curant parva neglegunt.*

[2] *Ep.* 95, 47-50. Cf. *Ep.* 41; *de Prov.* i, 5. A very close parallel, with a strong Stoic tinge, in Minucius Felix, 32, 2, 3, ending *Sic apud nos religiosior est ille qui iustior.*

This is not merely a statement of Stoic dogma ; it was a proclamation of freedom. Line after line of this fine passage directly counters what was asserted and believed throughout the world by the adherents of the Eastern religions. Hear Seneca once more.

" We understand Jove to be ruler and guardian of the whole, mind and breath of the Universe (*animum spiritumque mundi*), lord and artificer of this fabric. Every name is his. Would you call him fate ? You will not err. He it is on whom all things depend, the cause of causes. Would you call him Providence ? You will speak aright. He it is whose thought provides for the universe that it may move on its course unhurt and do its part. Would you call him Nature ? you will not speak amiss. He it is of whom all things are born, by whose breath (*spiritu*) we live. Would you call him Universe ? You will not be deceived. He himself is this whole that you see, fills his own parts, sustains himself and what is his." [1]

Some one asked Epictetus one day how we can be sure that all our actions are under the inspection of God. " Do you think," said Epictetus, " that all things are a unity ? " (*i.e.* in the polity of the cosmos). " Yes." " Well then, do you not think that things earthly are in sympathy (συμπαθεῖν) with things heavenly ? " " Yes." Epictetus reminded his listener of the harmony of external nature, of flowers and moon and sun. " But are leaves and our bodies so bound up and united with the whole, and are not our souls much more ? and are our souls so bound up and in touch with God (συναφεῖς τῷ θεῷ) as parts of Him and portions of Him, and can it be that God does not perceive every motion of these parts as being His own motion cognate with Himself (συμφυοῦς) ? " [2] He bade the man reflect upon his own power of grasping in his mind ten thousand things at once under divine administration ; " and is not God able to oversee all things, and to be present with them, and to receive from all a certain communication ? " The man replied that he could not comprehend all these things at once. " And who tells you this—that *you* have equal power with Zeus ? Nevertheless, he has placed by every man a guardian (ἐπίτροπον), each man's

---

[1] *Nat. Quæst.* ii, 45. Cf. Tertullian, *Apol.* 21, on Zeno's testimony to the Logos, as creator, fate, God, *animus Iovis* and *necessitas omnium rerum.*

[2] Cf. Sen. *Ep.* 41, 1. *Prope est a te deus, tecum est, intus est. Ita dico, Lucili, sacer intra nos spiritus sedet malorum bonorumque nostrorum observator et custos.*

Dæmon, to whom he has committed the care of the man, a guardian who never sleeps, is never deceived. For to what better and more careful watch (φύλακι) could He have entrusted each of us? When then you (plural) have shut your doors and made darkness within, remember never to say that you are alone, for you are not; but God is within and your Dæmon (ὁ ὑμέτερος δαίμων); and what need have they of light to see what you are doing?"[1]

Here another feature occurs—the question of the dæmons. Seneca once alludes to the idea—"for the present," he writes to Lucilius, "set aside the view of some people, that to each individual one of us a god is given as a pedagogue, not indeed of the first rank, but of an inferior brand, of the number of those whom Ovid calls 'gods of the lower order' (de plebe deos); yet remember that our ancestors who believed this were so far Stoics, for to every man and woman they gave a Genius or a Juno. Later on we shall see whether the gods have leisure to attend to private people's business."[2] But before we pursue a side issue, which we shall in any case have to examine at a later point, let us look further at the central idea.

The thoughtful man finds himself, as we have seen, in a polity of gods and men, a cosmos, well-ordered in its very essence. "In truth," says Epictetus, "the whole scheme of things (τὰ ὅλα) is badly managed, if Zeus does not take care of his own citizens, so that they may be like himself, happy."[3] The first lesson of philosophy is that "there is a God and that he provides for the whole scheme of things, and that it is not possible to conceal from him our acts—no, nor our intentions or thoughts."[4] "God," says Seneca, "has a father's mind towards the good, and loves them stoutly—'let them,' he says, 'be exercised in work, pain and loss, that they may gather true strength.'" It is because God is in love with the good (bonorum amantissimus) that he gives them fortune to wrestle with. " There is a match worth God's sight (par deo dignum)—a brave man paired with evil fortune—especially if he is himself the challenger."[5] He goes on to show that what appear to be evils are not so; that misfortunes are at once for the advantage of those whom

---

[1] Epict. D. i, 14. See Clem. Alex. Strom. vii, 37, for an interesting account of how φθάνει ἡ θεία δύναμις, καθάπερ φῶς, διϊδεῖν τὴν ψυχήν.

[2] Ep. 110, 1, pædagogum dari deum. [3] D. iii, 24.

[4] D. ii, 14. [5] de providentia, 2, 6-9.

they befall and of men in general or the universe (*universis*),
"for which the gods care more than for individuals"; that those
who receive them are glad to have them—"and deserve evil if
they are not"; that misfortunes come by fate and befall men by
the same law by which they are good. "Always to be happy
and to go through life without a pang of the mind (*sine morsu
animi*) is to know only one half of Nature."[1] "The fates lead
us: what time remains for each of us, the hour of our birth
determined. Cause hangs upon cause. . . . Of old it was
ordained whereat you should rejoice or weep; and though the
lives of individuals seem marked out by a great variety, the sum
total comes to one and the same thing—perishable ourselves we
receive what shall perish."[2] "The good man's part is then to
commit himself to fate—it is a great comfort to be carried along
with the universe. Whatever it is that has bidden us thus to
live and thus to die, by the same necessity it binds the gods.
An onward course that may not be stayed sweeps on human
and divine alike. The very founder and ruler of all things has
written fate, but he follows it: he ever obeys, he once com-
manded."[3] To the good, God says, "To you I have given
blessings sure and enduring; all your good I have set within
you. Endure! herein you may even out-distance God; he is
outside the endurance of evils and you above it.[4] Above all I
have provided that none may hold you against your will; the
door is open; nothing I have made more easy than to die; and
death is quick."[5]

Epictetus is just as clear that we have been given all we need.
"What says Zeus? Epictetus, had it been possible, I would
have made both your little body and your little property free,
and not exposed to hindrance. . . . Since I was not able to do
this, I have given you a little portion of us, this faculty of
pursuing or avoiding an object, the faculty of desire and

---

[1] *de Prov.* 4, 1.

[2] *de Prov.* 5, 7. See Justin Martyr's criticism of Stoic fatalism, *Apol.* ii, 7. It
involves, he says, either God's identity with the world of change, or his implication
in all vice, or else that virtue and vice are nothing—consequences which are alike
contrary to every sane ἔννοια, to λόγος and to νοῦς.

[3] *de Prov.* 5, 8.

[4] Plutarch, *adv. Stoicos*, 33, on this Stoic paradox of the equality of God and the
sage.

[5] *de Prov.* 6, 5-7. This Stoic justification of suicide was repudiated alike by
Christians and Neo-Platonists.

aversion and in a word the faculty of using the appearances of things."[1] "Must my leg then be lamed? Slave! do you then on account of one wretched leg find fault with the cosmos? Will you not willingly surrender it for the whole? . . . Will you be vexed and discontented with what Zeus has set in order, with what he and the Moiræ, who were there spinning thy nativity (γένεσιν), ordained and appointed? I mean as regards your body ; for so far as concerns reason you are no worse than the gods and no less."[2]

In language curiously suggestive of another school of thought, Seneca speaks of God within us, of divine help given to human effort. "God is near you, with you, within you. I say it, Lucilius ; a holy spirit sits within us (*sacer intra nos spiritus sedet*), spectator of our evil and our good, and guardian. Even as he is treated by us, he treats us. None is a good man without God.[3] Can any triumph over fortune unless helped by him? He gives counsel, splendid and manly ; in every good man,

> What god we know not, yet a god there dwells."[4]

"The gods," he says elsewhere, "are not scornful, they are not envious. They welcome us, and, as we ascend, they reach us their hands. Are you surprised a man should go to the gods? God comes to men, nay! nearer still! he comes *into* men. No mind (*mens*) is good without God. Divine seeds are sown in human bodies," and will grow into likeness to their origin if rightly cultivated.[5] It should be noted that the ascent is by the route of frugality, temperance and fortitude. To this we must return.

Man's part in life is to be the "spectator and interpreter" of "God"[6] as he is the "son of God";[7] to attach himself to God;[8] to be his soldier, obey his signals, wait his call to

---

[1] *D.* i, 1.

[2] *D.* i, 12. See also *D.*i i, 16 "We say 'Lord God! how shall I *not* be anxious?' Fool, have you not hands, did not God make them for you? Sit down now and pray that your nose may not run."

[3] Cf. Cicero's Stoic, *N.D.* ii, 66, 167, *Nemo igitur vir magnus sine aliquo afflatu divino unquam fuit.*

[4] *Ep.* 41, 1, 2. (The line is from Virgil, *Aen.* viii, 352.) The rest of the letter develops the idea of divine dependence. *Sic animus magnus ac sacer et in hoc demissus ut propius quidem divina nossemus, conversatur quidem nobiscum sed hæret origini suæ, etc.*

[5] *Ep.* 73, 15, 16.　　[6] Epictetus, *D.* i, 6.　　[7] *D.* i, 9.　　[8] *D.* iv, 1.

retreat; or (in the language of the Olympian festival) to "join with him in the spectacle and the festival for a short time" (συμπομπεύσοντα αὐτῷ καὶ συνεορτάσοντα πρὸς ὀλίγον), to watch the pomp and the panegyris, and then go away like a grateful and modest man;[1] to look up to God and say "use me henceforth for what thou wilt. I am of thy mind; I am thine."[2] "If we had understanding, what else ought we to do, but together and severally, hymn God, and bless him (εὐφημεῖν) and tell of his benefits? Ought we not, in digging or ploughing or eating, to sing this hymn to God? 'Great is God who has given us such tools with which to till the earth; great is God who has given us hands, the power of swallowing, stomachs, the power to grow unconsciously, and to breathe while we sleep.' . . . What else can I do, a lame old man, but hymn God? If I were a nightingale, I would do the part of a nightingale . . . but I am a rational creature, and I ought to hymn God; this is my proper work; I do it; nor will I quit my post so long as it is given me; and you I call upon to join in this same song."[3] Herakles in all his toils had nothing dearer to him than God, and "for that reason he was believed to be the son of God and he was."[4] "Clear away from your thoughts sadness, fear, desire, envy, avarice, intemperance, etc. But it is not possible to eject all these things, otherwise than by looking away to God alone (πρὸς μόνον τὸν θεὸν ἀποβλέποντα) by fixing your affections on him only, by being dedicated to his commands."[5] This is "a peace not of Cæsar's proclamation (for whence could he proclaim it?) but of God's—through reason."[6]

The man, who is thus in harmony with the Spermaticos, Logos, who has "put his 'I' and 'mine'"[7] in the things of the will, has no quarrel with anything external. He takes a part in the affairs of men without aggression, greed or meanness. He submits to what is laid upon him. His peace none can take away, and none can make him angry. There is a fine passage in Seneca's ninety-fifth letter, following his account of right worship already quoted, in which he proceeds to deduce from this the right attitude to men. A sentence or two

---

[1] D. iv, 1.

[2] D. ii, 16 end, with a variant between σὸς εἰμι and ἴσος εἰμι, the former of which, Long says, is certain.

[3] D. i, 16. Contrast the passage of Clement quoted on p. 286.

[4] D. ii, 16.   [5] D. ii, 16.   [6] D. iii, 13.   [7] D. ii, 22.

must suffice. "How little it is not to injure him, whom you ought to help! Great praise forsooth, that man should be kind to man! Are we to bid a man to lend a hand to the shipwrecked, point the way to the wanderer, share bread with the hungry? . . . This fabric which you see, wherein are divine and human, is one. We are members of a great body. Nature has made us of one blood, has implanted in us mutual love, has made us for society (*sociabiles*). She is the author of justice and equity. . . . Let that verse be in your heart and on your lip.

> *Homo sum, humani nihil a me alienum puto."* [1]

"Unhappy man! will you ever love? (*ecquando amabis*)" he says to the irritable.[2] A little before, he said, "Man, a sacred thing to man, is slain for sport and merriment; naked and un-armed he is led forth; and the mere death of a man is spectacle enough." [3] This was the Stoic's condemnation of the gladiatorial shows. Nor was it only by words that Stoicism worked for humanity, for it was Stoic lawyers who softened and broadened and humanized Roman law.[4]

Yet Stoicism in Seneca and Epictetus had reached its zenith. From now onward it declined. Marcus Aurelius, in some ways the most attractive of all Stoics, was virtually the last. With the second century Stoicism ceased to be an effective force in occupying and inspiring the whole mind of men, though it is evident that it still influenced thinkers. Men studied the Stoics and made fresh copies of their books, as they did for a thousand years; they borrowed and adapted; but they were not Stoics. Stoicism had passed away as a system first and then as a religion; and for this we have to find some reason or reasons.

It may well be true that the environment of the Stoics was not fit for so high and pure a philosophy. The broad gulf between the common Roman life and Stoic teaching is evident enough. The intellectual force of the Roman world moreover was ebbing, and Stoicism required more strength of mind and character than was easily to be found. That a religion or a philosophy

---

[1] *Ep.* 95, 51-53.   [2] *de ira*, iii, 28, 1.
[3] *Ep.* 95, 33, *homo sacra res homini.*
[4] See Lecky, *European Morals*, i, 294 ff. : Maine, *Ancient Law*, p. 54 f.

fails to hold its own is not a sure sign that it is unfit or untrue ;
it may only be premature, and it may be held that at another
stage of the world's history Stoicism or some similar scheme of
thought,—or, better perhaps, some central idea round which a
system and a life develop—may yet command the assent of
better men in a better age.   At the same time, it is clear that
when Stoicism re-emerges,—if it does,—it will be another thing.
Already we have seen in Wordsworth, and (so far as I understand him) in Hegel, a great informing conception which seems
to have clear affinity with the Spermaticos Logos of the Stoics.
The passage from the " Lines written above Tintern Abbey "
(quoted in the previous chapter) may be supplemented by
many from the " Prelude " and other poems to illustrate at
once the likeness and the difference between the forms the
thought has taken.   It is, however, a certain condemnation of
a philosophic school when we have to admit that, whatever
its apprehension of truth, it failed to capture its own generation, either because of some error of presentment, or of some
fundamental misconception.   When we find, moreover, that
there is not only a refusal of Stoicism but a reaction from it,
conscious or unconscious, we are forced to inquire into the
cause.

We shall perhaps be right in saying, to begin with, that
the doctrine of the Generative Reason, the Spermaticos Logos,
is not carried far enough.   The immense practical need, which
the Stoic felt, of fortifying himself against the world, is not
unintelligible, but it led him into error.   He employed his
doctrine of the Spermaticos Logos to give grandeur and
sufficiency to the individual, and then, for practical purposes,
cut him off from the world.   He manned and provisioned the
fortress, and then shut it off from supplies and from relief.   It
was a necessary thing to assert the value and dignity of the
mere individual man against the despotisms, but to isolate the
man from mankind and from the world of nature was a fatal
mistake.   Of course, the Stoic did not do this in theory, for he
insisted on the polity of gods and men, the " one city," [1] and the
duty of the " citizen of the universe " ($\kappa \acute{o} \sigma \mu \iota o s$)—a man is not an
independent object ; like the foot in the body he is essenti-

---

[1] See, by the way, Plutarch's banter on this " polity "—the stars its tribesmen, the
sun, doubtless, councillor, and Hesperus *prytanis* or *astynomus*, *adv. Sto.* 34.

ally a "part."[1] In practice, too, Stoics were human. Seneca tells us to show clemency but not to feel pity, but we may be sure that the human heart in him was far from observing the distinction—he "talked more boldly than he lived," he says—he was "among those whom grief conquered,"[2] and, though he goes on to show why he failed in this way, he is endeared to us by his failure to be his own ideal Stoic. Yet it remains that the chapters, with which his book on Clemency ends, are a Stoic protest against pity, and they can be re-inforced by a good deal in Epictetus. If your friend is unhappy, "remember that his unhappiness is his own fault, for God has made all men to be happy, to be free from perturbations."[3] Your friend has the remedy in his own hands; let him "purify his dogmata."[4] Epictetus would try to heal a friend's sorrow "but not by every means, for that would be to fight against God (θεομαχεῖν)," and would involve daily and nightly punishment to himself[5]—and "no one is nearer me than myself."[6] In the *Manual* the same thought is accentuated. "Say to yourself 'It is the opinion about this thing that afflicts the man.' So far as words go, do not hesitate to show sympathy, and even, if it so happen, to lament with him. Take care, though, that you do not lament internally also (μὴ καὶ ἔσωθεν στενάξῃς)."[7] We have seen what he has to say of a lost child. In spite of all his fine words, the Stoic really knows of nothing between the individual and the cosmos, for his practical teaching deadens, if it does not kill, friendship and family love.

Everything with the Stoic turns on the individual. Τὰ ἐπὶ σοι, "the things in your own power," is the refrain of Epictetus' teaching. All is thrown upon the individual will, upon "the universal" working in the individual, according to Stoic theory, "upon me" the plain man would say. If the gods, as Seneca says, lend a hand to such as climb, the climber has to make his own way by temperance and fortitude. The "holy spirit within us" is after all hardly to be distinguished from conscience, intellect and will.[8] God, says Epictetus, ordains "if you wish good, get it from yourself."[9] Once the will (προαίρεσις) is right,

---

[1] Epict. *D.* ii, 5 ; M. Aurelius, viii, 34. [2] *Ep.* 63, 14.
[3] *D.* iii, 24. [4] *D.* iv, 1. [5] *ib.* [6] *D.* iv, 6. [7] *M.* 16.
[8] Cf. Theophilus (the apologist of about 160 A.D.), ii, 4, who, though not always to be trusted as to the Stoics, remarks this identification of God and conscience. [9] *D.* i, 29.

all is achieved.[1] " You must exercise the will (θελῆσαι)—and
the thing is done, it is set right ; as on the other hand, only fall
a nodding and the thing is lost.   For from within (ἔσωθεν) comes
ruin, and from within comes help."[2] " What do you want
with prayers ? " asks Seneca, " make yourself happy."[3] The
old Stoic paradox about the " folly " of mankind, and the
worthlessness of the efforts of all save the sage, was by now
chiefly remembered by their enemies.[4]

All this is due to the Stoic glorification of reason, as the
embodiment in man of the Spermaticos Logos.   Though Nous
with the Stoics is not the pure dry light of reason, they tended
in practice to distinguish reason from the emotions or passions
(πάθη), in which they saw chiefly " perturbations," and they held
up the ideal of freedom from them in consequence (ἀπάθεια).[5]
To be godlike, a man had to suppress his affections just as he
suppressed his own sensations of pain or hunger.   Every human
instinct of paternal or conjugal love, of friendship, of sympathy,
of pity, was thus brought to the test of a Reason, which had
two catch-words by which to try them—the " Universe " and
" the things in your own power "—and the sentence was swift
and summary enough.   They did not realize that for most men
—and probably it is truest of the best men—Life moves onward
with all its tender and gracious instincts, while Analysis limps
behind.   The experiment of testing affection and instinct by
reason has often been tried, and it succeeds only where the
reason is willing to be a constitutional monarch, so to say,
instead of the despot responsible only to the vague concept of
the Universe, whom the Stoics wished to enthrone.   They
talked of living according to Nature, but they were a great deal
too quick in deciding what was Nature.   If the centuries have
taught us anything, it is to give Nature more time, more study
and more respect than even yet we do.   There are words

---

[1] Cf. *D.* i, 1 ; iii, 19 ; iv, 4 ; iv, 12, and very many other passages.

[2] *D.* iv, 9, end.   [3] *Ep.* 31, 5.

[4] Plutarch, *Progress in Virtue*, c. 2, 76 A, on the absurdity of there being no
difference between Plato and Meletus.   Cf. also *de repugn. Stoic.* 11, 1037 D.

[5] " Unconditional eradication," says Zeller, *Eclectics*, p. 226. " I do not hold with
those who hymn the savage and hard Apathy (τὴν ἄγριον καὶ σκληρὰν)," wrote
Plutarch. *Cons. ad Apoll.* 3, 102 C. See Clem. Alex. *Str.* ii, 110, on πάθη as
produced by the agency of spirits, and note his talk of Christian Apathy. *Str.* vi,
71-76.

at the beginning of the thirteenth book of the "Prelude" wiser and truer than anything the Stoics had to say of her with their "excessive zeal" and their "quick turns of intellect." Carried away by their theories (none, we must remember as we criticize them, without some ground in experience and observation), the Stoics made solitude in the heart and called it peace. The price was too high ; mankind would not pay it, and sought a religion elsewhere that had a place for a man's children.

Again, in their contempt for the passions the Stoics underestimated their strength. How strong the passions are, no man can guess for another, even if he can be sure how strong his own are. Perhaps the Stoics could subordinate their passions to their reason ;—ancient critics kept sharp eyes on them and said they were not always successful.[1] But there is no question that for the mass of men, the Stoic account of reason is absurd. "I see another law in my members," said a contemporary of Seneca's, "warring against the law of my mind and bringing me into captivity." Other men felt the same and sought deliverance in the sacraments of all the religions. That Salvation was *not* from within, was the testimony of every man who underwent the *taurobolium*. So far as such things can be, it is established by the witness of every religious mind that, whether the feeling is just or not the feeling is invincible that the will is inadequate and that religion begins only when the Stoic's ideal of saving oneself by one's own resolve and effort is finally abandoned. Whether this will permanently be true is another question, probably for us unprofitable. The ancient world, at any rate, and in general the modern world, have pronounced against Stoic Psychology—it was too quick, too superficial. The Stoics did not allow for the sense of Sin.[2] They recognized the presence of evil in the world ; they felt that "it has its seat within us, in our inward part" ;[3] and they remark the effect of evil in the blunting of the faculties—let the guilty, says Persius, "see virtue, and pine that they have lost her forever."[4] While Seneca finds himself "growing better and becoming changed," he still feels there may be much more needing amendment.[5] He often

---

[1] Justin Martyr (*Apol.* ii, 8) praises Stoic morality and speaks of Stoics who suffered for it.

[2] Cf. Epict. *D.* iii, 25.

[3] Sen. *Ep.* 50, 4.

[4] Persius, iii, 38.

[5] *Ep.* 6, 1.

expresses dissatisfaction with himself.[1] But the deeper realization of weakness and failure did not come to the Stoics, and what help their teaching of strenuous endeavour could have brought to men stricken with the consciousness of broken will-power, it is hard to see. "Filthy Natta," according to Persius, was "benumbed by vice" (*stupet hic vitio*).[2] "When a man is hardened like a stone (ἀπολιθωθῇ), how shall we be able to deal with him by argument?" asks Epictetus, arguing against the Academics, who "opposed evident truths"—what are we to do with necrosis of the soul?[3] But the Stoics really gave more thought to fancies of the sage's equality with God and occasional superiority—so confident were they in the powers of the individual human mind. Plutarch, indeed, forces home upon them as a deduction from their doctrine of "the common nature" of gods and men the consequence that sin is not contrary to the Logos of Zeus—and yet they say God punishes sin.[4]

Yet even the individual, much as they strove to exalt his capabilities, was in the end cheapened in his own eyes.[5] As men have deepened their self-consciousness, they have yielded to an instinctive craving for the immortality of the soul.[6] Whether savages feel this or not, it is needless to argue. No religion apart from Buddhism has permanently held men which had no hopes of immortality; and how far the corruptions of Buddhism have modified its rigour for common people, it is not easy to say. In one form or another, in spite of a terrible want of evidence, men have clung to eternal life. The Stoics themselves used this consensus of opinion as evidence for the truth of the belief.[7] "It pleased me," writes Seneca, "to inquire of the eternity of souls (*de æternitate animarum*)—nay! to believe in it. I surrendered myself to that great hope."[8]

[1] *e.g. Ep.* 57, 3, he is not even *homo tolerabilis*. On the bondage of the soul within the body, see *Ep.* 65, 21-23.

[2] Cf. Seneca, *Ep.* 53, 7, 8—*quo quis peius habet minus sentit.* "The worse one is, the less he notices it."

[3] *D.* i, 5.

[4] Plut. *de repugn. Stoic.* 34, 1050 C. Cf. Tert. *de exh. castit.* 2.

[5] Cf. Plutarch, *non suaviter*, 1104 F. καταφρονοῦντες ἑαυτῶν ὡς ἐφημέρων κτἑ—of the Epicureans.

[6] Cf. Plutarch, *non suaviter*, 1104 C. τῆς ἀιδιότητος ἐλπὶς καὶ ὁ πόθος του εἶναι πάντων ἐρώτων πρεσβύτατος ὢν καὶ μέγιστος. Cf. *ib.* 1093 A.

[7] Sen. *Ep.* 117, 6.

[8] *Ep.* 102, 2.

"How natural it is!" he says, "the human mind is a great and generous thing; it will have no bounds set to it unless they are shared by God."[1] "When the day shall come, which shall part this mixture of divine and human, here, where I found it, I will leave my body, myself I will give back to the gods. Even now I am not without them." He finds in our birth into this world an analogy of the soul passing into another world, and in language of beauty and sympathy he pictures the "birthday of the eternal," the revelation of nature's secrets, a world of light and more light. "This thought suffers nothing sordid to dwell in the mind, nothing mean, nothing cruel. It tells us that the gods see all, bids us win their approval, prepare for them, and set eternity before us."[2] Beautiful words that wake emotion yet!

But is it clear that it is eternity after all? In the *Consolation* which Seneca wrote for Marcia, after speaking of the future life of her son, he passed at last to the Stoic doctrine of the first conflagration, and described the destruction of the present scheme of things that it may begin anew. "Then we also, happy souls who have been assigned to eternity (*felices animæ et æterna sortitæ*), when God shall see fit to reconstruct the universe, when all things pass (*labentibus*), we too, a little element in a great catastrophe, shall be resolved into our ancient elements. Happy is your son, Marcia, who already knows this."[3] Elsewhere he is still less certain. "Why am I wasted for desire of him, who is either happy or non-existent? (*qui aut beatus aut nullus est*)."[4]

That in later years, in his letters to Lucilius, Seneca should lean to belief in immortality, is natural enough. Epictetus' language, with some fluctuations, leans in the other direction. "When God does not supply what is necessary, he is sounding the signal for retreat—he has opened the door and says to you, Come! But whither? To nothing terrible, but whence you came, to the dear and kin [both neuters], the elements. What in you was fire, shall go to fire, earth to earth, spirit to spirit [perhaps, breath ὅσον πνευματίου εἰς πνευμάτιον], water to water;

---

[1] *Ep.* 102, 21; the following passages are from the same letter. Note the Stoic significance of *naturale*.

[2] Compare *Cons. ad Marc.* 25, 1, *integer ille, etc.*

[3] The last words of the "*Consolation*." Plutarch on resolution into πῦρ νοερὸν, *non suaviter*, 1107 B.   [4] *ad Polyb.* 9, 3.

no Hades, nor Acheron, nor Cocytus, nor Pyriphlegethon ; but all things full of gods and dæmons. When a man has such things to think on, and sees sun and moon and stars, and enjoys earth and sea, he is not solitary or even helpless."[1]　"This is death, a greater change, not from what now is into what is not, but into what now is not. Then shall I no longer be? You will be, but something else, of which now the cosmos has no need. For you began to be (ἐγένου), not when *you* wished, but when the cosmos had need."[2]

On the whole the Stoic is in his way right, for the desire for immortality goes with the instincts he rejected—it is nothing without the affections and human love.[3]　But once more logic failed, and the obscure grave witnesses to man's instinctive rejection of Stoicism, with its simple inscription *taurobolio in æternum renatus.*

Lastly we come to the gods themselves, and here a double question meets us. Neither on the plurality nor the personality of the divine does Stoicism give a certain note. In the passages already quoted it will have been noticed how interchangeably "God," "the gods" and "Zeus" have been used. It is even a question whether "God" is not an identity with fate, providence, Nature and the Universe.[4]　Seneca, as we have seen, dismisses the theory of dæmons or *genii* rather abruptly—"that is what some think." Epictetus definitely accepts them, so far as anything here is definite, and with them, or in them, the ancestral gods. Seneca, as we have seen, is contemptuous of popular ritual and superstition. Epictetus inculcates that "as to piety about the gods, the chief thing is to have right opinions about them," but, he concludes, "to make libations and to sacrifice according to the custom of our fathers, purely and not meanly, nor carelessly, nor scantily, nor above our ability, is a thing which belongs to all to do.[5]　"Why do you," he asks, "act the part of a Jew, when you are a Greek?"[6]　He also accepts the

---

[1] *D.* iii, 13.　Plutarch (*non suaviter*, 1106 E) says Cocytus, etc., are not the chief terror but ἡ τοῦ μὴ ὄντος ἀπειλή.

[2] *D.* iii, 24.

[3] See Plutarch on this, *non suaviter*, 1105 E.　　　　[4] Seneca, *N.Q.* ii, 45.

[5] *Manual*, 31.　Plutarch, *de repugn. Stoic.* 6, 1034 B, C, remarks on Stoic inconsistency in accepting popular religious usages.

[6] *D.* ii, 9.　In *D.* iv, 7, he refers to "Galilaeans," so that it is quite possible he has Christians in view here.

fact of divination.[1]   Indeed, aside perhaps from conspicuous extravagances, the popular religion suffices. Without enthusiasm and without clear belief, the Stoic may take part in the ordinary round of the cults.   If he did not believe himself, he pointed out a way to the reflective polytheist by which he could reconcile his traditional faith with philosophy—the many gods were like ourselves manifestations of the Spermaticos Logos ; and he could accept tolerantly the ordinary theory of dæmons, for Chrysippus even raised the question whether such things as the disasters that befall good men are due to negligence on the part of Providence, or to evil dæmons in charge of some things.[2] While for himself the Stoic had the strength of mind to shake off superstition, the common people, and even the weaker brethren of the Stoic school, remained saddled with polytheism and all its terrors and follies.   Of this compromise Seneca is guiltless.[3]   It was difficult to cut the connexion with Greek tradition—how difficult, we see in Plutarch's case.   The Stoics, however, fell between two stools, for they had not enough feeling for the past to satisfy the pious and patriotic, nor the resolution to be done with it.   After all, more help was to be had from Lucretius than from Epictetus in ridding the mind of the paralysis of polytheism.

But the same instinct that made men demand immortality for themselves, a feeling, dim but strong, of the value of personality and of love, compelled them to seek personality in the divine.   Here the Stoic had to halt, for after all it is a thing beyond the power of reason to demonstrate, and he could not here allege, as he liked, that the facts stare one in the face.   So, with other thinkers, impressed at once by the want of evidence, and impelled by the demand for some available terms, he wavered between a clear statement of his own uncertainty, and the use of popular names.   " Zeus " had long before been adopted by Cleanthes in his famous hymn, but this was an element of weakness ; for the wall-paintings in every great house gave another account of Zeus, which belied every attribute with which the Stoics credited him.   The apologists and the Stoics

---

[1] *M.* 32 ; *D.* iii, 22.

[2] Plut. *de repugn. Stoic.* 37, 1051 C.

[3] Tertullian, *Apol.* 12, *idem estis qui Senecam aliquem pluribus et amarioribus de vestra superstitione perorantem reprehendistis.*

explained the legends by the use of allegory, but, as Plato says, children cannot distinguish between what is and what is not allegory—nor did the common people. The finer religious tempers demanded something firmer and more real than allegory. They wanted God or Gods, immortal and eternal; and at best the Stoic gods were to "melt like wax or tin" in their final conflagration, while Zeus too, into whom they were to be resolved, would thereby undergo change, and therefore himself also prove perishable.[1]

"I put myself in the hands of a Stoic," writes Justin Martyr, "and I stayed a long time with him, but when I got no further in the matter of God—for he did not know himself and he used to say this knowledge was not necessary—I left him."[2] Other men did not, like Justin, pursue their philosophic studies, and when they found that, while the Stoic's sense of truth would not let him ascribe personality to God, all round there were definite and authoritative voices which left the matter in no doubt, they made a quick choice. What authority means to a man in such a difficulty, we know only too well.

The Stoics in some measure felt their weakness here. When they tell us to follow God, to obey God, to look to God, to live as God's sons, and leave us not altogether clear what they mean by God, their teaching is not very helpful, for it is hard to follow or look to a vaguely grasped conception. They realized that some more definite example was needed. "We ought to choose some good man," writes Seneca, "and always have him before our eyes that we may live as if he watched us, and do everything as if he saw."[3] The idea came from Epicurus. "Do everything, said he, as if Epicurus saw. It is without doubt a good thing to have set a guard over oneself, to whom you may look, whom you may feel present in your thoughts."[4] "Wherever I am, I am consorting with the best men. To them, in whatever spot, in whatever age they were, I send my mind."[5] He recommends Cato, Lælius, Socrates, Zeno. Epictetus has the same advice. What would Socrates do? is the canon he recommends.[6] "Though you are not yet a Socrates, you

---

[1] See Plutarch, *de comm. not. adv. Stoicos*, c. 31, and *de def. orac.* 420 A, c. 19 ; Justin M. *Apol.* ii, 7.

[2] *Dial. c. Tryphone*, 2.

[3] Sen. *Ep.* 11, 8.   [4] *Ep.* 25, 5.   [5] *Ep.* 62, 2, cf. 104, 21.

[6] *M.* 33, τὶ ἂν ἐποίησεν ἐν τούτῳ Σωκράτης ἢ Ζήνων.

ought to live as one who wishes to be a Socrates."[1] "Go away to Socrates and see him . . . think what a victory he felt he won over himself."[2] Comte in a later day gave somewhat similar advice. It seems to show that we cannot do well without some sort of personality in which to rest ourselves.

When once this central uncertainty in Stoicism appeared, all the fine and true words the Stoics spoke of Providence lost their meaning for ordinary men who thought quickly. The religious teachers of the day laid hold of the old paradoxes of the school and with them demolished the Stoic Providence. "Chrysippus," says Plutarch, "neither professes himself, nor any one of his acquaintances and teachers, to be good ($\sigma\pi o\nu\delta a\hat{\iota}o\nu$). What then do they think of others, but precisely what they say —that all men are insane, fools, unholy, impious, transgressors, that they reach the very acme of misery and of all wretchedness? And then they say that it is by Providence that our concerns are ordered—and we so wretched! If the Gods were to change their minds and wish to hurt us, to do us evil, to overthrow and utterly crush us, they could not put us in a worse condition; for Chrysippus demonstrates that life can admit no greater degree either of misery or unhappiness."[3] Of course, this attack is unfair, but it shows how men felt. They demanded to know how they stood with the gods—were the gods many or one? were they persons or natural laws[4] or even natural objects? did they care for mankind? for the individual man? This demand was edged by exactly the same experience of life which made Stoicism so needful and so welcome to its followers. The pressure of the empire and the terrors of living drove some to philosophy and many more to the gods—and for these certainty was imperative and the Stoics could not give it.

It is easy, but not so profitable as it seems, to find faults in the religion of other men. Their generation rejected the Stoics, but they may not have been right. If the Stoics were too hasty in making reason into a despot to rule over the

---

[1] *M.* 50.

[2] *D.* ii, 18. The tone of Tertullian, *e.g.* in *de Anima*, 1, on the *Phædo*, suggests that Socrates may have been over-preached. What too (*ib.* 6) of barbarians and their souls, who have no " prison of Socrates," etc?

[3] Plut. *de Stoic. repugnantiis*, 31, 1048 E. Cf. *de comm. not.* 33.

[4] Plutarch, *Amat.* 13, 757 C. ὁρᾷς δήπου τὸν ὑπολαμβάνοντα βύθον ἡμᾶς ἀθεότητος, ἂν εἰς πάθη καὶ δυνάμεις καὶ ἀρετὰς διαγράφωμεν ἕκαστον τῶν θεῶν.

emotions, their contemporaries were no less hasty in deciding, on the evidence of emotions and desires, that there were gods, and these the gods of their fathers, because they wished for inward peace and could find it nowhere else. The Stoics were at least more honest with themselves, and though their school passed away, their memory remained and kept the respect of men who differed from them, but realized that they had stood for truth.

CHAPTER III

PLUTARCH

STOICISM as a system did not capture the ancient world, and even upon individuals it did not retain an undivided hold. To pronounce with its admirers to-day that it failed because the world was not worthy of it, would be a judgment, neither quite false nor altogether true, but at best not very illuminative. Men are said to be slow in taking in new thoughts, and yet it is equally true that somewhere in nearly every man there is something that responds to ideas, and even to theories ; but if these on longer acquaintance fail to harmonize with the deeper instincts within him, they alarm and annoy, and the response comes in the form of re-action.

In modern times, we have seen the mind of a great people surrendered for a while to theorists and idealists. The thinking part of the French nation was carried away by the inspiration of Rousseau into all sorts of experiments at putting into hasty operation the principles and ideas they had more or less learnt from the master. Even theories extemporized on the moment, it was hoped, might be made the foundations of a new and ideal social fabric. The absurdities of the old religion yielded place to Reason—embodied symbolically for the hour in the person of Mme Momoro—afterwards, more vaguely, in Robespierre's Supreme Being, who really came from Rousseau. And then —" avec ton Être Suprème tu commences à m'embêter," said Billaud to Robespierre himself. Within a generation Chateaubriand, de Maistre, Bonald, and de la Mennais were busy refounding the Christian faith. " The rites of Christianity," wrote Chateaubriand, " are in the highest degree moral, if for no other reason than that they have been practised by our fathers, that our mothers have watched over our cradles as Christian women, that the Christian religion has chanted its psalms over our parents' coffins and invoked peace upon them in their graves."

Alongside of this let us set a sentence or two of Plutarch. "Our father then, addressing Pemptides by name, said, 'You seem to me, Pemptides, to be handling a very big matter and a risky one—or rather, you are discussing what should not be discussed at all (τὰ ἀκίνητα κινεῖν), when you question the opinion we hold about the gods, and ask reason and demonstration for everything. For the ancient and ancestral faith is enough (ἀρκεῖ γὰρ ἡ πάτριος καὶ παλαιὰ πίστις), and no clearer proof could be found than itself—

Not though man's wisdom scale the heights of thought—

but it is a common home and an established foundation for all piety ; and if in one point its stable and traditional character (τὸ βέβαιον αὐτῆς καὶ νενομισμένον) be shaken and disturbed, it will be undermined and no one will trust it. . . . If you demand proof about each of the ancient gods, laying hands on everything sacred and bringing your sophistry to play on every altar, you will leave nothing free from quibble and cross-examination (οὐδὲν ἀσυκοφάντητον οὐδ' ἀβασάνιστον). . . . Others will say that Aphrodite is desire and Hermes reason, the Muses crafts and Athene thought. Do you see, then, the abyss of atheism that lies at our feet, if we resolve each of the gods into a passion or a force or a virtue ? ' "[1]

Such an utterance is unmistakeable—it means a conservative re-action, and in another place we find its justification in religious emotion. "Nothing gives us more joy than what we see and do ourselves in divine service, when we carry the emblems, or join in the sacred dance, or stand by at the sacrifice or initiation. . . . It is when the soul most believes and perceives that the god is present, that she most puts from her pain and fear and anxiety, and gives herself up to joy, yes, even as far as intoxication and laughter and merriment. . . . In sacred processions and sacrifices not only the old man and the old woman, nor the poor and lowly, but

The thick-legged drudge that sways her at the mill,

and household slaves and hirelings are uplifted by joy and triumph. Rich men and kings have always their own banquets and feasts—but the feasts in the temples and at initiations, when men seem to touch the divine most nearly in their thought,

[1] *Amatorius*, 13, 756 A, D ; 757 B. The quotation is from Euripides, *Bacchæ*, 203.

with honour and worship, have a pleasure and a charm far more exceeding. And in this no man shares who has renounced belief in Providence. For it is not abundance of wine, nor the roasting of meat, that gives the joy in the festivals, but also a good hope, and a belief that the god is present and gracious, and accepts what is being done with a friendly mind." [1]

One of Chateaubriand's critics says that his plea could be advanced on behalf of any religion ; and Plutarch had already made it on behalf of his own. He looks past the Stoics, and he finds in memory and association arguments that outweigh anything they can say. The Spermaticos Logos was a mere Être Suprême—a sublime conception perhaps, but it had no appeal to emotion, it waked no memories, it touched no chord of personal association. We live so largely by instinct, memory and association, that anything that threatens them seems to strike at our life,

> So was it when my life began ;
> So is it now I am a man ;
> So be it when I shall grow old,
>   Or let me die !
> The Child is father of the Man ;
> And I could wish my days to be
> Bound each to each by natural piety.

Some such thought is native to every heart, and the man who does not cling to his own past seems wanting in something essentially human. The gods were part of the past of the ancient world, and if Reason took them away, what was left? There was so much, too, that Reason could not grasp ; so much to be learnt in ritual and in mystery that to the merely thinking mind had no meaning,—that must be received. Reason was invoked so lightly, and applied so carelessly and harshly, that it could take no account of the tender things of the heart. Reason destroyed but did not create, questioned without answering, and left life without sanction or communion. It was too often a mere affair of cleverness. It had its use and place, no doubt, in correcting extravagances of belief, but it was by no means the sole authority in man's life, and its function was essentially to be the handmaid of religion. "We must take

---

[1] *Non suaviter*, 21, 1101 E—1102 A.

Reason from philosophy to be our mystagogue and then in holy reverence consider each several word and act of worship."[1]

Plutarch is our representative man in this revival of religion, and some survey of his life and environment will enable us to enter more fully into his thought, and through him to understand better the beginnings of a great religious movement, of which students too often have lost sight.

For centuries the great men of Greek letters were natives of every region of the eastern Mediterranean except Greece, and Plutarch stands alone in later literature a Hellen of the motherland—Greek by blood, birth, home and instinct, proud of his race and his land, of their history, their art and their literature. When we speak of the influence of the past, it is well to remember to how great a past this man looked back, and from what a present. Long years of faction and war, as he himself says, had depopulated Greece, and the whole land could hardly furnish now the three thousand hoplites that four centuries before Megara alone had sent to Platæa. In regions where oracles of note had been, they were no more; their existence would but have emphasized the solitude—what good would an oracle be at Tegyra, or about Ptoum, where in a day's journey you might perhaps come on a solitary shepherd?[2] It was not only that wars and faction fights had wasted the life of the Greek people, but with the opening of the far East by Alexander, and the development of the West under Roman rule, Commerce had shifted its centres, and the Greeks had left their old homes for new regions. Still keen on money, philosophy and art, they thronged Alexandria, Antioch and Rome, and a thousand other cities. The Petrie papyri have revealed a new feature of this emigration, for the wills of the settlers often mention the names of their wives, and these were Greek women and not Egyptian, as the names of their fathers and homes prove.[3] Julius Cæsar had restored Corinth a century after Mummius destroyed it, and Athens was still as she had been and was to be for centuries, the resort of every one who loved philosophy and literature.[4] These were the two

---

[1] de Iside, 68, 378 A. [2] de def. orac. 8, 414 A.
[3] Mahaffy, Silver Age of Greek World, p. 45.
[4] Horace is the best known of Athenian students. The delightful letters of Synesius show the hold Athens still retained upon a very changed world in 400 A.D

cities of Greece; the rest were reminders of what had been. In one of these forsaken places Plutarch was born, and there he was content to live and die, a citizen and a magistrate of Chæronea in Bœotia.

His family was an old one, long associated with Chæronea. From childhood his life was rooted in the past by the most natural and delightful of all connexions. His great-grand-father, Nicarchus, used to tell how his fellow-citizens were commandeered to carry wheat on their own backs down to Anticyra for Antony's fleet—and were quickened up with the whip as they went; and "then when they had taken one consignment so, and the second was already done up into loads and ready, the news came that Antony was defeated, and that saved the city; for at once Antony's agents and soldiers fled, and they divided the grain among themselves."[1] The grand-father, Lamprias, lived long and saw the grandson a grown man. He appears often in Plutarch's *Table Talk*—a bright old man and a lively talker—like incense, he said, he was best when warmed up.[2] He thought poorly of the Jews for not eating pork—a most righteous dish, he said.[3] He had tales of his own about Antony, picked up long ago from one Philotas, who had been a medical student in Alexandria and a friend of one of the royal cooks, and eventually medical attendant to a son of Antony's by Fulvia.[4] Plutarch's father was a quiet, sensible man, who maintained the practice of sacrificing,[5] kept good horses,[6] knew his Homer, and had something of his son's curious interest in odd problems. It is perhaps an accident that Plutarch never mentions his name, but, though he often speaks of him, it is always of "my father" or "our father"— the lifelong and instinctive habit. There were also two brothers. The witty and amiable Lamprias loved laughter and was an expert in dancing—a useful man to put things right when the dance went with more spirit than music.[7] Of Timon we hear less, but Plutarch sets Timon's goodness of heart among the very best gifts Fortune has sent him.[8] He emphasizes the bond that brothers have in the family sacrifices,

[1] *Life of Antony*, 68. [2] *Symp.* i, 5, 1. [3] *Symp.* iv, 4, 4.
[4] *v. Ant.* 28. [5] *Symp.* iii, 7, 1. [6] *Symp.* ii, 8, 1.
[7] *Symp.* viii, 6, 5, ὑβριστὴς ὢν καὶ φιλογέλως φύσει. *Symp.* ix, 15, 1.
[8] *de fraterno amore*, 16, 487 E. Volkmann, *Plutarch*, i, 24, suggests he was the Timon whose wife Pliny defended on one occasion, *Epp.* i, 5, 5.

ancestral rites, the common home and the common grave.[1]
That Plutarch always had friends, men of kindly nature and
intelligence, and some of them eminent, is not surprising.
Other human relationships, to be mentioned hereafter, com-
pleted his circle. He was born, and grew up, and lived, in a
network of love and sympathy, the record of which is in all his
books.

Plutarch was born about the year 50 A.D., and, when Nero
went on tour through Greece in 66 A.D., he was a student at
Athens under Ammonius.[2] He recalls that among his fellow-
students was a descendant of Themistocles, who bore his
ancestor's name and still enjoyed the honours granted to him
and his posterity at Magnesia.[3] Ammonius, whom he honoured
and quoted throughout life, was a Platonist [4] much interested in
Mathematics.[5] He was a serious and kindly teacher with a
wide range of interests, not all speculative. Plutarch records a
discussion of dancing by "the good Ammonius." [6] He was
thrice "General" at Athens,[7] and had at any rate once the
experience of an excited mob shouting for him in the street,
while he supped with his friends indoors.

Plutarch had many interests in Athens, in its literature, its
philosophy and its ancient history—in its relics, too, for he
speaks of memorials of Phocion and Demosthenes still extant.
But he lingers especially over the wonders of Pericles and
Phidias, "still fresh and new and untouched by time, as if a
spirit of eternal youth, a soul that was ageless, were in the work
of the artist." [8] Athens was a conservative place, on the whole,
and a great resort for strangers. The Athenian love of talk is
noticed by Luke with a touch of satire, and Dio Chrysostom
admitted that the Athenians fell short of the glory of their city
and their ancestors.[9] Yet men loved Athens.[10] Aulus Gellius in
memory of his years there, called his book of collections *Attic
Nights*, and here and there he speaks of student life—"It was
from Ægina to Piræus that some of us who were fellow-
students, Greeks and Romans, were crossing in the same ship.

---

[1] *de frat. am.* 7, 481 D.   [2] *de E.* 1, 385 B.   [3] *v. Them.* 32, end.
[4] Zeller, *Eclectics*, 334.
[5] *de E.* 17, 391 E.   Imagine the joys of a Euclid, says Plutarch, in *non suaviter*,
11, 1093 E.
[6] *Symp.* ix, 15.   [7] *Symp.* viii, 3, 1.   [8] *Pericles* 13.
[9] Dio Chr. *Rhodiaca, Or.* 31, 117.   [10] Cf. the *Nigrinus*.

It was night. The sea was calm. It was summertime and the sky was clear and still. So we were sitting on the poop, all of us together, with our eyes upon the shining stars," and fell to talking about their names.[1]

When his student days were over, Plutarch saw something of the world. He alludes to a visit to Alexandria,[2] but, though he was interested in Egyptian religion, as we shall see, he does not speak of travels in the country. He must have known European Greece well, but he had little knowledge, it seems, of Asia Minor and little interest in it. He went once on official business for his city to the pro-consul of Illyricum—and had a useful lesson from his father who told him to say "We" in his report, though his appointed colleague had failed to go with him.[3] He twice went to Italy in the reigns of Vespasian and Domitian, and he seems to have stayed for some time in Rome, making friends in high places and giving lectures. Of the great Latin writers of his day he mentions none, nor is he mentioned by them. But he tells with pride how once Arulenus Rusticus had a letter from Domitian brought him by a soldier in the middle of one of these lectures and kept it unopened till the end.[4] The lectures were given in Greek. He confesses to his friend Sossius Senecio that, owing to the pressure of political business and the number of people who came about him for philosophy, when he was in Rome, it was late indeed in life that he attempted to learn Latin ; and when he read Latin, it was the general sense of a passage that helped him to the meaning of the words. The niceties of the language he could not attempt, he says, though it would have been a graceful and pleasant thing for one of more leisure and fewer years.[5] That this confession is a true one is shown by the scanty use he makes of Roman books in his biographies, by his want of acquaintance with Latin literature, poetry and philosophy, and by blunders in detail noted by his critics. *Sine patris* is a poor attempt at Latin grammar for a man of his learning, and in his life of Lucullus he has turned the streets of Rome into villages through inattention to the various meanings of *vicus*.[6]

---

[1] Gellius, *N.A.* ii, 21, 1, *vos opici*, says Gellius to his friends—Philistines.
[2] *Symp.* v, 5, 1.   [3] *Polit. præc.* 20, 816 D.   [4] *de curiositate*, 15.
[5] *Demosthenes*, 2.
[6] See Volkmann, i, 35, 36 ; *Rom. Qu.* 103 ; *Lucullus*, 37, end.

But, as he says, he was a citizen of a small town, and he did not wish to make it smaller,[1] and he went back to Chæronea and obscurity. A city he held to be an organism like a living being,[2] and he never cared for a man on whom the claims of his city sat loosely—as they did on the Stoics.[3]   The world was full of Greek philosophers and rhetoricians, lecturing and declaiming, to their great profit and glory, but Plutarch was content to stay at home, to be magistrate and priest. If men laughed to see him inspecting the measurement of tiles and the carrying of cement and stones—"it is not for myself, I say, that I am doing this but for my native-place." [4]   This was when he was Telearch—an office once held by Epameinondas, as he liked to remember.   Pliny's letters show that this official inspection of municipal building operations by honest and capable men was terribly needed. But Plutarch rose to higher dignities, and as Archon Eponymos he had to preside over feasts and sacrifices.[5] He was also a Bœotarch.   The Roman Empire did not leave much political activity even to the free cities, but Plutarch loyally accepted the new era as from God, and found in it many blessings of peace and quiet, and some opportunities still of serving his city.   He held a priesthood at Delphi, with some charge over the oracle and a stewardship at the Pythian games. He loved Delphi, and its shrine and antiquities,[6] and made the temple the scene of some of his best dialogues. "The kind Apollo (ὁ φίλος)," he says, "seems to heal the questions of life, and to resolve them, by the rules he gives to those who ask; but the questions of thought he himself suggests to the philosophic temperament, waking in the soul an appetite that will lead it to truth." [7]

He does not seem to have gained much public renown, but he did not seek it. The fame in his day was for the men of rhetoric, and he was a man of letters. If he gave his time to municipal duties, he must have spent the greater part of his days in reading and writing. He says that a biographer needs a great many books and that as a rule many of them will not be readily accessible—to have the abundance he requires, he ought really to be in some " famous city where learning is loved and

---

[1] *Demosthenes*, 2.   [2] *de sera*, 15, 559 A.   [3] *de Stoic. rep.* 2, 1033 B, C.
[4] *Pol. Præc.* 15, 811 C.   [5] *Symp.* ii, 10, 1 ; vi, 8, 1.
[6] Reference to Polemo's hand-book to them, *Symp.* v, 2, 675 B.   [7] *de E.* 384 F.

men are many " ; though, he is careful to say, a man may be happy and upright in a town that is " inglorious and humble." [1]

He must have read very widely, and he probably made good use of his stay in Rome. In philosophy and literature it is quite probable that he used hand-books of extracts, though this must not imply that he did not go to the original works of the greater writers. But his main interest lay in memoirs and travels. He had an instinct for all that was characteristic, or curious, or out-of-the-way ; and all sorts of casual references show how such things attached themselves to his memory. Discursive in his reading, as most men of letters seem to be, with a quick eye for the animated scene, the striking figure, the strange occurrence, he read, one feels, for enjoyment—he would add, no doubt, for his own moral profit ; indeed he says that he began his Biographies for the advantage of others and found them to be much to his own.[2] He was of course an inveterate moralist ; but unlike others of the class, he never forgets the things that have given him pleasure. They crowd his pages in genial reminiscence and apt allusion. There is always the quiet and leisurely air of one who has seen and has enjoyed, and sees and enjoys again as he writes. It is this that has made his Biographies live. They may at times exasperate the modern historian, for he is not very systematic—delightful writers rarely are. He rambles as he likes and avowedly passes the great things by and treasures the little and characteristic. " I am not writing histories but lives," he says, " and it is not necessarily in the famous action that a man's excellence or failure is revealed. But some little thing—a word or a jest—may often show character better than a battle with its ten thousand slain." [3]

But, after all, it is the characteristic rather than the character that interests him. He is not among the greatest who have drawn men, for he lacks the mind and patience to go far below the surface to find the key to the whole nature. When he has shown us one side of the hero, he will present another and a very different one, and leave us to reconcile them if we can. The contradictions remain contradictions, and he wanders pleasantly on. The Lives of Pericles and Themistocles, for instance, are little more than mere collectanea from sources widely discrepant, and often quite worthless. Of the mind of Pericles he had little

---

[1] *Demosthenes*, 2 ; and 1.   [2] *Timoleon*, pref.   [3] *Alexander*, 1.

conception, he gathered up and pleasantly told what he had read in books. He had too little of the critical instinct and took things too easily to weigh what he quoted.

Above all, despite his "political" energy and enthusiasm, it was impossible for a Greek of his day to have the political insight that only comes from life in a living state. How could the Telearch of Chæronea under the Roman Empire understand Pericles? Archbishop Trench contrasts his enthusiasm about the gift of liberty to Greece by Flamininus with the reflection of Wordsworth that it is a thing

> which is not to be given
> By all the blended powers of Earth and Heaven.

Plutarch really did not know what liberty is; Wordsworth on the other hand had taken part in the French Revolution, and watched with keen and sympathetic eyes the march of events throughout a most living epoch. It is worth noting that indirectly Plutarch contributed to the disasters of that epoch, for his *Lycurgus* had enormous influence with Rousseau and his followers who took it for history. Here was a man who made laws and constitutions in his own head and imposed them upon his fellow-countrymen. So Plutarch wrote and believed, and so read and believed thinking Frenchmen of the eighteenth century, like himself subjects of a despotism and without political experience.

Besides Biographies he wrote moral treatises—some based on lectures, others on conversation, others again little better than note-books—pleasant and readable books, if the reader will forgive a certain want of humour, and a tendency to ramble, and will surrender his mind to the long and leisurely sentences, for Plutarch is not to be hurried. Everything he wrote had some moral or religious aim. He was a believer, in days of doubt and perplexity. The Epicurean was heard at Delphi. Even in the second century, when the great religious revival was in full swing, Lucian wrote and found readers. Men brought their difficulties to Plutarch and he went to meet them—ever glad to do something for the ancestral faith. Nor was he less ready to discuss—or record discussions of—questions much less serious. Was the hen or the egg first? Does a varied diet or a single dish help the digestion more? Why is fresh water better than salt for washing clothes? Which of Aphrodite's hands did Diomed wound?

It is always the same man, genial, garrulous, moral and sensible. There are no theatricalities in his style—he is not a rhetorician even on paper.[1] He discards the tricks of the school, adoxography, epigram and, as a rule, paradox. His simplicity is his charm. He is really interested in his subject whatever it is; and he believes in its power of interesting other men, too much to think it worth while to trick it out with extraneous prettinesses. Yet after he has discussed his theme, with excursions into its literary antecedents and its moral suggestions, we are not perhaps much nearer an explanation of the fact in question,[2] nor always quite sure that it is a fact. Everything interests him, but he is in no hurry to get at the bottom of anything; just as in the *Lives* he is occupied with everything except the depths of his hero's personality. It remains that in his various works he has given us an unexampled pageant of antiquity over a wide reach of time and many lands, and always bright with the colour of life—the work of a lover of men. " I can hardly do without Plutarch," wrote Montaigne; "he is so universal and so full, that upon all occasions, and what extravagant subject soever you take in hand, he will still intrude himself into your business, and holds out to you a liberal and not to be exhausted hand of riches and embellishments." What Shakespeare thought of him is written in three great plays.[3]

But so far nothing has been said of Plutarch's own home. The lot of the wife of a great preacher or moralist is not commonly envied; and the tracts which Plutarch wrote upon historic women and their virtues, and on the duties of married life, on diet and on the education of the young, suggest that Timoxena must have lived in an atmosphere of high moral elevation, with a wise saw and an ancient instance for every occurrence of the day. But it is clear that he loved her, and his affection for their four little boys must have been as plain to her as to his readers—and his joy when, after long waiting, at last a little girl was born. " You had longed for a daughter

---

[1] *de tranqu. animi*, i, 464 F, οὐκ ἀκροάσεως ἕνεκα θηρωμένης καλλιγραφίαν — a profession often made, but in Plutarch's case true enough as a rule.

[2] See, *e.g.*, variety of possible explanations of the E at Delphi, in tract upon it.

[3] Stapfer, *Shakespeare and Classical Antiquity* (tr.), p. 299. " It may be safely said he followed Plutarch far more closely than he did even the old English chroniclers."

after four sons,' he writes to her, "and I was glad when she came and I could give her your name." The little Timoxena lived for two years, and the letter of consolation which Plutarch wrote her mother tells the story of her short life. "She had by nature wonderful good temper and gentleness. So responsive to affection, so generous was she that it was a pleasure to see her tenderness. For she used to bid her nurse give the breast to other children and not to them only, but even to toys and other things in which she took delight. She was so loving that she wished everything that gave her pleasure to share in the best of what she had. I do not see, my dear wife, why things such as these, which gave us so much happiness while she lived, should give us pain and trouble now when we think of them." [1] He reminds her of the mysteries of Dionysus of which they were both initiates. In language that recalls Wordsworth's great Ode on the Intimations of Immortality, he suggests that old age dulls our impressions of the soul's former life, and that their little one is gone from them, before she had time to fall in love with life on earth. "And the truth about this is to be seen in the ancient use and wont of our fathers," who did not observe the ordinary sad rites of burial for little children, "as if they felt it not right in the case of those who have passed to a better and diviner lot and place. . . . And since to disbelieve them is harder than to believe, let us comply with the laws in outward things, and let what is within be yet more stainless, pure and holy." [2]

Two of the sons had previously died—the eldest Soclaros, and the fourth, "our beautiful Chæron"—the name is that of the traditional founder of Chæronea. The other two, Autobulus and Plutarch grew up. Some of these names appear in the *Table Talk*, while others of his works were written at the suggestion of his sons.

From the family we pass to the slaves, and here, as we should expect, Plutarch is an advocate of gentleness. In the tract *On Restraining Anger* a high and humane character is drawn in Fundanus, who had successfully mastered a naturally passionate temper. It has been thought that Plutarch was draw-

---

[1] *Cons. ad Ux.* 2-3, 608 C, D.
[2] *Cons. ad Ux.* 11. 612 A, B. Cf. *non suaviter*, 26, 1104 C, on the loss of a child or a parent.

ing his own portrait over his friend's name.   A naïve tendency to idealise his own virtues he certainly shares with other moralists. Fundanus urges that, while all the passions need care and practice if they are to be overcome, anger is the failure to which we are most liable in the case of our slaves.   Our authority over them sets us in a slippery place ; temper here has nothing to check it, for here we are irresponsible and that is a position of danger.   A man's wife and his friends are too apt to call gentleness to the slaves mere easy-going slackness (ἀτονίαν καὶ ῥᾳθυμίαν).   " I used to be provoked by such criticism myself against my slaves.   I was told they were going to pieces for want of correction.   Later on I realized that, first of all, it is better to let them grow worse through my forbearance than by bitterness and anger to pervert oneself for the reformation of others.   And, further, I saw that many of them, through not being punished, began to be ashamed of being bad, and that forgiveness was more apt than punishment to be the beginning of a change in them—and indeed that they would serve some men more readily for a silent nod than they would others for blows and brandings.   So I persuaded myself that reasoning does better than temper." [1]   It will be remarked that Fundanus, or his recording friend, does not here take the Stoic position that the slave is as much a son of God as the master,[2] nor does he spare the slave for the slave's sake but to overcome his own temper.   So much for theory ; but men's conduct does not always square with their theories, and in life we see men guilty of kind-heartedness and large-mindedness not at all to be reconciled with the theories which they profess, when they remember them.

It is curious that one of the few stories of Plutarch that come from outside sources should concern this very tract and the punishment of a slave.   Gellius heard it from the philosopher Taurus after one of his classes.   Plutarch, Taurus said, had a worthless slave and ordered him a flogging.   The man loudly protested he had done no wrong, and at last, under the stimulus of the lash, taunted his master with inconsistency—what about the fine book on controlling Anger ? he was angry enough now.

[1] *de coh. ira.* 11, 459 C ; cf. *Progress in Virtue*, 80 B, 81 C, on ἐπιείκεια and πρᾳότης as signs of moral progress.
[2] Cf. Sen. *Ep.* 47 ; Clem. Alex. *Pad.* iii, 92.

" Then Plutarch, slowly and gently " asked what signs of anger
he showed in voice or colour or word ?   " My eyes, I think, are
not fierce ; nor my face flushed ; I am not shouting aloud ;
there is no foam on my lip, no red in my cheek ; I am saying
nothing to be ashamed of ; nothing to regret ; I am not excited
nor gesticulating.   All these, perhaps you are unaware, are the
signs of anger." [1]   Then turning to the man who was flogging
the slave, he said, " In the meantime, while I and he are debating, *you* go on with your business." [2]   The story is generally
accepted, and it is certainly characteristic.   The philosopher,
feeling his pulse, as it were, to make sure that he is not angry,
while his slave is being lashed, is an interesting and suggestive
picture, which it is well to remember.

How long Plutarch lived we do not know.   He refers to
events of the year 104 or 105, and in his *Solon* he speaks of
Athens and Plato each having an unfinished masterpiece, so
that he cannot have known of the intention of the Emperor
Hadrian to finish the temple of Zeus Olympios.[3]   All that this
need imply is that the *Solon* was written before 125 A.D.   As
to his death, it is certainly interesting when we recall how full
of dreams and portents his Biographies are, to learn from
Artemidorus' great work on the Interpretation of Dreams
(written some forty years later) that Plutarch, when ill, dreamed
that he was ascending to heaven, supported by Hermes.   Next
day he was told that this meant great happiness.   " Shortly
after he died, and this was what his dream and the interpretation
meant.   For ascent to heaven means destruction to a sick man,
and the great happiness is a sign of death." [4]   Plutarch might
well have accepted this himself.

Such was Plutarch's life—the life of a quiet and simple-
minded Greek gentleman, spent amid scenes where the past
predominated over the present,—*nullum sine nomine saxum*,
where Antiquity claimed him for her own by every right that it
has ever had upon man.   The land of his fathers, the literature,
the art, the philosophy, the faith, and the reproduction of the

---

[1] A curious parallel to this in Tert. *de Patientia*, 15, where Tertullian draws the
portrait of Patience—perhaps from life, as Dean Robinson suggests—after Perpetua
the martyr.

[2] Gellius, *N.A.* i, 26.

[3] *Solon*, 32.

[4] Artemidorus, *Oneirocritica*, iv, 72.   On this author see chapter vii.

good old life in the pleasant household [1]—everything conspired to make him what he was. We now come to his significance in the story of the conflict of religions in the Roman Empire.

A good deal has been written about Plutarch's philosophy. His works are full of references to philosophy and philosophers, and he leaves us in no doubt as to his counting himself a disciple of Plato ; his commentaries on Platonic doctrines give him a place in the long series of Plato's expositors. But no one would expect a writer of the first century to be a man of one allegiance, and Plutarch modifies the teaching of Plato with elements from elsewhere. It has then been debated whether he should, or should not, be called an Eclectic, but not very profitably. The essential thing to note is that he is not properly a philosopher at all, much as the statement would have astonished him.[2] His real interest is elsewhere ; and while he, like the Greeks of his day, read and talked Philosophy interminably, as men in later ages have read and talked Theology, it was not with the philosophic spirit. Philosophy is not the mistress—rather, he avows, the servant of something else ; and that means that it is not Philosophy. His test of philosophic thought and doctrine was availability for the moral and religious life—a test which may or may not be sound, as it is applied. But Plutarch was an avowed moralist, didactic in every fibre ; and everything he wrote betrays the essential failure of the practical man and the moralist—impatience, the short view. From his experience of human life in its manifold relations of love and friendship, he came to the conclusion that "the ancient faith of our fathers suffices." It is also plain that he was afraid of life without religion. So far as a man of his training would— a man familiar with the history of philosophy, but without patience or depth enough to be clear in his own mind, he associated truth with his religion ; at all events it was "sufficient," for this he had found in his course through the world. Definite upon this one central point, he approached philosophy, but not with the true philosopher's purpose of examining his experience, in accordance with the Platonic

---

[1] See *non suaviter*, 17, 1098 D, on the unspeakably rich joy of such a life of friendly relations with gods and men.

[2] *Progress in Virtue*, 4, 77 C, Love of Philosophy compared to a lover's passion, to "hunger and thirst."

suggestion [1]; rather, with the more practical aim of profiting by every serviceable thought or maxim which he could find. And he certainly profited. If he started with preconceptions, which he intended to keep, he enlarged and purified them—in a sense, we may say, he adorned and enriched them. For wherever he found a moving or suggestive idea, a high thought, he adopted it and found it a place in his mind, though without inquiring too closely whether it had any right to be there. In the end, it is very questionable whether the sum of his ideas will hold together at all, if we go beyond the quick test of a rather unexamined experience. We have already seen how he protested against too curious examination. "There is no philosophy possible," wrote John Stuart Mill, "where fear of consequences is a stronger principle than love of truth."

But to such criticisms a reply is sometimes suggested, which is best made in the well-known words of Pascal—"the heart has its reasons which the reason does not know." [2] The experience which led Plutarch to his conclusion was real and sound. There is an evidential value in a good father, in wife and children—even in a telearchy with its tiles and cement— which is apt to be under-estimated. For with such elements in life are linked passions and emotions, which are deeply bound up with human nature, and rule us as instincts—blind reasons of the heart. Like all other things they require study and criticism if they are not to mislead, and those who most follow them are sometimes the worst judges of their real significance. On the other hand the danger of emotion, instinct and intuition as guides to truth is emphasized enough,— it was emphasized by the Stoics; and a contribution is made to human progress, when the value of these guides to truth is re-asserted, even to the extent of obvious exaggeration, by some one, who, like Plutarch, has had a life rich in various human experience. It remains however, in Plutarch's case as in all such cases, the fundamental question, whether the supposed testimony of instinct and intuition is confirmed. If it is not confirmed, it may be taken to have been misunderstood.

Keeping the whole life of this man in view, and realizing its soundness, its sweetness and its worth, we must see what

---

[1] Plato, *Apology*, 38 A, ὁ δὲ ἀνεξέταστος βίος οὐ βιωτὸς ἀνθρώπῳ.

[2] *Pensées*, Art. xxiv, 5.

he made of the spiritual environment of man's life in general—laying stress on what in his system, or his attempt at a system, is most significant, and postponing criticism. It should be said once for all that a general statement of Plutarch's views cannot be quite faithful, for he was a man of many and wandering thoughts, and also something of an Academic; and whatever he affirmed was with qualifications, which in a short summary must be understood rather than repeated.

Our knowledge of God and of things divine comes to us, according to Plutarch, from various sources. There is the consensus of mankind. "Of all customs first and greatest is belief in gods. Lycurgus, Numa, Ion and Deucalion, alike sanctified men, by prayers and oaths and divinations and oracles bringing them into touch with the divine in their hopes and fears. You might find communities without walls, without letters, without kings, without houses, without money, with no need of coinage, without acquaintance with theatres and gymnasia; but a community without holy rite, without a god, that uses not prayer nor oath, nor divination, nor sacrifice to win good or avert evil—no man ever saw nor will see. . . . This is what holds all society together and is the foundation and buttress of all law." [1]

This evidence from the consensus of mankind is brought to a higher point in the body of myth inherited from the past, and in custom and law—and is so far confirmed by reason. But we can go further and appeal to the highest and best minds of antiquity, who in their own highest moments of inspiration confirmed the common view. "In the matter of belief in gods, and in general, our guides and teachers have been the poets and the lawgivers, and, thirdly, the philosophers—all alike laying down that there are gods, though differing among themselves as to the number of the gods and their order, their nature and function. Those of the philosophers are free from pain and death; toil they know not, and are clean escaped the roaring surge of

---

[1] *Adv. Coloten* (the Epicurean), 31, 1125 D, E. For this argument from consensus, see Seneca, *Ep.* 117, 6, *Multum dare solemus præsumptioni omnium hominum et apud nos veritatis argumentum est aliquid omnibus videri: tanquam deos esse inter alia hoc colligimus, quod omnibus insita de dis opinio est, nec ulla gens usquam est adeo extra leges moresque projecta ut non aliquos deos credat.* This consensus rests (with the Stoics) on the common preconceptions of the mind, which are natural. For ridicule of the doctrine of consensus, see Lucian, *Zeus Tragœdus*, 42.

Acheron."[1] "It is likely that the word of ancient poets and philosophers is true," he says.[2]   Plutarch was a lover of poetry and of literature, and he attributed to them a value as evidence to truth, which is little intelligible to men who have not the same passion.[3]   Still the appeal to the poets in this connexion was very commonly made.

But men are not only dependent on the tradition of their fathers and the inspiration of poets and philosophers, much as they should, and do, love and honour these.   The gods make themselves felt in many ways.   There was abundant evidence of this in many established cases of theolepsy, enthusiasm ($\check{\epsilon}\nu\theta\epsilon$ος) and possession.   Again there were the oracles, in which it was clear that gods communicated with men and revealed truths not otherwise to be gained—a clear demonstration of the spiritual.   Men were " in anguish and fear lest Delphi should lose its glory of three thousand years," but Delphi has not failed ; for " the language of the Pythian priestess, like the right line of the Mathematicians—the shortest between two points, makes neither declension nor winding, has neither double meaning nor ambiguity, but goes straight to the truth.   Though hard to believe and much tested, she has never up to now been convicted of error,—on the contrary she has filled the shrine with offerings and gifts from barbarians and Greeks, and adorned it with the beautiful buildings of the Amphictyons."[4]   The revival of Delphi in Plutarch's day, " in so short a time," was not man's doing— but " the God came here and inspired the oracle with his divinity." And Delphi was not the only oracle.   The Stoics perhaps had pointed the way here with their teaching on divination, but as it stands the argument (such as it is) is said to be Plutarch's own.[5]   Lastly in this connexion, the mysteries offered evidence, but here he is reticent.   " As to the mysteries, in which we may receive the greatest manifestations and illuminations of the truth

---

[1] *Amatorius*, 18, 763 C. Cf. view of Celsus *ap*. Orig. *c. Cels*. vii, 41.

[2] *Consol. ad Apoll.* 34, 120 B.

[3] *Quomodo Poetas*, 1, 15 E, F, poetry a preliminary study to philosophy, προφιλοσοφητέον τοῖς ποιήμασιν.

[4] *de Pyth. orac.* 29, 408 F. Cf. the pagan's speech in Minucius Felix, 7, 6, *pleni et mixti deo vates futura præcerpunt . . . etiam per quietem deos videmus. . . .*

[5] So Volkmann, *Plutarch*, ii, 290 n. Cf. a passage of Celsus, Orig. *c. Cels.* viii, 45.

concerning dæmons — like Herodotus, I say, 'Be it un-spoken.'"[1]

Philosophy, poetry, tradition, oracles and mysteries[2] bring Plutarch to belief in gods. "There are not Greek gods and barbarian, southern or northern; but just as sun, moon, sky, earth and sea are common to all men and have many names, so likewise it is one Reason that makes all these things a cosmos; it is one Providence that cares for them, with ancillary powers appointed to all things; while in different people, different honours and names are given to them as customs vary. Some use hallowed symbols that are faint, others symbols more clear, as they guide their thought to the divine."[3] This one ultimate Reason is described by Plutarch in terms borrowed from all the great teachers who had spoken to the Greeks of God. The Demiurge, the One and Absolute, the World-Soul and the rest all contribute features.[4]

"We," he says, "have really no share in Being, but every mortal nature, set between becoming and perishing, offers but a show and a seeming of itself, dim and insecure"; and he quotes the famous saying of Heraclitus that it is impossible to descend into the same river twice, and develops the idea of change in the individual. "No one remains, nor is he one, but we become many as matter now gathers and now slips away about one phantasm and a common form (or impress). . . . Sense through ignorance of Being is deceived into thinking that the appearance is. What then indeed is Being? The eternal, free from becoming, free from perishing, for which no time brings change. . . . It is even impious to say 'Was' or 'Will be' of Being; for these are the varyings and passings and changings of that which by nature cannot abide in Being. But God *is*, we must say, and that *not* in time, but in the æon that knows no motion, time or variation, where is neither former

---

[1] *de def. or.* 14, 417 C, ἐμφάσεις and διαφάσεις.

[2] Tertullian sums up the pagan line of argument and adds a telling criticism in his book *adversus Nationes*, ii, 1: *adversus hæc igitur nobis negotium est, adversus institutiones maiorum, auctoritates receptorum, leges dominantium, argumentationes prudentium, adversus vetustatem consuetudinem necessitatem, adversus exempla prodigia miracula, quæ omnia adulterinam istam divinitatem corroboraverint. . . . Maior in huiusmodi penes vos auctoritas litterarum quam rerum est.*

[3] *de Iside*, 67, 377 F—378 A

[4] Oakesmith, *Religion of Plutarch*, p. 88—a book which I have found of great use.

nor latter, future nor past, older nor younger; but God is one, and with one Now he has filled Always, and is alone therein the one that Is." [1]

The symbol E at Delphi affords him a text here. It is one of "the kind Apollo's" riddles to stimulate thought. Plutarch read it as Epsilon and translates it "Thou Art," and from this as from the very name of Apollo he draws a lesson as to the nature of real Being. The name Ἀ-πολλ-ων means of itself the "Not-Many," and the symbol E is the soul's address to God—God is, and God is one. Not every one understands the nature of the divine; men confuse God with his manifestations. "Those who suppose Apollo and the sun to be one and the same, we should welcome and love for their pious speech, because they attach the idea (ἐπίνοια) of God to that thing which they honour most of all they know and crave for," but we should point them higher, "bid them go upward and see the truth of their dream, the real Being (τὴν οὐσίαν)." They may still honour the image—the visible sun. But that a god should do the work of the sun, that there should be changes and progressions in a god, that he should project fire from himself and extend himself into land, sea, winds and animals, and into all the strange experiences of animals and plants (as the Stoics taught) —it is not holy even to hear such things mentioned. No, God is not like Homer's child playing on the sand, making and un-making; all this belongs to another god, or rather dæmon, set over nature with its becomings and perishings.[2] To confuse gods and dæmons is to make disorder of everything.

It is here that the real interest of Plutarch's theology begins; for, as Christian apologists were quick to point out, all the philosophers were in the last resort monotheists. But the ultimate One God is by common consent far from all direct contact with this or any other universe of becoming and perish-ing. For it was questioned how many universes (κόσμοι) there might be [1]—some conjecturing there would be one hundred and eighty-three—and if there were more than one, the Stoics asked what became of Fate and Destiny, and would there not be many "Zeuses or Zênes"? Why should there be? asked

---

[1] *de E.* 18-20. Cf. Clem. Alex. *Protr.* 84. The true To-day of God is eternity. Also Tert. *ad Natt.* ii, 6, on the axiom of no change in God.

[2] *de E.* 21.   [3] Cf. Plato, *Timæus*, 55 D.

Plutarch; why not in each universe a guide and ruler with mind and reason, such as he who in our universe is called lord and father of all? What hinders that they should all be subjects of the Fate and Destiny that Zeus controls; that he should appoint to each several one of them his own realm, and the seeds and reasons of everything achieved in it; that he should survey them, and they be responsible to him? That in the whole scheme of things there should be ten universes, or fifty, or a hundred, all governed by one Reason, all subordinate to one rule, is not impossible. The Ultimate God rules through deputies.[1]

These deputies are Plutarch's chief concern in theology. The Stoics and he were at one about the Supreme and Ultimate God, waiving the matter of personality, which he asserted and which they left open. But when the Stoics turned the deputy gods into natural forces, which we might call laws of nature, or, still worse, into natural objects like wine and grain,[2] Plutarch grew angry and denounced such teaching as atheism. "We must not as it were turn them into queen-bees who can never go out, nor keep them shut up in the prison of matter, or rather packed up, as they (the Stoics) do, when they turn the gods into conditions of the atmosphere and mingled forces of water

[1] Plutarch, *de. def. orac.* 29, 425 F—426 A. Celsus has the same view; (Origen, *c. Cels.* v, 25; vii, 68): the world's regions are severally allotted to *epoptai* under Providence; so that local usages may well be maintained in such form as pleases them; to alter these would be impious, while to worship the dæmons is to honour God, who is not jealous of them. Cf. Plutarch, *de fortuna Romanorum*, 11, 324 B, ὁ Ῥωμαίων μέγας δαίμων . . . τῇ πόλει συνηβήσας καὶ συναυξηθείς, κτἑ—the tract is a poor and rhetorical one, and the phrase may be merely a synonym for "luck." See also Celsus (Orig. *c. Cels.* viii, 58) on the Egyptian attribution of the human body to thirty-six "dæmons or gods of æther," so that by prayer to the right one disease in any part of the body may be cured; Celsus gives some of their names. The Christians assumed a somewhat similar scheme with a rather different development. Athenagoras, an apologist of the second century, gives the following account in his *Presbeia*, 24-27. A system of angels under Providence existed, some good and some bad, enjoying free-will as men also do; "the ruler of matter and of the forms in it" lusted after virgins and succumbed to flesh, and neglected the administration entrusted to him; others fell with him; they cannot regain heaven but meantime occupy the air; their children by mortal women were giants and the souls of these are the dæmons; the ruler of matter directs all things against God; with matter are connected the soul's worse impulses. See also Clem. Alex. *Strom.* vi, 157, on angelic governance of individual nations and cities; and Lactantius, *Instit.* ii, 8, 14, whose account fairly resembles that of Athenagoras. Tertullian, however, suggests (*Apol.* 11) that the Creator had no need of ancillary gods to complete his work.

[2] For a summary of Stoic teaching here, see Cicero, *N.D.* ii, 60-70.

and fire, and thus beget them with the universe and again burn them up with it; they do not leave the gods at liberty and free to move, as if they were charioteers or steersmen; no! like images they are nailed down, even fused to their bases, when they are thus shut up into the material, yes, and riveted to it, by being made partakers with it in destruction and resolution and change."[1] This is one of many assertions of the existence of ancillary gods, who are not metaphors, nor natural laws, but personal rulers of provinces, which may very well be each a universe, free and independent. "The true Zeus" has a far wider survey than "the Homeric Zeus" who looked away from Troy to Thrace and the Danube, nor does he contemplate a vacant infinite without, nor yet (as some say) himself and nothing else. To judge from the motions of the heavens, the divine really enjoys variety, and is glad to survey movement, the actions of gods and men, the periods of the stars.[2]

Thus under the Supreme is a hierarchy of heavenly powers or gods, and again between them and men is another order of beings, the dæmons.[3] These, unlike the gods, are of mixed nature, for while the gods are emanations or Logoi of the Supreme, the dæmons have something of the perishable. "Plato and Pythagoras and Xenocrates and Chrysippus, following the ancient theologians, say that dæmons are stronger than men and far excel us in their natural endowment; but the divine element in them is not unmixed nor undiluted, but partakes of the soul's nature and the body's sense-perception, and is susceptive of pleasure and pain, while the passions which attend these mutations affect them, some of them more and others less. For there are among dæmons, as among men, differences of virtue and wickedness."[4] "It can be proved on the testimony of wise and ancient witnesses that there are natures, as it were on the frontiers of gods and men, that admit mortal passions and inevitable changes, whom we may rightly, after the custom of

---

[1] *de def. orac.* 29, 426 B. Cf. *de Iside*, 66, 377 D, E. "You might as well give the name of steersman to sails, ropes or anchor."

[2] *de def. orac.* 30, 246 D, E.

[3] This triple government of the Universe is worked out in *de fato* (a tract whose authorship is questioned), but from one passage and another of Plutarch's undoubted works it can be established, though every statement has a little fringe of uncertainties.

[4] *de Iside*, 25, 360 E.

our fathers, consider to be dæmons, and so calling them, worship them "[1] If the atmosphere were abolished between the earth and the moon (for beyond air and moon it was generally supposed that the gods lived [2]), the void would destroy the unity of the universe ; and in precisely the same way "those who do not leave us the race of dæmons, destroy all intercourse and contact between gods and men, by abolishing what Plato called the interpretive and ancillary nature, or else they compel us to make confusion and disorder of everything, by bringing God in among mortal passions and mortal affairs, fetching him down for our needs, as they say the witches in Thessaly do with the moon."[3] And "he, who involves God in human needs, does not spare his majesty, nor does he maintain the dignity and greatness of God's excellence."[4] The Stoic teaching that men are "parts of God" makes God responsible for every human act of wickedness and sin—the common weakness of every pantheistic system.[5]

Thus the dæmons serve two purposes in religious philosophy. They safeguard the Absolute and the higher gods from contact with matter, and they relieve the Author of Good from responsibility for evil. At the same time they supply the means of that relation to the divine which is essential for man's higher life—"passing on the prayers and supplications of men thitherward, and thence bringing oracles and gifts of blessing."[6] "They say well, who say that when Plato discovered the element underlying qualities that are begotten—what nowadays they call matter and nature—he set philosophers free from many great difficulties ; but to me they seem to solve more difficulties and greater ones, who set the race of dæmons between gods and

---

[1] de def. orac. 12, 416 C.

[2] Cf. Athenagoras, Presb. 24 (quoted in note 1 on p. 95) ; and Apuleius, de deo Socr. 6, 132, cited on p. 232.

[3] de def. orac. 13, 416 F.   [4] de def. orac. 9, 414 F.

[5] See de comm. not. adv. Stoicos, 33, and de Stoicorum repugn. 33, 34—three very interesting chapters. Clement of Alexandria has the same tone in criticizing this idea—οὐκ οἶδ' ὅπως ἀνέξεταί τις ἐπαΐων τούτου θεὸν ἐγνωκὼς ἀπιδὼν εἰς τὸν βίον τὸν ἡμέτερον ἐν ὅσοις φυρόμεθα κακοῖς. εἴη γὰρ ἂν οὕτως, ὃ μηδ' εἰπεῖν θέμις, μερικῶς ἁμαρτάνων ὁ θεὸς, κτέ. Strom. ii, 74.

[6] de Iside, 26, 361 C. Cf. Plato, Sympos. 202 E, 203 A (referred to above), for the functions of τὸ δαιμόνιον, which is μεταξὺ θεοῦ τε καὶ θνητοῦ . . . ἑρμηνεῦον καὶ διαπορθμεῦον θεοῖς τὰ παρ' ἀνθρώπων καὶ ἀνθρώποις τὰ παρὰ θεῶν κτέ . . . θεὸς δὲ ἀνθρώπῳ οὐ μίγνυται . . οὗτοι δὴ οἱ δαίμονες πολλοὶ καὶ παντοδαποί εἰσιν, εἷς δὲ τούτων ἐστὶ καὶ ὁ Ἔρως

men and discovered that in some such way it made a community of us and brought us together, whether the theory belongs to the Magians who follow Zoroaster, or is Thracian and comes from Orpheus, or is Egyptian, or Phrygian."[1] Homer, he adds, still uses the terms "gods" and "dæmons" alike; "it was Hesiod who first clearly and distinctly set forth the four classes of beings endowed with reason, gods, dæmons, heroes and finally men."

The dæmons, then, are the agents of Providence, of the One Reason, which orders the universe; they are the ministers of the divine care for man. And here perhaps their mediation is helped by the fact that the border lines between themselves and the gods above on the one hand, and men below on the other, are not fixed and final. Some dæmons, such as Isis, Osiris, Herakles and Dionysos, have by their virtue risen to be gods,[2] while their own numbers have been recruited from the souls of good men.[3] "Souls which are delivered from becoming (γενέσεως) and thenceforth have rest from the body, as being utterly set free, are the dæmons that care for men, as Hesiod says";[4] and, just as old athletes enjoy watching and encouraging young ones, "so the dæmons, who through worth of soul are done with the conflicts of life," do not despise what they have left behind, but are kindly minded to such as strive for the same goal,—especially when they see them close upon their hope, struggling and all but touching it. As in the case of a shipwreck those on shore will run out into the waves to lend a hand to the sailors they can reach (though if they are out on the sea, to watch in silence is all that can be done), so the dæmons help us "while the affairs of life break over us (βαπτιζομένους ὑπὸ τῶν πραγμάτων) and we take one body after another as it were carriages." Above all they help us if we strive of our own virtue to be saved and reach the haven.[5]

But this is not all, for in his letter written to console Apollonios Plutarch carries us further. There was, he says, a

---

[1] de def. orac. 10, 414 F—415 A.

[2] de Iside, 27, 361 E ; de def. orac. 10, 415 C ; cf. Tert. ad Natt. ii, 2.

[3] Romulus, 28 ; de def. orac. 10, 415 B.

[4] Hesiod, Works and Days, 121. "But," asks Tatian (c. 16), "why should they get δραστικωτέρας δυνάμεως after death?" See the reply given by Plutarch, de def. orac. 39, 431 E. Compare also views of Apuleius (de deo Socr. 15) cited on p. 233.

[5] de genio Socratis, 24, 593 D-F. He is thinking of the series of rebirths.

man who lost his only son—he was afraid, by poison. It perhaps adds confidence to the story that Plutarch gives his name and home; he was Elysios of Terina in Southern Italy. The precision is characteristic. Elysios accordingly went to a *psychomanteion*, a shrine where the souls of the dead might be consulted.[1] He duly sacrificed and went to sleep in the temple. He saw in a dream his own father with a youth strikingly like the dead son, and he was told that this was "the son's dæmon,"[2] and that the death had been natural, and right for the lad and for his parents. Elsewhere Plutarch quotes the lines of Menander—

> By each man standeth, from his natal hour,
> A dæmon, his kind mystagogue through life—[3]

but he prefers the view of Empedocles that there are two such beings in attendance on each of us.[4] The classical instance of a guardian spirit was the "daimonion" of Socrates, on which both Plutarch and Apuleius wrote books.[5] Plutarch discusses many theories that had been given of it, but hardly convinces the reader that he really knew what Socrates meant.

In a later generation it was held that if proper means were taken the guardian spirit would come visibly before a man's eyes. So Apuleius held, and Porphyry records that when an Egyptian priest called on the dæmon of Plotinus to manifest himself in the temple of Isis (the only "pure" spot the Egyptian

---

[1] On such places and on necromancy in general see Tertullian, *de anima*, 57, who puts it down to illusion of the evil one—*nec magnum illi exteriores oculos circumscribere cui interiorem mentis aciem excæcare perfacile est.*

[2] Cf. p. 15 on the *genius* and the *fravashi*.

[3] *de tranqu. animi*, 15, 474 B.

[4] Cf. the story of the appearance to Brutus of his evil genius—ὁ σός, ὦ Βροῦτε, δαίμων κακός, *Brutus*, 36. Basilides the Gnostic (the father of Isidore) is credited with describing Man as a sort of Wooden Horse with a whole army of different spirits in him (Clem. Alex. *Strom.* ii, 113). Plutarch makes a similar jibe at the Stoic account of arts, virtues, vices, etc., as corporeal or even animate and rational beings—making a man "a Paradise, or a cattle-pen, or a Wooden Horse," *de commun. notit. adv. Stoicos*, 45, 1084 B. There was a tendency in contemporary psychology to attribute all feelings, etc., to dæmonic influence ; cf. Clem. Alex. *Strom.* ii, 110, who suggests that all πάθη are imprints (as of a seal) made on the soul by the spiritual powers against which we have to wrestle. Cf. Tert. *de Anima*, 41, the evil of soul in part due to evil spirit.

[5] Clement says (*Strom.* vi, 53) that Isidore the Gnostic "in the first book of the expositions of Parchor the Prophet" dealt with the dæmon of Socrates and quoted Aristotle's authority for such tutelary spirits. For the book of Apuleius, see ch. vii.

could find in Rome), there came not a dæmon but a god; so great a being was Plotinus.[1] Plutarch discusses the question of such bodily appearances in connexion with the legend of Numa and Egeria.   He can believe that God would not disdain the society of a specially good and holy man, but as for the idea that god or dæmon would have anything to do with a human body—"that would indeed require some persuasion."   "Yet the Egyptians plausibly say that it is not impossible for the spirit of a god to have intercourse with a woman and beget some beginnings of life," though Plutarch finds a difficulty in such a union of unequals.[2]

Plutarch has comparatively little to say of visible appearances of tutelary or other dæmons.   To what lengths of credulity men went in this direction will be shown in a later chapter. Yet a guardian who does not communicate in some way with the person he guards, and a series of dæmonic and divine powers content to be inert and silent, would be futile; and in fact there was, Plutarch held, abundance of communication between men and the powers above them.   It was indeed one of the main factors of his religion that man's life is intimately related to the divine.

Plutarch, of course, could know nothing of the language in use to-day, but it is clear that he was familiar with some or all of the phænomena, which in our times have received a vocabulary of their own, for the moment very impressive.   Psychopathic, auto-suggestion, telepathy, the subliminal self—the words may tell us something ; whether what they tell us is verifiable, remains to be seen.   Plutarch's account of the facts, for the description of which this language has been invented, seems even more fantastic to a modern reader, but it must be remembered that he and his contemporaries were led to it at once by observation of psychical phænomena, still to be observed, and by philosophic speculation on the transcendence of God. As a body of theories, the ancient system holds together as well as most systems in the abstract.   It was not in theory that it broke down.   Plutarch as usual presents it with reservations.

---

[1] Porphyry, *v. Plotini*, 10.   Cf. Origen, *c. Cels.* vii, 35, for Celsus' views on the visibility of dæmons, *e.g.* in the cave of Trophonius.

[2] *Life of Numa*, 4—a most interesting chapter, when it is remembered what other works were being written contemporaneously.

The dæmons are not slow to speak; it is we who are slow to hear. "In truth we men recognize one another's thoughts, as it were feeling after them in the dark by means of the voice. But the thoughts of the dæmons are luminous and shine for those who can see; and they need no words or names, such as men use among themselves as symbols to see images and pictures of what is thought, while, as for the things actually thought, those they only know who have some peculiar and dæmonic light. The words of the dæmons are borne through all things, but they sound only for those who have the untroubled nature and the still soul—those, in fact, whom we call holy and happy (δαιμονίους)."[1] Most people think the dæmon only comes to men when they are asleep, but this is due to their want of harmony. "The divine communicates immediately (δι' αὐτοῦ) with few and but rarely; to most men it gives signs, from which rises the so-called Mantic art"[2]—prophecy or sooth-saying. All souls have the "mantic" faculty—the capacity for receiving impressions from dæmons—though not in an equal degree. A dæmon after all is, from one point of view, merely a disembodied soul, and it may meet a soul incorporated in a body; and thus, soul meeting soul, there are produced "impressions of the future,"[3] for a voice is not needed to convey thought.

But if a disembodied soul can foresee the future, why should not a soul in a body also be able? In point of fact, the soul has this power, but it is dulled by the body. Memory is a parallel gift. Some souls only shake off the influence of the body in dreams, some at the approach of death.[4] The mantic element is receptive of impressions and of anticipations by means of feelings, and without reasoning process (ἀσυλλογίστως) it touches the future when it can get clear of the present. The state, in which this occurs, is called "enthusiasm," god-possession—and into this the body will sometimes fall of itself, and sometimes it is cast into it by some vapour or ex-halation sent up by the earth. This vapour or whatever it is (τὸ μαντικὸν ῥεῦμα καὶ πνεῦμα) pervades the body, and produces

---

[1] de genio Socr. 20, 588 D, 589 D.   [2] de gen. Socr. 24, 593 D.

[3] de def. orac. 38, 431 C, φαντασίας τοῦ μέλλοντος.

[4] Cf. Clem. Alex. Strom. vi, 46, on preaching of Christ in Hades, where souls, rid of the flesh, see more clearly.

in the soul a disposition, or combination (κρᾶσιν), unfamiliar
and strange, hard to describe, but from what is said it may
be divined. "Probably by heat and diffusion it opens pores
[or channels] whereby impressions of the future may be received."[1] Such a vapour was found to issue from the ground
at Delphi—the accidental discovery of a shepherd, Coretas
by name, who spoke "words with God in them." (φωνὰς
ἐνθουσιώδεις) under its influence ; and it was not till his words
proved true that attention was paid to the place and the
vapour. There is the same sort of relation between the soul
and the mantic vapour as between the eye and light.

But does not this vapour theory do away with the other
theory that divination is mediated to us by the gods through
the dæmons ? Plutarch cites Plato's objection to Anaxagoras
who was "entangled in natural causes" and lost sight of better
causes and principles beyond them. There are double causes
for everything. The ancients said that all things come from
Zeus ; those who came later, natural philosophers (φυσικοὶ),
on the contrary "wandered away from the fair and divine
principle," and made everything depend on bodies, impacts,
changes and combinations (κρᾶσις) ; and both miss something of
the truth. "We do not make Mantic either godless or void of
reason, when we give it the soul of man as its material, and
the enthusiastic spirit and exhalation as its tool or plectron.
For, first, the earth that produces these exhalations—and the
sun, who gives the earth the power of combination (κρᾶσις) and
change, is by the tradition of our fathers a god ; and then we
leave dæmons installed as lords and warders and guards of
this combination (κράσεως), now loosening and now tightening
(as if it were a harmony), taking away excessive ecstasy and
confusion, and gently and painlessly blending the motive
power for those who use it. So we shall not seem guilty of
anything unreasonable or impossible."[2]

[1] de def. orac. 40, 432 C-E, θερμότητι γὰρ καὶ διαχύσει πόρους τινὰς ἀνοίγειν
φαντασικοὺς τοῦ μέλλοντος εἰκός ἐστιν. For these πόροι cf. Clem. Alex. Strom. vii,
36, with J. B. Mayor's note.

[2] de def. orac. 46-48, 435 A—437 A (referring to Phædo, 97 D). The curious mixture of metaphors, the double suggestion of κρᾶσις, the parallel from music, and the
ambiguity of τὸ ἐνθουσιαστικὸν πνεῦμα (characteristic of the confusion of spiritual and
material then prevalent) make a curious sentence in English. On the relation of
dæmons to oracles, see also de facie in orbe lunæ, 30, 944 D ; also Tertullian, de Anima,

Plutarch gives an interesting account of a potion, which will produce the same sort of effect. The Egyptians compound it in a very mystical way of sixteen drugs, nearly all of which are fragrant, while the very number sixteen as the square of a square has remarkable properties or suggestions. The mixture is called Kyphi, and when inhaled it calms the mind and reduces anxiety, and "that part of us which receives impressions (φανταστικὸν) and is susceptive of dreams, it rubs down and cleans as if it were a mirror."[1]

The gods, he says, are our first and chiefest friends.[2] Not every one indeed so thinks—"for see what Jews and Syrians think of the gods!"[3] But Plutarch insists that there is no joy in life apart from them. Epicureans may try to deliver us from the wrath of the gods, but they do away with their kindness at the same moment; and Plutarch holds it better that there should even be some morbid element (πάθος) of reverence and fear in our belief than that, in our desire to avoid this, we should leave ourselves neither hope, nor kindness, nor courage in prosperity, nor any recourse to the divine when we are in trouble.[4] Superstition is a rheum that gathers in the eye of faith, which we do well to remove, but not at the cost of knocking the eye out or blinding it.[5] In any case, its inconvenience is outweighed "ten thousand times" by the glad and joyous hopefulness that counts all blessing as coming from the gods. And he cites in proof of this that joy in temple-service, to which reference has already been made. Those who abolish Providence need no further punishment than to live without it.[6]

46, who gives a lucid account of dæmons as the explanation of oracles, and *Apol.* 22 —dæmons inhabiting the atmosphere have early knowledge of the weather, and by their incredible speed can pass miraculously quickly from one end of the earth to the other, and so bring information—strange, he adds (*c.* 25), that Cybele took a week to inform her priest of the death of Marcus Aurelius—*o somniculosa diplomata !* ("sleepy post").

[1] *de Iside*, 80, 383 E. Clem. Alex. *Strom.* i, 135, says Greek prophets of old were "stirred up by dæmons, or disordered by waters, fragrances or some quality of the air," but the Hebrews spoke "by the power and mind of God."

[2] *Præc. Conj.* 19. Cf. Plato, *Laws*, 906 A, σύμμαχοι δὲ ἡμῖν θεοί τε ἅμα καὶ δαίμονες, ἡμεῖς δ᾽ αὖ κτῆμα θεῶν καὶ δαιμόνων.

[3] *de repugn. Stoic.* 38, 1051 E. [4] *non suaviter,* 20, 1101 B.

[5] *non suaviter* 21, 1101 C. Clem. Alex. *Pæd.* ii, 1, says it is "peculiar to man to cleanse the eye of the soul."

[6] *non suaviter,* 22, 1102 F.

But the pleasures of faith are not only those of imagination or emotion. For while the gods give us all blessings, there is none better for man to receive or more awful for God to bestow than truth. Other things God gives to men, mind and thought he shares with them, for these are his attributes, and " I think that of God's own eternal life the happiness lies in his knowledge being equal to all that comes; for without knowledge and thought, immortality would be time and not life." [1] The very name of Isis is etymologically connected with knowing (εἰδέναι); and the goal of her sacred rites is " knowledge of the first and sovereign and intelligible, whom the goddess bids us seek and find in her." [2] Her philosophy is " hidden for the most part in myths, and in true tales (λόγοις) that give dim visions and revelations of truth." [3] Her temple at Sais bears the inscription : " I am all that has been and is and shall be, and my veil no mortal yet has lifted." [4] She is the goddess of " Ten Thousand Names." [5]

Plutarch connects with his belief in the gods " the great hypothesis " of immortality. " It is one argument that at one and the same time establishes the providence of God and the continuance of the human soul, and you cannot do away with the one and leave the other." [6] If we had nothing divine in us, nothing like God, if we faded like the leaves (as Homer said), God would hardly give us so much thought, nor would he, like women with their gardens of Adonis, tend and culture " souls of a day," growing in the flesh which will admit no "strong root of life." The dialogue, in which this is said, is supposed to have taken place in Delphi, so Plutarch turns to Apollo. " Do you think that, if Apollo knew that the souls of the dying perished at once, blowing away like mist or smoke from their bodies, he would ordain so many propitiations for the dead, and ask such great gifts and honours for the departed—that he would cheat and humbug believers? For my part, I will never let go the continuance of the soul, unless some Herakles shall come and take away the Pythia's tripod and abolish and destroy the oracle. For as long as so many oracles of this kind are given even in our day, it is not holy to condemn the soul to

---

[1] de Iside, 1, 351 D.   [2] de Iside, 2, 352 A.
[3] de Iside, 9, 354 C, ἐμφάσεις καὶ διαφάσεις.   [4] de Iside, 9, 354 C.
[5] de Iside, 53, 372 E, Μυριώνυμος.   [6] de ser. num. vind. 18, 560 F

death."[1]   And Plutarch fortifies his conviction with stories of
oracles, and of men who had converse with dæmons, with
apocalypses and revelations, among which are two notable
Descents into Hades,[2] and a curious account of dæmons in the
British Isles.[3]

The theory of dæmons lent itself to the explanation of the
origin of evil, but speculation in this direction seems not to
have appealed to Plutarch.   He uses bad dæmons to explain
the less pleasant phases of paganism, as we shall see, but the
question of evil he scarcely touches.   In his book on Isis and
Osiris he discusses Typhon as the evil element in nature, and
refers with interest to the views of " the Magian Zoroaster who,
they say, lived about five hundred years before the Trojan War."
Zoroaster held that there were two divine beings, the better being
a god, Horomazes (Ormuzd), the other a dæmon Areimanios
(Ahriman), the one most like to light of all sensible things, the
other to darkness and ignorance, " and between them is Mithras,
for which reason the Persians call Mithras the Mediator."   But
the hour of Mithras was not yet come, and in all his writings
Plutarch hardly alludes to him more than half a dozen times.[4]
It should be noted that, whatever his interest in Eastern dualism with its Western parallels, Plutarch does not abandon his
belief in the One Ultimate Good God.

This then in bare outline is a scheme of Plutarch's religion,
though, as already noted, the scheme is not of his own making,
but is put together from incidental utterances, all liable to
qualification.   It is not the religion of a philosopher ; and the
qualifications, which look like concessions to philosophic
hesitation, mean less than they suggest.   They are entrench-
ments thrown up against philosophy.   He is an educated Greek
who has read the philosophers, but he is at heart an apologist—
a defender of myth, ritual, mystery and polytheism.   He has

[1] *de ser. num. vind.* 17, 560 B-D. Justin, *Apology*, i, 18, appeals to the belief in the
continuance of the soul, which pagans derive from necromancy, dreams, oracles and
persons " dæmoniolept."

[2] In *de sera numinum vindicta* and *de genio Socratis.*   Cf. also the account of the
souls of the dead given in *de facie in orbe lunæ*, c. 28 ff.

[3] *de def. orac.* 18, 419 E.   Another curious tale of these remote islands is in Clem.
Alex. *Strom.* vi, 33.

[4] Cumont, *Mysteries of Mithra* (tr.), p. 35. Mithraism began to spread under the
Flavians, but (p. 33) " remained for ever excluded from the Hellenic world."

compromised where Plato challenged. His front (to carry out the military metaphor) extends over a very long line—a line in places very weakly supported, and the dæmons form its centre. It is the dæmons who link men to the gods, and through them to the Supreme, making the universe a unity; who keep the gods immune from contact with matter and from the suggestion of evil; and what is more, they enable Plutarch to defend the myths of Greek and Egyptian tradition from the attack of philosopher and unbeliever. And this defence of myth was probably more to him than the unity of the universe. Every kind of myth was finding a home in the eventual Greek religion, many of them obscene, bestial and cruel—revolting to the purity and the tenderness developing more and more in the better minds of Greece. They could not well be detached from the religion, so they had to be defended.

There are, for example, many elements in the myth of Isis and Osiris that are disgusting. Plutarch recommends us first of all, by means of the preconceptions supplied by Greek philosophy upon the nature of God, to rule out what is objectionable as unworthy of God, but not to do this too harshly. Myth after all is a sort of rainbow to the sun of reason,[1] and should be received "in a holy and philosophic spirit."[2] We must not suppose that this or the other story "happened so and was actually done." Many things told of Isis and Osiris, if they were supposed to have truly befallen "the blessed and incorruptible nature" of the gods, would be "lawless and barbarous fancy" which, as Æschylus says—

You must spit out and purify your mouth.[3]

But, all the same, myth must be handled tenderly and not in too rationalistic a spirit—for that might be opening the doors to "the atheist people." Euhemerus, by recklessly turning all the gods into generals and admirals and kings of ancient days, has covered the whole world with atheism,[4] and the Stoics, as we have seen, are not much better, who turn the gods into their own gifts. No, we may handle myth far too freely—"ah! yet

---

[1] de Iside, 20, 358 F.   [2] de Iside, 11, 355 C.
[3] de Iside, 20, 358 E. Cf. the language of Clement in dealing with expressions in the Bible that seem to imply an anthropomorphic conception of God. See p. 291.
[4] de Iside, 23, 360 A.

consider it again!" There are so many possibilities of acceptance.
And "in the rites of Isis there is nothing unreasonable, nothing
fictitious, nor anything introduced by superstition, but some
things have an ethical value, others a historical or physical
suggestion."[1]

In the second place, if nothing can be done for the myth or
the rite—if it is really an extreme case—Plutarch falls back upon
the dæmons. There are differences among them as there are
among men, and the elements of passion and unreason are
strong in some of them; and traces of these are to be found in
rites and initiations and myths here and there. Rituals in
which there is the eating of raw flesh, or the rending asunder
of animals, fasting or beating of the breast, or again the narra-
tion of obscene legends, are to be attributed to no god but to
evil dæmons. How many such rituals survived, Plutarch does
not say and perhaps he did not know; but the Christain
apologists were less reticent, and Clement of Alexandria and
Firmicus Maternus and the rest have abundant evidence about
them. Some of these rites, Plutarch says, must have been
practised to *avert* the attention of the dæmons. "The human
sacrifices that used to be performed," could not have been welcome
to the gods, nor would kings and generals have been willing to
sacrifice their own children unless they had been appeasing the
anger of ugly, ill-tempered, and vengeful spirits, who would
bring pestilence and war upon a people till they obtained what
they sought. "Moreover as for all they say and sing in myth
and hymn, of rapes and wanderings of the gods, of their hiding,
of their exile and of their servitude, these are not the experiences of gods but of dæmons." It is not right to say that
Apollo fought a dragon for the Delphic shrine.[2]

But some such tales were to be found in the finest literature
of the Greeks, and they were there told of the gods.[3] In reply
to this, one of Plutarch's characters quotes the narrative of a
hermit by the Red Sea.[4] This holy man conversed with men
once a year, and the rest of the time he consorted with wander-

---

[1] *de Iside*, 8, 353 E.

[2] *de def. orac.* 14, 15, 417 B-F. Cf. Clem. Alex. *Protr.* 42, ἀπάνθρωποι καὶ
μισάνθρωποι δαίμονες enjoying ἀνθρωποκτονίας.

[3] So Tertullian urges, *ad Natt.* ii, 7.

[4] This man, or somebody very like him, appears as a Christian hermit in Sulpicius
Severus, *Dial.* i, 17 ; only there he is reported to consort with angels.

ing nymphs and dæmons—"the most beautiful man I ever saw, and quite free from all disease." He lived on a bitter fruit which he ate once a month. This sage declared that the legends told of Dionysus and the rites performed in his honour at Delphi really pertained to a dæmon. "If we call some dæmons by the names that belong to gods,—no wonder," said this stranger, "for a dæmon is constantly called after the god, to whom he is assigned, and from whom he has his honour and his power"—just as men are called Athenæus or Dionysius—and many of them have no sort of title to the gods' names they bear.[1]

With Philosophy so ready to be our mystagogue and to lead us into the true knowledge of divine goodness, and with so helpful a theory to explain away all that is offensive in traditional religion, faith ought to be as easy as it is happy and wholesome. But there is another danger beside Atheism—its exact opposite, superstition; and here—apart from philosophical questions— lay the practical difficulty of Plutarch's religion. He accepted almost every cult and mythology which the ancient world had handed down ; Polytheism knows no false gods. But to guide one's course aright, between the true myth and the depraved, to distinguish between the true and good god and the pseudo- nymous dæmon, was no easy task. The strange mass of Egyptian misunderstandings was a testimony to this—some in their ignorance thought the gods underwent the actual experi- ence of the grain they gave men to sow, just as untaught Greeks identified the gods with their images; and some Egyptians worshipped the animals sacred to the gods; and so religion was brought into contempt, while "the weak and harmless" fell into unbounded superstition, and the shrewder and bolder into "beastly and atheistic reflections."[2] And yet on second thoughts Plutarch has a kindly apology for animal-worship.[3]

Plutarch himself wrote a tract on superstition in which some have found a note of rhetoric or special pleading, for he decidedly gives the atheist the superiority over the superstitious,

---

[1] *de def. orac.* 21, 421 A-E. Cf. Tert. *de Spect.* 10. The names of the dead and their images are nothing, but we know *qui sub istis nominibus institutis simulacris operentur et gaudeant et divinitatem mentiantur, nequam spiritus scilicet, dæmones.* He holds the gods to have been men, long deceased, but agrees in believing in dæmonic operations in shrines, etc.

[2] *de Iside,* 70, 71, 379 B-E.   [3] *de Iside,* 76, 382 A

a view which Amyot, his great translator, called dangerous, for "it is certain that Superstition comes nearer the mean of true Religion than does Atheism."[1] Perhaps it did in the sixteenth century, but in Plutarch's day superstition was the real enemy to be crushed. Nearly every superstitious practice he cites appears in other writers.

Superstition, the worst of all terrors, like all other terrors kills action. It makes no truce with sleep, the refuge from other fears and pains. It invents all kinds of strange practices, immersions in mud, baptisms,[2] prostrations, shameful postures, outlandish worships. He who fears "the gods of his fathers and his race, saviours, friends and givers of good"—whom will he not fear? Superstition adds to the dread of death "the thought of eternal woes." The atheist lays his misfortunes down to accident and looks for remedies. The superstitious makes all into judgments, "the strokes of God," and will have no remedies lest he should seem "to fight against God" ($\theta\epsilon o\mu\alpha\chi\epsilon\hat{\iota}\nu$). "Leave me, Sir, to my punishment!" he cries, "me the impious, the accursed, hated of Gods and dæmons" —so he sits in rags and rolls in the mud, confessing his sins and iniquities, how he ate or drank or walked when the dæmonion forbade. "Wretched man!" he says to himself, "Providence ordains thy suffering; it is God's decree." The atheist thinks there are no gods; the superstitious wishes there were none. It is they who have invented the sacrifices of children that prevailed at Carthage[3] and other things of the kind. If Typhons and Giants were to drive out the gods and become our rulers, what worse could they ask?

A hint from the *Conjugal Precepts* may be added here, as it suggests a difficulty in practice. "The wife ought not to have men friends of her own but to share her husband's; and the gods are our first and best friends. So those gods whom the the husband acknowledges, the wife ought to worship and own, and those alone, and keep the great door shut on superfluous devotions and foreign superstitions. No god really enjoys the

---

[1] See discussion in Oakesmith, *Religion of Plutarch*, p. 185. Gréard, *de la Morale de Plutarque*, p. 269, ranks it with the best works that have come down to us from Antiquity.

[2] Tertullian on pagan baptisms—Isis and Mithras, *de Baptismo*, 5 ; *de Præscr. Hær.* 40.

[3] Cf. Tert. *Apol.* 9, on these sacrifices, in Africa, and elsewhere, and see p. 26.

stolen rites of a woman in secret."[1]   This is a counsel of peace, but if "ugly, ill-tempered and vengeful spirits" seem to the mother to threaten her children, who will decide what are superfluous devotions?

The religion of Plutarch is a different thing from his morality.   For his ethics rest on an experience much more easy to analyse, and like every elderly and genial person he has much that he can say of the kindly duties of life.   Every reader will own the beauty and the high tone of much of his teaching, though some will feel that its centre is the individual, and that it is pleasant rather than compulsive and inevitable.   After all nearly every religion has, somewhere or other, what are called "good ethics," but the vital question is, "What else?"   In the last resort is ecstasy, independently of morality, the main thing?   Are words and acts holy as religious symbols which in a society are obviously vicious?   What propellent power lies behind the morals?   And where are truth and experience?

What then is to be said of Plutarch's religion?   Here his experience was not so readily intelligible, and every inherited and acquired instinct within him conspired to make him cling to tradition and authority as opposed to independent judgment. His philosophy was not Plato's, in spite of much that he borrowed from Plato, for its motive was not the love of truth. The stress he lays upon the pleasure of believing shows that his ultimate canon is emotion.   He does not really wish to find truth on its own account, though he honestly would like its support.   He wishes to believe, and believe he will—*sit pro ratione voluntas.*   "There is something of the woman in Plutarch," says Mr Lecky.   Like men of this temperament in every age, he surrenders to emotion, and emotion declines into sentimentalism.   He cannot firmly say that anything, with which religious feeling has ever been associated, has ceased to be useful and has become false.   He may talk bravely of shutting the great door against Superstition, but Superstition has many entrances—indeed, was indoors already.

We have only to look at his treatise on Isis and Osiris to see the effects of compromise in religion.   He will never take a firm stand ; there are always possibilities, explanations, parallels, suggestions, symbolisms, by which he can escape from facing

[1] *Conjug. Præc.* 19.

definitely the demand for a decisive reformation of religion. As a result, in spite of the radiant mist of amiability, which he diffuses over these Egyptian gods, till the old myths seem capable of every conceivable interpretation, and everything a symbol of everything else, and all is beautiful and holy—the foolish and indecent old stories remain a definite and integral part of the religion, the animals are still objects of worship and the image of Osiris stands in its original naked obscenity.[1] And the Egyptian is not the only religion, for, as Tertullian points out, the old rites are still practised everywhere, with unabated horrors, symbol or no symbol.[2] Plutarch emphasizes the goodness and friendliness of the gods, but he leaves the evil dæmons in all their activity. Strange and awful sacrifices of the past he deprecates, but he shows no reason why they should not continue. God, he says, is hardly to be conceived by man's mind as in a dream; and he thanks heaven for its peculiar grace that the oracles are reviving in his day; he believes in necromancy, theolepsy and nearly every other grotesque means of intercourse with gods and dæmons. He calls himself a Platonist; he is proud of the great literature of Greece; but nearly all that we associate in religious thought with such names as Xenophanes, Euripides and Plato, he gently waves aside on the authority of Apollo. It raises the dignity of Seneca when we set beside him this delightful man of letters, so full of charm, so warm with the love of all that is beautiful, so closely knit to the tender emotions of ancestral piety—and so unspeakably inferior in essential truthfulness.

The ancient world rejected Seneca, as we have seen, and chose Plutarch. If Plutarch was not the founder of Neo-Platonism, he was one of its precursors and he showed the path. Down that path ancient religion swung with deepening emotion into that strange medley of thought and mystery, piety, magic and absurdity, which is called the New Platonism and has nothing to do with Plato. Here and there some fine spirit emerged into clearer air, and in some moment of ecstasy

---

[1] Cf. *de Iside*, 55, 373 C ; 18, 358 B ; the image of Osiris, 36, 365 B. Origen (*c. Cels.* v, 39) remarks that Celsus is quite pleased with those who worship crocodiles "in the ancestral way."

[2] If the legend is *mere* fable, he asks, *cur rapitur sacerdos Cereris, si non tale Ceres passa est? cur Saturno alieni liberi immolantur . . . cur Idææae masculus amputatur? ad Natt.* ii, 8.

achieved "by a leap" some fleeting glimpse of Absolute Being, if there is such a thing. But the mass of men remained below in a denser atmosphere, prisoners of ignorance and of fancy—in an atmosphere not merely dark but tainted, full of spiritual and intellectual death.

CHAPTER IV

JESUS OF NAZARETH

When we hear any other speaker, even a very good one, he produces absolutely no effect upon us, or not much, whereas the mere fragments of you and your words, even at second-hand, and however imperfectly repeated, amaze and possess the souls of every man, woman and child who comes within hearing of them.—Plato, *Symposium*, 215 D (Jowett).

Dominus noster Christus veritatem se non consuetudinem cognominavit.—Tertullian, *de virg. vel.* 1.

TOWARDS the end of the first century of our era, there began to appear a number of little books, written in the ordinary Greek of every-day life, the language which the common people used in conversation and correspondence. It was not the literary dialect, which men of letters affected—a mannered and elaborate style modelled on the literature of ancient Greece and no longer a living speech. The books were not intended for a lettered public, but for plain people who wanted a plain story, which they knew already, set down in a handy and readable form. The writers did their work very faithfully—some of them showing a surprising loyalty to the story which they had received. Like other writers they were limited by considerations of space and so forth, and this involved a certain freedom of choice in selecting, omitting, abridging and piecing together the material they gathered. Four only of the books survive intact; of others there are scanty fragments; and scholars have divined at least one independent work embodied in two that remain. So far as books can, three of them represent very fairly the ideas of an earlier generation, as it was intended they should, and tell their common story, with the variations natural to individual writers, but with a general harmony that is the pledge of its truth.

At an early date, these books began to be called Gospels [1] and by the time they had circulated for a generation they were

---

[1] Justin, *Apology*, i, 66.

very widely known and read among the community for which they were written. Apart from a strong instinct which would allow no conscious change to be made in the lineaments of the central figure of the story, there was nothing to safeguard the little books from the fate of all popular works of their day. Celsus, at the end of the second century, maintained that a good deal of the story was originally invention; and he added that the "believers" had made as free as drunk men with it and had written the gospel over again—three times, four times, many times—and had altered it to meet the needs of controversy.[1] Origen replied that Marcion's followers and two other schools had done so, but he knew of no others. It may to-day be taken as established that the four gospels, as we know them, stand substantially as near the autograph of their authors as most ancient books which were at all widely read, though here and there it is probable, or even certain, that changes on a slight scale have been made in the wording to accommodate the text to the development of Christian ideas.[2] This is at first sight a serious qualification, but it is not so important as it seems. By comparison of the first three gospels with one another, with the aid of the history of their transmission in the original Greek and in many versions and quotations, it is not very difficult to see where the hand of a later day has touched the page and to break through to something in all probability very near the original story.

This is the greatest problem of literary and historical criticism to-day. All sorts of objections have been raised against the credibility of the gospels from the time of Celsus— they were raised even earlier; for Celsus quotes them from previous controversialists—and they are raised still. We are sometimes told that we cannot be absolutely certain of the authenticity of any single saying of Jesus, or perhaps of any recorded episode in his life. A hypertrophied conscience might admit this to be true in the case of any word or deed of Jesus that might be quoted, and yet maintain that we have not lost much. For, it is a commonplace of historians that an anecdote, even if false in itself, may contain historical truth; it

---

[1] Quoted by Origen, *contra Celsum*, ii, 26, 27.
[2] Cf. Mr F. C. Conybeare's article on the remodelling of the baptismal formula in Matthew xxviii after the Council of Nicæa, *Hibbert Journal*, Oct. 1902.

may be evidence, that is, to the character of the person of whom it is told; for a false anecdote depends, even more than a true story, upon keeping the colour of its subject. It may be added that, as a rule, false anecdotes are apt to be more highly coloured than true stories, just as a piece of colour printing is generally a good deal brighter than nature. The reader, who, by familiarity with books, and with the ways of their writers, has developed any degree of literary instinct, will not be inclined to pronounce the colours in the first three gospels at least to be anything but natural and true. However, even if one were to concede that all the recorded sayings and doings of Jesus are fabrications (a wildly absurd hypothesis), there remains a common element in them, a unity of tone and character, which points to a well-known and clearly marked personality behind them, whose actual existence is further implied by the Christian movement. In other words, whether true or false in detail, the statements of the gospels, if we know how to use them aright, establish for us the historicity of Jesus, and leave no sort of doubt as to his personality and the impression he made upon those who came into contact with him.

We may not perhaps be able to reconstruct the life of Jesus as we should wish—it will not be a biography, and it will have no dates and hardly any procession of events. We shall be able to date his birth and death, roughly in the reigns of Augustus and Tiberius, more exactly fixing in each case a period of five years or so within which it must have happened. Of epochs and crises in his life we can say little, for we do not know enough of John the Baptist and his work to be able to make clear his relations with Jesus, nor can we speak with much certainty of the development of the idea of Messiahship in the mind of Jesus himself. But we can with care re-capture something of the experience of Jesus; we can roughly outline his outward life and environment. What is of more consequence, we can realize that, whatever the particular facts of his own career which opened the door for him, he entered into the general experience of men and knew human life deeply and intimately. And, after all, in this case as in others, it is not the facts of the life that matter, but the central fact that this man did know life as it is before he made judgment upon it. It is this alone that makes his judgment—or any other man's—of consequence to us. It is not his individual life, full of endless significance as that is, but his realization thereby of man's life and his attitude toward it that is the real gift of the great man—his thought, his character, himself in fact. And here our difficulty vanishes, for no one, who has cared to study the gospels with any degree of intelligent sympathy, has failed to realize the personality there revealed and to come in some way or other under its influence.

So far in dealing with the religious life of the ancient world, we have had to do with ideas and traditions—with a well thought-out scheme of philosophy and with an ancient and impressive series of mysteries and cults. The new force that now came into play is something quite different. The centre in the new religion is not an idea, nor a ritual act, but a personality. As its opponents were quick to point out,—and they still find a curious pleasure in rediscovering it—there was little new in Christian teaching. Men had been monotheists before, they had worshipped, they had loved their neighbours, they had displayed the virtues of Christians—what was there peculiar in Christianity? Plato, says Celsus, had taught long ago everything of the least value in the Christian scheme of things. The Talmud, according to the modern Jew, contains a parallel to everything that Jesus said—("and how much else!" adds Wellhausen). What was new in the new religion, in this "third race" of men? The Christians had their answer ready. In clear speech, and in aphasia, they indicated their founder. He was new. If we are to understand the movement, we must in some degree realize him—in himself and in his influence upon men.

In every endeavour made by any man to reconstruct another's personality, there will always be a subjective and imaginative element. Biography is always a work of the imagination. The method has its dangers, but without imagination the thing is not to be done at all. A great man impresses men in a myriad of different ways—he is as various and as bewilderingly suggestive as Nature herself—and no two men will record quite the same experience of him. Where the imagination has to penetrate an extraordinary variety of impressions, to seize, not a series of forces each severally making its own impression, but a single personality of many elements and yet a unity, men may well differ in the pictures they make. Even the same man will at different times be differently impressed and not always be uniformly able to grasp and order his impressions. Hence it is that biographies and portraits are so full of surprises and disappointments, while even the writer or the painter will not always accept his own interpretation—he outgrows it and detests it. And if it is possible to spend a life in the realization of the simplest human nature, what is to be said of an attempt to make a final picture of Jesus of Nazareth? Still the effort must be made to apprehend what he was to those with whom he lived, for from that comes the whole Christian movement.

Celsus denounced Jesus in language that amazes us; but when he was confronted with the teaching of Jesus, the moral worth of which a mind so candid could not deny, he admitted its value, but he attributed it to the fact that Jesus plagiarized largely from Greek philosophy and above all from Plato. He did not grasp, Celsus adds, how good what he stole really was, and he spoiled it by his vulgarity of phrase. In particular, Celsus denounced the saying "Whosoever shall smite thee on the right cheek, turn to him the other also." The idea came from the *Crito*, where Socrates compels Crito to own that we must do evil to no one—not even by way of requital. The passage is a fine one, and Celsus quoted it in triumph and asked if there were not something coarse and clownish in the style of Jesus.[1]

Celsus forgot for the moment that the same sort of criticism had been made upon Socrates. "'You had better be done,' said Critias, 'with those shoemakers of yours, and the carpenters and coppersmiths. They must be pretty well down at the heel by now—considering the way you have talked them round.' 'Yes,' said Charicles, 'and the cowherds too.'"[2] But six centuries had made another man of Socrates. His ideas, interpreted by Plato and others, had altered the whole thinking of the Greek world; his Silenus-face had grown beautiful by

---

[1] Origen, *c. Cels.* vii, 58, ἀγροικότερον.
[2] Xen. *Mem*, i, 2, 37. Cf. Plato, *Symp*. 221 E. *Gorgias*, 491 A. See Forbes, *Socrates*, 128 ; Adam, *Religious Teachers of Greece*, i, 338.

association; the physiognomy of his mind and speech was no longer so striking; he was a familiar figure, and his words and phrases were current coin, accepted without question. But to Celsus Jesus was no such figure; he had not the traditions and preconceptions which have in turn obscured for us the features of Jesus; there was nothing in Jesus either hallowed or familiar, and one glance revealed a physiognomy. That he did not like it is of less importance.

Taking the saying in question, we find, as Celsus did, absurdity upon the face of it, and, as he also did, something else at the heart of it—a contrast between surface and inner value broad as the gulf between the common sense which men gather from experience and the morality which Jesus read beneath human nature. Among the words of Jesus there are many such sayings, and it is clear that he himself saw and designed the contrasts which we feel as we read them. This sense of contrast is one of the ground-factors of humour generally, perhaps the one indispensable factor; it is always present in the highest humour. If we then take the words of Jesus, as they struck those who first heard them—or as they struck Celsus—we cannot help remarking at once a strong individual character in them, one element in which is humour, —always one of the most personal and individual of all marks of physiognomy.

Humour, in its highest form, is the sign of a mind at peace with itself, for which the contrasts and contradictions of life have ceased to jar, though they have not ceased to be,—which accepts them as necessary and not without meaning, indeed as adding charm to life, when they are viewed from above. It is the faculty which lets a man see what Plato called "the whole tragedy and comedy of life" [1]—the one in the other. Is it not humour that saw the Pharisee earnestly rinsing, rubbing and polishing the *outside* of his cup, forgetful of the fact that he drank from the inside? that saw the simple-minded taking their baskets to gather the grape-harvest from bramble-bushes? That pleaded with a nation, already gaining a name for being sordid, *not* to cast pearls before swine, and to forsake caring for the morrow, because such care was the mark of the *Gentile* world—the distinguishing sign between Gentile and Jew?

[1] Plato, *Philebus*, 50 B.

That told the men he knew so well—men bred in a rough world—to "turn the other cheek,"—to yield the cloak to him who took the coat, not in irony, but with the brotherly feeling that "his necessity is greater than mine" — to go when "commandeered" not the required mile, making an enemy by sourness of face, but to go two—"two additional," the Syriac version says—and so soften the man and make him a friend ? [1]

What stamps the language of Jesus invariably is its delicate ease, implying a sensibility to every real aspect of the matter in hand—a sense of mastery and peace. Men marvelled at the *charm* of his words—Luke using the Greek χάρις to express it.[2] The homely parable may be in other hands coarse enough, but the parables of Jesus have a quality about them after all these years that leaves one certain he smiled as he spoke them. There is something of the same kind to be felt in Cowper's letters, but in the stronger nature the gift is of more significance. At the cost of a little study of human character, and close reading of the Synoptists, and some careful imagination, it is possible to see him as he spoke,—the flash of the eye, the smile on the lip, the gesture of the hand, all the natural expression of himself and his thought that a man unconsciously gives in speaking, when he has forgotten himself in his matter and his hearer—his physiognomy, in fact. We realize very soon his complete mastery of the various aspects of what he says. That he realizes every implication of his words is less likely, for there is a spontaneity about them—they are "out of the abundance of his heart"; the form is not studied ; they are for the man and the moment. But they imply the speaker and his whole relation to God and man—they cannot help implying this, and that is their charm. Living words, flashed out on the spur of the moment from the depths of him, they *are* the man. It was not idly that the early church used to say "Remember the words of the Lord Jesus." On any showing, it is of importance to learn the mind of one whose speech is so full of life, and it is happily possible to do this from even the small collections we possess of his recorded sayings.

[1] On "playfulness" in the words of Jesus, see Burkitt, the *Gospel History*, p. 142. See also *Life of Abp Temple*, ii. 681 (letter to his son 18 Dec. 1896), on the "beam in the eye" and the "eye of the needle"—"that faint touch of fun which all Oriental teachers delight in."

[2] Luke iv, 22, ἐθαύμαζον ἐπὶ τοῖς λόγοις τῆς χάριτος.

Quite apart from the human interest which always clings about the childhood of a significant man, the early years of Jesus have a value of their own, for it was to them that he always returned when he wished to speak his deepest thought on the relations of God and man. In the life and love of the home he found the truest picture of the divine life. This we shall have to consider more fully at a later point. Very little is said by the evangelists of the childhood and youth at Nazareth, but in the parables we have Jesus' own reminiscences, and the scenes and settings of the stories he tells fit in easily and pleasantly with the framework of the historical and geographical facts of his life at Nazareth.

The town lies in a basin among hills, from the rim of which can be seen the historic plain of Esdraelon toward the South, Eastward the Jordan valley and the hills of Gilead, and to the West the sea. " It is a map of Old Testament history." [1] On great roads North and South of the town's girdle of hills passed to and fro, on the journey between Egypt and Mesopotamia, the many-coloured traffic of the East—moving no faster than the camel cared to go, swinging disdainfully on, with contempt on its curled lip for mankind, its work and itself. Traders, pilgrims and princes—the kingdoms of the world and the glory of them—all within reach and in no great hurry, a panorama of life for a thoughtful and imaginative boy.

The history of his nation lay on the face of the land at his feet, and it was in the North that the Zealots throve. Was it by accident that Joseph the carpenter gave all his five sons names that stood for something in Hebrew history? Jesus himself says very little, if anything, of the past of his people, and he does not, like some of the Psalmists, turn to the story of Israel for the proof of his thoughts upon God. But it may be more than a coincidence that his countrymen were impressed with his knowledge of the national literature ; and traces of other than canonical books have been found in his teaching. It implies a home of piety, where God was in all their thoughts.

The early disappearance of the elder Joseph has been explained by his death, which seems probable. The widow was

---

[1] George Adam Smith, *Historical Geography of the Holy Land,* ad loc.

left with five sons and some daughters.[1] The eldest son was, according to the story, more than twelve years old, and he had probably to share the household burden. The days were over when he played with the children in the market at weddings and at funerals, and while he never forgot the games and kept something of the child's mind throughout, he had to learn what it was to be weary and heavy-laden. His parables include pictures of home-life—one of a little house, where the master in bed can argue with an importunate friend outside the door, who has come on a very homely errand.[2] In a group of stories, parables of the mother, we see the woman sweeping the house till she finds a lost drachma, the recovery of which is joyful enough to be told to neighbours. We see her hiding leaven in three measures of meal, while the eldest son sat by and watched it work. He never forgot the sight of the heaving, panting mass, the bubbles swelling and bursting, and all the commotion the proof of something alive and at work below; and he made it into a parable of the Kingdom of God—associated in the minds of the weary with broken bubbles, and in the mind of Jesus with the profoundest and most living of realities. It was perhaps Mary, too, who explained to him why an old garment will not tolerate a new patch. Whatever is the historical value of the fourth Gospel, it lays stress on the close relation between Jesus and his mother.

One of the Aramaic words, which the church cherished from the first as the *ipsissima verba* of Jesus, was *Abba*. It was what Mary had taught him as a baby to call Joseph. The fact that in manhood he gave to God the name that in his childhood he had given to Joseph, surely throws some light upon the homelife. To this word we shall return.

Jesus had always a peculiar tenderness for children. "Suffer little children to come unto me," is one of his most familiar sayings, though in quoting it we are apt to forget that "come" is in Greek a verb carrying volition with it, and that Mark uses another noticeable word, and tells us that Jesus put his arms round the child.[3] Little children, we may be sure, came to him of their own accord and were at ease with him;

---

[1] Matthew xiii, 56 says πᾶσαι, and Mark uses a plural.
[2] Luke xi, 5.   [3] Mark ix, 36, ἐναγκαλισάμενος.

and it has been suggested that the saying goes back to the Nazareth days, and that the little children came about their brother in the workshop there. Mr Burkitt has recently remarked [1] that we may read far and wide in Christian Literature before we find any such feeling for children as we know so well in the words of Jesus ; and in Classical Literature we may look as far. To Jesus the child is not unimportant—to injure a child was an unspeakable thing. Indeed, if the Kingdom of God meant anything, it was that we must be children again—God's little children, to whom their Father is the background of everything. The Christian phrase about being born again may be Jesus' own, but if so, it has lost for us something of what he intended by it, which survives in more authentic sayings. We have to recover, he said, what we lost when we outgrew the child ; we must have the simplicity and frankness of children —their instinctive way of believing all things and hoping all things. All things are new to the child ; it is only for grown-up people that God has to " *make* all things new." Paul has not much to say about children, but he has this thought— " if any man be in Christ, it is a new creation, all things are made new." Probably the child's habit of taking nothing for granted—except the love that is all about it—is what Jesus missed most in grown men. Every idealist and every poet is a child from beginning to end—and something of this sort is the mark of the school of Jesus.

The outdoor life of Jesus lies recorded in his parables. Weinel has said that Paul was a man of a city—Paul said so himself. But Jesus is at home in the open air. The sights and sounds of the farm are in his words—the lost sheep, the fallen ox, the worried flock, the hen clucking to her chickens. This last gave a picture in which his thought instinctively clothed itself in one of his hours of deepest emotion. It is perhaps a mark of his race and land that to " feed swine " is with him a symbol of a lost life, and that the dog is an unclean animal—as it very generally is elsewhere. He speaks of ploughing, clearly knowing how it should be done ; and like other teachers, he uses the analogies of sowing and harvest. The grain growing secretly, and the harvest, over-ripe and spilling its wheat, were to him pictures of human life.

[1] *Gospel History*, p. 285.

Wild nature, too, he knew and loved. The wild lily, which the women used to burn in their ovens never thinking of its beauty, was to him something finer than King Solomon, and he probably had seen Herodian princes on the Galilean roads. (It is a curious thing that he has more than one allusion to royal draperies.) He bade men study the flowers (καταμαν-θάνειν). It is perhaps worth remark that flower-poetry came into Greek literature from regions familiar to us in the life of Jesus; Meleager was a Gadarene. The Psalmist long ago had said of the birds that they had their meat from God; but Jesus brought them into the human family—"Your Heavenly Father feedeth them." Even his knowledge of weather signs is recorded. Not all flowers keep in literature the scent and colour of life; they are a little apt to become "natural objects." But if they are to retain their charm in print, something is wanted that is not very common—the open heart and the open eye, to which birds and flowers are willing to tell their secret. There are other things which point to the fact that Jesus had this endowment,—and not least his being able to find in the flower a link so strong and so beautiful between God and man. Here as elsewhere he was in touch with his environment, for he loved Nature as Nature, and was true to it. His parables are not like Æsop's Fables. His lost sheep has no arguments; his lily is not a Solomon, though it is better dressed; and his sparrows are neither moralists nor theologians—but sparrows, which might be sold at two for a farthing, and in the meantime are chirping and nesting. And all this life of Nature spoke to him of the character of God, of God's delight in beauty and God's love. God is for him the ever-present thought in it all—real too, to others, whenever he speaks of him.

An amiable feeling for Nature is often to be found in senti-mental characters. But sentimentalism is essentially self-deception; and the Gospels make it clear that of all human sins and weaknesses none seems to have stirred the anger of Jesus as did self-deception. When the Pharisees in the synagogue watched to see whether Jesus would heal on the Sabbath, he "looked round about upon them all with anger," says Mark. This gaze of Jesus is often mentioned in the Gospels—almost unconsciously—but Luke and Matthew drop the last two words in quoting this passage, and do so at the cost of a most characteristic touch.　Matthew elsewhere, in accordance with his habit of grouping his matter by subject, gathers together a collection of the utterances of Jesus upon the Pharisees, with the recurring refrain "Scribes and Pharisees, actors."　The Mediterranean world was full of Greek actors ; we hear of them even among the Parthians in 53 B.C., and in Mesopotamia for centuries ; and as there had long been Greek cities in Palestine, and a strong movement for generations toward Greek ways of life, the actor cannot have been an unfamiliar figure.　To call the Pharisees "actors" was a new and strong thing to say, but Jesus said such things.　Of the grosser classes of sinners he was tolerant to a point that amazed his contemporaries and gave great occasion of criticism to such enemies as Celsus and Julian.　He had apparently no anger for the woman taken in adultery ; and he was the "friend of publicans and sinners"—even eating with them.

The explanation lies partly in Jesus' instinct for reality and truth.　Sensualist and money-lover were at least occupied with a sort of reality ; pleasure and money in their way are real, and the pursuit of them brings a man, sooner or later, into contact with realities genuine enough.　Whatever illusions publican and harlot might have, the world saw to it that they did not keep them long.　The danger for such people was that they might be disillusioned overmuch.　But the Pharisee lied with himself.　If at times he traded on his righteousness to over-reach others, his chief victim was himself, as Jesus saw, and as Paul found.　Paul, brought up in their school to practise righteousness, gave the whole thing up as a pretence and a lie —he would no longer have anything to do with "his own righteousness."　But he was an exception ; Pharisees in general believed in their own righteousness ; and, by tampering with their sense of the proportions of things, they lost all feeling for reality, and with it all consciousness of the value and dignity of man and the very possibility of any conception of God.

Jesus had been bred in another atmosphere, in a school of realities.　When he said "Blessed are ye poor, for yours is the Kingdom of heaven," his words were the record of experience— the paradox was the story of his life.　He had known poverty and hand-labour ; he had been "exposed to feel what wretches feel."　Whatever criticism may make of the story of his feeding multitudes, it remains that he was markedly sensitive to the idea of hunger—over and over he urged the feeding of the poor, the maimed and the blind ; he suggested the payment of a day's wage for an hour's work, where a day's food was needed and only an hour's work could be had ; he even reminded a too happy father that his little girl would be the better of food. No thinker of his day, or for long before and after, was so deeply conscious of the appeal of sheer misery, and this is one of the things on which his followers have never lost the mind of Jesus. Poverty was perhaps even for himself a key to the door into the Kingdom of God. At any rate, he always emphasizes the advantage of disadvantages, for they at least make a man in earnest with himself.

There is a revelation of the seriousness of his whole mind and nature in his reply to the follower who would go away and return. "No man, having put his hand to the plough and looking back, is *fit* for the Kingdom of God." This every one knows who has tried to drive a furrow, and all men of action know only too well that the man, whom Jesus so describes, is fit for no kind of Kingdom. It is only the sentimentalism of the church that supposes the flabby-minded to be at home in the Kingdom of God. Jesus did not. The same kind of energy is in the parables. The unjust steward was a knave, but he was in earnest ; and so was the questionably honest man who found treasure in a field. The merchant let everything go for the one pearl of great price. Mary chose "the one thing needful." We may be sure that in one shop in Nazareth benches were made to stand on four feet and doors to open and shut. The parables from nature, as we have seen, are true to the facts of nature. They too stand on four feet. The church laid hold of a characteristic word, when it adopted for all time Jesus' *Amen*—"in truth." Jesus was always explicit with his followers—they should know from the first that their goal was the cross, and that meantime they would have no place where to lay their heads. They were to begin with hard realities, and to consort with him on the basis of the real.

The world in the age of Jesus was living a good deal upon its past, looking to old books and old cults, as we see in Plutarch and many others. The Jews no less lived upon their great books. Even Philo was fettered to the Old Testament, except when he could dissolve his fetters by allegory, and even then he believed himself loyal to the higher meaning of the text. But nothing of the kind is to be seen in Jesus. His knowledge of Psalmist and Prophet excited wonder; but in all his quotations of the Old Testament that have reached us, there is no trace of servitude to the letter and no hint of allegory. He does not quote Scripture as his followers did. Here too he spoke as having authority. If sometimes he quoted words for their own sake, it was always as an *argumentum ad hominem*. But his own way was to grasp the writer's mind—a very difficult thing in his day, and little done—and to go straight to the root of the matter, regardless of authority and tradition. Like draws to like, and an intensely real man at once grasped his kinship with other intensely real men ; and he found in the prophets, not reeds shaken with the wind, courtiers of king or of people, but men in touch with reality, with their eyes open for God, friends and fore-runners, whose experience illumined his own. This type of manhood needed no explanation for him. The other sort perplexed him—"Why can you not judge for yourselves?" how was it that men could see and yet not see? From his inner sympathy with the prophetic mind, came his freedom in dealing with the prophets. He read and understood, and decided for himself. No sincere man would ever wish his word to be final for another. Jesus was conscious of his own right to think and to see and to judge, and for him, as for the modern temper, the final thing was not opinion, nor scripture, nor authority, but reality and experience. There lay the road to God. Hence it is that Jesus is so tranquil,—he does "not strive nor cry"—for the man who has experienced in himself the power of the real has no doubts about it being able to maintain itself in a world, where at heart men want nothing else.

When so clear an eye for reality is turned upon the great questions of man's life and of man's relations with God, it is apt here too to reach the centre. From the first, men lingered over the thought that Jesus had gone to the bottom of human experience and found in this fact his power to help them. He was made like to his brethren ; he was touched with the feeling of our infirmities; he was "able to sympathize" (δυνάμενον συμπαθῆσαι) for he was "tempted in all respects like us." In the Gospel, as it is handed down to us, the temptation of Christ is summed up in three episodes set at the beginning of the story and told in a symbolic form, which may or may not have been given to them by Jesus himself.   Then " the devil left him "—Luke adding significantly " till a time."   The interpretation is not very clear.   Strong men do not discuss their own feelings very much, but it is possible now and then to divine some experience from an involuntary tone, or the unconscious sensitiveness with which certain things are mentioned ; or, more rarely, emotion may open the lips for a moment of self-revelation, in which a word lays bare a lifetime's struggle.   It will add to the significance of his general attitude toward God and man's life, if we can catch any glimpse of the inner mind of Jesus.

We have records of his being exhausted and seeking quiet. Biographers of that day concealed such things in their heroes, but the Gospels freely reveal what contemporary critics counted weaknesses in Jesus.   He weeps, he hungers, he is worn out. He has to be alone—on the mountain by night, in a desert-place before dawn.   Such exhaustion is never merely physical or merely spiritual ; the two things are one.   Men crowded upon Jesus, till he had not leisure to eat ; he came into touch with a ceaseless stream of human personalities; and those who have been through any such experience will understand what it cost him.   To communicate an idea or to share a feeling is exhausting work, and we read further of deeds of healing, which, Jesus himself said, took " virtue " ($\delta\acute{v}\nu\alpha\mu\iota\nu$) out of him, and he had to withdraw.   When the Syro-Phœnician woman called for his aid, it was a question with him whether he should spend on a foreigner the " virtue " that could with difficulty meet the claims of Israel, for he was not conscious of the " omnipotence " which has been lightly attributed to him.   It was the woman's brilliant answer about the little dogs eating the children's crumbs that gained her request.   The turn of speech showed a vein of humour, and he consented " for this saying." [1]   If human experience goes for anything in such a case, contact with a spirit so delicate and sympathetic gave him something of the

---

[1] I believe that the allusion to dogs has been thrown back into Jesus' words from the woman's reply, and that she was the first to mention them.   Note Mark's emphatic phrase διὰ τοῦτον τὸν λόγον ; vii, 29.

strength he spent. The incident throws light upon the " fluxes and refluxes of feeling " within him, and the effect upon him of a spirit with something of his own tenderness and humour. For the moment, though, his sense of having reached his limits should be noticed.

The church has never forgotten the agony in the garden, but that episode has lost some of its significance because it has not been recognized to be one link in a chain of experience, which we must try to reconstruct. It has been assumed that Jesus never expected to influence the Pharisees and scribes; but this is to misinterpret the common temper of idealists, and to miss the pain of Jesus' words when he found his hopes of the Pharisees to be vain. Gradually, from their pressure upon his spirit, he grew conscious of the outcome—they would not be content with logomachies; the end might be death. Few of us have any experience to tell us at what cost to the spirit such a discovery is made. The common people he read easily enough and recognized their levity. And now, in exile, as Mr Burkitt has lately suggested,[2] he began to concentrate himself upon the twelve. It was not till Peter, by a sudden flash of insight, grasped his Messiahship—a character, which Jesus had realized already, though we do not know by what process, and had for reasons of his own concealed,—it was not till then that Jesus disclosed his belief that he would be killed at last. From that moment we may date the falling away of Judas, and what this man's constant presence must have meant to Jesus, ordinary experience may suggest. Shrewd, clever and disappointed, he must have been a chill upon his Master at all hours. His influence upon the rest of the group must have been consciously and increasingly antipathetic. Night by night Jesus could read in the faces which of them had been with Judas during the day. The sour triumph of Judas when the Son of man was told to go on to another village after a day's journey, and the uncomfortable air of one or more of the others, all entered into Jesus' experience; and night by night he had to undo Judas' work. He "learnt by what he suffered" from the man's tone and look that there would be desertion, perhaps betrayal. The daily suffering involved in trying to recapture the man, in going to seek the lost sheep in the wilderness of bitterness, may be

---

[1] *Gospel History*, p. 93 f. (with map).

imagined. Side by side, King, Pharisee and disciple are against him, and the tension, heightened by the uncertainty as to the how, when and where of the issue must have been great. Luke's graphic word says his face was "set" for Jerusalem—it would be, he knew, a focus for the growing forces of hatred.

Day by day the strain increased. Finally Jesus spoke. The where and how of the betrayal he could not determine; the when he could. At the supper, he looked at Judas and then he spoke.[1] "What thou doest, do quickly." The man's face as he hurried out said "Yes" to the unspoken question—and for the moment it brought relief. This is the background of the garden-scene. What the agony meant spiritually, we can hardly divine. The physical cost is attested by the memory of his face which haunted the disciples. The profuse sweat that goes with acute mental strain is a familiar phenomenon, and its traces were upon him—visible in the torchlight. Last of all, upon the cross, Nature reclaimed her due from him. Jesus had drawn, as men say, upon the body, and in such cases Nature repays herself from the spirit. The worn-out frame dragged the spirit with it, and he died with the cry—"My God, my God, why hast thou forsaken me?"

Turning back, we find in Luke[2] that Jesus said to his disciples "Ye are they that have continued with me in my temptations." Dr John Brown[3] used to speak of Jesus having "a disposition for private friendships." A mind with the genius for friendliness is not only active but passive. We constantly find in history instances of men with such a gift failing in great crises because of it—they yield to the friendly word; it means so much to them. Thus when Peter, a friend of old standing and of far greater value since his confession at Philippi, spoke and reinforced the impressions made on Jesus' mind by his prevision of failure and death, the temptation was of a terrible kind. The sudden rejoinder, in which Jesus identifies the man he loved with Satan, shows what had happened. But, if friend-ship carried with it temptation, yet when physical exhaustion brought spiritual exhaustion in its train, the love and tenderness

---

[1] The steady gaze and the pause are mentioned by the Gospels, in more than one place, as preceding utterance. There are of course great variations in the accounts of the last supper.

[2] xxii, 28.   [3] The author of *Rab and his Friends.*

of his friends upheld him. But, more still, their belief in him and in his ideas, their need of him, drove the tempter away. He could not disappoint them. The faces that softened to him,—all that came to his mind as he thought of his friends name by name—gave him hope and comfort, though the body might do its worst. It was perhaps in part this experience of the friendship of simple and commonplace men that differentiated the teaching of Jesus from the best the world had yet had. No other teacher dreamed that common men could possess a tenth part of the moral grandeur and spiritual power, which Jesus elicited from them—chiefly by believing in them. Here, to any one who will study the period, the sheer originality of Jesus is bewildering. This belief in men Jesus gave to his followers and they have never lost it.

It was in the new life and happiness in God that he was bringing to the common people that Jesus saw his firmest credentials. He laid stress indeed upon the expulsion of devils and the cure of disease—matters explained to-day by "suggestion." But the culmination was "the good news for the poor." "Gospel" and "Evangelical" have in time become technical terms, and have no longer the pulse of sheer happiness which Jesus felt in them, and which the early church likewise experienced. "Be of good cheer!" is the familiar English rendering of one of the words of Jesus, often on his lips—"Courage!" he said. One text of Luke represents him as saying it even on the cross, when he spoke to the penitent thief.

Summing up what we have so far reached, we may remark the broad contrast between the attitude of Jesus to human life and the views of the world around him. A simple home with an atmosphere of love and truth and intelligence, where life was not lost sight of in its refinements, where ordinary needs and common duties were the daily facts, where God was a constant and friendly presence—this was his early environment. Later on it was the carpenter's bench, the fisherman's boat, wind on the mountain and storm on the lake, leaven in the meal and wheat in the field. Everywhere his life is rooted in the normal and the natural, and everywhere he finds God filling the meanest detail of man's life with glory and revelation.

Philosophers were anxious to keep God clear of contact with matter; Marcus Aurelius found "decay in the substance

of all things—nothing but water, dust, bones, stench."[1] Jesus
saw life in all things—God clothing the grass and watching
over little birds. To-day the old antithesis of God and matter
is gone, and it comes as a relief to find that Jesus anticipated
its disappearance. The religious in his day looked for God in
trance and ritual, in the abnormal and unusual, but for him, as
for every man who has ever helped mankind, the ordinary and
the commonplace were enough. The Kingdom of God is
among you, or even within you—in the common people, of
whom all the other teachers despaired.

We come now to the central question of man's relation
with God, never before so vital a matter to serious people in the
Mediterranean world. Jew and Greek and Egyptian were all
full of it, and men's talk ran much upon it. Men were anxious
to be right with God, and sought earnestly in the ways of their
fathers for the means of communion with God and the attainment of some kind of safety in their position with regard to him
Jew and Greek alike talked of heaven and hell and of the ways
to them. They talked of righteousness and holiness—" holy " is
one of the great words of the period—and they sought these
things in ritual and abstinence. Modern Jews resent the
suggestion that the thousand and one regulatious as to ceremonial purity, and the casuistries, as many or more, spun out of
the law and the traditions, ranked with the great commandments
of neighbourly love and the worship of the One God. No
doubt they are right, but it is noticeable that in practice the
common type of mind is more impressed with minutiæ than
with principles. The Southern European to-day will do murder
on little provocation, but to eat meat in Lent is sin. But,
without attributing such conspicuous sins as theft and adultery
and murder to the Pharisees, it is clear that in establishing
their own righteousness they laid excessive stress on the details
of the law, on Sabbath-keeping (a constant topic with the
Christian apologists), on tithes, and temple ritual, on the
washing of pots and plates—still rigorously maintained by the
modern Jew—and all this was supposed to constitute holiness.
Jesus with the clear incisive word of genius dismissed it all as
" acting." The Pharisee was essentially an actor—playing to
himself the most contemptible little comedies of holiness.

[1] ix, 36.

Listen, cries Jesus, and he tells the tale of the man fallen among thieves and left for dead, and how priest and Levite passed by on the other side, fearing the pollution of a corpse, and how they left mercy, God's own work—"I will have mercy and not sacrifice" was one of his quotations from Hosea,—to be done by one unclean and damned—the Samaritan. Whited sepulchres! he cries, pretty to look at, but full of what? of death, corruption and foulness. "How *can* you escape from the judgment of hell?" he asked them, and no one records what they answered or could answer.

It is clear, however, that, outside Palestine, the Jews in the great world were moving to a more purely moral conception of religion—their environment made mere Pharisaism impossible, and Greek criticism compelled them to think more or less in the terms of the fundamental. The debt of the Jew to the Gentile is not very generously acknowledged. None the less, the distinctive badge of all his tribe was and remained what the Greeks called fussiness (τὸ ψοφοδεές).[1] The Sabbath, circumcision, the blood and butter taboos remained—as they still remain in the most liberal of "Liberal Judaisms"—tribe marks with no religious value, but maintained by patriotism. And side by side with this lived and lives that hatred of the Gentile, which is attributed to Christian persecution, but which Juvenal saw and noted before the Christian had ceased to be persecuted by the Jew. The extravagant nonsense found in Jewish speculation as to how many Gentile souls were equivalent in God's sight to that of one Jew is symptomatic. To this day it is confessedly the weakness of Judaism that it offers no impulse and knows no enthusiasm for self-sacrificing love where the interests of the tribe are not concerned.[2]

The great work of Jesus in this matter was the final and decisive cleavage with antiquity. Greek rationalism had long since laughed at the puerilities of the Greek cults; but rationalism and laughter are unequally matched against Religion, and it triumphed over them, and, as we see in Plutarch

---

[1] Cf. *ad Diognetum*, cited on p. 177.

[2] I quote this from a friend to whom a Jew said as much; of course every general statement requires modification. Still the predominantly tribal character of Judaism implies contempt for the spiritual life of the Gentile Christian and pagan. If the knowledge of God was or is of value to the Jew, he has made little effort to share it.

and the Neo-Platonists, it imposed its puerilities—yes, and its obscenities — upon Philosophy and made her in sober truth "procuress to the lords of hell." It was a new thing when Religion, in the name of truth and for the love of God, abolished the connexion with a trivial past. Jesus cut away at once every vestige of the primitive and every savage survival—all natural growths perhaps, and helpful too to primitive man and to the savage, but confusing to men on a higher plane,—either mere play-acting or the " damnation of hell." Pagan cults he summed up as much speaking. Once for all he set Religion free from all taboos and rituals. Paul, once, on the spur of the moment, called Jesus the "Yes" of all the promises of God—a most suggestive name for the vindicator and exponent of God's realities. It is such a man as this who liberates mankind, cutting us clear of make-believes and negations and taboos, and living in the open-air, whether it is cloud or sun. That Jesus shocked his contemporaries with the abrupt nakedness of his religious ideas is not surprising. The church made decent haste to cover a good many of them up, but not very successfully. A mind like that of Jesus propagates itself, and reappears with startling vitality, as history in many a strange page can reveal.

We must now consider what was the thought of Jesus upon God and how he conceived of the relation between God and man. He approached the matter originally from the standpoint of Judaism, and no attempt to prove the influence of Greek philosophy is likely to succeed. The result of Greek speculation upon God—where it did not end in pure pantheism—was that of God nothing whatever could be predicated—not even being, but that he was to be expressed by the negation of every idea that could be formed of him. To this men had been led by their preconception of absolute being, and so strong was the influence of contemporary philosophy that Christian thinkers adopted the same conclusion, managing what clumsy combinations they could of it and of the doctrine of incarnation. Clement of Alexandria is a marked example of this method.

To the philosophic mind God remains a difficult problem, but to the religious temper things are very different. To it God is the one great reality never very far away, and is conceived not as an abstraction, nor as a force, but as a personality.

It has been and is the strength and redemption of Judaism, that God is the God of Israel—"Oh God, thou art my God!" How intuition is to be reconciled with philosophy has been the problem of Christian thinkers in every age, but it may be remarked that the varying term is philosophy. To the intuition of Jesus Christians have held fast—though Greeks and others have called it "folly"; and in the meantime a good many philosophies have had their day.

The central thought of Jesus is the Fatherhood of God. For this, as for much else, parallels have been found in the words of Hebrew thinkers, ancient and contemporary, and we may readily concede that it was not original with Jesus to call God Father. The name was given to God by the prophets, but it was also given to him by the Stoics—and by Homer; so that to speak of God's Fatherhood might mean anything between the two extremes of everything and nothing. Christian theology, for instance, starting with the idea of the Fatherhood of God, has not hesitated to speak in the same breath of his "vindicating his majesty"—a phrase which there is no record or suggestion that Jesus ever used. There may be fathers who vindicate their majesty, as there are many other kinds, but until we realize the connotation of the word for men who speak of God as Father, it is idle to speak of it being a thought common to them. The name may be in the Old Testament and in Homer, but the meaning which Jesus gave to it is his own.

Jesus never uses the name Father without an air of gladness. Men are anxious as to what they shall eat, and what they shall drink, and wherewithal they shall be clothed—"your heavenly Father knoweth that ye have need of all these things." Children ask father and mother for bread—will they receive a stone? The women had hid the leaven in the three measures of meal long before the children began to feel hungry. And as to clothes—God has clothed the flower far better than Solomon ever clothed himself, "and shall he not much more clothe you, O ye of little faith?" The picture is one of the strong and tender parent, smiling at the child's anxiety with no notion of his own majesty or of anything but love. So incredibly simple is the relation between God and man—simple, unconstrained, heedless and tender as the talk round a table in Nazareth. Jesus is greater than the men who have elaborated

his ideas, and majesty is the foible of little minds. The great
man, if he thinks of his dignity, lets it take care of itself; he is
more interested in love and truth, and he forgets to think of
what is due to himself. Aristotle said that his "magnificent
man" would never run ; but, says Jesus, when the prodigal son
was yet a great way off, "his father saw him, and ran, and fell
on his neck, and kissed him." This contrast measures the
distance between the thought of Jesus and some Christian
theologies. It is worth noting that in the two parables, in
which a father directly addresses his son, it is with the tender
word τέκνον, which is more like a pet name. It adds to the
meaning of the parable of the prodigal, when the father calls
the elder brother by the little name that has come down from
childhood. It was a word which Jesus himself used in speaking
to his friends.[1] The heavenly Father does not cease to be a
father because his children are ungracious and bad. He sends
rain and sun—and all they mean—to evil and to good. The
whole New Testament is tuned to the thought of Jesus—"the
philanthropy of God our saviour."[2]

Plato had long before defined the object of human life as
"becoming like to God." Jesus finds the means to this likeness
to God in the simplest of every day's opportunities. "Love
your enemies and do good, and ye shall be sons of the
Highest, for he is good and pitiful." "Blessed are the peacemakers," he said, "for they shall be called children of God."
This is sometimes limited to the reconciliation of quarrels, but
the worst of quarrels is the rift in a man's own soul, the
"division of his spiritual substance against itself" which is the
essence of all tragedy. There are some whose least word, or
whose momentary presence, can somehow make peace wherever
they go, and leave men stronger for the rest they have found
in another's soul. This, according to Jesus, is the family likeness by which God's children are recognized in all sorts of
company. To have the faculty of communicating peace of
mind—and it is more often than not done unconsciously, as
most great things are—is no light or accidental gift.

Jesus lays a good deal more stress upon unconscious instinct
than most moralists do. Once only he is reported to have
spoken of the Last Judgment, which was a favourite theme

---

[1] *e.g.* Mark x, 24.   [2] Titus iii, 4.

with the eschatologists of his period, Jewish, pagan, and Christian. He borrowed the whole framework of the scene, but he changed, and doubly changed, the significance of it. For he discarded the national or political criterion which the Jew preferred, and he did not have recourse to the rather individualistic moral test which Greek thinkers proposed, in imitation of Plato; still less did it occur to him to suggest a *Credo*. With him the ultimate standard was one of sheer kindness and good-heartedness—"inasmuch as ye did it to one of the least of these my brethren." But it is still more interesting to note how this standard is applied. Every one at the Last Judgment accepts it, just as every one accepts the propositions of moralists in general. But the real cleavage between the classes of men does not depend on morality, as the chilly suggestion of the mere word reminds us. Men judge other men not by their morality, professed or practised, so much as by their unconscious selves—by instinct, impulse and so forth, the things that really give a clue to the innermost man. The most noticeable point then in Jesus' picture of the Last Judgment is that, when "sheep" and "goats" are separated, neither party at once understands the reasons of the decision. These are conscious of duties done; the others have no very clear idea about it. Elsewhere Jesus suggests that, when men have done all required of them, they may still have the feeling that they are unprofitable servants; and it is precisely the peacemakers and the pure in heart who do not realize how near they come to God. The priest and the Levite in the parable were conscious of their purity, but Jesus gives no hint that they saw God. The Samaritan lived in another atmosphere, but it was natural to him and he breathed it unconsciously. The cultivation of likeness to God by Greek philosophers and their pupils was very different. Plutarch has left a tract, kindly and sensible, on "How a man may recognize his own progress in virtue," but there is no native Christian product of the kind.

From what Jesus directly says of God, and from what he says of God's children, we may conclude that he classes God with the strong and sunny natures; with the people of bright eyes who see through things and into things, who have the feeling for reality, and love every aspect of the real. God has that sense which is peculiar to the creative mind—the keen joy in beauty, that loves star and bird and child. God has the father's instinct, a full understanding of human nature, and a heart open for the prodigal son, the publican and the woman with seven devils. "In his will is our peace," wrote the great Christian poet of the middle ages. "Doing the will we find rest," said a humble and forgotten Christian of the second century.[1] They both learnt the thought from Jesus, who set it in the prayer beginning with *Abba* which he taught his disciples, and who prayed it himself in the garden with the same *Abba* in his heart. "In the Lord's prayer," said Tertullian, "there is an epitome of the whole Gospel."[2]

At this point two questions rise, which are of some historical importance, and bear upon Jesus' view of God. It is clear, first of all, that the expression "the Kingdom of God" was much upon the lips of Jesus, at least in the earlier part of his ministry. It was not of his own coining, and scholars have differed as to what he really meant. Such controversy always rises about the terms in which a great mind expresses itself. The great thinker, even the statesman, has to use the best language he can find to convey his ideas, and if the ideas are new, the difficulty of expression is sometimes very great. The words imply one thing to the listener, and another to the speaker who is really trying (as Diogenes put it) to "re-mint the currency," and how far he succeeds depends mostly upon his personality. To-day "the Kingdom," or more accurately "the Kingship of God," is in some quarters interpreted rather vigorously in the sense which the ordinary Jew gave to the phrase in the age of Jesus; but it is more than usually unsound criticism to take the words of such a man as meaning merely what they would in the common talk of unreflective persons, who use words as counters and nothing else. There was a vulgar interpretation of the "Kingship of God," and there was a higher one, current among the better spirits; and it is only reasonable to interpret this phrase, or any other, in the light of the total mind of the man who uses it. It is clear then that, when Jesus used "the Kingship of God," he must have subordinated it to his general idea of God; and what

---

[1] *Second Clement* (so-called), 6, 7.
[2] Tert. *de Or.* 1 (end). Cf. also c. 4, on the prayer in the Garden; and *de fuga*, 8.

that was, we have seen. To-day the phrase is returning into religious speech to signify the permeation of society by the mind of Christ, which cannot be far from what it meant to the earliest disciples. It is significant that the author of the fourth gospel virtually dropped the phrase altogether, that Paul preferred other expressions as a rule, and that it was merged and lost in the idea of the church.

Closely bound up with the "Kingdom of God" is the name Messiah, with a similarly wide range of meanings. The question has also been raised as to how far Jesus identified himself with the Messiah. It might be more pertinent to ask with which Messiah. On the whole, the importance of the matter can be gauged by the fate of the word. It was translated into Greek, and very soon Christos, or Chrestos, was a proper name and hardly a title at all except in apologetics, where alone the conception retained some importance. The Divine Son and the Divine Logos—terms which Jesus did not use—superseded the old Hebrew title, at any rate in the Gentile world, and this could hardly have occurred if the idea had been of fundamental moment in Jesus' mind and speech. If he used the name, as seems probable, it too must have been subordinated to his master-thought of God's fatherhood. It would then imply at most a close relation to the purposes of God, and a mission to men, the stewardship of thoughts that would put mankind on a new footing with God. The idea of his being a mediator in the Pauline sense is foreign to the gospels, and the later conception of a purchase of mankind from the devil, or from the justice of God, by the blood of a victim is still more alien to Jesus' mind.

These are some of the features of the founder of the new religion as revealed in the Gospels—features that permanently compel attention, but after all it was not the consideration of these that conquered the world. Of far more account in winning the world was the death of this man upon the cross. It was the cross that gave certainty to all that Jesus had taught about God. The church sturdily and indignantly repudiated any suggestion, however philosophic, that in any way seemed likely to lessen the significance of the cross. That he should taste the ultimate bitterness of death undisguised, that he should refuse the palliative wine and myrrh (an action symbolic of his

whole attitude to everything and to death itself), that with
open eyes he should set his face for Jerusalem, and with all the
sensitiveness of a character, so susceptive of impression and so
rich in imagination, he should expose himself to our experience
—to the foretaste of death, to the horror of the unknown, and
to the supreme fear—the dread of the extinction of personality ;
and that he should actually undergo all he foresaw, as the last
cry upon the cross testified—all this let the world into the real
meaning of his central thought upon God.   It was the pledge
of his truth, and thus made possible our reconciliation with God.

If we may take an illustration from English literature,
Shakespeare's *Julius Cæsar* may suggest something here.   It
has been noticed how small a part Cæsar plays in the drama—
how little he speaks ; what weakness he shows—epilepsy, deaf-
ness, arrogance, vacillation ; and how soon he disappears.
Would not the play have been better named *Brutus*?   Yet
Shakespeare knew what he was doing ; for the whole play *is*
Julius Cæsar, from the outbreak of Cassius at the beginning—

> Why ! man he doth bestride the narrow world
> Like a colossus,

to the bitter cry of Brutus at the end—

> O Julius Cæsar, thou art mighty yet !

Cæsar determines everything in the story.   Every character in
it is a mirror in which we see some figure of him, and the life
of every man there is made or unmade by his mind toward
Cæsar.   Cæsar is the one great determining factor in the story ;
living and dead, he is the centre and explanation of it all.

What was written in the Gospels of the life and death of
Jesus, might by now be ancient history, if the Gospels had told
the whole story.   But they did not tell the whole story ; and
they neither were, nor are, the source of the Christian movement, great as their influence is and has been.   The Jesus who
has impressed himself upon mankind is not a character, however strong and beautiful, that is to be read about in a book.
Before the Gospels were written, men spoke of the "Spirit of
Jesus" as an active force amongst them.   We may criticize
their phrase and their psychology as we like, but they were
speaking of something they knew, something they had seen

and felt, and it is that "something" which changed the course of history. Jesus lives for us in the pages of the Gospels, but we are not his followers on that account, nor were the Christians of the first century. They, like ourselves, followed him under the irresistible attraction of his character repeating itself in the lives of men and women whom they knew. The Son of God, they said, revealed himself in men, and it was true. Of his immediate followers we know almost nothing, but it was they who passed him on to the next generation, consciously in their preaching, which was not always very good ; and unconsciously in their lives, which he had transformed, and which had gained from him something of the power of his own life. The church was a nexus of quickened and redeemed personalities,—men and women in whom Christ lived. So Paul wrote of it. A century later another nameless Christian spoke of Christ being "new born every day over again in the hearts of believers," and it would be hard to correct the statement. If we are to give a true account of such men as Alexander and Cæsar, we consider them in the light of the centuries through which their ideas lived and worked. In the same way, the life, the mind and the personality of Jesus will not be understood till we have realized by some intimate experience something of the worth and beauty of the countless souls that in every century have found and still find in him the Alpha and Omega of their being. For the Gospels are not four but "ten thousand times ten thousand, and thousands of thousands," and the last word of every one of them is "Lo, I am with you alway, even unto the end of the world."

CHAPTER V

THE FOLLOWERS OF JESUS

TWO things stand out, when we study the character of the early church—its great complexity and variety, and its unity in the personality of Jesus of Nazareth. In spite of the general levelling which Greek culture and Roman government had made all over the Mediterranean world, the age-long influences of race and climate and cult were still at work. Everywhere there was a varnish of Greek literature; everywhere a tendency to uniformity in government, very carefully managed with great tenderness for local susceptibilities, but none the less a fixed object of the Emperors; everywhere cult was blended with cult with the lavish hospitality of polytheism; and yet, apart from denationalized men of letters, artists and dilettanti, the old types remained and reproduced themselves. And when men looked at the Christian community, it was as various as the Empire—" Thou wast slain," runs the hymn in the Apocalypse, " and thou hast redeemed us to God by thy blood out of every kindred and tongue and people and nation." There soon appeared that desire for uniformity which animated the secular government, and which appears to be an ineradicable instinct of the human mind. Yet for the first two centuries—the period under our discussion—the movement toward uniformity had not grown strong enough to overcome the race-marks and the place-marks. There are great areas over which in Christian life and thought the same general characteristics are to be seen, which were manifested in other ways before the Christian era. There is the great West of Italy, Gaul and Africa, Latin in outlook, but with strong local variations. There is the region of Asia Minor and Greece,—where the church is Hellenistic in every sense of the word, very Greek upon the surface and less Greek underneath, again with marked contrasts due to geography and race-distribution. Again there is the Christian South—Alexandria, with its Christian community, Greek and

Jewish, and a little known hinterland, where Christian thought spread, we do not know how.   There was Palestine with a group of Jewish Christians, very clearly differentiated.   And Eastward there rose a Syrian Christendom, which as late as the fourth century kept a character of its own.[1]

Into all these great divisions of the world came men eager to tell "good news"—generally quite commonplace and unimportant people with a "treasure in earthen vessels."   Their message they put in various ways, with the aphasia of ill-educated men, who have something to tell that is far too big for any words at their command.   It was made out at last that they meant a new relation to God in virtue of Jesus Christ. From a philosophic point of view they talked "foolishness," and they lapsed now and then, under the pressure of what was within them, into inarticulate and unintelligible talk, from which they might emerge into utterance quite beyond their ordinary range.   Such symptoms were familiar enough, but these people were not like the usual exponents of "theolepsy" and "enthu-siasm."   They were astonishingly upright, pure and honest; they were serious; and they had in themselves inexplicable reserves of moral force and a happiness far beyond anything that the world knew.   They were men transfigured, as they owned.   Some would confess to wasted and evil lives, but something had happened,[2] which they connected with Jesus or a holy spirit, but everything in the long run turned upon Jesus.

Clearer heads came about them, and then, as they put it, the holy spirit fell upon them also.   These men of education and ideas were "converted," and began at once to analyse their experience, using naturally the language with which they were familiar.   It was these men who gave the tone to the groups of believers in their various regions, and that tone varied with the colour of thought in which the more reflective converts had grown up.   A great deal, of course, was common to all regions of the world,—the new story and the new experience, an un-philosophized group of facts, which now, under the stimulus of man's unconquerable habit of speculation, began to be interpreted

[1] See Burkitt's *Early Eastern Christianity*.

[2] See Justin, *Apology*, i, 14, a vivid passage on the change of character that has been wrought in men by the Gospel. Cf. Tert. *ad Scap.* 2, *nec aliunde noscibiles quam de emendatione vitiorum pristinorum.*

and to be related in all sorts of ways to the general experience of men. No wonder there was diversity. It took centuries to achieve a uniform account of the Christian faith.

The unity of the early church lay in the reconciliation with God, in the holy spirit, and Jesus Christ,—a unity soon felt and treasured. "There is one body and one spirit, even as ye are called in one hope of your calling; one Lord, one faith, one baptism, one God and Father of all, who is above all and through all and in you all." [1] The whole body of Christians was conscious of its unity, of its distinctness and its separation. It was a "peculiar people" [2]—God's own; a "third race," as the heathen said. [3]

To go further into detail we may consider the recruits and their experience, their explanations of this experience, and the new life in the world.

The recruits came, as the Christians very soon saw, from every race of mankind, and they brought with them much that was of value in national preconceptions and characteristics. The presence of Jew, Greek, Roman, Syrian and Phrygian, made it impossible for the church to be anything but universal; and if at times her methods of reconciling somewhat incompatible contributions were unscientific, still in practice she achieved the task and gained accordingly. Where the Empire failed in imposing unity by decree, the church produced it instinctively.

It was on Jewish ground that Christianity began, and it was from its native soil and air that it drew, transmuting as it drew them, its passionate faith in One God, its high moral standard and its lofty hopes of a Messianic age to come. For no other race of the Mediterranean world was the moral law based on the "categoric imperative." Nowhere else was that law written in the inward parts, in the very hearts of the people, [4] and nowhere was it observed so loyally. The absurdity and scrupulosity which the Greek ridiculed in the Jew, were the outcome of his devotion to the law of the Lord; and, when once the law was reinterpreted and taken to a higher plane by Jesus, the

---

[1] Ephesians iv, 4.   [2] I Peter ii, 7.

[3] Tertullian, *ad Nationes*, i, 8, *Plane, tertium genus dicimur . . . verum recogitate ne quos tertium genus dicitis principem locum obtineant, siquidem non ulla gens non Christiana.*

[4] Cf. Jeremiah xxxi, 31—a favourite passage with Christian apologists.

old passion turned naturally to the new morality. It was the Jew who brought to the common Christian stock the conception of Sin, and the significance of this is immense in the history of the religion. It differentiated Christianity from all the religious and philosophical systems of the ancient world.

> 'Tis the faith that launched point-blank her dart
> At the head of a lie—taught Original Sin,
> The Corruption of Man's Heart.

Seneca and the Stoics played with the fancy of man's being equal, or in some points superior, to God—a folly impossible for a Jewish mind. It was the Jews who gave the world the "oracles of God" in the Old Testament, who invested Christianity for the moment with the dignity of an ancient history and endowed it for all time with a unique inheritance of religious experience. Nor is it only the Old Testament that the church owes to the Jew ; for the Gospels are also his gift —anchors in the actual that have saved Christianity from all kinds of intellectual, spiritual and ecclesiastical perils. And, further, at the difficult moment of transition, when Christian ideas passed from the Jewish to the Gentile world, there were Jews of the Hellenistic type ready to mediate the change They of all men stood most clearly at the universal point of view ; they knew the grandeur and the weakness of the law ; they understood at once the Jewish and the Greek mind. It is hard to exaggerate what Christianity owes to men of this school—to Paul and to "John," and to a host of others, Christian Jews of the Dispersion, students of Philo, and followers of Jesus. On Jewish soil the new faith died ; it was transplantation alone that made Christianity possible ; for it was the true outcome of the teaching of Jesus, that the new faith should be universal.

The chief contribution of the Greek was his demand for this very thing—that Christianity must be universal. He made no secret of his contempt for Judaism, and he was emphatic in insisting on a larger outlook than the Jewish. No man could seem more naturally unlikely to welcome the thoughts of Jesus than the "little Greek" (*Græculus*) of the Roman world ; yet he was won ; and then by making it impossible for Christianity to remain an amalgam of the ideas of Jesus and of Jewish law, the Greek really secured the triumph of Jesus. He eliminated the tribal and the temporary in the Gospel as it came from purely Jewish teachers, and, with all his irregularities of conduct and his flightiness of thought, he nevertheless set Jesus before the world as the central figure of all history and of all existence.[1] Even the faults of the Greek have indirectly served the church ; for the Gospels gained their place in men's minds and hearts, because they were the real refuge from the vagaries of Greek speculation, and offered the ultimate means of verifying every hypothesis. The historic Jesus is never of such consequence to us as when the great intellects tell us that the true and only heaven is Nephelococcygia. For Aristophanes was right—it was the real Paradise of the Greek mind. What relief the plain matter-of-fact Gospel must have brought men in a world, where nothing throve like these cities of the clouds, would be inconceivable, if we did not know its value still. While we recognize the real contribution of the Greek Christians, it is good to see what Christianity meant to men who were not Greeks.

There was one Christian of some note in the second century, whose attitude toward everything Greek is original and interesting. Tatian was "born in the land of the Assyrians."[2] He travelled widely in the Græco-Roman world,[3] and studied rhetoric like a Greek ; he gave attention to the great collections of Greek art in Rome—monuments of shame, he called them. He was admitted to the mysteries, but he became shocked at the cruelty and licentiousness tolerated and encouraged by paganism. While in this mind, seeking for the truth, "it befel that I lit upon some barbarian writings, older than the dogmata of the Greeks, divine in their contrast with Greek error ; and it befel too that I was convinced by them, because their style was simple, because there was an absence of artifice in the speakers, because the structure of the whole was intelligible, and also because of the fore-knowledge of future

---

[1] Professor Percy Gardner (*Growth of Christianity*, p. 49) illustrates this by comparison of earlier and later stages in Christian Art. On some early Christian sarcophagi Jesus is represented with markedly Jewish features ; soon however he is idealized into a type of the highest humanity.

[2] Tatian, 42.   [3] *Id.* 35.

events, the excellence of the precepts and the subordination of the whole universe to One Ruler (τὸ τῶν ὅλων μοναρχικόν). My soul was taught of God, and I understood that while Greek literature (τὰ μὲν) leads to condemnation, this ends our slavery in the world and rescues us from rulers manifold and ten thousand tyrants." [1] He now repudiated the Greeks and all their works, the grammarians who "set the letters of the alphabet to quarrel among themselves," [2] the philosophers with their long hair and long nails and vanity, [3] the actors, poets and legislators; and "saying good-bye to Roman pride and Attic pedantry (ψυχρολογία) I laid hold of our barbarian philosophy." [4] He made the first harmony of the Gospels—an early witness to the power of their sheer simplicity in a world of literary affectations.

Another famous Syrian of the century was Ignatius of Antioch, whose story is collected from seven letters he wrote, in haste and excitement, as he travelled to Rome to be thrown to the beasts in the arena—his guards in the meantime being as fierce as any leopards. The burden of them all is that Jesus Christ *truly* suffered on the cross. Men around him spoke of a phantom crucified by the deluded soldiers amid the deluded Jews.—No! cries Ignatius, over and over, he *truly* suffered, he *truly* rose, ate and drank, and was no dæmon without a body (δαιμόνιον ἀσώματον)—none of it is *seeming*, it is all truly, truly, truly. [5] He has been called hysterical, and his position might make any nervous man hysterical—death before him, his Lord's reality denied, and only time for one word—*Truly*. Before we pass him by, let us take a quieter saying of his to illustrate the deepest thought of himself and his age—" He that hath the word of Jesus truly can hear his silence also." [6]

The Roman came to the Church as he came to a new province. He gravely surveyed the situation, considered the existing arrangements, accepted them, drew up as it were a *lex provinciæ* to secure their proper administration, and thereafter interpreted it in accordance with the usual principles of Roman

---

[1] Tatian, 29. Cf. the account Theophilus gives of the influence upon him of the study of the prophets, i, 14.

[2] 26. [3] 25. [4] 35.

[5] Ignatius, *Magn.* 11 ; *Trall.* 9, 10 ; *Smyrn.* 1, 2, 3, 12.

[6] Ignatius, *Eph.* 15, ὁ λόγον Ἰησοῦ κεκτημένος ἀληθῶς δύναται καὶ τῆς ἡσυχίας αὐτοῦ ἀκούειν.

law, and, like the procurator in Achæa, left the Greeks to discuss any abstract propositions they pleased. Tertullian and Cyprian were lawyers, and gave Latin Christendom the language, in which in later days the relations of man with his Divine Sovereign were worked out by the great Latin Fathers.

The confession of Tatian, above cited, emphasizes as one of the great features of the barbarian literature—its "monarchic" teaching—"it sets man free from ten thousand tyrants"—and this may be our starting-point in considering the new experience. To be rid of the whole dæmon-world, to have left the dæmons behind and their "hatred of men,"[1] their astrology,[2] their immorality and cruelty, their sacrifices, and the terror of "possession" and theolepsy and enchantment,[3] was happiness in itself. "We are above fate," said Tatian, "and, instead of dæmons that deceive, we have learnt one master who deceiveth not."[4] "Christ," wrote an unknown Christian of a beautiful spirit—"Christ wished to save the perishing, and such mercy has he shown us that we the living do not serve dead gods, but through him we know the Father of truth."[5] "Orpheus sang to beguile men, but my Singer has come to end the tyranny of dæmons," said Clement.[6] The perils of "meats offered to idols" impressed some, who feared that by eating of them they would come under dæmoniac influence. With what relief they must have read Paul's free speech on the subject—"the earth is the Lord's and the fullness thereof"—"for us there is one God, the Father, and one Lord, Jesus Christ, through whom are all things, and we through him."[7] "Even the very name of Jesus is terrible to the dæmons"[8]—the "name that is above every name." In no other name was there salvation from dæmons, for philosophy had made terms with them.

No one can read the Christian Apologists without remarking the stress which they lay upon the *knowledge* of God, which the new faith made the free and glad possession of the humblest.

---

[1] Tatian, 16, 17. Cf. Plutarch (cited on p. 107) on malignant dæmons. See Tertullian, *Apol.* 22 ; Justin, *Apol.* ii. 5 ; Clem. Alex. *Protr.* 3, 41, on the works of dæmons.

[2] Tatian, 7, 8.

[3] See Tertullian, *de Idol.* 9, on the surprising case of a Christian who wished to pursue his calling of astrologer—a claim Tertullian naturally will not allow.

[4] Tatian, 9.   [5] The so-called second letter of Clement of Rome, c. 3.

[6] Clem. Alex. *Protr.* 3.   [7] 1 Cor. vi, etc.   [8] Justin, *Dial. c. Tryph.* 30.

"They say of us that we babble nonsense among females, half-grown people, girls and old people. No! all our women are chaste and at their distaffs our maidens sing of things divine," said Tatian, and rejoined with observations on famous Greek women, Lais, Sappho and others. Justin, always kindlier, speaks of Socrates who urged men to seek God, yet owned that "it would be a hard task to find the father and maker of this All, and when one had found him, it would not be safe to declare him to all,"[1] but, he goes on, " our Christ did this by his power. No man ever believed Socrates so much as to die for his teaching. But Christ, who was known to Socrates in part, (for he was and is the Word that is in everything . . .)—on Christ, I say, not only philosophers and scholars ($\phi\iota\lambda\delta\lambda\sigma\gamma\omicron\iota$) believed, but artisans, men quite without learning ($\iota\delta\iota\hat\omega\tau\alpha\iota$), and despised glory and fear and death." " There is not a Christian workman but finds out God and manifests him," said Tertullian.[2] This knowledge of God was not merely a desirable thing in theory, for it is clear that it was very earnestly sought. To Justin's quest for God, allusion has been made—" I hoped I should have the vision of God at once ($\kappa\alpha\tau\delta\psi\epsilon\sigma\theta\alpha\iota$)" he says. " Who among men had any knowledge of what God was, before he came?" [3] " This," wrote the fourth evangelist, " is eternal life—that they may know thee, the one true God and Jesus Christ whom thou hast sent."

But it is one thing to be a monotheist, and another to be a child of " Abba Father," and this is one of the notes of the early Christian. It is impossible to over-emphasize the significance of Christian happiness amid the strain and doubt of the early Empire. Zeno and Isis each had something to say, but who had such a message of forgiveness and reconciliation and of the love of God? " God is within you," said Seneca ; but he knew nothing of such an experience as the Christian summed up as the " grace of God," " grace sufficient " and " grace abound-

[1] Tatian, 33 ; Justin, *Apol.* ii, 10. It may be noted that Justin quotes the famous passage in the *Timæus* (28 C) not quite correctly. Such passages " familiar in his mouth as household words " are very rarely given with verbal accuracy. Tertullian, *Apol.* 46, and Clement, *Strom.* v, 78, 92, also quote this passage.

[2] *Apol.* 46. Compare Theophilus, i, 2 ; " If you say 'Show me your God,' I would say to you, 'Show me your man and I will show you my God,' or show me the eyes of your soul seeing, and the ears of your heart hearing."

[3] *ad Diogn.* 8, 1.

ing." It is hard to think of these familiar phrases being new and strange—the coining of Paul to express what no man had said before—and this at the moment when Seneca was writing his "moral letters" to Lucilius. Verbal coincidences may be found between Paul and Seneca, but they are essentially verbal. The Stoic Spermaticos Logos was a cold and uninspiring dogma compared with "Abba Father" and the Spirit of Jesus—it was not the same thing at all. The one doctrine made man self-sufficient—in the other, "our sufficiency (ἱκανότης) is of God." It was the law of nature, contrasted with the father of the prodigal son—"our kind and tender-hearted father" as Clement of Rome calls him [1]—the personal God, whose "problem is ever to save the flock of men ; that is why the good God has sent the good shepherd." [2]

The more lettered of Christian writers like to quote Plato's saying that man was born to be at home with God (οἰκείως ἔχειν πρὸς θεὸν) and that he was "a heavenly plant." Falsehood, they say, and error obscured all this, but now "that ancient natural fellowship with heaven" has "leapt forth from the darkness and beams upon us." [3] "God," says Clement, "out of his great love for men, cleaves to man, and as when a little bird has fallen out of the nest, the mother-bird hovers over it, and if perchance some creeping beast open its mouth upon the little thing,

> Wheeling o'er his head, with screams the dam
> Bewails her darling brood ;

so God the Father seeks his image, and heals the fall, and chases away the beast, and picks up the little one again." [4]

God has "anointed and sealed" his child and given him a pledge of the new relation—the holy spirit. This is distinctly said by St Paul,[5] and the variety of the phenomena, to which he refers, is a little curious. Several things are covered by the phrase, and are classed as manifestations with a common origin. There are many allusions to "speaking with tongues" ; Paul, however, clearly shows that we are not to understand a miraculous gift in using actual languages, reduced to grammar and

---

[1] Clem. R. 29, 1, τὸν ἐπιεικῆ καὶ εὔσπλαγχνον πατέρα ἡμῶν.
[2] Clem. Alex. *Protr.* 116.   [3] Clem. Alex. *Protr.* 25, ἔμφυτος ἀρχαία κοινωνία.
[4] Clem. Alex. *Protr.* 91, citing *Iliad*, 2, 315 (Cowper).   [5] 2 Cor. i, 22 ; v, 5.

spoken by men, as the author of the *Acts* suggests with a possible reminiscence of a Jewish legend of the law-giving from Sinai. The "glossolaly" was inarticulate and unintelligible; it was a feature of Greek "mantic," an accompaniment of over-strained emotion, and even to be produced by material agencies, as Plutarch lets us see. Paul himself is emphatic upon its real irrelevance to the Christian's main concern, and he deprecates the attention paid to it. Other "spiritual" manifestations were visions and prophecies. With these Dr William James has dealt in his *Varieties of Religious Experience*, showing that in them, as in "conversion," there is nothing distinctively Christian. The content of the vision and the outcome of the conversion are the determining factors. Where men believe that an ordinary human being can be temporarily transformed by the presence within him of a spirit, the very belief produces its own evidence. If the tenet of the holy spirit rested on nothing else, it would have filled a smaller place in Christian thought.

But when Paul speaks of the holy spirit whereby the Christians are sealed, calling it now the spirit of God and now the spirit of Jesus, he is referring to a profounder experience. Explain conversion as we may, the word represents a real thing. Men were changed, and were conscious of it. Old desires passed away and a new life began, in which passion took a new direction, finding its centre of warmth and light, not in morality, not in religion, but in God as revealed in Jesus Christ. "To me to live is Christ," cried Paul, giving words to the experience of countless others. Life had a new centre; and duty, pain and death were turned to gladness. The early Christian was con-scious of a new spirit within him. It was by this spirit that they could cry "Abba, Father"; it was the spirit that guided them into all truth; it was the spirit that united them to God,[1] that set them free from the law of sin and death, that meant life and peace and joy and holiness. Paul trusted everything to what we might call the Christian instinct and what he called the holy spirit, and he was justified. No force in the world has done so much as this nameless thing that has controlled and guided and illumined—whatever we call it. Any one who has breathed the quiet air of a gathering of men and women con-sciously surrendered to the influence of Jesus Christ, with all its

[1] Cf. Tatian, 15.

sobering effect, its consecration, its power and gladness, will know what Paul and his friends meant. It is hardly to be known otherwise. In our documents the spirit is closely associated with the gathering of the community in prayer.

Freedom from dæmons, forgiveness and reconciliation with God, gladness and moral strength and peace in the holy spirit —of such things the early Christians speak, and they associate them all invariably with one name, the living centre of all. "Jesus the beloved" is a phrase that lights up one of the dullest of early Christian pages.[1] "No! you do not so much as listen to anyone, if he speaks of anything but Jesus Christ in truth," says Ignatius.[2] "What can we give him in return? He gave us light . . . he saved us when we were perishing . . . We were lame in understanding, and worshipped stone and wood, the works of men. Our whole life was nothing but death. . . . He pitied us, he had compassion, he saved us, for he saw we had no hope of salvation except from him; he called us when we were not, and from not being he willed us to be."[3] "The blood of Jesus, shed for our salvation, has brought to all the world the grace of repentance."[4] "Ye see what is the pattern that has been given us; what should we do who by him have come under the yoke of his grace?"[5] "Let us be earnest to be imitators of the Lord."[6] These are a few words from Christians whose writings are not in the canon. Jesus is pre-eminently and always the Saviour; the author of the new life; the revealer of God; the bringer of immortality. It made an immense impression upon the ancient world to see the transformation of those whom it despised,—women, artisans, slaves and even slave-girls. Socrates with the hemlock cup and the brave Thrasea were figures that men loved and honoured. But here were all sorts of common people doing the same thing as Socrates and Thrasea, cheerfully facing torture and death "for the name's sake"—and it was a name of contempt, too. "Christ's people" — *Christianoi* — was a bantering improvisation by the people of Antioch, who were notorious in antiquity for impudent wit:[7] it was a happy shot

[1] Barnabas, 4, 8.
[2] Ign. *Eph.* 6, 2.
[3] II. Clem. 1, 3-7 (abridged a little).
[4] Clem. R. 7, 4.
[5] Clem. R. 16, 17.
[6] Ign. *Eph.* 10, 3.
[7] Cf. Socr. *e.h.* iii, 17, 4, the Antiochenes mocked the Emperor Julian, εὐρίπιστοι γὰρ οἱ ἄνθρωποι εἰς ὕβρεις.

and touched the very centre of the target. "The name" and "his name," are constantly recurring phrases. But it was not only that men would die for the name—men will die for anything that touches their imagination or their sympathy—but they lived for it and showed themselves to be indeed a "new creation." "Our Jesus"[1] was the author of a new life, and a very different one from that of Hellenistic cities. That Christianity retained its own character in the face of the most desperate efforts of its friends to turn it into a philosophy congenial to the philosophies of the day, was the result of the strong hold it had taken upon innumerable simple people, who had found in it the power of God in the transformation of their own characters and instincts, and who clung to Jesus Christ—to the great objective facts of his incarnation and his death upon the cross—as the firm foundations laid in the rock against which the floods of theory might beat in vain. For now we have to consider another side of early Christian activity—the explanation of the new experience.

The early Christian community found "the unexamined life" as impossible as Plato had, and they framed all sorts of theories to account for the change in themselves. Of most immediate interest are the accounts which they give of the holy spirit and of Jesus. Here we must remember that in all definition we try to express the less known through the more known, and that the early Christians necessarily used the best language available to them, and tried to communicate a new series of experiences by means of the terms and preconceptions of the thinking world of their day—terms and preconceptions long since obsolete.

Much in the early centuries of our era is unintelligible until we form some notion of the current belief in spiritual beings, evidence of which is found in abundance in the literature of the day, pagan and Christian. A growing consensus among philosophers made God more and more remote, and emphasized the necessity for intermediaries. We have seen how Plutarch pronounced for the delegation of rule over the universe and its functions to ministering spirits. The Jews had a parallel belief in angels, and had come to think of God's spirit and God's intelligence as somehow detachable from his being. In abstract

[1] II. Clem. 14, 2.

thought this may be possible just as we think of an angle without reference to matter. The great weakness in the speculation of the early Empire was this habit of supposing that men can be as certain of their deductions as of their premises ; and God's Logos, being conceivable, passed into common religious thought as a separate and proven existence.

At the same time there was abundant evidence of devil-possession as there is in China to-day. Modern medicine distinguishes four classes of cases which the ancients (and their modern followers) group under this one head :—Insanity, Epilepsy, Hysteria major and the mystical state. To men who had no knowledge of modern medicine and its distinctions, the evidence of the " possessed " was enough, and it was apt to be quite clear and emphatic as it is in such cases to-day. The man said he " had a devil "—or even a " legion of devils." The priestess at the oracle said that a god was within her (ἔνθεος). In both cases the ocular evidence was enough to convince the onlookers of the truth of the explanation, for the persons concerned were clearly changed and were not themselves.[1] Plato played with the idea that poetry even might be, as poets said, a matter of inspiration. The poet could not be merely himself when he wrote or sang words of such transforming power. The Jews gave a similar account of prophecy—the Spirit of the Lord descended upon men, as we read in the Old Testament. The Spirit, says Athenagoras to the Greeks, used the Hebrew prophets, as a flute-player does a flute, while they were in ecstasy (κατ' ἔκστασιν)[2]—the holy spirit, he adds, is an effluence (ἀπόρροια) of God.[3]

The Christians, finding ecstasy, prophecy, trance, and glossolaly among their own members, and having before them the parallel of Greek priestesses and Hebrew prophets, and making moreover the same *very* slight distinction as their pagan

---

[1] See Tertullian, *Apol.* 22.   [2] Athenagoras, *Presbeia*, 9.

[3] See a very interesting chapter in Philo's *de migr. Abr.* 7 (441 M), where he gives a very frequent experience of his own (μυριάκις παθών) as a writer. Sometimes, though he " saw clearly " what to say, he found his mind " barren and sterile " and went away with nothing done, with " the womb of his soul closed." At other times he " came empty and suddenly became full, as thoughts were imperceptibly sowed and snowed upon him from above, so that, as if under Divine possession (κατοχῆς ἐνθέου), he became frenzied (κορυβαντιᾶν) and utterly knew not the place, nor those present, nor himself, nor what was said or written." See Tert. *de Anima*, 11, on the spirits of God and of the devil that may come upon the soul.

neighbours between matter and spirit, and, finally, possessing all the readiness of unscientific people in propounding theories,— they assumed an "effluence" from God, a spirit which entered into a man, just as in ordinary life evil demons did, but here it was a holy spirit. This they connected with God after the manner familiar to Jewish thinkers, and following the same lead, began to equate it with God, as a separate being. It is not at first always quite clear whether it is the spirit of God or of Jesus —or even a manifestation of the risen Jesus.[1]

When we pass to the early explanations of Jesus, we come into a region peculiarly difficult. A later age obscured the divergences of early theory. Some opinions the church decisively rejected—Christians would have nothing to do with a Jesus who was an emanation from an absolute and inconceivable Being, a Jesus who in that case would be virtually indistinguishable from Asclepios the kindly-natured divine healer. Nor would they tolerate the notion of a phantom-Jesus crucified in show, while the divine Christ was far away—like Helen in Euripides' play.[2] "Spare," says Tertullian, "the one hope of all the world."[3] They would not have a "daimonion without a body." But two theories, one of older Jewish, and the other of more recent Alexandrian origin, the church accepted and blended, though they do not necessarily belong to each other.

The one theory is especially Paul's—sacred to all who lean with him to the Hebrew view of things, to all who, like him, are touched with the sense of sin and feel the need of another's righteousness, to all who have come under the spell of the one great writer of the first century. A Jew, a native of a Hellenistic city—and " no mean one "[4]—a citizen of the Roman Empire, a man of wide outlooks, with a gift for experience, he passed from

---

[1] It may be remarked, in passing, that the contemporary worship of the Emperor is to be explained by the same theory of the possibility of an indwelling daimonion. It was helped out by the practice, which had never so far died out in the East and in Egypt, of regarding the King and his children as gods incarnate. See J. G. Frazer, *Early History of Kingship.*

[2] Tertullian, *adv. Marc.* iii, 8, *nihil solidum ab inani, nihil plenum a vacuo perfici licuit . . . imaginarius operator, imaginariæ operæ.*

[3] Tertullian, *de carne Christi*, 5.

[4] His Tarsiot feeling is perhaps shown by his preference that women should be veiled. Dio Chrysostom (*Or.* 33, 48) mentions that in Tarsus there is much conservatism shown in the very close veiling of the women's faces.

Pharisaism to Christ. The mediating idea was righteousness. He knew his own guilt before God, and found that by going about to establish his own righteousness he was achieving nothing.

At the same time a suffering Messiah was a contradiction in terms, unspeakably repulsive to a Jew. We can see this much in the tremendous efforts of the Apologists to overcome Jewish aversion by producing Old Testament prophecies that Christ was to suffer. Παθητός (subject to suffering) was a word that waked rage and contempt in every one, who held to contemporary views of God, or even had dabbled in Stoic or similar conceptions of human greatness. But it seems that the serenity and good conscience of Christian martyrs impressed their persecutor, who was not happy in his own conscience ; and at last the thought came—along familiar lines—that Christ's sufferings might be for the benefit of others. And then he saw Jesus on the road to Damascus. What exactly happened is a matter of discussion, but Paul was satisfied—he was "a man in Christ."

Much might be said in criticism of Paul's Christology—if it were not for Paul and his followers. They have done too much and been too much for it to be possible to dissect their great conception in cold blood. Paul's theories are truer than another man's experiences—they pulse with life, they have (in Luther's phrase) hands and feet to carry a man away. The man is so large and so strong, so simple and true, so various in his knowledge of the world, so tender in his feeling for men— "all things to all men"—such a master of language, so sympathetic and so open—he is irresistible. The quick movement of his thought, his sudden flashes of anger and of tenderness, his apostrophes, his ejaculations—one feels that pen and paper never got such a man written down before or since. Every sentence comes charged with the whole man—half a dozen Greek words, and not always the best Greek—and the Christian world for ever will sum up its deepest experience in " God forbid that I should glory save in the cross of our Lord Jesus Christ, by whom the world is crucified unto me and I unto the world."

Close examination reveals a good deal of Judaism surviving in Paul,—a curious way of playing with the text of Scripture, odd reminiscences of old methods, and deeper infiltrations of a Jewish thought which is not that of Jesus. Yet it does not affect our feeling for him—he stands too close to us as a man, too much over us as the teacher of Augustine, Calvin and Luther—a man, whom it took more genius to explain than the church had for fifteen centuries, and yet the man to whom the church owes its universal reach and unity, its theology and the best of the language in which it has expressed its love for his master.

Paul went back to the Jewish conception of a Messiah, modified, in the real spirit of Jesus, by the thought of suffering. But when we put side by side the Messiah of Jesus and the Messiah of Paul, we become conscious of a difference. The latter is a mediator between God and man, making atonement, transferring righteousness by a sort of legal fiction, and implying a conception of God's fatherhood far below that taught by Jesus. At the same time Paul has other thoughts of a profounder and more permanent value. It is hard, for instance, to imagine that any change, which time and thought may bring, can alter a word in his statement that "God was in Christ, reconciling the world to himself"—here there is no local or temporal element even in the wording. It may be noted that Paul has his own names for Jesus, for while he uses "Messiah" (in Greek) and "Son of God," he is the first to speak of "the Lord" and "the Saviour." Paul held the door open for the other great theory of the early church, when he emphasized the pre-existence of the heavenly Christ and made him the beginning, the centre and the end of all history.

The Logos, as we have seen, was not an original idea of the Christian world. It was long familiar to Greek philosophy, and Philo and the Stoics base much of their thought upon it. It must have come into the church from a Greek or Hellenistic source, perhaps as a translation of Paul's "heavenly Christ." As it stands, it is a peculiarly bold annexation from Philosophy. No Stoic would have denied that the Spermaticos Logos was in Jesus, but the bold identification of the Logos with Jesus must have been "foolishness to the Greek." Still in contemporary thought there was much to dispose men to believe in such an incarnation of the Logos in a human being, though there is no suggestion that a spiritual being of any at all commensurate greatness was ever so incarnated before. But the thought appealed to the Christian mind, when once the shock to Greek susceptibilities was overcome. Once accepted, it "solved all questions in the earth and out of it." It permitted the congenial idea of Greek theology to remain—the transcendence of God being saved by this personification of his Thought. It was a final blow to all theories that made Jesus an emanation, a phantom or a demi-god, and it kept his historic personality well in the centre of thought, though leaving it now comparatively much less significance.

Surveying the two accounts, Jewish and Greek, we cannot help remarking that they belong to other ages of thought than our own. Columbus, Copernicus and Darwin were neither philosophers nor theologians, but they have changed the perspectives of philosophy and theology, and we think to-day with a totally different series of preconceptions from those of Jew and Greek of the first century. The Greek himself never thought much of the "chosen race," and it was only when he realized that Jesus was not a tribal hero, that he accepted him. To the Greek the Messiah was as strange a thought as to ourselves. To us the Logos is as strange as the Messiah was to the Greek. We have really at present no terms in which to express what we feel to be the permanent significance of Jesus, and the old expressions may repel us until we realize, first, that they are not of the original essence of the Gospel, and second, that they represent the best language which Greek and Jew could find for a conviction which we share—that Jesus of Nazareth does stand in the centre of human history, that he has brought God and man into a new relation, that he is the personal concern of everyone of us, and that there is more in him than we have yet accounted for.

Into the question of the organization adopted by the early Christians and the development of the idea of the church, it is not essential to our present purpose to inquire. Opinion varies as to how far we should seek the origin of the church in the teaching and work of Jesus. If his mind has been at all rightly represented in this book, it seems to follow that he was not responsible either for the name or the idea of the church. Minds of the class to which his belongs have as a rule little or no interest in organizations and arrangements, and nothing can be more alien to the tone and spirit of his thinking than the ecclesiastical idea as represented by Cyprian and Ignatius. That out of the group of followers who lived with Jesus, a society should grow, is natural ; and societies instinctively organize themselves.   The Jew offered the pattern of a theocracy, and the Roman of a hierarchy of officials, but it took two centuries to produce the church of Cyprian.   The series of running fights with Greek speculation in the second century contributed to the natural and acquired instincts for order and system,—particularly in a world where such instincts had little opportunity of exercise in municipal, and less in political, life. The name was, as Harnack says, a masterly stroke—the "ecclesia of God " suggested to the Greek the noble and free life of a self-governing organism such as the ancient world had known, but raised to a higher plane and transfigured from a Periclean Athens to a Heavenly Jerusalem.   Fine conceptions and high ideals clung about the idea of the church in the best minds,[1] but in practice it meant the transformation of the gospel into a code, the repression of liberty of thought, and the final extinction of prophecy.   For the view that every one of these results was desirable, reason might be shown in the vagaries of life and speculation which the age knew, but it was obviously a departure from the ideas of Jesus.

The rise of the church was accompanied by the rise of mysteries.   There is a growing consensus of opinion among independent scholars that Jesus instituted no sacraments, yet Paul found the rudiments of them among the Christians and believed he had the warrant of Jesus for the heightening which he gave to them.   Ignatius speaks of the Ephesians " breaking one bread, which is the medicine of immortality ($\phi\acute{\alpha}\rho\mu\alpha\kappa\sigma\nu$ $\dot{\alpha}\theta\alpha\nu\alpha\sigma\acute{\iota}\alpha\varsigma$) and the antidote that we should not die "—the former phrase reappearing in Clement of Alexandria.[2]   That such ideas should emerge in the Christian community is natural enough, when we consider its environment—a world without natural science, steeped in belief in every kind of magic and enchantment, and full of public and private religious societies, every one of which had its mysteries and miracles and its blood-bond with its peculiar deity.   It was from such a world

---

[1] Tert. *Apol.* 39, *Corpus sumus de conscientia religionis et disciplinæ* **unitate et** *spei foedere.*   [2] Ign. *Eph.* 20 ; Clem. Alex. *Protr.* 106.

and such societies that most of the converts came and brought
with them the thoughts and instincts of countless generations,
who had never conceived of a religion without rites and
mysteries. Baptism similarly took on a miraculous colour—men
were baptized for the dead in Paul's time—and before long
it bore the names familiarly given by the world to all such
rituals of admission—enlightenment (φωτισμός) and initiation ;
and with the names came many added symbolic practices in its
administration. The Christians readily recognized the parallel
between their rites and those of the heathen, but no one seems
to have perceived the real connexion between them. Quite
naively they suggest the exact opposite—it was the dæmons,
who foresaw what the Christian rites (ἱερά) would be, and fore-
stalled them with all sorts of pagan parodies.[1]

But, after all, the force of the Christian movement lay neither
in church, nor in sacrament, but in men. " How did Christianity
rise and spread among men?" asks Carlyle, "was it by institutions,
and establishments, and well arranged systems of mechanism ?
No! . . . It arose in the mystic deeps of man's soul ; and was
spread by the ' preaching of the word,' by simple, altogether
natural and individual efforts ; and flew, like hallowed fire, from
heart to heart, till all were purified and illuminated by it. Here
was no Mechanism ; man's highest attainment was accomplished
Dynamically, not Mechanically."[2] Nothing could be more just.
The Gospel set fire to men's hearts, and they needed to do nothing but live to spread their faith. The ancient evidence is
abundant for this. The Christian had an " insatiable passion for
doing good "[3]—not as yet a technical term—and he "did good "
in the simplest kind of ways. " Even those things which you
do after the flesh are spiritual," says Ignatius himself, "for you
do all things in Jesus Christ."[4] "Christians," says a writer
whose name is lost, "are not distinguishable from the rest of
mankind in land or speech or customs. They inhabit no
special cities of their own, nor do they use any different form of
speech, nor do they cultivate any out-of-the-way life. . . . But
while they live in Greek and barbarian cities as their lot may be

---

[1] Justin, *Apol.* i, 66, the use of bread and cup in the mysteries of Mithras ;
Tertullian, *de Bapt.* 5, on baptism in the rites of Isis and Mithras, the mysteries of
Eleusis, etc.

[2] Carlyle, *Signs of the Times.* (Centenary edition of *Essays,* ii, p. 70.)

[3] Clem. R. 2, 2, ἀκόρεστος πόθος εἰς ἀγαθοποιίαν.   [4] Ign. *Eph.* 8, 2.

cast, and follow local customs in dress and food and life generally, . . . yet they live in their own countries as sojourners only; they take part in everything as citizens and submit to everything as strangers. Every strange land is native to them, and every native land is strange. They marry and have children like everyone else—but they do not expose their children. They have meals in common, but not wives. They are in the flesh, but they do not live after the flesh. They continue on earth, but their citizenship is in heaven. They obey the laws ordained, and by their private lives they overcome the laws. . . . In a word, what the soul is in the body, that is what Christians are in the world."[1]

"As a rule," wrote Galen, "men need to be educated in parables. Just as in our day we see those who are called Christians[2] have gained their faith from parables. Yet they sometimes act exactly as true philosophers would. That they despise death is a fact we all have before our eyes; and by some impulse of modesty they abstain from sexual intercourse —some among them, men and women, have done so all their lives. And some, in ruling and controlling themselves, and in their keen passion for virtue, have gone so far that real philosophers could not excel them."[3]   So wrote a great heathen, and Celsus admits as much himself.   In life at least, if not in theory, the Christians daily kept to the teaching of their Master. "Which is ampler?" asks Tertullian, "to say, Thou shalt not kill; or to teach, Be not even angry?   Which is more perfect, to forbid adultery or to bid refrain from a single lustful look?"[4] There was as yet no flight from the world, though Christians had no illusions about it or about the devil who played so large a part in its affairs.   They lived in an age that saw Antinous deified.[5] They stood for marriage and family life, while all around "holy" men felt there was an unclean and dæmonic element in marriage.[6]   One Christian writer even speaks of women being

---

[1] Auctor *ad Diognetum*, 5-6.

[2] He apologizes for the use of the name, as educated people did in his day, when it was awkward or impossible to avoid using it.   It was a vulgarism.

[3] Galen, extant in Arabic in *hist. anteislam. Abulfedæ* (ed. Fleischer, p. 109), quoted by Harnack, *Expansion of Christianity*, i, p. 266.

[4] Tertullian, *Apol.* 45 ; cf. Justin, *Apol.* i, 15.   [5] Cf. Justin, *Apol.* i, 29.

[6] The feeling referred to is associated with the primitive sense of the mystery of procreation and conception surviving, it is said, among the Arunta of Australia, and very widely in the case of twins ; see Rendel Harris, *Cult of the Dioscuri*.

saved *by* child-bearing.[1]   Social conditions they accepted—
even slavery among them—but they brought a new spirit into
all ; love and the sense of brotherhood could transform every
thing.   Slavery continued, but the word " slave " is not found
in Christian catacombs.[2]

Above all, they were filled with their Master's own desire to
save men.   " I am debtor," wrote Paul, " both to Greeks and to
barbarians, wise and unwise." [3]   If modern criticism is right in
detaching the " missionary commission " (in Matthew) from the
words of Jesus, the fact remains that the early Christians were
" going into all the world " and " preaching the gospel to every
creature " for half a century before the words were written.
Why?   " He that has the word of Jesus truly can hear his
silence," said Ignatius ; and if Jesus did not speak these words,
men heard his silence to the same effect.   Celsus, like Julian
long after him, was shocked at the kind of people to whom
the gospel was preached.[4]

The Christian came to the helpless and hopeless, whom men
despised, and of whom men despaired, with a message of the
love and tenderness of God, and he brought it home by a new
type of love and tenderness of his own.   Kindness to friends
the world knew ; gentleness, too, for the sake of philosophic
calm ; clemency and other more or less self-contained virtues.
The " third race " had other ideas—in all their virtues there
was the note of " going out of oneself," the unconsciousness
which Jesus loved—an instinctive habit of negating self
($\dot{\alpha}\pi\alpha\rho\nu\dot{\eta}\sigma\alpha\sigma\theta\alpha\iota$ $\dot{\epsilon}\alpha\upsilon\tau\dot{o}\nu$), which does not mean medieval asceticism,
nor the dingy modern virtue of self-denial.   There was no
sentimentalism in it ; it was the spirit of Jesus spiritualizing
and transforming and extending the natural instinct of brother-
liness by making it theocentric.   Christians for a century or two
never thought of *ataraxia* or apathy, and, though Clement of
Alexandria plays with them, he tries to give them a new turn.
Fortunately the Gospels were more read than the *Stromateis*
and " Christian apathy " never succeeded.   The heathen recognized sympathy as a Christian characteristic—" How these

---

[1] Tim. 2, 15.   Cf. Tert. *adv. Marc.* iv, 17, *nihil impudentius si ille nos sibi filio faciet qui nobis filios facere non permisit auferendo conubium.*

[2] de Rossi, cited by Harnack, *Expansion*, i, 208 n.

[3] Romans 1, 14.   [4] See p. 241 ; and cf. Justin, *Apol.* i, 15.

Christians love each other ! " they said. Lucian bears the same testimony to the mutual care and helpfulness of Christians. " You see," wrote Lucian, " these poor creatures have persuaded themselves that they are immortal for all time and will live for ever, which explains why they despise death and voluntarily give themselves up, as a general rule ; and then their original law-giver persuaded them that they are all brothers, from the moment that they cross over and deny the gods of Greece and worship their sophist who was gibbeted, and live after his laws. All this they accept, with the result that they despise all worldly goods alike and count them common property." In a later century Julian, perhaps following Maximin Daza, whom he copied in trying to organize heathenism into a new catholic church, urged benevolence on his fellow-pagans, if they wished to compete with the Christians. It was the only thing, he felt, that could revive paganism, and his appeal met with no response. "Infinite love in ordinary intercourse" is the Christian life, and it must come from within or nowhere. No organization can produce it, and, however much we may have to discount Christian charity in some directions as sometimes mechanical, the new spirit of brotherhood in the world presupposed a great change in the hearts of men.

It was not Stoic cosmopolitanism. The Christian was not " the citizen of the world " nor " the Friend of Man "; he was a plain person who gave himself up for other people, cared for the sick and the worthless, had a word of friendship and hope for the sinful and despised, would not go and see men killed in the amphitheatre, and—most curious of all—was careful to have indigent brothers taught trades by which they could help themselves. A lazy Christian was no Christian, he was a "trader in Christ."[1] If the Christians' citizenship was in heaven, he had a social message for this world in the meantime.

Every great religious movement coincides with a new discovery of truth of some kind, and such discoveries induce a new temper. Men inquire more freely and speak more freely the truth they feel. Mistakes are made and a movement begins

---

[1] *Didache*, 12. εἰ δὲ οὐκ ἔχει τέχνην, κατὰ τὴν σύνεσιν ὑμῶν προνοήσατε, πῶς μὴ ἀργὸς μεθ' ὑμῶν ζήσεται χριστιανός. εἰ δὲ οὐ θέλει οὕτω ποιεῖν, χριστέμπορός ἐστιν· προσέχετε ἀπὸ τῶν τοιούτων. See Tert. *Apol.* 39, on provision for the needy and the orphan, the shipwrecked, and those in jails and mines.

for " quenching the spirit." But the gains that have been made by the liberated spirits are not lost. Thus the early Christian rose quickly to a sense of the value of woman. Dr Verrall pronounces that "the radical disease, of which, more than of anything else, ancient civilization perished " was "an imperfect ideal of woman."[1] In the early church woman did a good many things, which in later days the authorities preferred not to mention. Thekla's name is prominent in early story, and the prophetesses of Phrygia, Prisca and Maximilla, have a place in Church History. They were not popular; but the church was committed to the Gospel of Luke and the ministry of women to the Lord. And whatever the Christian priesthood did or said, Jesus and his followers had set woman on a level with man. "There is neither male nor female." The same freedom of spirit is attested by the way in which pagan prophets and their dupes classed Christians with Epicureans [2]—they saw and understood too much. The Christians were the only people (apart from the Jews) who openly denounced the folly of worshipping and deifying Emperors. Even Ignatius, who is most famous for his belief in authority, breaks into independence when men try to make the Gospel dependent on the Old Testament—"for me the documents ($\tau\grave{a}$ $\dot{a}\rho\chi\epsilon\hat{i}a$) are Jesus Christ; my unassailable documents are his cross, and his death and resurrection, and the faith that is through him; in which things I hope with your prayers to be saved."[3] "Where the spirit of the Lord is, there is liberty," as Paul said.

God and immortality were associated in Christian thought. Christians, said a writer using the name of Peter, are to be "partakers of the divine nature." " If the soul," says Tatian, "enters into union with the divine spirit, it is no longer helpless, but ascends to regions whither the spirit guides it; for the dwelling-place of the spirit is above, but the origin of the soul is from beneath."[4] " God sent forth to us the Saviour and Prince of immortality, by whom he also made manifest to us the truth and the heavenly life."[5] The Christian's life is " hid with Christ in God," and Christ's resurrection is to the

---

[1] *Euripides the Rationalist*, p. 111 n.

[2] Lucian, *Alexander*, 38, Alexander said : "If any atheist, or Christian, or Epicurean comes as a spy upon our rites let him flee !" He said ἔξω χριστιανούς, and the people responded ἔξω Ἐπικουρείους.

[3] Ignatius, *Philad.* 8.   [4] Tatian, 13.   [5] II. Clem. 20, 5.

early church the pledge of immortality—"we shall be ever
with the Lord." For the transmigration of souls and "eternal
re-dying," life was substituted.[1]   "We have believed," said
Tatian, "that there will be a resurrection of our bodies, after
the consummation of all things—not, as the Stoics dogmatize,
that in periodic cycles the same things for ever come into being
and pass out of it for no good whatever,—but once for all," and
this for judgment.   The judge is not Minos nor Rhadamanthus,
but "God the maker is the arbiter." [2]   "They shall see him
(Jesus) then on that day," wrote the so-called Barnabas, "wearing
the long scarlet robe upon his flesh, and they will say ' Is this not
he whom we crucified, whom we spat upon, and rejected ? ' " [3]
Persecution tempted the thought of what " that day " would mean
for the persecutor.   But it was a real concern of the Christian himself.   " I myself, utterly sinful, not yet escaped from temptation,
but still in the midst of the devil's engines,—I do my diligence
to follow after righteousness that I may prevail so far as at
least to come near it, fearing the judgment that is to come." [4]
Immortality and righteousness—the two thoughts go together,
and both depend upon Jesus Christ.   He is emphatically called
" our Hope "—a favourite phrase with Ignatius.[5]

Some strong hope was needed—some "anchor of the soul,
sure and steadfast." [6]   Death lay in wait for the Christian at
every turn, never certain, always probable.   The dæmons whom
he had renounced took their revenge in exciting his neighbours
against him.[7]   The whim of a mob [8] or the cruelty of a governor[9]
might bring him face to face with death in no man knew what
horrible form.   One writer spoke of "the burning that came
for trial," [10] and the phrase was not exclusively a metaphor.

---

[1] See Tertullian, de Testim. Animæ, 4, the Christian opinion much nobler than the
Pythagorean.

[2] Tatian, 6. Cf. Justin, Apol. i, 8; and Tertullian, de Spectaculis, 30, quoted on p. 305.

[3] Barnabas, 7, 9. Cf. Rev. i, 7. Behold he cometh with the clouds and every eye
shall see him—and they that pierced him. Cf. Tertullian, de Spect. 30, once more.

[4] II. Clem. 18, 2.   [5] Ignatius, Eph. 21 ; Magn. 11 ; Trall. int. 2, 2 ; Philad. 11.
[6] Hebrews 6, 19.

[7] Justin, Apol. i, 5, the dæmons procured the death of Socrates, καὶ ὁμοίως ἐφ᾽ ἡμῶν
τὸ αὐτὸ ἐνεργοῦσι : 10, they spread false reports against Christians ; Apol. ii, 12 ;
Minucius Felix, 27, 8.

[8] The mob, with stones and torches, Tert. Apol. 37 ; even the dead Christian was
dragged from the grave, de asylo quodam mortis, and torn to pieces.

[9] Stories of governors in Tert. ad Scap. 3, 4, 5 ; one provoked by his wife becoming
a Christian.   [10] I. Peter 4, 12.

"Away with the atheists—where is Polycarp?" was a sudden shout at Smyrna—the mob already excited with sight of "the right noble Germanicus fighting the wild beasts in a signal way." The old man was sought and found—with the words "God's will be done" upon his lips. He was pressed to curse Christ. "Eighty-six years I have been his slave," he said, "and he has done me no wrong. How can I blaspheme my King who saved me?"[1]   The suddenness of these attacks, and the cruelty, were enough to unnerve anyone who was not "built upon the foundation." Nero's treatment of the Christians waked distaste in Rome itself. But it was the martyrdoms that made the church. Stephen's death captured Paul. "I delighted in Plato's teachings," says Justin, "and I heard Christians abused, but I saw they were fearless in the face of death and all the other things men count fearful."[2]   Tertullian and others with him emphasize that "the blood of martyrs is the seed of the church." It was the death of Jesus over again—the last word that carried conviction with it.

With "the sentence of death in themselves" the early Christians faced the world, and astonished it by more than their "stubbornness." They were the most essentially happy people of the day—Jesus was their hope, their sufficiency was of God, their names were written in heaven, they were full of love for all men—they had "become little children," as Jesus put it, glad and natural. Jesus had brought them into a new world of possibilities. A conduct that ancient moralists dared not ask, the character of Jesus suggested, and the love of Jesus made actual. "I can do all things," said Paul, "in him that strengtheneth me." They looked to assured victory over evil and they achieved it. "This is the victory that *has* overcome the world—our faith." Very soon a new note is heard in their words. Stoicism was never "essentially musical"; Epictetus announces a hymn to Zeus,[3] but he never starts the tune. Over and over again there is a sound of singing in Paul—as in the eighth chapter of the *Romans*, and the thirteenth of *First Corinthians*,[4] and it repeats itself. "Children of joy" is Barnabas' name for his friends.[5]

---

[1] *Martyrium Polycarpi*, 3, 7-11.   [2] Justin, *Apol.* ii, 12.

[3] *D.* i, 16, the hymn he proposes is quoted on p. 62. It hardly sings itself, and he does not return to it. The verbal parallel of the passage with that in Clement, *Strom.* vii, 35, heightens the contrast of tone.

[4] See Norden, *Kunstprosa*, ii, 509.   [5] Barnabas, 7, 1.

"Doing the will of Christ we shall find rest," wrote the unknown author of "Second Clement."[1]   "Praising we plough ; and singing we sail," wrote the greater Clement.[2]   "Candidates for angelhood, even here we learn the strain hereafter to be raised to God, the function of our future glory," said Tertullian.[3] "Clothe thyself in gladness, that always has grace with God and is welcome to him—and revel in it.   For every glad man does what is good, and thinks what is good. . . . The holy spirit is a glad spirit . . . yes, they shall all live to God, who put away sadness from themselves and clothe themselves in all gladness."   So said the angel to Hermas,[4] and he was right. The holy spirit was a glad spirit, and gladness—joy in the holy spirit—was the secret of Christian morality.   Nothing could well be more gay and happy than Clement's *Protrepticus*. Augustine was attracted to the church because he saw it *non dissolute hilaris*.   Such happiness in men is never without a personal centre, and the church made no secret that this centre was "Jesus Christ, whom you have not seen, but you love him ; whom yet you see not, but you believe in him and rejoice with joy unspeakable and glorified."[5]

---

[1] II. Clem. 6, 7.   [2] *Strom.* vii, 35.   [3] *de orat.* 3.

[4] Hermas, *M.* 10, 31,—the word is ἱλαρὸς ; which Clement (*l.c.*) also uses, conjoining it with σεμνός.   Cf. Synesius, *Ep.* 57, p. 1389, Migne, who says that when he was depressed about becoming a bishop (410 A.D.), old men told him ὡς ἱλαρόν ἐστι τὸ πνεῦμα τὸ ἅγιον καὶ ἱλαρύνει τοὺς μετόχους αὐτοῦ.

[5] I Peter, 1, 8.

CHAPTER VI

THE CONFLICT OF CHRISTIAN AND JEW

IT is a much discussed question as to how far Jesus realized the profound gulf between his own religious position and that of his contemporaries. Probably, since tradition meant more to them, they were quicker to see declension from orthodox Judaism than a mind more open and experimental; and when they contrived his death, it was with a clear sense of acting in defence of God's Law and God's Covenant with Israel. From their own point of view they were right, for the triumph of the ideas of Jesus was the abolition of tribal religions and their supersession by a new mind or spirit with nothing local or racial about it.

The death of Jesus meant to the little community, which he left behind him, a final cleavage with the system of their fathers, under which they had been born, and with which was associated every religious idea they had known before their great intimacy began. It was a moment of boundless import in the history of mankind. Slowly and reluctantly they moved out into the great unknown,—pilgrim fathers, unconscious of the great issues they carried, but obedient to an impulse, the truth of which history has long since established. Once again it was their opponents who were the quickest to realize what was involved, for affection blinded their own eyes.

The career of Paul raised the whole question between Judaism and Christianity. He was the first to speak decisively of going to the Gentiles. The author of the *Acts* cites precedents for his action; and, as no great movement in man's affairs comes unheralded, it is easy to believe that even before Paul "the word" reached Gentile ears. None the less the leader in the movement was Paul; and whatever we may imagine might have been the history of Christianity without him, it remains that he declared, decisively and for all time, the church's independence of the synagogue. It is not unlikely that, even before his conversion, he had grasped the fact that church and synagogue were not to be reconciled, and that, when "it pleased God to reveal his Son in him," he knew at once that he was in "a new creation" and that he was to be a prophet of a new dispensation.

There is no doubt that the hostile Jews very quickly realised Paul's significance, but the Christians were not so quick. Paul was a newcomer and very much the ablest man among them—they were "not many wise, not many learned," and Paul, though he does not mention it, was both. He was moreover proposing to take them into regions far beyond their range ; he had not personally known "the Lord" and they had ; and there was no clear word of Jesus on the Gentile question. There was a conference. What took place, Paul tries in the *Galatians* to tell ; but he is far too quick a thinker to be a master of mere narrative ; the question of Christian freedom was too hot in his heart to leave him free for reminiscence, and the matter is not very clear. The author of the *Acts* was not at the council, and, whatever his authorities may have been, there is a constant suggestion in his writing that he has a purpose in view—a purpose of peace between parties. Whether they liked the result or not, the Christian community seem loyally to have submitted themselves to "the Spirit of Jesus." "It seemed good to the holy spirit and to us" tells the story of their deliberations, whether they put the phrase at the top of a resolution or did not. Paul came to the personal followers of Jesus with a new and strange conception of the religion of their Master. They laid it alongside of their memories of their Master, and they heard him say "Go ye into all the world" ; and they went.

The natural outcome of this forward step at once became evident. Paul did not go among the Gentiles to "preach circumcision," and there quickly came into being, throughout Asia Minor and in the Balkan provinces, many groups of Christians of a new type—Gentile in mind and tradition, and in Christian life no less Gentile. They remained uncircumcised, they did not observe the Sabbath nor any other distinctive usage of Judaism—they were a new people, a "third race." Their very existence put Judaism on the defensive ; for, if their position was justified, it was hard to see what right Judaism had to be. It was not yet quite clear what exactly the new religion was, nor into what it might develope ; but if, as the Gentile Christians and their Apostle claimed, they stood in a new relation to God, a higher and a more tender than the greatest and best spirits in Israel had known, and this without the seal of God's covenant with Israel and independently of his law, then it was evident that the unique privileges of Israel were void, and that, as Paul put it, " there is neither Jew nor Greek."

That part of the Jewish race, and it was the larger part, which did not accept the new religion, was in no mind to admit either Paul's premisses or his conclusions. They stood for God's covenant with Israel. Nor did they stand alone, for it took time to convince even Christian Jews that the old dispensation had yielded to a new one, and that the day of Moses was past. To the one class the rise of the Christian community was a menace, to the other a problem. The one left no means untried to check it. By argument, by appeals to the past, by working on his superstitions, they sought to make the Christian convert into a Jew ; and, when they failed, they had other methods in reserve. Themselves everywhere despised and hated, as they are still, for their ability and their foreign air, they stirred up their heathen neighbours against the new race. Again and again, in the *Acts* and in later documents, we read of the Jews being the authors of pagan persecution.[1] The " unbelieving Jew " was a spiritual and a social danger to the Christian in every city of the East. The converted Jew was, in his way, almost as great a difficulty within the community.

It is not hard to understand the feeling of the Jews within or without the Church. Other races had their ancient histories, and the Jew had his—a history long and peculiar. From the day of Abraham, the friend of God, the chosen race had been the special care of Jehovah. Jehovah had watched over them ; he had saved them from their enemies ; he had visited them for their iniquities ; he had sent them prophets ; he had given them his law. In a long series of beautiful images, which move us yet, Jehovah had spoken, through holy men of old, of his love for Israel. To Israel belonged the oracles of God

[1] Justin, *Trypho*, c. 17 ; Tert. *adv. Jud.* 13.

and his promises. For here again the national consciousness of Israel differed from that of every other race. It was something that in the past God had spoken to no human family except the seed of Abraham ; it was more that to them, and to them alone, he had assured the future. Deeply as Israel felt the trials of the present, the Roman would yet follow the Persian and the Greek, and the day of Israel would dawn. The Messiah was to come and restore all things.

" He shall destroy the ungodly nations with the word of his mouth, so that at his rebuke the nations may flee before him, and he shall convict the sinners in the thoughts of their hearts.

" And he shall gather together a holy people whom he shall lead in righteousness ; and shall judge the tribes of his people that hath been sanctified by the Lord his God.

" And he shall not suffer iniquity to lodge in their midst, and none that knoweth wickedness shall dwell with them. . . .

" And he shall possess the nations of the heathen to serve him beneath his yoke ; and he shall glorify the Lord in a place to be seen of the whole earth ;

" And he shall purge Jerusalem and make it holy, even as it was in the days of old.

" So that the nations may come from the ends of the earth to see his glory, bringing as gifts her sons that had fainted,

" And may see the glory of the Lord, wherewith God hath glorified her."

So runs one of the *Psalms of Solomon* written between 70 and 40 B.C.[1] Parallel passages might be multiplied, but one may suffice, written perhaps in the lifetime of Jesus.

" Then thou, O Israel, wilt be happy, and thou wilt mount upon the neck of the eagle, and [the days of thy mourning] will be ended,

" And God will exalt thee, and he will cause thee to approach to the heaven of the stars, and he will establish thy habitation among them.

" And thou wilt look from on high, and wilt see thine

[1] *Psalm. Solom.* xvii, 27-35. Ed. Ryle and James.

enemies in Ge[henna], and thou wilt recognize them and rejoice, and wilt give thanks and confess thy Creator." [1]

No people in the Mediterranean world had such a past behind them, and none a future so sure and so glorious before them—none indeed seems to have had any great hope of the future at all ; their Golden Ages were all in the past, or far away in mythical islands of the Eastern seas or beyond the Rhine. And if the Christian doctrine was true, that great past was as dead as Babylon, and the Messianic Kingdom was a mockery—Israel was "feeding on the east wind," and the nation was not Jehovah's chosen. At one stroke Israel was abolished, and every national memory and every national instinct, rooted in a past of suffering and revelation, and watered with tears in a present of pain, were to wither like the gardens of Adonis. No man with a human heart but must face the alternative of surrendering national for Christian ideals, or hating and exterminating the enemy of his race.

So much for the nation, and what Christianity meant for it, but much beside was at stake. There was the seal of circumcision, the hereditary token of God's covenant with Abraham, a sacrament passed on from father to son and associated with generations of faith and piety. Week by week the Sabbath came with its transforming memories—the "Princess Sabbath," for Heine was not the first to feel the magic that at sunset on Friday restores the Jew to the "halls of his royal father, the tents of Jacob." Every one of their religious usages spoke irresistibly of childhood. "When your children shall say unto you 'What mean ye by this service,' ye shall say . . . ," so ran the old law, binding every Jew to his father by the dearest and strongest of all bonds. To become a Christian was thus to be alienated from the commonwealth of Israel, to renounce a father's faith and his home. If the pagan had to suffer for his conversion, the Jew's heritage was nobler and holier, and the harder to forego. Even the friendly Jew pleads, "Cannot a man be saved who trusts in Christ and also keeps the law—keeps it so far as he

---

[1] *Assumption of Moses*, x, 8-10, tr. R. H. Charles.   "Gehenna" is a restoration which seems probable, the Latin *in terram* representing what was left of the word in Greek.   See Dr Charles' note.

can under the conditions of the dispersion,—the Sabbath, circumcision, the months, and certain washings?"[1]

But this was not all. Israel had stood for monotheism and that not the monotheism of Greek philosophy, a dogma of the schools consistent with the cults of Egypt and Phrygia, with hierodules and a deified Antinous. The whole nation had been consecrated to the worship of One God, a personal God, who had, at least where Israel was concerned, no hint of philosophic Apathy. The Jew was now asked by the Christian to admit a second God—a God beside the Creator (ἄλλος θεὸς παρὰ τὸν ποιητὴν τῶν ὅλων[2])—and such a God! The Jews knew all about Jesus of Nazareth—it was absurd to try to pass him off even as the Messiah. "Sir," said Trypho, "these scriptures compel us to expect one glorious and great, who receives from 'the Ancient of Days' the 'eternal Kingdom' as 'Son of Man'; but this man of yours—your so-called Christ—was unhonoured and inglorious, so that he actually fell under the extreme curse that is in the law of God; for he was crucified."[3] The whole thing was a paradox, incapable of proof.[4] "It is an incredible thing, and almost impossible that you are trying to prove—that God endured to be begotten and to become a man."[5]

The Jews had a propaganda of their own about Jesus. They sent emissaries from Palestine to supply their country-men and pagans with the truth.[6] Celsus imagines a Jew disputing with a Christian,—a more life-like Jew, according to Harnack, than Christian apologists draw,—and the arguments he uses came from Jewish sources. Jesus was born, they said, in a village, the bastard child of a peasant woman, a poor person who worked with her hands, divorced by her husband (who was a carpenter) for adultery.[7] The father was a soldier called Panthera. As to the Christian story, what could have attracted the attention of God to her? Was she pretty? The carpenter at all events hated her and cast her out.[8]

---

[1] Justin, *Trypho*, 46, 47. The question is still asked ; I have heard it asked.

[2] Justin, *Trypho*, 50.   [3] Justin, *Trypho*, 32 ; the quotations are from Daniel

[4] Justin, *Trypho*, 48.   [5] Justin, *Trypho*, 68.

[6] Justin, *Trypho*, 17, 108.

[7] Cf. Tert. *de Spect.* 30, *fabri aut quæstuariæ filius.*

[8] Origen, *c. Cels.* i, 28, 32, 39. The beauty of the woman is an element in the stories of Greek demi-gods.

("I do not think I need trouble about this argument," is all
Origen says.) Who saw the dove, or heard the voice from
heaven, at the baptism? Jesus suffered death in Palestine for
the guilt he had committed ($\pi\lambda\eta\mu\mu\epsilon\lambda\dot{\eta}\sigma\alpha\nu\tau\alpha$). He convinced
no one while he lived ; even his disciples betrayed him—a
thing even brigands would not have done by their chief—
so far was he from improving them, and so little ground is
there for saying that he foretold to them what he should suffer.
He even complained of thirst on the cross. As for the
resurrection, that rests on the evidence of a mad woman
($\pi\dot{\alpha}\rho o\iota\sigma\tau\rho o\varsigma$)—or some other such person among the same
set of deceivers, dreaming, or deluded, or "wishing to startle
the rest with the miracle, and by a lie of that kind to give
other impostors a lead." Does the resurrection of Jesus at all
differ from those of Pythagoras or Zamolxis or Orpheus or
Herakles—" or do you think that the tales of other men both
are and seem myths, but that the catastrophe of your play is a
well-managed and plausible piece of invention—the cry upon
the gibbet, when he died, and the earthquake and the
darkness?"[1] The Christians systematically edited and
altered the Gospels to meet the needs of the moment;[2] but
Jesus did not fulfil the prophecies of the Messiah—"the
prophets say he shall be great, a dynast, lord of all the earth
and all its nations and armies."[3] There are ten thousand
other men to whom the prophecies are more applicable than
to Jesus,[4] and as many who in frenzy claim to "come from
God."[5] In short the whole story of the Christians rests on no
evidence that will stand investigation.

Even men who would refrain from the hot-tempered
method of controversy, which these quotations reflect, might
well feel the contrast between the historic Jesus and the expected Messiah—between the proved failure of the cross and
the world-empire of a purified and glorious Israel. And when
it was suggested further that Jesus was God, an effluence
coming from God, as light is lit by light—even if this were
true, it would seem that the Jew was asked to give up the
worship of the One God, which he had learnt of his fathers,
and to turn to a being not unlike the pagan gods around him
in every land, who also, their apologists said, came from the

[1] *c. Cels.* ii, 55. [2] ii, 27. [3] ii, 29. [4] ii, 28. [5] i, 50.

Supreme, and were his emanations and ministers and might therefore be worshipped.

Thus everything that was distinctive of their race and their religion—the past of Israel, the Messiah and the glorious future, the beautiful symbols of family religion, and the One God Himself—all was to be surrendered by the man who became a Christian. We realize the extraordinary and compelling force of the new religion, when we remember that, in spite of all to hold them back, there were those who made the surrender and "suffered the loss of all things to win Christ and be found in him." Paul however rested, as he said, on revelation, and ordinary men, who were not conscious of any such distinction, who mistrusted themselves and their emotions, and who rested most naturally upon the cumulative religious experience of their race, might well ask whether after all they were right in breaking with a sacred past—whether, apart from subjective grounds, there were any clear warrant from outside to enable them to go forward. The Jew had of course oracles of God given by inspiration ($\theta\epsilon\acute{o}\pi\nu\epsilon\upsilon\sigma\tau\sigma$[1]), written by "holy men of God, moved by the holy spirit." These were his warrant. Here circumcision, the Sabbath, the Passover, and all his religious life was definitely and minutely prescribed in what was almost, like the original two tables, the autograph of the One God. The law had its own history bound up with that of the race, and the experience and associations of every new generation made it more deeply awful and mysterious. Had the Christian any law? had he any oracles, apart from the unintelligible glossolalies of men possessed ($\dot{\epsilon}\nu\theta\sigma\upsilon\sigma\iota\hat{\omega}\nu\tau\epsilon\varsigma$)? When Justin spoke of the gifts of the Spirit, Trypho interjected, "I should like you to know that you are talking nonsense." [2]

Not unnaturally then did men say to Ignatius (as we have seen), "If I do not find it in the ancient documents, I do not believe it in the gospel." And when Ignatius rejoined, "It is written"; "That is the problem," said they.[3] It was their problem, though it was not his. For him Judaism is "a leaven old and sour," and "to use the name of Jesus Christ and yet observe Jewish customs is absurd ($\breve{\alpha}\tau\sigma\pi\sigma\nu$)" or really "to confess we have not received grace." [4] His documents were

---

[1] 2 Tim. 3, 15.
[2] *Trypho*, 39.
[3] Ign. *Philad.* 8, 2.
[4] Ign. *Magn.* 10, 3; 8, 1.

Jesus Christ, his cross and death and resurrection, and faith through him.

" That is the problem "—can it be shown from the infallible Hebrew Scriptures that the crucified Jesus is the Messiah of prophecy, that he is a " God beside the Creator," that Sabbath and Circumcision are to be superseded, that Israel's covenant is temporary, and that the larger outlook of the Christian is after all the eternal dispensation of which the Jewish was a copy made for a time? If this could be shown, it might in some measure stop the mouths of hostile Jews, and calm the uneasy consciences of Jews and proselytes who had become Christians. And it might serve another and a distinct purpose. It was one of the difficulties of the Christian that his religion was a new thing in the world. Around him were men who gloried in ancient literatures and historic cults. All the support that men can derive from tradition and authority, or even from the mere fact of having a past behind them, was wanting to the new faith, as its opponents pointed out. If, by establishing his contention against the Jew, the Christian could achieve another end, and could demonstrate to the Greek that he too had a history and a literature, that his religion was no mere accident of a day, but was rooted in the past, that it had been foretold by God himself, and was part of the divine scheme for the destiny of mankind, then, resting on the sure ground of Providence made plain, he could call upon the Greek in his turn to forsake his errors and superstitions for the first of all religions, which should also be the last—the faith of Jesus Christ.

The one method thus served two ends. Justin addressed an *Apology* to Antoninus Pius, and one-half of his book is occupied with the demonstration that every major characteristic of Christianity had been prophesied and was a fulfilment. The thirty chapters show what weight the sheer miracle of this had with the apologist, though, if the Emperor actually read the *Apology*, it was probably his first contact with Jewish scripture. Some difference of treatment was necessary, according as the method was directed to Jew or Gentile. For the Jew it was axiomatic that Scripture was the word of God, and, if he did not grant the Christian's postulate of allegory, he was withholding from an opponent what had been allowed to Philo

The Greek would probably allow the allegory, and the first task in his case was to show by chronological reckoning that the greater prophets, and above all Moses, antedated the bloom of Greek literature, and then to draw the inference that it was from Hebrew sources that the best thoughts of Hellas had been derived. Here the notorious interest of early Greek thinkers in Egypt helped to establish the necessary, though rather remote, connexion. When once the priority of the Hebrew prophets had been proved, and, by means of allegory, a coincidence (age by age more striking) had been established between prophecy and event, the demonstration was complete. There could be only one interpretation of such facts.

A number of these refutations of the Jew survive from early times. Justin's *Dialogue with Trypho* is the most famous, as it deserves to be. It opens in a pleasant Platonic style with a chance meeting one morning in a colonnade at Ephesus.[1] Trypho accosts the philosopher Justin—"When I see a man in your garb, I gladly approach him, and that is why I spoke to you, hoping to hear something profitable from you." When Trypho says he is a Jew, Justin asks in what he expects to be more helped by philosophy than by his own prophets and law-giver. Is not all the philosophers' talk about God? Trypho asks. Justin then tells him of his own wanderings in philosophy,—how he went from school to school, and at last was directed by an old man to read the Jewish prophets, and how "a fire was kindled in my soul, and a passion seized me for the prophets and those men who are Christ's friends ; and so, discussing their words with myself, I found this philosophy alone to be safe and helpful. And that is how and why I am a philosopher."[2] Trypho smiled, but, while approving Justin's ardour in seeking after God, he added that he would have done better to philosophize with Plato or one of the others, practising endurance, continence and temperance, than "to be deceived by lies and to follow men who are worthless." Then the battle begins, and it is waged in a courteous and kindly spirit, as befits philosophers, till after two days they part with prayers and goodwill for each other—Trypho unconvinced. Other writers have less

---

[1] So says Eusebius, *E.H.* iv, 18. Justin does not name the city.
[2] *Trypho*, 8.

skill, and the features of dialogue are sadly whittled away. Others again abandon all pretence of discussion and frankly group their matter as a scheme of proof-texts. In what follows, Justin shall be our chief authority.

We may start with the first point that Trypho raises. "If you will listen to me (for I count you a friend already), first of all be circumcised, and then keep, in the traditional way, the Sabbath and the feasts and new moons of God, and, in a word, do all that is written in the law, and then perhaps God will have mercy upon you. As for Christ, if indeed he has been born and already exists, he is unknown—nay! he does not even know himself yet, nor has he any power, till Elijah come and anoint him and make him manifest to all men. You people have accepted an empty tale, and are imagining a Christ for yourselves, and for the sake of him you are perishing quite aimlessly." [1]

Salvation, according to the Jew, was inconceivable outside the pale of Judaism. "Except ye be circumcised, ye cannot be saved," men had said in Paul's time. Paul's repudiation of this assertion is to be read in his Epistle to the *Galatians*—in his whole life and mind. But genius such as Paul's was not to be found in the early church, and men looked outside of themselves for arguments to prove what he had seen and known of his own experience and insight.

Some apologists merely laughed at the Jew. Thus the brilliant and winsome writer known only by his *Epistle to Diognetus* has a short and ready way of dealing with Jewish usages, which is not conciliatory. "In the next place I think you wish to hear why Christians do not worship in the same way as the Jews. Now the Jews do well in abstaining from the mode of service I have described [paganism], in that they claim to reverence One God of the universe and count Him their master; but, in offering this worship to Him in the same way as those I have mentioned, they go far astray. For the Greeks offer those things to senseless and deaf images and so give an exhibition of folly, while the Jews—considering they are presenting them to God as if He had need of them—ought in all reason to count it foolery and not piety. For He that made the heaven and the earth and all

[1] Justin, *Trypho*, 8.

that is in them, and gives freely to every one of us what we need, could not Himself need any of the things which He Himself actually gives to those who imagine they are giving them to Him. . . .

"But again of their nervousness (ψοφοδεὲς) about meats, and their superstition about the Sabbath, and the quackery (ἀλαζονεία) of circumcision, and the pretence (εἰρωνεία) of fasts and new moons—ridiculous and worthless as it all is, I do not suppose you wish me to tell you. For to accept some of the things which God has made for man's need as well created, and to reject others as useless and superfluous, is it not rebellion (ἀθέμιστον)? To lie against God as if He forbade us to do good on the Sabbath day, is not that impiety? To brag that the mutilation of the flesh is a proof of election—as if God specially loved them for it—ridiculous! And that they should keep a look-out on the stars and the moon and so observe months and days and distinguish the ordinances of God and the changes of the seasons, as their impulses prompt them to make some into feasts and some into times of mourning—who would count this a mark of piety towards God and not much rather of folly?

"That Christians are right to keep aloof from the general silliness and deceit of the Jews, their fussiness and quackery, I think you are well enough instructed. The mystery of their own piety towards God you must not expect to be able to learn from man."[1]

This was to deal with the distinctive usages of Judaism on general principles and from a standpoint outside it. It would doubtless be convincing enough to men who did not need to be convinced, but of little weight with those to whom the Scriptures meant everything. Accordingly the Apologists went to the Scriptures and arrayed their evidence with spirit and system.

We may begin, as the writer to Diognetus begins, with sacrifices. Here the Apologists could appeal to the Prophets, who had spoken of sacrifice in no sparing terms. Tertullian's fifth chapter in his book *Against the Jews* presents the evidence shortly and clearly. I will give the passages cited in a tabular form :—

[1] *ad Diogn.* 3, 4.

Malachi 1, 10 : I will not receive sacrifice from your hands, since from the rising sun to the setting my name is glorified among the Gentiles, saith the Lord Almighty, and in every place they offer pure sacrifices to my name.

Psalm 96, 7 : Offer to God glory and honour, offer to God the sacrifices of his name ; away with victims (*tollite*) and enter into his court.

Psalm 51, 17 : A heart contrite and humbled is a sacrifice for God.

Psalm 50, 14 : Sacrifice to God the sacrifice of praise and render thy vows to the Most High.

Isaiah 1, 11 : Wherefore to me the multitude of your sacrifices ? . . . . Whole burnt offerings and your sacrifices and the fat of goats and the blood of bulls I will not . . . Who has sought these from your hands ?

Justin has other passages as decisive. Does not God say by Amos (5, 21) " I hate, I loathe your feasts, and I will not smell [your offerings] in your assemblies. When ye offer me your whole burnt offerings and your sacrifices, I will not receive them," and so forth, in a long passage quoted at length. And again

Jeremiah 7, 21-22 : Gather your flesh and your sacrifices and eat, for neither concerning sacrifices nor drink offerings did I command your fathers in the day that I took them by the hand to lead them out of Egypt.[1]

Next as to circumcision and the Sabbath. " You need a second circumcision," says Justin, " and yet you glory in the flesh ; the new law bids you keep a perpetual Sabbath, while you idle for one day and suppose you are pious in so doing ; you do not understand why it was enjoined upon you. And, if you eat unleavened bread, you say you have fulfilled the will of God."[2] Even by Moses, who gave the law, God cried " You shall circumcise the hardness of your hearts and stiffen your necks no more " ;[3] and Jeremiah long afterwards said the same more than once.[4] On the Sabbath question, Tertullian and the others distinguished two Sabbaths, an eternal and a temporal,[5] citing :—

---

[1] *Trypho*, 22. [2] *Ibid.* 12. [3] *Deut.* 10, 16, 17 ; *Trypho*, 16.
[4] *Jerem.* 4, 4; 9, 25 ; *Trypho*, 28. [5] Tert. *adv. Jud.* 4.

Isaiah 1, 14 : My soul hates your sabbaths.
Ezekiel 22, 8 : Ye have profaned my sabbath.

The Jew is referred back to the righteous men of early days—
Was Adam circumcised, or did he keep the Sabbath ? or Abel,
or Noah, or Enoch, or Melchizedek ? Did Abraham keep the
Sabbath, or any of the patriarchs down to Moses ?[1] " But,"
rejoins the Jew, " was not Abraham circumcised ? Would not
the son of Moses have been strangled, had not his mother
circumcised him ? "[2]

To this the Christian had several replies. Circumcision
was merely given for a sign, as is shown by the fact that a
woman cannot receive it, " for God has made women as well
able as men to do what is just and right." There is no
righteousness in being of one sex rather than of the other.[3]
Circumcision then was imposed upon the Jews " to mark you
off from the rest of the nations and from us, that you alone
might suffer what now you are suffering, and so deservedly
suffering—that your lands should be desolate and your cities
burnt with fire, that strangers should eat your fruits before
your faces, and none of you set his foot in Jerusalem. For in
nothing are you known from other men apart from the circumcision of your flesh. None of you, I suppose, will venture to
say that God did not foresee what should come to pass. And
it is all deserved ; for you slew the Righteous one and his
prophets before him ; and now you reject and dishonour—so
far as you can—those who set their hopes on him and on the
Almighty God, maker of all things, who sent him ; and in your
synagogues you curse those who believe on Christ."[4] The
Sabbath was given to remind the Jews of God ; and restrictions
were laid on certain foods because of the Jewish proclivity to
forsake the knowledge of God.[5] In general, all these commands were called for by the sins of Israel,[6] they were signs
of judgment.

On the other hand the so-called Barnabas maintains that
the Jews never had understood their law at all. Fasts, feasts

---

[1] Justin, *Trypho*, 19 ; Tert. *adv. Jud.* 2 ; Cyprian, *Testim.* I, 8. Tertullian had
to face a similar criticism of Christian life—was Abraham *baptized*? *de Bapt.* 13.

[2] Tert. *adv. Jud.* 3.   [3] *Trypho*, 23 ; Cyprian, *Testim.* I, 8.

[4] *Trypho*, 16 (slightly compressed).

[5] *Trypho*, 19, 20 ; cf. Tert. *adv. Jud.* 3.   [6] *Trypho*, 22.

and sacrifices were prescribed, not literally, but in a spiritual sense which the Jews had missed. The taboos on meats were not prohibitions of the flesh of weasels, hares and hyænas and so forth, but were allegoric warnings against fleshly lusts, to which ancient zoologists and modern Arabs have supposed these animals to be prone.[1] Circumcision was meant, as the prophets showed, to be that of the heart ; evil dæmons had misled the Jews into practising it upon the flesh.[2] The whole Jewish dispensation was a riddle, and of no value, unless it is understood as signifying Christianity.

This line of attack was open to the criticism that it robbed the religious history of Israel of all value whatever, and the stronger Apologists do not take it. They will allow the Jews to have been so far right in observing their law, but they insist that it had a higher sense also, which had been overlooked except by the great prophets. The law was a series of types and shadows, precious till the substance came, which the shadows foretold. That they were mere shadows is shown by the fact that Enoch walked with God and Abraham was the friend of God. For this could not have been, if the Jewish contention were true that without Sabbath and circumcision man cannot please God. Otherwise, either the God of Enoch was not the God of Moses—which was absurd ; or else God had changed his mind as to right and wrong—which was equally absurd.[3] No, the legislation of Moses was for a people and for a time ; it was not for mankind and eternity. It was a prophecy of a new legislator, who should repeal the carnal code and enact one that should be spiritual, final and eternal.[4] Here, following the writer to the Hebrews, the Apologists quote a great passage of Jeremiah, with the advantage (not always possible) of using it in the true sense in which it was written. " Behold ! the days come, saith the Lord, when I will make a new covenant with the house of Israel and with the house of Judah ; not that which I made with their fathers in the day when I took them by the hand to lead them out of Egypt ; which my covenant they brake, although I was an

---

[1] Barnabas, 10 ; cf. Pliny, *N.H.* 8, 218, on the hare ; and Plutarch, *de Iside et Osiride*, 353 F, 363 F, 376 E, 381 A (weasel), for similar zoology and symbolism. Clem. Alex. *Str.* ii, 67 ; v, 51 ; refers to this teaching of Barnabas (cf. *ib.* ii, 105).

[2] Barnabas, 9.　　　[3] *Trypho*, 23.　　　[4] *Ibid.* 11.

husband unto them, saith the Lord. But this shall be the covenant that I will make with the house of Israel: After those days, saith the Lord, I will put my law in their inward parts and write it in their hearts, and I will be their God and they shall be my people."[1]

With the law, the privilege of Israel passes away and the day of the Gentiles comes. It was foretold that Israel would not accept Christ—"their ears they have closed";[2] "they have not known nor understood";[3] "who is blind but my servants?"[4] "all these words shall be unto you as words of a book that is sealed."[5] "By Isaiah the prophet, God, knowing beforehand what you would do, cursed you thus";[6] and Justin cites Isaiah 3, 9-15, and 5, 18-25. Leah is the type of the synagogue and of the Jewish people and Rachel of "our church"; the eyes of Leah were weak, and so are the eyes of your soul—very weak.[7] No less was it prophesied that the Gentiles should believe on Christ—"in thee shall all tribes of the earth be blest"; "Behold! I have manifested him as a witness to the nations, a prince and a ruler to the races. Races which knew thee not shall call upon thee and peoples who were ignorant of thee shall take refuge with thee."[8]

"By David He said 'A people I knew not has served me, and hearkened to me with the hearing of the ear.' Let us, the Gentiles gathered together, glorify God," says Justin, "because he has visited us . . . for he is well pleased with the Gentiles, and receives our sacrifices with more pleasure than yours. What have I to do with circumcision, who have the testimony of God? What need of that baptism to me, baptized with the holy spirit? These things, I think, will persuade even the slow of understanding. For these are not arguments devised by me, nor tricked out by human skill,—nay! this was the theme of David's lyre, this the glad news Isaiah brought, that Zechariah proclaimed and Moses wrote. Do you recognize them, Trypho? They are in your books—no! not yours, but ours—for we believe them—and you, when you

---

[1] *Jerem.* 31, 31 ; *Trypho*, 11 ; Tert. *adv. Jud.* 3.
[2] *Is.* 6, 10 ; *Trpyho* 12 ; Cyprian, *Testim.* i, 3.
[3] *Ps.* 82, 5 ; *Trypho*, 124 ; Cyprian, *Testim.* i, 3.
[4] *Is.* 42, 19 ; *Trypho*, 123, where the plural is used.
[5] *Is.* 29, 11 ; Cyprian, *Testim.* i, 4.   [6] *Trypho*, 133.   [7] *Trypho*, 134.
[8] Cyprian, *Testim.* i, 21 ; Justin, *Trypho*, 12 ; Tert. *adv. Marc.* iii, 20.

read, do not understand the mind that is in them." [1] And with that Justin passes on to discuss whether Jesus is the Messiah. Such a passage raises the question as to how far he is reporting an actual conversation. In his 80th chapter he says to Trypho that he will make a book (σύνταξις) of their conversation—of the whole of it—to the best of his ability, faithfully recording all that he concedes to Trypho. Probably he takes Plato's liberty to develop what was said—unless indeed the dialogue is from beginning to end merely a literary form imposed upon a thesis. In that case, it must be owned that Justin manages to give a considerable suggestion of life to Trypho's words.

But, even if the law be temporary, and the Sabbath spiritual, if Israel is to be rejected and the Gentiles chosen, we are still far from being assured on the warrant of the Old Testament that Jesus is the Messiah, who shall accomplish this great change. Why he rather than any of the "ten thousand others" who might much more plausibly be called the Messiah ? [2]

To prove the Messiahship of Jesus, a great system of Old Testament citations was developed, the origins of which are lost to us. Paul certainly applied Scripture to Jesus in a free way of his own, though he is not more fanciful in quotation than his contemporaries. But he never sought to base the Christian faith on a scheme of texts. Lactantius, writing about 300 A.D., implies that Jesus is the author of the system. " He abode forty days with them and interpreted the Scriptures, which up to that time had been obscure and involved." [3] Something of the kind is suggested by Luke (24, 27). But it is obvious that the whole method is quite alien to the mind and style of Jesus, in spite of quotations in the vein of the apologists which the evangelists here and there have attributed to him.

We may discover two great canons in the operations of the Apologists. In the first place, they seek to show that all things prophesied of the Messiah were fulfilled in Jesus of Nazareth ; and, secondly, that everything which befel Jesus was prophesied of the Messiah. These canons need only to be stated to show the sheer impossibility of the enterprise to any-

---

[1] *Trypho*, 29.   [2] *c. Cels.* ii, 28.   [3] Lactantius, *de mort. persec.* 2.

one who attaches meaning to words. But in the early centuries of our era there was little disposition with Jew or Greek to do this where those books were concerned, whose age and beauty gave them a peculiar hold upon the mind. In each case the preconception had grown up, as about the myths of Isis, for example, that such books were in some way sacred and inspired. The theory gave men an external authority, but it presented some difficulties; for, both in Homer and in *Genesis* as in the Egyptian myths, there were stories repugnant to every idea of the divine nature which a philosophic mind could entertain. They were explained away by the allegoric method. Plutarch shows how the grossest features of the Isis legend have subtle and spiritual meanings and were never meant to be taken literally—that the myths are *logoi* in fact; and Philo vindicates the Old Testament in the same way.[1] The whole procedure was haphazard and unscientific; it closely resembled the principles used by Artemidorus for the interpretation of dreams—a painful analogy. But, in the absence of any kind of historic sense, it was perhaps the only way in which the continuity of religious thought could then be maintained. It is not surprising in view of the prevalence of allegory that the Christians used it—they could hardly do anything else. Thus with the fatal aid of allegory, the double thesis of the Apologists became easier and easier to maintain.

The most accessible illustration of this line of apology is to be found in the second chapter of *Matthew*. We may set out in parallel columns the events in the life of Jesus and the prophecies which they fulfil.

(*a*) The Virgin-Birth.	*Isaiah* 7, 14 : Behold a virgin shall conceive.
(*b*) Bethlehem.	*Micah* 5, 2 : And thou, Bethlehem, etc.
(*c*) The Flight into Egypt.	*Hosea* 11, 1 : Out of Egypt have I called my son.
(*d*) The Murder of the children.	*Jerem.* 31, 15 : Rachel weeping.
(*e*) Nazareth.	*Judges* 13, 5 : A Nazarene.

[1] Tertullian lays down the canon (*adv. Marc.* iii, 5) *pleraque figurate portenduntur per ænigmata et allegorias et parabolas, aliter intelligenda quam scripta sunt*; but (*de resurr. carnis*, 20) *non omnia imagines sed et veritates, nec omnia umbræ sed et corpora, e.g.* the Virgin-birth is not foretold in figure.

It is hardly unfair to say that the man who cited these passages in these connexions had no idea whatever of their original meaning, even where he quotes them correctly.

Here is a fuller scheme taken from the *Apology* which Justin addressed to the Emperor Antoninus Pius. (The numbers on the left refer to the chapter in the first *Apology*.)

32. Jesus Christ foretold by Moses.	*Gen.* 49, 10 f : (the blessing of Judah). *Numbers* 24, 17 : There shall dawn a star, etc.
Jesus Christ foretold by Isaiah.	*Isaiah* 11, 1 : the rod of Jesse, etc.
33. Jesus Christ to be born of a virgin.	*Is.* 7, 14 : (the sign to Ahaz).
34. Jesus Christ to be born at Bethlehem.	*Micah* 5, 2 : Thou, Bethlehem, etc.
35. The triumphal entry into Jerusalem.	*Zech.* 9, 9 : Thy king cometh riding on an ass, etc.
The Crucifixion: the Cross.	*Is.* 9, 6 : The government upon his shoulders. *Is.* 65, 2 : I have stretched out my hands, etc.
The Crucifixion : the mockery.	*Is.* 58, 2 : They ask me for judgment, etc.
The Crucifixion : the nails and the casting of lots.	*Psalm* 22, 16, 18 : They pierced my feet and my hands ; they cast lots upon my raiment.
38. The Crucifixion : the scourging.	*Is.* 50, 6-8 : I gave my back to the lashes and my cheeks to blows, etc.
The Crucifixion : the mocking.	*Ps.* 22, 7 : they wagged the head, saying, etc.
The Crucifixion : the resurrection.	*Ps.* 3, 5 : I slept and slumbered and I rose up ($\dot{\alpha}\nu\acute{\epsilon}\sigma\tau\eta\nu$) because the Lord laid hold of me.

39. The sending of the twelve Apostles.	*Is.* 2, 3 f.: Out of Sion shall go forth the law.
40. The proclamation of the Gospel. Christ, Pilate, the Jews and Herod.	*Ps.* 19, 2-5 : Day unto day, etc. *Psalms* 1 and 2 : cited *in extenso.*
41. Christ to reign after the Crucifixion.	I *Chron.* 16, 23, 25-31 : (a psalm). Cf. *Ps.* 96, 1, 2, 4-10, with ending : " The Lord hath reigned from the tree."
45. The Ascension.	*Ps.* 110, 1-3 : Sit thou at my right hand, etc.
47. The desolation of Jerusalem.	*Is.* 64, 10-12 : Sion has become desert, etc. *Is.* 1, 7, and *Jer.* 50, 3 : Their land is desert.
48. The miracles of Christ.	*Is.* 35, 5, 6 : The lame shall leap ... the dead shall rise and walk, etc.
Christ's death.	*Is.* 57, 1 f.: Behold, how the Just Man has perished, etc.
49. The Gentiles to find Christ but not the Jews.	*Is.* 65, 1-3 : I was visible to them that asked not for me ... I spread out my hands to a disobedient people.
50. Christ's humiliation and the glorious second advent.	*Is.* 53, 12 : For that they gave his soul to death ... he shall be exalted. *Is.* 52, 13-53, 8 : ... he was wounded, etc.
51. His sufferings, origin, reign and ascension. His second coming.	*Is.* 53, 8-12. "Jeremiah " = *Daniel* 7, 13, as it were a son of man cometh upon the clouds and his angels with him.

52. The final resurrection.	*Ezek.* 37, 7-8 : Bone shall be joined to bone.
	Is. 45, 23 : Every knee shall bow to the Lord.
	Is. 66, 24 : The worm shall not sleep nor the fire be quenched.
	Also a composite quotation with phrases mingled from Isaiah and Zechariah, attributed to the latter.
53. More Gentiles than Jews will believe.	*Is.* 54, 1 : Rejoice, O barren, etc.
	"Isaiah " = *Jerem.* 9, 26 : Israel uncircumcised in heart.
60. The Cross foretold in the brazen serpent.	*Num.* 21, 8 : If ye look at this type($τύπῳ$) I believe ye shall be saved in it ($ἐν αὐτῷ$).
61. Baptism.	*Is.* 1, 16 : Wash you . . . I will whiten as wool.

What in the *Apology* is a bare outline, is developed at great length and with amazing ingenuity in the dialogue with Trypho. We may begin with the question of a "God beside the Creator."

When Moses wrote in *Genesis* (1, 26) " And God said, 'Let us make man in our image after our likeness,'" and again (3, 22) " And the Lord God said, 'Behold the man is become as one of us,'"[1] why did he use the plural, unless there is a God beside God? Again, when Sodom is destroyed why does the holy text say " The Lord rained upon Sodom and Gomorrha sulphur and fire from the Lord from heaven "?[2] And again in the *Psalms* (110) what is meant by " The Lord said unto my Lord "?[3] and by " Thy throne, O God, is for ever and ever . . . therefore God, thy God, hath anointed thee with the oil of gladness above thy fellows? "[4]

The Old Testament abounds in theophanies, which are

---

[1] *Trypho*, 62, 129 ; Barnabas, 5, 5 ; Tert. *adv. Prax.* 12.
[2] *Trypho*, 56.   [3] *Ibid.* 56.   [4] *Ibid.* 56.

brought up in turn. Justin cites the three men who appeared
to Abraham—"they were angels," says Trypho, and a long
argument follows to show from the passage that one of them
is not to be explained as an angel,[1] nor of course as the Creator
of all things. Trypho owns this. Justin pauses at his suggestion to discuss the meal which Abraham had served, but is
soon caught up with the words : " Now, come, show us that
this God who appeared to Abraham and is the servant of God,
the Maker of all, was born of a virgin, and became, as you
said, a man of like passions with all men." But Justin has
more evidence to unfold before he reaches that stage. Without
following the discussion as it sways from point to point, we may
take the passage in which he recapitulates this line of argument.
" I think I have said enough, so that, when my God says ' God
went up from Abraham,' or ' The Lord spoke to Moses,' or
' The Lord descended to see the tower which the sons of men
had built,' or ' The Lord shut the ark of Noah from without,'
you will not suppose the unbegotten God Himself went down
or went up. For the ineffable Father and Lord of all neither
comes anywhere, nor ' walks ' [as in the garden of Eden], nor
sleeps, nor rises, but abides in his own region wherever it is,
seeing keenly and hearing keenly, but not with eyes or ears,
but by power unspeakable ; and he surveys all things and
knows all things, and none of us escapes his notice ; nor does
he move, nor can space contain him, no, nor the whole
universe, him, who was before the universe was made."[2]

Who then was it who walked in the garden, who wrestled with
Jacob, who appeared in arms to Joshua, who spoke with Moses and
with Abraham, who shut Noah into the ark, who was the fourth
figure in the fiery furnace ? Scripture gives us a key. Can the
Jew say, who it is whom Ezekiel calls the "angel of great counsel;"
and the " man " ; whom Daniel describes " as the Son of man " ;
whom Isaiah called " child," and David " Christ " and " God
adored " ; whom Moses called " Joseph " and " Jacob " and
" the star " ; whom Zechariah called " the daystar " ; whom

---

[1] *Trypho*, 56, 57.

[2] *Trypho*, 127. Tert. *adv. Marc.* ii, 27. *Quæcunque exigitis deo digna, habebuntur
in patre invisibili incongressibilique et placido et, ut ita dixerim, philosophorum deo.
Quæcunque autem ut indigna reprehenditis, deputabuntur in filio*, etc. Cf. on the dis
tinction Tert. *adv. Prax.* 14 ff. Cf. the language of Celsus on God "descending," see
p. 248.

Isaiah again called the "sufferer" ($\pi\alpha\theta\eta\tau\acute{o}s$), "Jacob" and "Israel"; whom others have named "the Rod," "the Flower," "the Chief Corner-stone" and "the Son of God"?[1] The answer is more clearly given by Solomon in the eighth chapter of *Proverbs*—it is the Divine Wisdom, to whom all these names apply. When it is said "Let *us* make man," it is to be understood that the Ineffable communicated his design to his Wisdom, his Logos or Son, and the Son made man. The Son rained upon Sodom the fire and brimstone from the Father. It was the Son who appeared to men in all the many passages cited—the Son, Christ the Lord, God and Son of God—inseparable and unseverable from the Father, His Wisdom and His Word and His Might ($\delta\acute{u}\nu\alpha\mu\iota s$).[2]

But, while all this might be accepted by a Jew, it still seemed to Trypho that it was "paradoxical, and foolish, too," to say that Christ could be God before all the ages, and then tolerate to be born a man, and yet "not a man of men." The offence of the Cross also remained. The Apologist began by explaining the mysteries of the two comings of Christ, first in humiliation, and afterwards in glory, as Jacob prophesied in his last words.[3] For the First Coming Tertullian quotes Isaiah—" he is led as a sheep to the slaughter"; and the *Psalms*—"made a little lower than the angels," "a worm and not a man"; while the Second Coming is to be read of in Daniel and the forty-fifth *Psalm*, and in the more awful passage of Zechariah "and then they shall know him whom they pierced."[4] The paschal lamb is a type of the First Coming—especially as it was to be roasted whole and trussed like a cross; and the two goats of *Leviticus* (16) are types of the two Comings.[5]

"And now," says Justin, "I took up the argument again to show that he was born of a virgin, and that it had been prophesied by Isaiah that he should be born of a virgin; and I again recited the prophecy itself. This is it: 'And the Lord said moreover unto Ahaz, saying: 'Ask for thyself a sign from the Lord thy God in the depth or in the height. And Ahaz

---

[1] *Trypho*, 126. Other titles are quoted by Justin, *Trypho*, 61.
[2] *Trypho*, 128. Cf. Tertullian, *adv. Marc.* ii, 27, *Ille est qui descendit, ille qui interrogat, ille qui postulat, ille qui jurat*; *adv. Prax.* 15, *Filius itaque est qui.* . . . .
[3] *Gen.* 49, 8-12; *Trypho*, 52, 53; *Apol.* i, 32; Cyprian, *Testim.* i, 21.
[4] Tert. *adv. Jud.* 14. [5] *Trypho*, 40; Tert. *adv. Jud.* 14; Barnabas, 7.

said : I will not ask nor tempt the Lord. And Isaiah said :
Hear ye then, O house of David ! Is it a little thing with you
to strive with men ? and how will ye strive with the Lord ?
Therefore shall the Lord himself give you a sign. Behold, the
virgin shall conceive and bear a son, and they shall call his
name Emmanuel. Butter and honey shall he eat. Before he
shall either have knowledge or choose evil, he shall choose
good ; because, before the child knows evil or good, he refuses
evil to choose good. Because, before the child knows to call
father or mother, he shall take the power of Damascus and the
spoils of Samaria before the King of the Assyrians. And the
land shall be taken, which thou shalt bear hardly from before
the face of two kings. But God will bring upon thee, and
upon thy people, and upon the house of thy father, days which
have never come, from the day when Ephraim removed from
Judah the King of the Assyrians.' And I added, ' That, in the
family of Abraham according to the flesh, none has ever yet
been born of a virgin, or spoken of as so born, except our
Christ, is manifest to all.' " It may be noted that the passage
is not only misquoted, but is a combination of clauses from
two distinct chapters.[1] The explanation is perhaps that Justin
found it so in a manual of proof-texts and did not consult the
original. Similar misquotations in other authors have suggested
the same explanation.

"Trypho rejoined : ' The scripture has not : Behold the
virgin shall conceive and bear a son ; but : Behold the young
woman shall conceive and bear a son : and the rest as you
said. The whole prophecy was spoken of Hezekiah and was
fulfilled of him. In the myths of the Greeks it is said that
Perseus was born of Danae, when she was a virgin—after their
so-called Zeus had come upon her in the form of gold. You
ought to be ashamed to tell the same story as they do. You
would do better to say this Jesus was born a man of men, and
—if you show from the Scriptures that he is the Christ—say
that it was by his lawful and perfect life that he was counted
worthy of being chosen as Christ. Don't talk miracles of that
kind, or you will be proved to talk folly beyond even that of
the Greeks.' "[2]

Trypho has the Hebrew text behind him, which says

---

[1] *Trypho*, 66. Isaiah vii and viii.   [2] *Trypho*, 67.

nothing about a virgin, though the Septuagint has the word. The sign given to Ahaz has a close parallel in a prophecy of Muhammad. Before he became known, an old man foretold that a great prophet should come, and on being challenged for a sign he pointed to a boy lying in rugs by the camp-fire—" That boy should *see* the prophet"; and he did. Isaiah's sign is much the same ; a young woman shall conceive and have a son, and before that son is two or three years old, Damascus and Syria will fall before the King of Assyria.

But Justin and the Apologists are not to be diverted. As for Danae, the Devil (διάβολος) has there anticipated the fulfilment of God's prophecy, as in many other instances, *e.g.* :— Dionysus rode an ass, he rose from the dead and ascended to heaven ; Herakles is a parody of the verse in *Psalm* xix—the strong man rejoicing to run a race, a Messianic text ; Æsculapius raised the dead ; and the cave of Mithras is Daniel's " stone cut without hands from the great mountains." " I do not believe your teachers; they will not admit that the seventy elders of Ptolemy, King of Egypt, translated well, but they try to translate for themselves. And I should like you to know that they have cut many passages out of the versions made by Ptolemy's elders which prove expressly that this man, who was crucified, was prophesied of as God and man, crucified and slain. I know that all your race deny this ; so, in discussions of this kind I do not quote those passages, but I have recourse to such as come from what you still acknowledge." [1]   The objection to the rendering " young woman " is that it completely nullifies the sign given to Ahaz, for children are born of young women every day—" what would really be a sign and would give confidence to mankind,—to wit, that the firstborn of all creations should take flesh and really be born a child of a virgin womb—*that* was what he proclaimed beforehand by the prophetic spirit." [2]

The whole story is parable. It would be absurd to suppose that an infant could be a warrior and reduce great states. The spoils are really the gifts of the Magi, as is indicated by passages in Zechariah (" he shall gather all the strength of the peoples round about, gold and silver," 14, 14) and the seventy second *Psalm* (" Kings of the Arabs and of Saba shall bring

[1] *Trypho*, 71.   [2] *Trypho*, 84.   Cf. **Tert.** *adv. Jud.* 9 = *adv. Marc.* iii, 13.

gifts to him; and to him shall be given gold from the East"). Samaria again is a common synonym with the prophets for idolatry. Damascus means the revolt of the Magi from the evil dæmon who misdirected their arts to evil. The King of Assyria stands, says Justin, for King Herod, and so says Tertullian, writing against Marcion, though in the tract *Against the Jews* (if it is Tertullian's) he says the devil is intended.[1] The usual passages from Micah and Jeremiah are cited to add Bethlehem and the Murder of the infants to the prophetic story.

"At this Trypho, with some hint of annoyance, but overawed by the Scriptures, as his face showed, said to me: 'God's words are holy, but your expositions [or translations] are artificial—or blasphemous, I should say.'"[2]

To complete the proof, it is shown that the very name of Jesus was foretold. When Moses changed the name of his successor from *Auses* to *Jesus*, it was a prophecy, as Scripture shows. "The Lord said unto Moses: Say to this people, Behold I send my angel before thy face that he may guard thee in the way, that he may lead thee into the land that I have prepared for thee. Give heed unto him . . . for he will not let thee go, for my name is in him."[3] This is confirmed by Zechariah's account of the High Priest Joshua. Furthermore, the chronology of the book of Daniel, when carefully worked out, proves to have contained the prediction of the precise date at which Christ should come, and at that precise date Christ came.

Barnabas discovers another prophecy of Jesus in an unlikely place. "Learn, children of love," he says, "that Abraham, who first gave circumcision, looked forward in spirit unto Jesus, when he circumcised, for he received dogmata in three letters. For it saith: And Abraham circumcised of his house men 18 and 300. What then was the knowledge given unto him? Mark that it says 18 first, and then after a pause 300. 18 [IH in Greek notation] there thou hast Jesus. And because the cross in T [= 300 in Greek notation] was to have grace, it

---

[1] *Trypho*, 77 : Tert. *adv. Jud.* 9=*adv. Marc.* iii, 13; both referring to *Psalm* 71.

[2] *Trypho*, 79.   [3] *Trypho*, 75 ; *Exodus* 23, 20.

saith 300 as well. It shows Jesus in the two letters, and in the one the cross." [1]

We now reach the prophecies of the cross, and, as the method is plain, a few references may suffice, taken this time from Tertullian (c. 10) :—

Genesis 22, 6 : Isaac carrying the wood for the sacrifice of himself.

Genesis 37, 28 : Joseph sold by his brethren.

Deuteronomy 33, 17 : Moses' blessing of Joseph. (The unicorn's horns, with some arrangement, form a cross : cf. *Psalm* 22).

Exodus 17, 11 : Moses with his arms spread wide.

Numbers 21, 9 : The brazen serpent.

Psalm 96, 10 : The Lord hath reigned *from the tree, e ligno* (though the Jews have cut out the last words).

Isaiah 9, 6 : The government upon his shoulder.

Jeremiah 11, 19 : Let us cast wood (*lignum*) into his bread.

Isaiah 53, 8, 9 : For the transgression of my people is he stricken . . . and his sepulture is taken from the midst (*i.e.* the resurrection).

Amos 8, 9 : I will cause the sun to go down at noon.

For a long time before Justin was done with his exposition, Trypho was silent—the better part, perhaps, in all controversy. At last, writes Justin, " I finished. Trypho said nothing for a while, and then he said, ' You see, we came to the controversy unprepared. Still, I own, I am greatly pleased to have met you, and I think my friends have the same feeling. For we have found more than we expected,—or anyone could have expected. If we could do it at more length, we might be better profited by looking into the passages themselves. But, since you are on the point of sailing and expect to embark every day now,—be sure you think of us as friends, if you go.' " [2] So, with kindly feelings, Trypho went away unconvinced. And there were others, as clear of mind, who were as little convinced,—Marcion, for instance, and Celsus. " The more reasonable among Jews and Christians," says Celsus, " try to allegorize them [the Scriptures], but they are beyond being

---

[1] Barnabas, 9, 8 (the subject of ' saith ' ay in each case be ' he '). Clement of Alexandria cites this and adds a mystic and mathematical account of this suggestive figure 318, *Strom.* vi, 84.   [2] *Trypho*, 142.

allegorized and are nothing but sheer mythology of the silliest type. The supposed allegories that have been made are more disgraceful than the myths and more absurd, in their endeavour to string together what never can in any way be harmonized—it is folly positively wonderful for its utter want of perception." [1] The modern reader may not be so ready as Origen was to suggest that Celsus probably had Philo in mind.[2]

It is clear that, in the endeavour to give Christianity a historical background and a prophetic warrant, the Apologists lost all perspective.[3] The compelling personality of Jesus receded behind the vague figure of the Christ of prophecy ; and, in their pre-occupation with what they themselves called "types and shadows," men stepped out of the sunlight into the shade and hardly noticed the change. Yet there is still among the best of them the note of love of Jesus—"do not speak evil of the crucified," pleads Justin, "nor mock at his stripes, whereby all may be healed, as *we* have been healed."[4] And after all it was an instinct for the truth and universal significance of Jesus that carried them away. He must be eternal ; and they, like the men of their day, thought much of the beginning and the end of creation, and perhaps found it easier than we do,—certainly more natural,—to frame schemes under which the Eternal Mind might manifest itself. Eschatology, purpose, foreknowledge, pervade their religious thought, and they speak with a confidence which the centuries since the Renaissance have made more and more impossible for us, who find it hard enough to be sure of the fact without adventuring ourselves in the possibilities that lie around it. None the less the centre of interest was the same for them as for us—what *is* the significance of Jesus of Nazareth ? For them the facts of his life and of his mind had often less value than the fancy that they fulfilled prophecy ; Celsus said outright that the Christians altered them, and there is some evidence that, in the accommodation of prophecy and history,

---

[1] Celsus *ap.* Orig. *c. Cels.* iv, 50, 51.

[2] Especially when he finds Celsus referring to the dialogue of Jason and Papiscus as " more worthy of pity and hatred than of laughter " ; *c. Cels.* iv, 52.

[3] Porphyry (cited by Euseb. *E.H.* vi, 19), says they made riddles of what was perfectly plain in Moses, their expositions would not hang together, and they cheated their own critical faculty, τὸ κριτικὸν τῆς ψυχῆς καταγοητεύσαντες.

[4] *Trypho,* 137.

the latter was sometimes over-developed. For us, the danger is the opposite ; we risk losing sight of the eternal significance in our need of seeing clearly the historic lineaments.

In the conflict of religions, Christianity had first to face Judaism, and, though the encounter left its record upon the conquering faith, it secured its freedom from the yoke of the past. It gained background and the broadening of the historic imagination. It made the prophets and psalmists of Israel a permanent and integral part of Christian literature— and in all these ways it became more fit to be the faith of mankind, as it deepened its hold upon the universal religious experience. Yet it did so at the cost of a false method which has hampered it for centuries, and of a departure (for too long a time) from the simplicity and candour of the mind of Jesus. In seeking to recover that mind to-day we commit ourselves to the belief that it is sufficient, and that, when we have rid ourselves of all that in the course of ages has obscured the great personality, in proportion as we regain his point of view, we shall find once more (in the words of a far distant age) that his spirit will guide us into all truth.

CHAPTER VII

"GODS OR ATOMS?"

IN the first two centuries of our era a great change came over the ancient world. A despised and traditional religion, under the stimulus of new cults coming from the East, revived and re-asserted its power over the minds of men. Philosophy, grown practical in its old age, forsook its youthful enthusiasm for the quest of truth, and turned aside to the regulation of conduct, by means of maxims now instead of inspiration, and finally, as we have seen, to apology for the ancient faith of the fathers. Its business now was to reconcile its own monotheistic dogma with popular polytheistic practice. It was perhaps this very reconciliation that threw open the door for the glowing monotheism of the disciples of Jesus; but, whatever the cause, Christianity quickly spread over the whole Roman Empire. We are apt to wonder to-day at the great political and national developments that have altered the whole aspect of Europe since the French Revolution, and to reflect rather idly on their rapidity. Yet the past has its own stories of rapid change, and not the least striking of them is the disappearance of that world of thought which we call Classical. By 180 A.D. nearly every distinctive mark of classical antiquity is gone—the old political ideas, the old philosophies, the old literatures, and much else with them. Old forms and names remain—there are still consuls and archons, poets and philosophers, but the atmosphere is another, and the names have a new meaning, if they have any at all. But the mere survival of the names hid for many the fact that they were living in a new era.

In the reign of Marcus Aurelius, however, the signs of change became more evident, and men grew conscious that some transformation of the world was in progress. A great plague, the scanty records of which only allow us to speak in vague terms of an immense reduction in population[1]—barbarism active upon the frontier of an Empire not so well able as it had fancied to defend itself—superstitions, Egyptian and Jewish, diverting men from the ordinary ways of civic duty—such were some of the symptoms that men marked. Under the weight of absurdity, quietism and individualism, the state seemed to be sinking, and all that freedom of mind which was the distinctive boast of Hellenism was rapidly being lost.

It happens that, while the historical literature of the period has largely perished, a number of authors survive, who from their various points of view deal with what is our most immediate subject—the conflict of religions. Faith, doubt, irritation and fatalism are all represented. The most conspicuous men of letters of the age are undoubtedly the Emperor Marcus Aurelius himself and his two brilliant contemporaries, Lucian of Samosata and Apuleius of Madaura.[2] Celsus, a man of mind as powerful as any of the three, survives in fragments, but fragments ample enough to permit of re-construction. Among the Christians too there was increased literary activity, but Tertullian and Clement will suffice for our purpose.

Though not in his day regarded as a man of letters, it is yet in virtue of his writing that Marcus Aurelius survives. His journal, with the title that tells its nature—" To Himself," is to-day perhaps the most popular book of antiquity with those whose first concern is not literature. It is translated again and again, and it is studied. The peculiar mind of the solitary Emperor has made him, as Mr F. W. H. Myers put it, "the saint and exemplar of Agnosticism." Meditative, tender and candid, yet hesitant and so far ineffectual, he is sensitive to so much that is positive and to so much that is negative, that the diary, in which his character is most intimately revealed, gives him a place of his own in the hearts of men perplext in the extreme. He is a man who neither believes, nor disbelieves,—"either gods or atoms "[3] seems to be the necessary antithesis, and there is so much to be said both for

---

[1] On the other hand see a very interesting passage in Tertullian, *de Anima*, 30, on the progress of the world in civilization, and population outstripping Nature, while plague, famine, war, etc., are looked on as *tonsura insolescentis generis humani*.

[2] Marcus Aurelius was born about 121 A.D. and died in 180. The other two were born in or about 125.

[3] *e.g.* viii, 17.

and against each of the alternatives that decision is impossible. He is attracted by the conception of Providence, but he hesitates to commit himself. There are arguments—at least of the kind that rest on probability—in favour of immortality, but they are insufficient to determine the matter. In his public capacity he became famous for the number and magnificence of his sacrifices to the gods of the state ; he owns in his journal his debt to the gods for warnings given in dreams, but he suspects at times that they may not exist. Meanwhile he persecutes the Christians for their disloyalty to the state. Their stubborn convictions were so markedly in contrast with his own wavering mind that he could not understand them— perhaps their motive was bravado, he thought ; they were too theatrical altogether ; their pose recalled the tragedies composed by the pupils of the rhetoricians—large language with nothing behind it.[1]

In the absence of any possibility of intellectual certainty, Marcus fell back upon conduct. Here his want of originality and of spiritual force was less felt, for conduct has tolerably well-established rules of neighbourliness, purity, good temper, public duty and the like. His Stoic guides, too, might in this region help him to follow with more confidence the voice of his own pure and delicate conscience—the conscience of a saint and a quietist rather than that of a man of action. Yet even in the realm of conduct he is on the whole ineffectual. Pure, truthful, kind, and brave he is, but he does not believe enough to be great. He is called to be a statesman and an administrator ; he does not expect much outcome from all his energies, and he preaches to himself the necessity of patience with his prospective failure to achieve anything beyond the infinitesimal.

"Ever the same are the cycles of the universe, up and down, for ever and for ever. Either the intelligence of the Whole puts itself in motion for each separate effect—in which case accept the result it gives ; or else it did so once for all, and everything is sequence, one thing in another . . . [The text is doubtful for a line] . . . In a word, either God, and all goes well ; or all at random—live not thou at random.

"A moment, and earth will cover us all ; then it too in its turn will change ; and what it changes to, will change again

---

[1] The one passage is in xi, 3.

and again for ever ; and again change after change to infinity. The waves of change and transformation—if a man think of them and of their speed, he will despise everything mortal.

" The universal cause is like a winter torrent ; it carries all before it. How cheap then these poor statesmen, these who carry philosophy into practical affairs, as they fancy—poor diminutive creatures. Drivellers. Man, what then ? Do what now Nature demands. Start, if it be given thee, and look not round to see if any will know. Hope not for Plato's Republic ;[1] but be content if the smallest thing advance ; to compass that one issue count no little feat.

" Who shall change one of their dogmata [the regular word of Epictetus]? And without a change of dogmata, what is there but the slavery of men groaning and pretending to obey ? Go now, and talk of Alexander, and Philip and Demetrius of Phalerum ; whether they saw the will of Nature and schooled themselves, is their affair ; if they played the tragic actor, no one has condemned me to copy them. Simplicity and modesty are the work of philosophy ; do not lead me astray into vanity.

" Look down from above on the countless swarms of men, their countless initiations, and their varied voyage in storm and calm, their changing combinations, as they come into being, meet, and pass out of being. Think too of the life lived by others of old, of the life that shall be lived by others after thee, of the life now lived among the barbarian nations ; and of how many have never heard thy name, and how many will at once forget it, and how many may praise thee now perhaps but will very soon blame thee ; and how neither memory is of any account, nor glory, nor anything else at all. . . .

"The rottenness of the material substance of every individual thing—water, dust, bones, stench. . . . And this breathing element is another of the same, changing from this to that. . . .

" Either the gods have no power, or they have power. If they have not, why pray ? If they have, why not pray for deliverance from the fear, or the desire, or the pain, which the thing causes, rather than for the withholding or the giving of the particular thing ? For certainly, if they can co-operate with men, it is for these purposes they can co-operate. But perhaps

---

[1] Or, the English equivalent, Utopia.

thou wilt say, The gods have put all these in my own power. Then is it not better to use what is in thine own power and be free, than to be set on what is not in thy power—a slave and contemptible? And who told thee that the gods do not help us even to what is in our own power?"[1]

This handful of short passages all from the same place, with a few omitted, may be taken as representing very fairly the mind of Marcus Aurelius. The world was his to rule, and he felt it a duty to remember how slight a thing it was. This was not the temper of Alexander or of Cæsar,—of men who make mankind, and who, by their belief in men and in the power of their own ideas to lift men to higher planes of life, actually do secure that advance is made,—and that advance not the smallest. Yet he speaks of Alexander as a "tragic actor."[1] For a statesman, the attitude of Marcus is little short of betrayal. He worked, he ruled, he endowed, he fought—he was pure, he was conscientious, he was unselfish—but he did not believe, and he was ineffectual. The Germans it might have been beyond any man's power to repel at that day, but even at home Marcus was ineffectual. His wife and his son were by-words. He had almost a morbid horror of defilement from men and women of coarse minds,—a craving too for peace and sympathy; he shrank into himself, condoned, ignored. Among his bene-factors he does not mention Hadrian, who really gave him the Empire—and it is easy to see why. In everything the two are a contrast. Hadrian's personal vices and his greatness as a ruler, as a man handling men and moving among ideas[3]— these were impossible for Marcus.

Nor was the personal religion of this pure and candid spirit a possible one for mankind. "A genuine eternal Gospel," wrote Renan of this diary of Marcus, "the book of the *Thoughts* will never grow old, for it affirms no dogma. The Gospel has grown old in certain parts; Science no longer allows us to admit the naive conception of the supernatural which is its base. . . . Yet Science might destroy God and the soul, and the book of the *Thoughts* would remain young in its life and truth."

---

[1] Marcus Aurelius, ix, 28-40, with omissions. Phrases have been borrowed from the translations of Mr Long and Dr Rendall.

[2] This sheds some light on his comparison of the Christians to actors, xi, 3.

[3] Cf. Tertullian, *Apol.* 5, *Hadrianus omnium curiositatum explorator.*

Renan is right; when Science, or anything else, " destroys God
and the soul," there is no Gospel but that of Marcus; and yet for
men it is impossible; and it is not young—it is senile. Duty
without enthusiasm, hope or belief—belief in man, of course,
for " God and the soul " are by hypothesis " destroyed "—duty,
that is, without object, reason or result, it is a magnificent fancy,
and yet one recurs to the criticism that Marcus passed upon
the Christians. Is there not a hint of the school about this?
Is it not possible that the simpler instincts of men,—instincts
with a history as ludicrous as Anthropologists sometimes sketch
for us,—may after all come nearer the truth of things than
semi-Stoic reflexion? At all events the instincts have ruled the
world so far with the co-operation of Reason, and are as yet
little inclined to yield their rights to their colleague. They
have never done so without disaster.

The world did not accept Marcus as a teacher. Men readily
recognized his high character, but for a thousand years and
more nobody dreamed of taking him as a guide—nobody, that
is, outside the schools. For the world it was faith or unbelief,
and the two contemporaries already mentioned represent the
two poles to which the thoughts of men gravitated, who were
not yet ready for a cleavage with the past.

" I am a Syrian from the Euphrates," [1] wrote Lucian of himself; and elsewhere he has a playful protest against a historian
of his day, magnificently ignorant of Eastern geography, who
" has taken up my native Samosata, and shifted it, citadel,
walls and all, into Mesopotamia," and by this new feat of
colonization has apparently turned him into a Parthian or
Mesopotamian.[2] Samosata lay actually in Commagene, and
there Lucian spent his boyhood talking Syriac, his native
language.[3] He was born about 125 A.D. His family were
poor, and as soon as he left school, the question of a trade was
at once raised, for even a boy's earnings would be welcome.
At school he had had a trick of scraping the wax from his
tablets and making little figures of animals and men, so his
father handed him over to his mother's brother, who was one of
a family of statuaries. But a blunder and a breakage resulted
in his uncle thrashing him, and he ran home to his mother. It
was his first and last day in the sculptor's shop, and he went to

---

[1] *Piscator*, 19. [2] *Quomodo historia*, 24. [3] *Bis accusatus*, 27.

bed with tears upon his face. In later life he told the story of a dream which he had that night—a long and somewhat literary dream modelled on Prodicus' fable of the *Choice of Herakles*. He dreamed that two women appeared to him, one dusty and workmanlike, the other neat, charming and noble. They were Sculpture and Culture, and he chose the latter. He tells the dream, he says, that the young may be helped by his example to pursue the best and devote themselves to Culture, regardless of immediate poverty.[1] He was launched somehow on the career of his choice and became a rhetorician. It may be noted however that an instinctive interest in art remained with him, and he is reckoned one of the best art-critics of antiquity.

Rhetoric, he says, "made a Greek of him," went with him from city to city in Greece and Ionia, "sailed the Ionian sea with him and attended him even as far as Gaul, scattering plenty in his path."[2] For, as he explains elsewhere, he was among the teachers who could command high fees, and he made a good income in Gaul.[3] But, about the age of forty, he resolved "to let the gentlemen of the jury rest in peace—tyrants enough having been arraigned and princes enough eulogized."[4] From now onward he wrote dialogues—he had at last found his proper work.

Dialogue in former days had been the vehicle of speculation —"had trodden those aerial plains on high above the clouds, where the great Zeus in heaven is borne along on winged car." But it was to do so no more, and in an amusing piece Lucian represents Dialogue personified as bringing a suit against him for outrage. Had Lucian debased Dialogue, by reducing him to the common level of humanity and making him associate with such persons as Aristophanes and Menippus, one a light-hearted mocker at things sacred, the other a barking, snarling dog of a Cynic,—thus turning Dialogue into a literary Centaur, neither fit to walk nor able to soar? Or was Dialogue really a musty, fusty, superannuated creature, and greatly improved now for having a bath and being taught to smile and to go genially in the company of Comedy? Between the attack and the defence, the case is fairly stated.[5] Lucian created a new

---

[1] *Somnium*, 18.   [2] *Bis Accusatus*, 30, 27.   [3] *Apology*, 15.

[4] *Bis Acc.* 32.   Cf. Juvenal, 7, 151, *perimit sævos classis numerosa tyrannos.*

[5] *Bis Acc.* 33, 34.

mode in writing—or perhaps he revived it, for it is not very clear how much he owes to his favourite Menippus, the Gadarene Cynic and satirist of four centuries before.

Menippus however has perished and Lucian remains and is read ; for, whatever else is to be said of him, he is readable. He has not lost all the traces of the years during which he consorted with Rhetoric ; at times he amplifies and exaggerates, and will strain for more point and piquancy than a taste more sure would approve. Yet he has the instinct to avoid travesty, and his style is in general natural and simple, despite occasional literary reminiscences. His characters talk,—as men may talk of their affairs, when they are not conscious of being overheard,— with a naive frankness not always very wise, with a freedom and common sense, and sometimes with a folly, that together reveal the speaker. They rarely declaim, and they certainly never reach any high level of thought or feeling. The talk is slight and easy—it flickers about from one idea to another, and gives a strong impression of being real. If it is gods who are talking, they become surprisingly human—and even *bourgeois*, they are so very much at home among themselves. Lucian's skill is amazing. He will take some episode from Homer and change no single detail, and yet, as we listen to the off-hand talk of the gods as they recount the occurrence, we are startled at the effect—the irony is everywhere and nowhere ; the surprises are irresistible. Zeus, for instance, turns out to have more literary interests than we suppose ; he will quote Homer and make a Demosthenic oration to the gods, though alas ! his memory fails him in the middle of a sentence ; [1] he laments that his altars are as cold as Plato's *Laws* or the syllogisms of Chrysippus. He is the frankest gentleman of heaven, and so infinitely obliging !

In short, for sheer cleverness Lucian has no rival but Aristophanes in extant Greek literature. His originality, his wit, his humour (not at all equal, it may be said, to his wit), his gifts of invention and fancy, his light touch, and his genius for lively narrative, mark him out distinctively in an age when literature was all rhetoric, length and reminiscence. But as we read him, we become sensible of defects as extraordinary as his gifts. For all his Attic style, he belongs to his age. He

---

[1] *Zeus Tragœdus*, 15.

may renounce Rhetoric, but no man can easily escape from his
past.   The education had intensified the cardinal faults of his
character, impatience, superficiality, a great lack of sympathy
for the more tender attachments and the more profound interests
of men—essential unbelief in human grandeur.   An expatriated
adventurer, living for twenty years on his eloquence, with the
merest smattering of philosophy and no interest whatever in
nature and natural science or mathematics, with little feeling
and no poetry,—it was hardly to be expected that he should
understand the depths of the human soul, lynx-eyed as he is
for the surface of things.   He had a very frank admiration for
his own character, and he drew himself over and over again
under various names.   Lykinos, for example, is hardly a dis-
guise at all.   " Free-Speech, son of True-man, son of Examiner,"
he calls himself in one of his mock trials, " hater of shams,
hater of impostors, hater of liars, hater of the pompous, hater
of every such variety of hateful men—and there are plenty of
them " ; conversely, he loves the opposites, when he meets them,
which, he owns, is not very often.[1]

With such a profession, it is not surprising that a man of
more wit than sympathy, found abundance of material in the
follies of his age.   Men were taking themselves desperately
seriously,—preaching interminable Philosophy, saving their
souls, and communing with gods and dæmons in the most
exasperating ways.   Shams, impostures, and liars—so Lucian
summed them up, and he did not conceal his opinion.   Granted
that the age had aspects quite beyond his comprehension, he
gives a very vivid picture of it from the outside.   This is what
men were doing and saying around him—but why?   Why,
but from vanity and folly?   Gods, philosophers, and all who
take human life seriously, are deluged with one stream of
badinage, always clever but not always in good taste.   He has
no purpose, religious or philosophic.   If he attacks the gods,
it is not as a Sceptic—the Sceptics are ridiculed as much as
any one else in the *Sale of Lives*—men who know nothing,
doubt of their own experience, and avow the end of their
knowledge to be ignorance.[2]   If he is what we nowadays
loosely call sceptical, it is not on philosophic grounds.   We
should hardly expect him in his satirical pamphlets really to

---

[1] *Piscator*, 19, 20.   [2] *Vit. auctio*, 27.

grapple with the question of Philosophy, but he seems not to understand in the least why there should be Philosophy at all. He is master of no single system, though he has the catchwords of them all at his finger-ends.

His most serious dialogue on Philosophy is the *Hermotimus.* " Lykinos " meets Hermotimus on his way to a lecture—a man of sixty who for many years has attended the Stoics. Into their argument we need not go, but one or two points may be noted.   Hermotimus is a disciple, simple and persevering, who owns that he has not reached the goal of Happiness and hardly expects to reach it, but he presses bravely on, full of faith in his teachers.   Under the adroit questions of Lykinos, he is forced to admit that he had chosen the Stoics rather than any other school by sheer intuition—or because of general notions acquired more or less unconsciously—like a man buying wine, he knew a good thing when he tasted it, and looked no further.   Yes, says Lykinos, take the first step and the rest is easy—Philosophy depends on a first assumption— take the Briareus of the poets with three heads and six hands, and then work him out,—six eyes, six ears, three voices talking at once, thirty fingers—you cannot quarrel with the details as they come ; once grant the beginning, and the rest comes flooding in, irresistible, hardly now susceptible of doubt.   So in Philosophy, your passion, like the longing of a lover, blinded you to the first assumptions, and the structure followed.[1]   " Do not think that I speak against the Stoics, through any special dislike of the school ; my arguments hold against all the schools." [2]   The end is that Hermotimus abandons all Philosophy for ever—not a very dramatic or probable end, as Plato and Justin Martyr could have told Lucian.

The other point to notice is the picture of Virtue under the image of a Celestial City, and here one cannot help wondering whether the irony has any element of personal reminiscence.   Virtue Lykinos pictures as a City, whose citizens are happy, wise and good, little short of gods, as the Stoics say.   All there is peace, unity, liberty, equality.   The citizens are all aliens and foreigners, not a native among them —barbarians, slaves, misformed, dwarfs, poor ; for wealth and birth and beauty are not reckoned there.   " In good truth, we

[1] *Hermot.* 74.   [2] *Ibid.* 85.

should devote all our efforts to this, and let all else go. We should take no heed of our native-land, nor of the clinging and weeping of children or parents, if one has any, but call on them to take the same journey, and then, if they will not or cannot go with us, shake them off, and march straight for the city of all bliss, leaving one's coat in their hands, if they won't let go, —for there is no fear of your being shut out there, even if you come without a coat." Fifteen years ago an old man had urged Lykinos to go there with him. "If the city had been near at hand and plain for all to see, long ago, you may be sure, with never a doubt I would have gone there, and had my franchise long since. But as you tell us, it lieth far away"—— and there are so many professed guides and so many roads, that there is no telling whether one is travelling to Babylon or to Corinth.[1] "So for the future you had better reconcile yourself to living like an ordinary man, without fantastic and vain hopes." [2]

Lucian never ceases to banter the philosophers. When he visits the Islands of the Blest, he remarks that, while Diogenes and the Epicureans are there, Plato prefers his own Republic and Laws, the Stoics are away climbing their steep hill of Virtue, and the Academics, though wishful to come, are still suspending their judgment, uncertain whether there really is such an island at all and not sure that Rhadamanthus himself is qualified to give judgment.[3] Diogenes in the shades, Pan in his grotto, Zeus in heaven, and the common man in the streets, are unanimous that they have had too much Philosophy altogether. The philosophers have indeed embarked on an impossible quest, for they will never find Truth. Once Lucian represents Truth in person, and his portrait is characteristic. She is pointed out to him—a female figure, dim and indistinct of complexion; "I do not see which one you mean," he says, and the answer is, "Don't you see the unadorned one there, the naked one, ever eluding the sight and slipping away?" [4]

But still more absurd than Philosophy was the growth of belief in the supernatural. Lucian's *Lover of Lies* is a most illuminating book. Here are gathered specimens of the various

---

[1] *Hermot.* 22-28. [2] *Ibid.* 84.
[3] *V.H.* ii, 18. [4] *Piscator*, 16.

types of contemporary superstition—one would suspect the author of the wildest parody, if it were not that point by point we may find parallels in the other writers of the day. Tychiades (who is very like Lucian himself) tells how he has been visiting Eucrates and has dropped into a nest of absurdities. Eucrates is sixty and wears the solemn beard of a student of philosophy. He has a ring made of iron from gibbets and is prepared to believe everything incredible. His house is full of professed philosophers, Aristotelian, Stoic, and Platonic, advising him how to cure the pain in his legs, by wrapping round them a lion's skin with the tooth of a field mouse folded within it.[1] Tychiades asks if they really believe that a charm hung on outside can cure the mischief within, and they laugh at his ignorance. The Platonist tells a number of stories to prove the reasonableness of the treatment,—how a vine-dresser of his father's had died of snake-bite and been re-covered by a Chaldæan, and how the same Chaldæan charmed (like the Pied Piper) all the snakes off their farm. The Stoic narrates how he once saw a Hyperborean flying and walking on water—" with those brogues on his feet that his countrymen habitually wear "—a man whose more ordinary feats were raising spirits, calling the dead from their graves, and fetching down the moon. Ion, the Platonist, confirms all this with an account of another miracle-worker—" everybody knows the Syrian of Palestine " who drives dæmons out of men ; " he would stand by the patient lying on the ground and ask whence they have come into the body ; and, though the sick person does not speak, the dæmon answers in Greek, or in some barbarian tongue, or whatever his own dialect may be, and explains how he entered into the man and whence he came. Then the Syrian would solemnly adjure him, or threaten him if he were obstinate, and so drive him out. I can only say I saw one, of a black smoky hue, in the act of coming out."[2] The Syrian's treatment was expensive, it appears. Celsus, as we shall see later on, has some evidence on this matter. The nationality of the magicians quoted in the book may be remarked—they are Libyan, Syrian, Arab, Chaldæan, Egyptian, and " Hyperborean."

Other tales of magical statues, a wife's apparition, an

[1] *Philopseudes*, 7. [2] *Ibid.* 16.

uneasy ghost,[1] a charm for bringing an absent lover, and the
familiar one of the man who learns the spell of three syllables
to make a pestle fetch water, but unhappily not that which will
make it stop, and who finds on cutting it in two that there are
now two inanimate water-carriers and a double deluge—these
we may pass over.   We may note that this water-fetching
spell came originally from a sacred scribe of Memphis, learned
in all the wisdom of the Egyptians, who lived underground in
the temple for three and twenty years and was taught his
magic there by Isis herself.[2]   Interviews with dæmons are so
common that instances are not given.[3]

More significant are the stories of the other world, for here
we come again, from a different point of approach, into a region
familiar to the reader of Plutarch.   Eucrates himself, out in
the woods, heard a noise of barking dogs; an earthquake
followed and a voice of thunder, and then came a woman more
than six hundred feet high, bearing sword and torch, and
followed by dogs "taller than Indian elephants, black in colour."
Her feet were snakes—here we may observe that Pausanias the
traveller pauses to dismiss "the silly story that giants have
serpents instead of feet," for a coffin more than eleven ells long
was found near Antioch and "the whole body was that of a
man."[4]   So the snake-feet are not a mere fancy of Lucian's.
The woman then tapped the earth with one of these feet of
hers, and disappeared into the chasm she made.   Eucrates,
peeping over the edge, "saw everything in Hades, the river of
fire and the lake, Cerberus and the dead"—what is more, he
recognized some of the dead.   "Did you see Socrates and
Plato?" asks Ion.   Socrates he thought he saw, "but Plato I
did not recognize; I suppose one is bound to stick to the
exact truth in talking to one's friends."   Pyrrhias the slave
confirms the story as an eye-witness.[5]   Another follows with
a story of his trance in illness, and how he saw the world below,
Fates, Furies, and all, and was brought before Pluto, who dis-

---

[1] This ghost appears rather earlier in a letter of Pliny's, vii, 27, who says he
believes the story and adds another of his own.

[2] *Philopseudes*, 34.   [3] *Ibid.* 17.

[4] Pausanias, viii, 29, 3.   Cf. Milton's *Ode on Nativity*, 25, "Typhon huge, ending
in snaky twine."   References to remains of giants, in Tertullian, *de resurr. carnis*, 42 ;
Pliny, *N.H.* vii, 16, 73.

[5] *Philopseudes*, 22-24.

missed him with some irritation, as not amenable yet to his Court, and called for the smith Demylos ; he came back to life and announced that Demylos would shortly die, and Demylos did die. "Where is the wonder?" says another—the physician, "I know a man raised from the dead twenty days after his burial, for I attended him both before his death and after his resurrection."[1]

In all this, it is clear that there is a strong element of mockery. Mockery was Lucian's object, but he probably kept in all these stories a great deal nearer to what his neighbours would believe than we may imagine. Ælian, for example, has a story of a pious cock, which made a point of walking gratefully in the processions that took place in honour of Æsculapius ; and he does not tell it in the spirit of the author of the *Jackdaw of Rheims*.

As one of the main preoccupations of his age was with the gods, Lucian of course could not leave them alone. His usual method is to accept them as being exactly what tradition made them, and then to set them in new and impossible situations. The philosopher Menippus takes "the right wing of an eagle and the left of a vulture," and, after some careful practice, flies up to heaven to interview Zeus. He has been so terribly distracted by the arguments of the schools, that he wants to see for himself—"I dared not disbelieve men of such thundering voices and such imposing beards." Zeus most amiably allows him to stand by and watch him at work, hearing prayers as they come up through tubes, and granting or rejecting them, then settling some auguries, and finally arranging the weather —"rain in Scythia, snow in Greece, a storm in the Adriatic, and about a thousand bushels of hail in Cappadocia."[2] Zeus asks rather nervously what men are saying about him nowadays— mankind is so fond of novelty. "There was a time," he says, "when I was everything to them—

Each street, each market-place was full of Zeus—-

and I could hardly see for the smoke of sacrifice " ; but other gods, Asklepios, Bendis, Anubis and others, have set up shrines and the altars of Zeus are cold — cold as Chrysippus.[3] Altogether the dialogue is a masterpiece of humour and irony.

In another piece, we find Zeus and the other gods in

---

[1] *Philopseudes*, 25, 26.   [1] *Icaromenippus*, 24 26.   [2] *Icaromen.* 24.

assembly listening to an argument going on at Athens. An Epicurean, Damis, and a singularly feeble Stoic are debating whether gods exist, and whether they exercise any providence for men. Poseidon recommends the prompt use of a thunderbolt "to let them see," but Zeus reminds him that it is Destiny that really controls the thunderbolts—and, besides, "it would look as if we were frightened." So the argument goes on, and all the familiar proofs from divine judgments, regularity of sun and season, from Homer and the poets, from the consensus of mankind and oracles, are produced and refuted there and then, while the gods listen, till it becomes doubtful whether they do exist. The Stoic breaks down and runs away. "What are we to do?" asks Zeus. Hermes quotes a comic poet in Hamlet's vein—"there is nothing either good or bad, but thinking makes it so"—and what does it matter, if a few men are persuaded by Damis? we still have the majority— "most of the Greeks and all the barbarians." [1]

In *Zeus Cross-examined* the process is carried further. Cyniscus questions Zeus, who is only too good-natured and falls into all the questioner's traps. He admits Destiny to be supreme, and gets entangled in a terrible net of problems about fore-knowledge, the value of sacrifice and of divination, divine wrath, sin and so forth, till he cries "You leave us nothing!—you seem to me to despise me, for sitting here and listening to you with a thunderbolt on my arm." "Hit me with it," says Cyniscus, "if it is so destined,—I shall have no quarrel with you for it, but with Clotho." At last Zeus rises and goes away and will answer no more. But perhaps, reflects Cyniscus, he has said enough, and it was "not destined for me to hear any more." [2] The reader feels that Zeus has said more than enough.

From the old gods of Greece, we naturally turn to the new-comers. When Zeus summoned the gods to discuss the question of atheism at Athens, a good many more came than understood Greek, and it was they who had the best seats as they were made of solid gold—Bendis, Anubis, Attis and Mithras for example. Elsewhere Momus (who is a divine Lucian) complains to Zeus about them—"that Mithras with his Persian robe and tiara, who can't talk Greek, nor even understand when one drinks

[1] *Zeus Tragœdus.*   [2] *Zeus Elenchomenos*

to him "—what is he doing in heaven ?   And then the dog-faced
Egyptian in linen—who is he to bark at the gods ?   " Of course,"
says Zeus, " Egyptian religion—yes ! but all the same there are
hidden meanings, and the uninitiated must not laugh at them."
Still Zeus is provoked into issuing a decree—on second thoughts,
he would not put it to the vote of the divine assembly, for he
felt sure he would be outvoted.   The decree enacts that, whereas
heaven is crowded with polyglot aliens, till there is a great rise in
the price of nectar, and the old and true gods are being crowded
out of their supremacy, a committee of seven gods shall be
appointed to sit on claims ; further, that each god shall attend
to his own function, Athene shall not heal nor Asklepios give
oracles, etc. ; that philosophers shall talk no more nonsense ;
and that the statues of deified men shall be replaced by those
of Zeus, Hera, etc., the said men to be buried in the usual way.[1]

More than one reference has been made to new gods and
new oracles.   Lucian in his *Alexander* gives a merciless
account of how such shrines were started.   He came into
personal contact—indeed into conflict—with Alexander, the
founder of the oracle of Abonoteichos, and his story is full of
detail.   The man was a quack of the vulgarest type, and, yet
by means of a tame snake and some other simple contrivances,
he imposed himself upon the faith of a community.   His
renown spread far and wide.   By recognizing other oracles he
secured their support.   Men came to him even from Rome.
Through one of these devotees, he actually sent an oracle to
Marcus Aurelius among the Marcomanni and Quadi, bidding
him throw two lions with spices into the Danube, and there
should be a great victory.   This was done, Lucian says ; the
lions swam ashore on the farther side, and the victory fell to
the Germans.[2]   Lucian himself trapped the prophet with some
cunningly devised inquiries, which quite baffled god, prophet,
snake and all.   He also tried to detach an eminent adherent.
Alexander realized what was going on, and Lucian got a guard
of two soldiers from the governor of Cappadocia.   Under their
protection he went to see the prophet who had sent for him
The prophet, as he usually did with his followers, offered him

---

[1] *Deor. Eccles.* 14-18.

[2] *Alexander*, 48.   The reader of Marcus will remember that his first book is dated
" Among the Quadi."

his hand to kiss, and Lucian records with satisfaction that he bit the proffered hand and nearly lamed it.   Thanks to his guard, he came away uninjured.   Alexander, however, after this tried still more to compass his death, which is not surprising.[1]   There is other evidence than Lucian's, though it is not unnaturally slight, for the existence of this remarkable impostor.

Lucian has one or two incidental references to Christians.[2] Alexander warned them, in company with the Epicureans, to keep away from his shrine.   But we hear more of them in connexion with Proteus Peregrinus.   Lucian is not greatly interested in them ; he ridicules them as fools for being taken in by the impostor ; for Peregrinus, he tells us, duped them with the greatest success.   He became a prophet among them, a thiasarch, a ruler of the synagogue, everything in fact ; he interpreted their books for them, and indeed wrote them a lot more ; and they counted him a god and a lawgiver.   "You know," Lucian explains, "they still worship that great man of theirs, who was put on a gibbet in Palestine, because he added this new mystery ($\tau\epsilon\lambda\epsilon\tau\dot{\eta}\nu$) to human life."   In his mocking way he gives some interesting evidence on the attention and care bestowed by Christians on those of their members who were thrown into prison.   He details what was done by the foolish community for "their new Socrates" when Peregrinus was a prisoner.   When he was released, Peregrinus started wandering again, living on Christian charity, till " he got into trouble with them, too,—he was caught eating forbidden meats."[3]

Lucian differs from Voltaire in having less purpose and no definite principles.   He had no design to overthrow religion in favour of something else ; it is merely that the absurdity of it provoked him, and he enjoyed saying aloud, and with all the vigour of reckless wit, that religious belief was silly.   If the effect was scepticism, it was a scepticism founded, not on

---

[1] *Alexander*, 53-56.

[2] Keim, *Celsus' Wahres Wort*, p. 233, suggests that Lucian was not quite clear as to the differences between Judaism and Christianity.   The reference to forbidden meat lends colour to this.

[3] *De morte Peregrini*, 11, 16 ; cf. the *Passio Perpetuæ*, 3 and 16, on attention to Christians in prison.   Tertullian, *de Jejunio*, 12, gives an extraordinary account of what might be done for a Christian in prison, though the case of Pristinus, which he quotes, must have been unusual, if we are to take all he says as literally true.

philosophy, but on the off-hand judgment of what is called common-sense. Hidden meanings and mysteries were to him nonsense. How little he was qualified to understand mysticism and religious enthusiasm, can be seen in his account of the self-immolation of Peregrinus on his pyre at the Olympian games [1]—perhaps the most insufficient thing he ever wrote, full of value as it is. Peregrinus was a wanderer among the religions of the age. Gellius, who often heard him at Athens, calls him a man *gravis atque constans*, and says he spoke much that was useful and honest. He quotes in his way a paragraph of a discourse on sin, which does not lack moral elevation.[2] To Lucian the man was a quack, an advertiser, a mountebank, who burnt himself to death merely to attract notice. Lucian says he witnessed the affair, and tells gaily how, among other jests, he imposed a pretty miracle of his own invention upon the credulous. He had taken no pains to understand the man —nor did he to understand either the religious temper in general, or the philosophic, or anything else. His habit of handling things easily and lightly did not help him to see what could not be taken in at a glance.

What then does Lucian make of human life? On this he says a great deal. His most characteristic invention perhaps is the visit that Charon pays to the upper world to see what it really is that the dead regret so much. It is indeed, as M. Croiset points out, a fine stroke of irony to take the opinion of a minister of Death upon Life. Charon has left his ferry boat and comes up to light. Hermes meets him and they pile up some mountains—Pelion on Ossa, and Parnassus on top, from the two summits of which they survey mankind—a charm from Homer removing Charon's difficulty of vision. He sees many famous people, such as Milo, Polycrates and Cyrus ; and he overhears Crœsus and Solon discussing happiness, while Hermes foretells their fates. He sees a varied scene, life full of confusion, cities like swarms of bees, where each has a sting and stings his neighbour, and some, like wasps, harass and plunder the rest ; over them, like a cloud, hang hopes and fears

---

[1] Cf. Tertullian, *ad Martyras*, 4, *Peregrinus qui non olim se rogo immisit.* Athenagoras, *Presb.* 26, Πρώτεως, τοῦτον δ' οὐκ ἀγνοεῖτε ῥίψαντα ἑαυτὸν εἰς τὸ πῦρ περὶ τὴν 'Ολυμπίαν.

[2] Gellius, *N.A.* xii, 11 ; and summary of viii, 3.

and follies, pleasures and passions and hatreds.   He sees the
Fates spinning slender threads, soon cut, from which men hang
with never a thought of how quickly death ends their dreams ;
and he compares them to bubbles, big and little inevitably
broken.   He would like to shout to them "to live with Death
ever before their eyes"—why be so earnest about what they
can never take away?—but Hermes tells him it would be
useless.   He is amazed at the absurdity of their burial rites, and
he astonishes Hermes by quoting Homer on the subject.   Last
of all he witnesses a battle and cries out at the folly of it.
"Such," he concludes, "is the life of miserable men—and not
a word about Charon."[1]

In the same way and in the same spirit Menippus visits the
Lower World, where he sees Minos judging the dead.   Minos
too seems to have been interested in literature, for he reduced
the sentence upon Dionysius, the tyrant of Syracuse, on the very
proper ground of his generosity to authors.   But the general
picture has less humour.   "We entered the Acherusian plain,
and there we found the demi-gods, and the heroines, and the
general throng of the dead in nations and tribes, some ancient
and mouldering, 'strengthless heads' as Homer says, others
fresh and holding together—Egyptians these in the main, so
thoroughly good is their embalming.   But to know one from
another was no easy task ; all become so much alike when the
bones are bared ; yet with pains and long scrutiny we began
to recognize them.   They lay pell-mell in undistinguishable
heaps, with none of their earthly beauties left.   With so many
skeletons piled together, all as like as could be, eyes glaring
ghastly and vacant, teeth gleaming bare, I knew not to tell
Thersites from Nireus the fair. . . . For none of their ancient
marks remained, and their bones were alike, uncertain, un-
labelled, undistinguishable.   When I saw all this, the life of
man came before me under the likeness of a great pageant,
arranged and marshalled by Chance," who assigns the parts
and reassigns them as she pleases ; and then the pageant ends,
every one disrobes and all are alike.   "Such is human life,
as it seemed to me while I gazed."[2]   Over and over again with
every accent of irony the one moral is enforced—sometimes
with sheer brutality as in the tract on *Mourning*.

---

[1] *Charon* is the title of the dialogue.   [2] *Menippus*, 15, 16.

Menippus asked Teiresias in the shades what was the best life. "He was a blind little old man, and pale, and had a weak voice." He said : " The life of ordinary people is best, and wiser ; cease from the folly of metaphysics, of inquiry into origins and purposes ; spit upon those clever syllogisms and count all these things idle talk ; and pursue one end alone, how you may well arrange the present and go on your way with a laugh for most things and no enthusiasms." [1] In fact, "the unexamined life" is the only one, as many a weary thinker has felt—if it were but possible.

Goethe's criticism on Heine may perhaps be applied to Lucian—" We cannot deny that he has many brilliant qualities, but he is wanting in love . . . and thus he will never produce the effect which he ought." [2] Various views have been held of Lucian's contribution to the religious movement of the age ; it has even been suggested that his Dialogues advanced the cause of Christianity. But when one reflects upon the tender hearts to be found in the literature of the century, it is difficult to think that Lucian can have had any effect on the mass of serious people, unless to quicken in them by repulsion the desire for something less terrible than a godless world of mockery and death, and the impulse to seek it in the ancestral faith of their fathers. He did not love men enough to understand their inmost mind. The instincts that drove men back upon the old religion were among the deepest in human nature, and of their strength Lucian had no idea. His admirers to-day speak of him as one whose question was always " Is it true ? " We have seen that it was a question lightly asked and quickly answered. It is evident enough that his mockery of religion has some warrant in the follies and superstitions of his day. But such criticism as his, based upon knowledge incomplete and sympathy imperfect, is of little value. If a man's judgment upon religion is not to be external, he must have felt the need of a religion,—he must have had at some time the consciousness of imperative cravings and instincts which only a religion can satisfy. Such cravings are open to criticism, but men can neither be laughed out of them, nor indeed reasoned out of them ; and however absurd a religion may seem, and however defective it may be, if it is

---

[1] *Menippus*, 21.　　　　[2] Eckermann, 25th Dec. 1825.

still the only available satisfaction of the deepest needs of which men are conscious, it will hold its own, despite mockery and despite philosophy—as we shall see in the course of the chapter, though two more critics of religion remain to be noticed.

Lucian was not the only man who sought to bring the age back to sound and untroubled thinking. There was a physician, Sextus—known from the school of medicine to which he belonged as Sextus Empiricus—who wrote a number of books about the end of the second century or the beginning of the third in defence of Scepticism. A medical work of his, and a treatise on the Soul are lost, but his *Pyrrhonean Sketches* and his books *Against the Dogmatists* remain—written in a Greek which suggests that he was himself a Greek and not a foreigner using the language. Physicists, mathematicians, grammarians, moralists, astrologers, come under his survey, and the particular attention which he gives to the Stoics is a material fact in fixing his date, for after about 200 A.D. they cease to be of importance. His own point of view a short extract from his sketches will exhibit fully enough for our present purpose.

" The aim of the Sceptic is ataraxia [freedom from mental perturbation or excitement] in matters which depend on opinion, and in things which are inevitable restraint of the feelings (μετριοπάθειαν). For he began to philosophise in order to judge his impressions (φαντασίας) and to discover which of them are true and which false, so as to be free from perturbation. But he came to a point where the arguments were at once diametrically opposite and of equal weight ; and then, as he could not decide, he suspended judgment (ἐπέσχεν), and as soon as he had done so, there followed as if by accident this very freedom from perturbation in the region of opinion. For if a man opines anything to be good or bad in its essential nature, he is always in perturbation. When he has not the things that appear to him to be good, he considers himself tortured by the things evil by nature, and he pursues the good (as he supposes them to be) ; but, as soon as he has them, he falls into even more perturbations, through being uplifted out of all reason and measure, and from fear of change he does everything not to lose the things that seem to him to be good. But the man, who makes no definitions as to what is good or bad by nature, neither avoids nor pursues anything with eagerness, and is therefore unperturbed. What is related of Apelles the painter has in fact befallen the Sceptic. The story goes that he was painting a horse and wished to represent the foam of its mouth in his picture; but he was so unsuccessful that he gave it up, and took the sponge, on which he used to wipe the colours from his brush, and threw it at the picture. The sponge hit the picture and produced a likeness of the horse's foam. The Sceptics then hoped to gain ataraxia by forming some decision on the lack of correspondence between things as they appear to the eye and to the mind; they were unable to do it, and so suspended judgment (ἐπέσχον); and then as if by accident the ataraxia followed—just as a shadow follows a body. We do not say that the Sceptic is untroubled in every way, but we own he is troubled by things that are quite inevitable. For we admit that the Sceptic is cold sometimes, and thirsty, and so forth. But even in these matters the uneducated are caught in two ways at once, viz.: by the actual feelings and (not less) by supposing these conditions to be bad by nature. The Sceptic does away with the opinion that any one of these things is evil in its nature, and so he gets off more lightly even in these circumstances."[1]

A view of this kind was hardly likely to appeal to the temper of the age, and the influence of Scepticism was practically none. Still it is interesting to find so vigorous and clear an exponent of the system flourishing in a period given over to the beliefs that Lucian parodied and Apuleius accepted. Sextus, it may be added, is the sole representative of ancient Scepticism whose works have come down to us in any complete form.

One very obscure person of this period remains to be noticed, who in his small sphere gave his views to mankind in a way of his own.

In 1884 two French scholars, MM. Holleaux and Paris were exploring the ruins of Oinoanda, a Greek city in Lycia, and they came upon a number of inscribed stones, most of them built in a wall. What was unusual was that these were neither fragments of municipal decrees nor of private monuments, but all formed part of one great inscription which dealt apparently with some philosophic subject. In June 1895 two Austrian

---

[1] Sextus Empiricus, *Hypotyposes*, i, 25-30.

scholars, MM. Heberdey and Kalinka, re-collated the inscription and found some further fragments, and now the story is tolerably clear, and a curious one it is.[1]

It appears that the fragments originally belonged to an inscription carved on the side of a colonnade, and they fall into three series according to their place on the wall—one above another. The middle series consists of columns of fourteen lines, the letters $1\frac{1}{2}$ to 2 centimetres high, fifteen or sixteen in a line,—each column forming a page, as it were ; and it extends over some twenty-one or two yards. The lowest series is in the same style. On top is a series of columns added later (as the inscription shows) and cut in letters of $2\frac{1}{2}$-3 centimetres, generally ten lines to the column—the larger size to compensate for the greater height above the ground, for it was all meant to be read. The inscription begins :—

" Diogenes to kinsmen, household and friends, this is my charge. Being so ill that it is critical whether I yet live or live no longer—for an affection of the heart is carrying me off—if I survive, I will gladly accept the life yet given to me ; if I do not survive, ΔO . . ."

There ends a column, and a line or two has been lost at the top of what seems to be the next, after which come the words " a kindly feeling for strangers also who may be staying here," and the incomplete statement which begins " knowing assuredly, that by knowledge of the matters relating to Nature and feelings, which I have set forth in the spaces below. . . ." It is evident that Diogenes had something to say which he considered it a duty to make known. This proves to have been the Epicurean theory of life ; and here he had carved up for all to read a simple exposition of the philosophy of his choice.

The uppermost row contains his account of his purpose and something upon old age—very fragmentary. There follow a letter of Epicurus to his mother, and another letter from some one unidentified to one Menneas, and then a series of apophthegms and sentences. Thus fragment 27 is a column of ten lines to this effect : " Nothing is so contributive to good spirits, as not to do many things, nor take in hand tiresome matters, nor force oneself in any way beyond one's own strength, for all these things perturb nature." Another column proclaims : " Acute

---

[1] See *Rheinisches Museum,* 1892, and *Bulletin de Correspondance Hellénique,* 1897.

pains cannot be long ; for either they quickly destroy life and are themselves destroyed with it, or they receive some abatement of their acuteness." These platitudes are, as we may guess, an afterthought.

The middle row, the first to be inscribed, deals with the Epicurean theory of atoms—not by apophthegm or aphorism, but with something of the fulness and technicality of a treatise. " Herakleitos of Ephesus, then, said fire was the element ; Thales of Miletus water ; Diogenes of Apollonia and Anaximenes air ; Empedocles of Agrigentum both fire and air and water and earth ; Anaxagoras of Clazomenæ the homœomeries of each thing in particular ; those of the Stoa matter and God. But Democritus of Abdera said atomic natures—and he did well ; but since he made some mistakes about them, these will be set right in our opinions. So now we will accuse the persons mentioned, not from any feeling of illwill against them, but wishing the truth to be saved ($\sigma\omega\theta\hat{\eta}\nu\alpha\iota$)." So he takes them in turn and argues at leisure. The large fragment 45 discusses astronomy in its four columns—in particular, the sun and its apparent distance and its nature. Fr. 48 (four columns) goes on to treat of civilization,—of the development of dress from leaves to skins and woven garments, without the intervention " of any other god or of Athena either." Need and time did all. Hermes did not invent language. In fr. 50, we read that Protagoras " said he did not know if there are gods. That is the same thing as saying he knew there are not." Fr. 51 deals with death—" thou hast even persuaded me to laugh at it. For I am not a whit afraid because of the Tityos-es and Tantalus-es, whom some people paint in Hades, nor do I dread decay, reflecting that the [something] of the body . . . [three broken lines] . . . nor anything else." At the end of the row another letter begins (fr. 56) " [Diogen]es to Anti[pater] greeting." He writes from Rhodes, he says, just before winter begins, to friends in Athens and elsewhere, whom he would like to see. Though away from his country, he knows he can do more for it in this way than by taking part in political life. He wishes to show that " that which is convenient to Nature, viz. Ataraxia is the same for all." He is now " at the sunset of life," and all but departing ; so, since most men, as in a pestilence, are diseased with false opinion, which is very infectious, he wishes

' to help those that shall be after us ; for they too are ours, even if they are not yet born "; and strangers too. " I wished to make use of this colonnade and to set forth in public the medicine of salvation " (τὰ τῆς σωτηρίας προθεῖναι φάρμακα, fr. 58). The idle fears that oppressed him, he has shaken off; as to pains—empty ones he has abolished utterly, and the rest are reduced to the smallest compass. He bewails the life of men, wasted as it is, and weeps for it ; and he has "counted it a good man's part" to help men as far as he can. That is why he has thought of this inscription which may enable men to obtain " joy with good spirits " (τῆ[ς μετ' εὐθυ]μίας χαρᾶ[ς]), rather than of a theatre or a bath or anything else of the kind, such as rich men would often build for their fellow-citizens (fr. 59).

The discussion which follows in the third series of columns need not here detain us. Diogenes appeals for its consideration—that it may not merely be glanced at in passing (fr. 61, col. 3) ; but it will suffice us at present to note his statement that his object is "that life may become pleasant to us " (fr. 63, col. 1), and his protest—"I will swear, both now and always, crying aloud to all, Greeks and barbarians, that pleasure is the objective of the best mode of life, while the virtues, which these people now unseasonably meddle with (for they shift them from the region of the contributive to that of the objective) are by no means an objective, but contributive to the objective " (fr. 67 col. 2, 3). Lastly we may notice his reference to the improvement made in the theory of Democritus by the discovery of Epicurus of the swerve inherent in the atoms (fr. 81).

Altogether the inscription is as singular a monument of antiquity as we are likely to find. What the fellow-citizens of Diogenes thought of it, we do not know. Perhaps they might have preferred the bath or other commonplace gift of the ordinary rich man. It is a pity that Lucian did not see the colonnade.

Side by side with Lucian, Sextus and Diogenes it is interesting to consider their contemporaries who were not of their opinion.

Perhaps, while the stone-masons were day by day carving up the long inscription at Oinoanda, others of their trade were

busy across the Ægæan with one of another character. At
any rate, the inscription which M. Julius Apellas set up in the
temple of Asklepios in Epidauros, belongs to this period.
Like Diogenes, he is not afraid of detail.

"In the priesthood of Poplius Ælius Antiochus.

"I, Marcus Julius Apellas of Idrias and Mylasa, was sent
for by the God, for I was a chronic invalid and suffered from
dyspepsia. In the course of my journey the God told me in
Ægina not to be so irritable. When I reached the Temple,
he directed me to keep my head covered for two days ; and for
these two days it rained. I was to eat bread and cheese, parsley
with lettuce, to wash myself without help, to practise running,
to drink citron-lemonade, to rub my body on the sides of the
bath in the bath-room, to take walks in the upper portico, to
use the trapeze, to rub myself over with sand, to go with bare
feet in the bath-room, to pour wine into the hot water before I
got in, to wash myself without help, and to give an Attic
drachma to the bath-attendant, to offer in public sacrifices to
Asklepios, Epione and the Eleusinian goddesses, and to take
milk with honey. When for one day I had drunk milk
alone, the god said to put honey in the milk to make it
digestible.

"When I called upon the god to cure me more quickly, I
thought it was as if I had anointed my whole body with
mustard and salt, and had come out of the sacred hall and
gone in the direction of the bath-house, while a small child was
going before holding a smoking censer. The priest said to
me : ' Now you are cured, but you must pay up the fees for
your treatment.' I acted according to the vision, and when
I rubbed myself with salt and moistened mustard, I felt the pain
still, but when I had bathed, I suffered no longer. These
events took place in the first nine days after I had come to
the Temple. The god also touched my right hand and my
breast.

"The following day as I was offering sacrifice, a flame
leapt up and caught my hand, so as to cause blisters. Yet
after a little my hand was healed.

"As I prolonged my stay in the Temple, the god told me
to use dill along with olive-oil for my head-aches. Formerly I
had not suffered from head-aches, but my studies had brought

on congestion. After I used the olive-oil, I was cured of head-aches. For swollen glands the god told me to use a cold gargle, when I consulted him about it, and he ordered the same treatment for inflamed tonsils.

" He bade me inscribe this treatment, and I left the Temple in good health and full of gratitude to the god." [1]

Pausanias speaks of " the buildings erected in our time by Antoninus a man of the Conscript Senate "—a Roman Senator in fact,[2]—in honour of Asklepios at Epidauros, a bath, three temples, a colonnade, and " a house where a man may die, and a woman lie in, without sin," for these actions were not " holy " within the sanctuary precincts, and had had to be done in the open air hitherto.

A more conspicuous patient of Asklepios is Ælius Aristides, the rhetorician. This brilliant and hypochondriacal person spent years in watching his symptoms and consulting the god about them. Early in his illness the god instructed him to record its details, and he obeyed with zest, though in after years he was not always able to record the minuter points with complete clearness. He was bidden to make speeches, to rub himself over with mud, to plunge into icy water, to ride, and, once, to be bled to the amount of 120 litres. As the human body does not contain anything like that amount of blood, and as the temple servants knew of no one ever having been " cut " to that extent—" at least except Ischyron, and his was one of the most remarkable cases," the god was not taken literally.[3] The regular plan was to sleep in the Temple, as already mentioned, and the god came. " The impression was that one could touch him, and perceive that he came in person ; as if one were between asleep and awake, and wished to look out and were in an agony lest he should depart too soon,—as if one held one's ear and listened—sometimes as in a dream, and then as in a waking vision—one's hair was on end, and tears of joy were shed, and one felt light-hearted. And who among

[1] C.I.G. iv, 955. Translation of Mary Hamilton, in her *Incubation*, p. 41 (1906).

[2] I agree with the view of Schubart quoted by J. G. Frazer on the passage (Pausan. ii, 27, 6) that this man was neither the Emperor Antoninus Pius nor Marcus. It is perhaps superfluous to call attention to the value of Dr Frazer's commentary, here and elsewhere.

[3] *Sacred Speech*, ii, § 47, p 301, λίτρας εἴκοσι καὶ ἑκατόν.

men could set this forth in words? Yet if there is one of the initiated, he knows and recognises [what I say]." [1]

None of the cases yet quoted can compare with the miracles of ancient days to be read in the inscriptions about the place— stories of women with child for three and five years, of the extraordinary surgery of the god, cutting off the head of a dropsical patient, holding him upside down to let the water run out and putting the head on again,—a mass of absurdities hardly to be matched outside *The Glories of Mary*. They make Lucian's *Philopseudes* seem tame.

There were other gods, beside Asklepios, who gave oracles in shrine and dream. Pausanias the traveller has left a book on Greece and its antiquities, temples, gods and legends of extraordinary value. "A man made of common stuff and cast in a common mould," as Dr Frazer characterizes him,—and therefore the more representative—he went through Greece with curious eyes and he saw much that no one else has recorded. At Sparta stood the only temple he knew of which had an upper story. In this upper story was an image of Aphrodite Morpho fettered [2]—a silly thing he thought it to fetter a cedar-wood doll. He particularly visited Phigalea, because of the "Black Demeter"—a curious enough image she had been, though by then destroyed.[3] He was initiated in the Eleusinian mysteries.[4] He tells us that the stony remnants of the lump of clay from which Prometheus fashioned the first man were still preserved,[5] and that the sceptre which Hephaistos made for Agamemnon received a daily sacrifice in Chæronea, Plutarch's city—"a table is set beside it covered with all sorts of flesh and cakes."[6] He has many such stories. He tells us too about a great many oracles of his day, of which that of Amphilochus at Mallus in Cilicia "is the most infallible"[7]—a curiously suggestive superlative (ἀψευδέστατον). He is greatly

---

[1] *Sacred Speech*, ii, § 33, p. 298. For Aristides see Hamilton, *Incubation*, pt. i. ch. 3, and Dill, *Roman Society from Nero to Marcus Aurelius*, bk. iv. ch. 1. See also Richard Caton, M.D., *The Temples and Ritual of Asklepios* (1900).

[2] Paus. iii, 15, 11. [3] Paus. viii, 42, 11. [4] Paus. i, 37, 4; 38, 7.

[5] Paus. x, 4, 4; they smell very like human flesh. [6] Paus. ix, 40, 11.

[7] Paus. i, 34, 3. Cf. Tertullian, *de Anima*, 46, a list of dream-oracles. Strabo, *c.* 761-2, represents the practice as an essential feature of Judaism, ἐγκοιμᾶσθαι δὲ καὶ αὐτοὺς ὑπὲρ ἑαυτῶν καὶ ὑπὲρ τῶν ἄλλων ἄλλους τοὺς εὐονείρους; he compares Moses to Amphiaraus, Trophonius, Orpheus, etc.

interested in Asklepios, but for our present purpose a few sentences from his elaborate account of the ceremony with which Trophonius is consulted at Lebadea must suffice.

After due rites the inquirer comes to the oracle, in a linen tunic with ribbons, and boots of the country. Inside bronze railings is a pit of masonry, some four ells across and eight deep, and he goes down into it by means of a light ladder brought for the occasion. At the bottom he finds a hole, a very narrow one. " So he lays himself on his back on the ground, and holding in his hand barley cakes kneaded with honey, he thrusts his feet first into the hole, and follows himself endeavouring to get his knees through the hole. When they are through, the rest of his body is immediately dragged after them and shoots in, just as a man might be caught and dragged down by the swirl of a mighty and rapid river. Once they are inside the shrine the future is not revealed to all in one and the same way, but to one it is given to see and to another to hear. They return through the same aperture feet foremost. . . . When a man has come up from Trophonius, the priests take him in hand again, and set him on what is called the chair of Memory, which stands not far from the shrine ; and, being seated there, he is questioned by them as to all he saw and heard. On being informed, they hand him over to his friends who carry him, still overpowered with fear, and quite unconscious of himself and his surroundings, to the building where he lodged before, the house of Good Fortune and the Good Dæmon. Afterwards, however, he will have all his wits as before, and the power of laughter will come back to him. I write not from mere hearsay : I have myself consulted Trophonius and have seen others who have done so. All who have gone down to Trophonius are obliged to set up a tablet containing a record of all they heard and saw." [1]

A man who has been through such an experience may be excused for believing much. While Pausanias kept his Greek habit of criticism and employs it on occasional myths and traditions, and particularly on stories of hell—though the fact of punishment after death he seems to accept—yet his travels and his inquiries made an impression on him. " When I began this work, I used to look on these Greek stories as little better

[1] Paus. ix, 39, 5-14. Frazer's translation.

than foolishness ; but now that I have got as far as Arcadia, my opinion about them is this : I believe that the Greeks who were accounted wise spoke of old in riddles, and not straight out ; and, accordingly, I conjecture that this story about Cronos [swallowing a foal instead of his child] is a bit of Greek philosophy.   In matters of religion I will follow tradition." [1]

Pausanias mentions several oracles and temples of Apollo in Greece and Asia Minor—one obscure local manifestation of the god he naturally enough omitted, but a fellow-citizen of the god preserves it.   " It was in obedience to him, the god of my land, that I undertook this treatise.   He often urged me to it, and in particular appeared visibly to me (ἐναργῶς ἐπιστάντι),[2] since I knew thee, and all but ordered me to write all this. No wonder that the Daldian Apollo, whom we call by the ancestral name of Mystes, urged me to this, in care for thy worth and wisdom, for there is an old friendship between Lydians and Phœnicians, as they tell us who set forth the legends of the land." [3]   So writes Artemidorus to his friend Cassius Maximus of his treatise on the scientific interpretation of dreams—a work of which he is very proud.   " Wonder not," he says, "at the title, that the name stands Artemidorus Daldianus, and not ' of Ephesus,' as on many of the books I have already written on other subjects.   For Ephesus, it happens, is famous on her own account, and she has many men of note to proclaim her.   But Daldia is a town of Lydia of no great renown, and, as she has had no such men, she has remained unknown till my day.   So I dedicate this to her, my native-place on the mother's side, as a parent's due (θρεπτήρια)." [4]

Marcus Aurelius records his gratitude " that remedies have been shown to me by dreams, both others, and against blood-spitting and giddiness." [5]   Plutarch, Pausanias, Aristides—

---

[1] Paus. viii, 8, 3 (Frazer).   τῶν μὲν δὴ ἐς τὸ θεῖον ἡκόντων τοῖς εἰρημένοις χρησόμεθα.

[2] The word of Luke 2, 9.

[3] Artemidorus Dald. ii, 70.   [4] Artem. Dald. iii, 66.

[5] Marcus, i, 17 ; George Long's rendering, here as elsewhere somewhat literal, but valuable as leaving the sharp edges on the thought of the Greek, which get rubbed off in some translations. See Tertullian, de Anima, cc. 44 and following, for a discussion of dreams, referring to the five volumes of Hermippus of Berytus for the whole story of them.

dreams come into the scheme of things divine with all the
devout of our period. Artemidorus is their humble brother
—not the first to give a whole book to dreams, but
proud to be a pioneer in the really scientific treatment of
them—"the accuracy of the judgments, that is the thing
for which, even by itself, I think highly of myself."[1] The
critic may take it "that I too am quite capable of neologisms and persuasive rhetoric (εὑρεσιλογεῖν καὶ πιθανεύεσθαι),
but I have not undertaken all this for theatrical effect
or to please the speech-mongers; I appeal throughout to
experience, as canon and witness of my words," and he begs
his readers neither to add to his books nor take anything
away.[2] His writing is, as he says, quite free from "the
stage and tragedy style."

Artemidorus takes himself very seriously. "For one thing,
there is no book on the interpretation of dreams that I have
not acquired, for I had great enthusiasm for this; and, in the
next place, though the prophets (μάντεων) in the market-place
are much slandered, and called beggars and quacks and
humbugs by the gentlemen of solemn countenance and lifted
eye-brows, I despised the slander and for many years I have
associated with them—both in Greece, in cities and at festivals,
and in Asia, and in Italy, and in the largest and most
populous of the islands, consenting to hear ancient dreams and
their results."[3] This patient research has resulted in principles
of classification.[4] There are dreams that merely repeat what
a man is doing (ἐνύπνια); and others (ὄνειροι) which are
prophetic. These last fall into two classes—theorematic
dreams, as when a man dreams of a voyage, and wakes to go
upon a voyage, and allegoric dreams. The latter adjective has
a great history in regions more august, but the allegoric
method is the same everywhere, as an illustration will show.
A man dreamed he saw Charon playing at counters with
another man, whom he called away on business; Charon grew
angry and chased him, till he ran for refuge into an inn called

---

[1] Artem. Dald. ii, pref., μέγα φρονῶ.

[2] Artem. Dald. ii, 70. Cf. v. pref., ἄνευ σκηνῆς καὶ τραγῳδίας.

[3] Artem. Dald. i, pref.

[4] A very different classification in Tertullian, de Anima, 47, 48. Dreams may be
due to demons, to God, the nature of the soul or ecstasy.

"The Camel," and bolted the door, whereupon "the dæmon" went away, but one of the man's thighs sprouted with grass. Shortly after this dream he had his thigh broken —the one and sole event foretold. For Charon and the counters meant death, but Charon did not catch him, so it was shown that he would not die; but his foot was threatened, since he was pursued. The name of the inn hinted at the thigh, because of the anatomy of a camel's thigh; and the grass meant disuse of the limb, for grass only grows where the earth is left at rest.[1] The passage is worth remembering whenever we meet the word allegory and its derivatives in contemporary literature. Artemidorus has five books of this stuff—the last two dedicated to his son, and containing instances "that will make you a better interpreter of dreams than all, or at least inferior to none; but, if published, they will show you know no more than the rest."[2] The sentence suggests science declining into profession.

Far more brilliant, more amusing and more attractive than any of these men, whom we have considered since we left Lucian, is Apuleius of Madaura. Rhetorician, philosopher and man of science, a story-teller wavering between Boccaccio and Hans Andersen, he is above all a stylist, a pietist and a humorist. For his history we depend upon himself, and this involves us in difficulties; for, while autobiography runs through two of his works, one of these is an elaboration of a defence he made on a charge of magic and the other is a novel of no discoverable class but its own, and through both runs a vein of nonsense, which makes one chary of being too literal.

The novel is the *Golden Ass*—that at least is what St Augustine tells us the author called it.[3] Passages from this have been seriously used as sources of information as to the author. But there is another *Ass*, long attributed to Lucian though probably not Lucian's, and in each case the hero tells the tale in the first person, and the co-incidences between the Greek and the Latin make it obvious that there is some

---

[1] Artem. Dald. i, 4.   [2] Artem. Dald. iv, pref.

[3] See Augustine, *C.D.* xviii, 18, *Apuleius in libris quos Asini aurei titulo inscripsit.* In the printed texts, it is generally called the *Metamorphoses.*

literary connexion between them, whatever it is. The scene is Greece and Thessaly, but not the Greece and Thessaly of geography, any more than the maritime Bohemia of Shakespeare. Yet in the last book Apuleius seems to have forgotten "Lucius of Patræ" and to be giving us experiences of his own which have nothing to do with the hero of the *Ass*, Greek or Latin.

In the *Apology* he comes closer to his own career and he tells us about himself. Here he does not venture on the delightful assertion that he is the descendant of the great Plutarch, as the hero of the *Ass* does, but avows that, as his native place is on the frontiers of Numidia and Gætulia, he calls himself "half Numidian and half Gætulian"—just as Cyrus the Greater was "half Mede and half Persian." His city is "a most splendid colony," and his father held in turn all its magistracies, and he hopes not to be unworthy of him.[1] He and his brother inherited two million sesterces, though he has lessened his share "by distant travel and long studies and constant liberalities." [2]   Elsewhere he tells us definitely that he was educated at Athens.[3]   Everybody goes to the *litterator* for his rudiments, to the grammarian next and then to the rhetorician—"but I drank from other vessels at Athens," so "Empedocles frames songs, Plato dialogues, Socrates hymns, Epicharmus measures, Xenophon histories, Xenocrates satires ; your Apuleius does all these and cultivates the nine Muses with equal zeal—with more will, that is, than skill."[4]

Like many brilliant men of his day he took to the strolling life of the rhetorician, going from city to city and giving displays of his powers of language, extemporizing wonderful combinations of words. Either he himself or some other admirer made a collection of elegant extracts from these exhibition-speeches, still extant under the title of *Florida*. His fame to-day rests on other works.   In the course of his travels he came to Oea in his native-land, and there married the widowed mother of a fellow-student of his Athenian days. Her late husband's family resented the marriage ; and affecting to believe that her affections had been gained by

---

[1] *Apol.* 24.   [2] *Apol.* 23.   [3] *Apol.* 72 ; *Flor.* 18.   [4] *Flor.* 20.

some sort of witchcraft, they prosecuted Apuleius on a charge
of magic. The charge was in itself rather a serious one,
though Apuleius made light of it.   His defence is an interesting document for the glimpses it gives into North African
society, with its Greek, Latin and Punic elements.   The
younger stepson has fallen into bad hands ; " he never speaks
except in Punic,—a little Greek, perhaps, surviving from what
he learnt of his mother ; Latin he neither will nor can speak." [1]
On family life, on marriage customs, on the registration of
births (c. 89) ;—on the personal habits of the defendant, his
toothpowder (and a verse he made in its praise) and his
looking-glass, we gain curious information.   Above all the
speech sheds great light on the inter-relations of magic and
religion in contemporary thought.   A few points may be
noticed.

What, asks the prosecution, is the meaning of this curious
interest Apuleius has in fish ?   It is zoological, says Apuleius ;
I have written books on fish, both in Greek and Latin,—and
dissected them.   That curious story, too, of the boy falling
down in his presence ?   As to that, Apuleius knows all about
divination by means of boys put under magical influence ; he
has read of it, of course, but he does not know whether to
believe or not ; " I do think with Plato," he owns to the
court (or to his readers), " that between gods and men, in nature
and in place intermediary, there are certain divine powers, and
these preside over all divinations and the miracles of magicians.
Nay, more, I have the fancy that the human soul, particularly
the simple soul of a boy, might, whether by evocation of
charm or by mollification of odour, be laid to sleep, and
so brought out of itself into oblivion of things present, and
for a brief space, all memory of the body put away, it
might be restored and returned to its own nature, which is
indeed immortal and divine, and thus, in a certain type of
slumber, foretell the future." [2]   As for the boy in question,
however, he is so ricketty that it would take a magician
to keep him standing.

Then those mysterious " somethings " which Apuleius keeps

---

[1] *Apol.* 98.   Cf. *Passio Perpetuæ*, c. 13, *et cœpit Perpetua Grœce cum eis loqui*, says
Saturus ; Perpetua uses occasional Greek words herself in recording her visions.

[2] *Apol.* 43.   Cf. Plutarch cited on p. 101.

wrapped up in a napkin? "I have been initiated in many of the mysteries of Greece. Certain symbols and memorials of these, given to me by the priests, I sedulously preserve. I say nothing unusual, nothing unknown. To take one instance, those among you who are *mystæ* of Father Liber [Bacchus] know what it is you keep laid away at home, and worship in secret, far from all profane eyes. Now, I, as I said, from enthusiasm for truth and duty toward the gods, I have learnt many sacred mysteries, very many holy rites, and divers ceremonies"—the audience will remember he said as much three years ago in his now very famous speech about Æsculapius—"then could it seem strange to anyone, who has any thought of religion, that a man, admitted to so many divine mysteries, should keep certain emblems of those holy things at home, and wrap them in linen, the purest covering for things divine?" Some men—the prosecutor among them—count it mirth to mock things divine ; no, he goes to no temple, has never prayed, will not even put his hand to his lips when he passes a shrine,—why ! he has not so much as an anointed stone or a garlanded bough on his farm.[1]

One last flourish may deserve quotation. If you can prove, says Apuleius, any material advantage accruing to me from my marriage, "then write me down the great Carmendas or Damigeron or *his* . . . Moses or Jannes or Apollobeches or Dardanus himself, or anyone else from Zoroaster and Ostanes downwards who has been famous among magicians."[2] Several of these names occur in other authors,[3] but the corruption is more interesting. Has some comparative fallen out, or does *his* conceal another name? Is it *ihs*, in fact,— a reference to Jesus analogous to the suggestion of Celsus that he too was a magician?

The philosophical works of Apuleius need not detain us, but a little space may be spared to his book *On the God of Socrates*, where he sets forth in a clear and vivid way that doctrine of dæmonic beings, which lies at the heart of ancient

---

[1] *Apol.* 55, 56. Cf. *Florida*, I, an ornamental passage on pious usage.

[2] *Apol.* 90. Many restorations have been attempted.

[3] *e.g.* Tertullian, *de Anima*, 57, *Ostanes et Typhon et Dardanus et Damigeron et Nectabis et Berenice.*

religion, pre-eminently in this period, from Plutarch onwards. His presentment is substantially the same as Plutarch's, but crisper altogether, and set forth in the brilliant rhetoric, to which the Greek did not aspire, and from which the African could not escape, nor indeed wished to escape.

Plato, he says, classifies the gods in three groups, distinguished by their place in the universe.[1] Of the celestial gods some we can see—sun, moon and stars[2] (on which, like a true rhetorician, he digresses into some fine language, which can be omitted). Others the mind alone can grasp (*intellectu eos rimabundi contemplamur*)—incorporeal natures, animate, with neither beginning nor end, eternal before and after, exempt from contagion of body; in perfect intellect possessing supreme beatitude; good, but not by participation of any extraneous good, but from themselves. Their father, lord and author of all things, free from every nexus of suffering or doing—him Plato, with celestial eloquence and language commensurate with the immortal gods, has declared to be, in virtue of the ineffable immensity of his incredible majesty, beyond the poverty of human speech or definition—while even to the sages themselves, when by force of soul they have removed themselves from the body, the conception of God comes, like a flash of light in thick darkness—a flash only, and it is gone.[3]

At the other extremity of creation are men—"proud in reason, loud in speech, immortal of soul, mortal of member, in mind light and anxious, in body brute and feeble, divers in character, in error the same, in daring pervicacious, in hope pertinacious, of vain toil, of frail fortune, severally mortal, generally continuous, mutable in the succession of offspring, time fleeting, wisdom lingering, death swift and life querulous, so they live."[4] Between such beings and the gods, contact cannot be. "To whom then shall I recite prayers? to whom tender vows? to whom slay victim? on whom shall I call, to

---

[1] Much of this material Apuleius has taken from the *Timaeus*, 40 D to 43 A.

[2] Cf. Lactantius, *Instit.* ii, *de origine erroris*, c. 5. Tertullian, *ad Natt.* ii, 2. Cicero, *N.D.* ii, 15, 39-44.

[3] *de deo Socr.* 3, 124. Cf. the account (quoted below) of what was experienced in initiation, which suggests some acquaintance with mystical trance—the confines of death and the sudden bright light look very like it.

[4] *de deo Socr.* 4, 126.

help the wretched, to favour the good, to counter the evil?
. . . . What thinkest thou? Shall I swear 'by Jove the
stone' (*per Iovem lapidem*) after the most ancient manner of
Rome? Yet if Plato's thought be true, that never god and
man can meet, the stone will hear me more easily than
Jupiter."[1]

"Nay, not so far—(for Plato shall answer, the thought is
his, if mine the voice) not so far, he saith, do I pronounce the
gods to be sejunct and alienate from us, as to think that not
even our prayers can reach them. Not from the care of
human affairs, but from contact, have I removed them. But
there are certain mediary divine powers, between æther above
and earth beneath, situate in that mid space of air, by whom
our desires and our deserts reach the gods. These the Greeks
call dæmons, carriers between human and heavenly, hence of
prayers, thence of gifts ; back and forth they fare, hence with
petition, thence with sufficiency, interpreters and bringers of
salvation."[2] To cut short this flow of words, the dæmons are,
as is familiar to us by now, authors of divination of all kinds,
each in its province. It would ill fit the majesty of the gods
to send a dream to Hannibal or to soften the whetstone for
Attius Navius—these are the functions of the intermediate
spirits.[3] Justin's explanation of the theophanies of the
Old Testament may recur to the reader's mind, and not
unjustly.[4]

The dæmons are framed of a purer and rarer matter than
we, "of that purest liquid of air, of that serene element,"
invisible therefore to us unless of their divine will they choose
to be seen.[5] From their ranks come those " haters and lovers "
of men, whom the poets describe as gods—they feel pity and
indignation, pain and joy and "every feature of the human
mind " ; while the gods above "are lords ever of one state in
eternal equability," and know no passions of any kind. The
dæmons share *their* immortality and *our* passion. Hence we
may accept the local diversities of religious cult, rites nocturnal
or diurnal, victims, ceremonies and ritual sad or gay, Egyptian

---

[1] *de deo Socr.* 5, 130-132.

[2] *de deo Socr.* 6, 132. Cf. Tert. *Apol.* 22, 23, 24, on nature and works of demons,
on lines closely similar.

[3] *de deo Socr.* 7, 136. [4] See chapter vi. p. 188. [5] *de deo Socr.* 11, 144.

or Greek,—neglect of these things the dæmons resent, as we learn in dream and oracle.

The human soul, too, is " a dæmon in a body "—the *Genius* of the Latins. From this we may believe that after death souls good and bad become good and bad ghosts—*Lares* and *Lemures*—and even gods, such as " Osiris in Egypt and Æsculapius everywhere." [1] Higher still are such dæmons as Sleep and Love, and of this higher kind Plato supposes our guardian spirits to be—" spectators and guardians of individual men, never seen, ever present, arbiters not merely of all acts, but of all thoughts," and after death witnesses for or against us. Of such was Socrates' familiar dæmon. Why should not we too live after the model of Socrates, studying philosophy and obeying our dæmon ?

The *Golden Ass* is the chief work of Apuleius. *Lector intende ; lætaberis*, he says in ending his short preface, and he judged his work aright. The hero, Lucius, is a man with an extravagant interest in magic, and he puts himself in the way of hearing the most wonderful stories of witchcraft and enchantment. Apuleius tells them with the utmost liveliness and humour. Magical transformations, the vengeance of witches, the vivification of waterskins—one tale comes crowding after another, real and vivid, with the most alarming and the most amusing details. For example, we are told by an eye-witness (like everybody else in the book he is a master-hand at story-telling) how he saw witches by night cut the throat of his friend, draw out the heart and plug the hole with a sponge ; how terrified he was of the hags to begin with, and then lest he should himself be accused of the murder ; how the man rose and went on his journey —somewhat wearily, it is true ; and how, as they rested, he stooped to drink, the sponge fell out and he was dead.

Lucius meddles with the drugs of a witch, and, wishing to transform himself to a bird, by the ill-luck of using the wrong box he becomes an ass. He is carried off by robbers, and, while he has the most varied adventures of his own, he is enabled to record some of the most gorgeous exploits that

[1] *de deo Socr.* 15.

brigands ever told one another in an ass's hearing.[1] What is more, a young girl is captured and held to ransom, and to comfort her for a little, the old woman who cooks the robbers' food—-"a witless and bibulous old hag"—tells her a story—"such a pretty little tale," that the ass, who is listening, wishes he had pen and paper to take it down. For, while in aspect Lucius is an ass, his mind remains human—human enough to reflect sometimes what "a genuine ass" he is— and his skin has not, he regrets, the proper thickness of true ass-hide. The tale which he would like to write down is *Cupid and Psyche*. "*Erant in quadam civitate,*" begins the old woman—"There were in a certain city a king and a queen."

The old and universal fairy-tales of the invisible husband, the cruel sisters, and the impossible quests are here woven together and brought into connexion with the Olympic pantheon, and through all runs a slight thread, only here and there visible, of allegory. But if Psyche is at times the soul, and if the daughter she bears to Cupid is Pleasure, the fairy-tale triumphs gloriously over the allegory, and remains the most wonderful thing of the kind in Latin. Here, and in the *Golden Ass* in general, the extraordinarily embroidered language of Apuleius is far more in keeping than in his philosophic writings. His hundreds of diminutives and neologisms, his antitheses, alliterations, assonances, figures and tropes, his brilliant invention, his fun and humour, here have full scope and add pleasure to every fresh episode of the fairy-tale and of the larger and more miscellaneous tale of adventure in which it is set—in the strangest setting conceivable. *Cupid and Psyche* is his own addition to the story of the Ass—quite irrelevant, and like many other irrelevant things in books an immense enrichment.

Another development of the original story which is similarly due to Apuleius alone is the climax in the last book. The ass, in the Greek story, becomes a man by eating roses. In the Latin, Lucius, weary of the life of an ass, finds himself by moonlight on the seashore near Corinth, and amid "the silent

---

[1] The story of Lamachus "our high-souled leader," now "buried in the entire element," would make anyone wish to become a brigand, Sainte-Beuve said. Here one must regretfully omit the robbers' cave altogether.

secrets of opaque night," he reflects that "the supreme goddess
rules in transcendent majesty and governs human affairs by her
providence." So he addresses a rather too eloquent prayer to
the Queen of Heaven under her various possible names, Ceres,
Venus, Diana and Proserpine. He then falls asleep, and at
once "lo! from mid sea, uplifting a countenance venerable
even to gods, emerges a divine form. Gradually the vision,
gleaming all over, and shaking off the sea, seemed to stand
before me." A crown of flowers rests on her flowing hair.
Glittering stars, the moon, flowers and fruits, are wrought into
her raiment, which shimmers white and yellow and red as the
light falls upon it. In one hand is a sistrum, in the other a
golden vessel shaped like a boat, with an asp for its handle.[1]
She speaks.

"Lo! I come in answer, Lucius, to thy prayers, I mother
of Nature, mistress of all the elements, initial offspring of ages,
chief of divinities, queen of the dead, first of the heavenly ones,
in one form expressing all gods and goddesses. I rule with
my rod the bright pinnacles of heaven, the healthful breezes of
the sea, the weeping silence of the world below. My sole
godhead, in many an aspect, with many a various rite, and
many a name, all the world worships." Some of these names
she recites, and then declares her "true name, Queen Isis."[2]
The next day is her festival, she says, and her priest, taught
by her in a dream, will tender Lucius the needful roses; he
will eat and be a man again. But hereafter all his life
must be devoted to the goddess, and then in the Elysian fields
he shall see her again, shining amid the darkness of Acheron,
propitious to him.

The next day all falls as predicted. The procession of Isis
is elaborately described.[3] The prelude of the pomp is a series
of men dressed in various characters,—one like a soldier,
another like a woman, others like a gladiator, a philosopher and
so forth. There is a tame bear dressed like a woman, and a
monkey "in a Phrygian garment of saffron." Then come
women in white, crowned with flowers, some with mirrors
hanging on their backs, some carrying ivory combs. Men
and women follow with torches and lamps; then a choir of

---

[1] *Metam.* xi, 3, 4. Apuleius had a fancy for flowing hair.
[2] *Metam.* xi, 5.   [3] *Metam.* xi, 8 ff.

youths in white, singing a hymn, and fluteplayers dedicated to Serapis.   After this a crowd of initiates of both sexes, of every age and degree, dressed in white linen and carrying sistra,—the men with shaven heads.   Then came five chief priests with emblems, and after them the images of the gods borne by other priests—Anubis with his dog's head, black and gold—after him the figure of a cow "the prolific image of the all-mother goddess" ("which one of this blessed ministry bore on his shoulder, with mimicking gait")—then an image of divinity, like nothing mortal, an ineffable symbol, worthy of all veneration for its exquisite art.   At this point came the priest with the promised roses—"my salvation"—and Lucius ate and was a man again.   The priest, in a short homily, tells him he has now reached the haven of quiet; Fortune's blindness has no more power over him; he is taken to the bosom of a Fortune who can see, who can illuminate even the other gods.   Let him rejoice and consecrate his life to the goddess, undertake her warfare and become her soldier.[1]

The pomp moves onward till they reach the shore, and there a sacred ship is launched — inscribed with Egyptian hieroglyphics, purified with a burning torch, an egg, and sulphur, on her sail a vow written in large letters.   She is loaded with aromatics; and "filled with copious gifts and auspicious prayers" she sails away before a gentle breeze and is lost to sight.   The celebrants then return to the temple, but we have perhaps followed them far enough.

From now on to the end of the book the reformed Lucius lives in the odour of sanctity.   He never sleeps without a vision of the goddess.   He passes on from initiation to initiation, though the service of religion is difficult, chastity arduous, and life now a matter of circumspection—it had not been before.   The initiations are, he owns, rather expensive.[2] "Perhaps, my enthusiastic reader, thou wilt ask—anxiously enough—what was said, what done.   I would speak if it were

---

[1] *Metam.* xi, 15, *da nomen sanctæ huic militiæ cuius . . . sacramento, etc.*

[2] Tertullian remarks that pagan rituals, unlike Christian baptism, owe much to pomp *and expense; de Bapt.* 2.   *Mentior si non e contrario idolorum sollemnia vel arcana de suggestu et apparatu deque sumptu fidem et auctoritatem sibi extruunt*

lawful to speak, thou shouldst know if it were lawful to hear. . . . Hear then, and believe, for it is true. I drew near to the confines of death ; I trod the threshold of Proserpine ; I was borne through all the elements and returned. At midnight I saw the sun flashing with bright light. Gods of the world below, gods of the world above, into their presence I came, I worshipped there in their sight." Garments, emblems, rites, purifications are the elements of his life now. Nor does he grudge the trouble and expense, for the gods are blessing him with forensic success. In a dream, Osiris himself " chief among the great gods, of the greater highest, greatest of the highest, ruler of the greatest," appears in person, and promises him—speaking with his own awful voice—triumphs at the bar, with no need to fear the envy his learning might rouse. He should be one of the god's own Pastophori, one of " his quinquennial decurions." So " with my hair perfectly shaved, I performed in gladness the duties of that most ancient college, established in Sulla's times, not shading nor covering my baldness, but letting it be universally conspicuous." And there ends the *Golden Ass.*

Was it true—this story of the ass ? Augustine says that Apuleius " either disclosed or made up " these adventures. Both he and Lactantius had to show their contemporaries that there was a difference between the miracles of Apuleius and those of Christ.[1] The Emperor Septimius Severus, on the other hand, sneered at his rival Albinus for reading " the Punic Milesian-tales of his fellow-countryman Apuleius and such literary trifles." [2]

Between these two judgments we may find Apuleius. He is a man of letters, but he has a taste for religion. Ceremony, mystery, ritual, sacraments, appeal to him, and there he stands with his contemporaries. But a man, in whose pages bandit and old woman, ass and Isis, all talk in one Euphuistic strain, was possibly not so pious as men of simpler speech. Yet his giving such a conclusion to such a tale is significant, and there is not an absurdity among all the many, in which he so gaily revels, but corresponded with something that men believed.

---

[1] Augustine, *C.D.* xviii, 18 ; and cf. *ib.* viii, 14 (on the *de deo Socr.*) ; and Lactantius, v, 3.

[2] Capitolinus *v. Albini*, 12.

In conclusion, we may ask what Lucian of Samosata and Diogenes of Oinoanda had to offer to Aristides and Pausanias and Apuleius; and what they in turn could suggest to men whose concern in religion goes deeper than the cure of physical disease, trance and self-conscious revelling in ceremony. Some spiritual value still clung about the old religion, or it could not have found supporters in a Plotinus and a Porphyry, but (to quote again a most helpful question) "how much else?"

CHAPTER VIII

CELSUS

Deliquit, opinor, divina doctrina ex Judæa potius quam ex Græcia oriens. Erravit et Christus piscatores citius quam sophistam ad præconium emittens.—TERTULLIAN, *de Anima*, 3.

AT the beginning of the last chapter reference was made to the spread of Christianity in the second century, and then a brief survey was given of the position of the old religion without reference to the new.   When one realizes the different habits of mind represented by the men there considered, the difficulties with which Christianity had to contend become more evident and more intelligible.   Lucian generally ignored it, only noticing it to laugh at its folly and to pass on—it was too inconspicuous to be worth attack.   To the others—the devout of the old religion, whose fondest thoughts were for the past, and for whom religion was largely a ritual, sanctified by tradition and by fancy,—the Christian faith offered little beyond the negation of all they counted dear. We are happily in possession of fragments of an anti-Christian work of the day, written by a man philosophic and academic in temperament, but sympathetic with the followers of the religion of his fathers—fragments only, but enough to show how Christianity at once provoked the laughter, incensed the patriotism, and offended the religious tastes of educated people.

It was for a man called Celsus that Lucian wrote his book upon the prophet Alexander and his shrine at Abonoteichos, and it has been suggested that Lucian's friend and the Celsus, who wrote the famous *True Word*, may have been one and the same.   The evidence is carefully worked out by Keim,[1] but it is not very strong, especially as some two dozen men of the name are known to the historians of the first three centuries of our era.   Origen himself knew little of Celsus—hardly more than we can gather from the quotations he made from the book

[1] Keim, *Celsus' Wahres Wort* (1873).

239

in refuting it. From a close study of his occasional hints at
contemporary history, Keim puts Celsus' book down to the
latter part of the reign of Marcus Aurelius, or, more closely, to
the year 178 A.D.[1] Celsus' general references to Christianity
and to paganism imply that period. He writes under the
pressure of the barbarian inroads on the Northern frontier, of
the Parthians in the East and of the great plague. His main
concern is the Roman State, shaken by all these misfortunes,
and doubly threatened by the passive disaffection of Christians
within its borders.[2] From what Turk and Mongol meant to
Europe in the Middle Ages and may yet mean to us, we may
divine how men of culture and patriotism felt about the white
savages coming down upon them from the North.

Of the personal history of Celsus nothing can be said, but
the features of his mind are well-marked. He was above all
a man of culture,—candid, scholarly and cool. He knew and
admired the philosophical writings of ancient Greece, he had
some knowledge of Egypt, and he also took the pains to read
the books of the Jews and the Christians. On the whole he
leant to Plato, but, like many philosophic spirits, he found
destructive criticism more easy than the elaboration of a system
of his own. Yet here we must use caution, for the object he
had set before him was not to be served by individual speculation. It was immaterial what private opinions he might hold,
for his great purpose was the abandonment of particularism and
the fusion of all parties for the general good. Private judgment
run mad was the mark of all Christians, orthodox and heretical,
—" men walling themselves off and isolating themselves from
mankind "[3]—and his thesis was that the whole spirit of the
movement was wrong. A good citizen's part was loyal
acceptance of the common belief, deviation from which was now
shown to impair the solidarity of the civilized world. Of course
such a position is never taken by really independent thinkers ;
but it is the normal standpoint of men to whom practical

---

[1] Keim, pp. 264-273.

[2] Tertullian, *Apol.* 38, *nec ulla res aliena magis quam publica.* Elsewhere
Tertullian explains this : *lædimus Romanos nec Romani habemur qui non
Romanorum deum colimus, Apol.* 24.

[3] Apud Origen, *c. Cels.* viii, 2. References in what follows will be made to the
book and chapter of this work without repetition of Origen's name. The text used
is that of Koetschau.

affairs are of more moment than speculative precision—men, who are at bottom sceptical, and have little interest in problems which they have given up as insoluble. Celsus was satisfied with the established order, alike in the regions of thought and of government. He mistrusted new movements—not least when they were so conspicuously alien to the Greek mind as the new superstition that came from Palestine. He has all the ancient contempt of the Greek for the barbarian, and, while he is influenced by the high motive of care for the State, there are traces of irritation in his tone which speak of personal feeling. The folly of the movement provoked him.

This, he says, is the language of the Christians : "'Let no cultured person draw near, none wise, none sensible ; for all that kind of thing we count evil ; but if any man is ignorant, if any is wanting in sense and culture, if any is a fool, let him come boldly.' Such people they spontaneously avow to be worthy of their God ; and, so doing, they show that it is only the simpletons, the ignoble, the senseless, slaves and women-folk and children, whom they wish to persuade, or can persuade."[1] Those who summon men to the other initiations (τελετὰς), and offer purification from sins, proclaim : " Whosoever has clean hands and is wise of speech," or " Whosoever is pure from defilement, whose soul is conscious of no guilt, who has lived well and righteously." " But let us hear what sort these people invite ; ' Whosoever is a sinner, or unintelligent, or a fool, in a word, whosoever is god-forsaken (κακοδαίμων), him the kingdom of God will receive.' Now whom do you mean by the sinner but the wicked, thief, housebreaker, poisoner, temple-robber, grave-robber ? Whom else would a brigand invite to join him ? "[2] But the Christian propaganda is still more odious. " We see them in our own houses, wool dressers, cobblers, and fullers, the most uneducated and vulgar persons, not daring to say a word in the presence of their masters who are older and wiser ; but when they get hold of the children in private, and silly women with them, they are wonderfully eloquent,—to the effect that the children must not listen to their father, but believe *them* and be taught by *them* ; . . . that they alone know how to live, and if the children will listen to them, they will be happy themselves, and will make

---

[1] *c. Cels.* iii, 44. [2] *Ibid.* iii, 59.

their home blessed. But if, while they are speaking, they see some of the children's teachers, some wiser person or their father coming, the more cautious of them will be gone in a moment, and the more impudent will egg on the children to throw off the reins—whispering to them that, while their father or their teachers are about, they will not and cannot teach them anything good . . . they must come with the women, and the little children that play with them, to the women's quarters, or the cobbler's shop, or the fuller's, to receive perfect knowledge. And that is how they persuade them." [1] They are like quacks who warn men against the doctor—" take care that none of you touches Science (ἐπιστήμη); Science is a bad thing; knowledge (γνῶσις) makes men fall from health of soul." [2] They will not argue about what they believe—" they always bring in their 'Do not examine, but believe,' and 'Thy faith shall save thee'" [3]—" believe that he, whom I set forth to you, is the son of God, even though he was bound in the most dishonourable way, and punished in the most shameful, though yesterday or the day before he weltered in the most disgraceful fashion before the eyes of all men—so much the more believe!" [4] So far all the Christian sects are at one.

And the absurdity of it! "Why was he not sent to the sinless as well as to sinners? What harm is there in not having sinned?" [5] Listen to them! "The unjust, if he humble himself from his iniquity, God will receive; but the just, if he look up to Him with virtue from beginning to end, him He will not receive." [6] Celsus' own view is very different —" It must be clear to everybody, I should think, that those, who are sinners by nature and training, none could change,

---

[1] iii, 55. I have omitted a clause or two.

Clem. A. *Strom.* iv, 67, on the other hand, speaks of the difficult position of wife or slave in such a divided household, and (68) of conversions in spite of the master of the house. Tert. *ad Scap.* 3, has a story of a governor whose wife became a Christian, and who in anger began a persecution at once.

[2] iii, 75.

[3] i, 9. Cf. Clem. Alex. *Strom.* i, 43, on some Christians who think themselves εὐφυεῖς and "ask for faith—faith alone and bare." In *Paed.* i, 27, he says much the same himself, τὸ πιστεῦσαι μόνον καὶ ἀναγεννηθῆναι τελείωσίς ἐστιν ἐν ζωῇ.

[4] vi, 10. Clem. Alex. *Strom.* ii, 8, " The Greeks think Faith empty and barbarous, and revile it," but (ii, 30) " if it had been a human thing, as they supposed, it would have been quenched."

[5] iii, 62.   [6] iii, 62.

not even by punishment—to say nothing of doing it by pity!
For to change nature completely is very difficult ; and those
who have not sinned are better partners in life." [1] Christians
in fact make God into a sentimentalist—" the slave of pity for
those who mourn " [2] to the point of injustice.

Jews and Christians seem to Celsus " like a swarm of bats
—or ants creeping out of their nest—or frogs holding a
symposium round a swamp — or worms in conventicle
(ἐκκλησιάζουσι) in a corner of the mud [3]—debating which of
them are the more sinful, and saying ' God reveals all things
to us beforehand and gives us warning ; he forsakes the whole
universe and the course of the heavenly spheres, and all this
great earth he neglects, to dwell with us alone ; to us alone he
despatches heralds, and never ceases to send and to seek how
we may dwell with him for ever.' "   " God is," say the worms,
" and after him come we, brought into being by him (ὑπ' αὐτοῦ
γεγονότες), in all things like unto God ; and to us all things
are subjected, earth and water and air and stars ; for our sake
all things are, and to serve us they are appointed."   " Some
of us," continue the worms (" he means us," says Origen)—
" some of us sin, so God will come, or else he will send his son,
that he may burn up the unrighteous, and that the rest of us
may have eternal life with him." [4]

The radical error in Jewish and Christian thinking is that
it is anthropocentric.   They say that God made all things for
man,[5] but this is not at all evident.   What we know of the
world suggests that it is not more for the sake of man than
of the irrational animals that all things were made.   Plants and
trees and grass and thorns—do they grow for man a whit
more than for the wildest animals?   " ' Sun and night serve
mortals,' says Euripides—but why us more than the ants or
the flies ?   For them, too, night comes for rest, and day for sight
and work."   If men hunt and eat animals, they in their turn
hunt and eat men ; and before towns and communities were
formed, and tools and weapons made, man's supremacy was
even more questionable.   " In no way is man better in God's

[1] iii, 65, τοὺς ἁμαρτάνειν πεφυκότας τε καὶ εἰθισμένους.   [2] iii, 71.
[3] Clement of Alexandria, *Protr.* 92, uses this simile of worms in the mud of swamps,
applying it to people who live for pleasure.
[4] iv. 23.   [5] iv, 74.

sight than ants and bees " (iv. 81). The political instinct of man is shared by both these creatures—they have constitutions, cities, wars and victories, and trials at law—as the drones know. Ants have sense enough to secure their corn stores from sprouting : they have graveyards ; they can tell one another which way to go—thus they have λόγος and ἔννοιαι like men. If one looked from heaven, would there be any marked difference between the procedures of men and of ants ?[1] But man has an intellectual affinity with God ; the human mind conceives thoughts that are essentially divine (θείας ἐννοίας).[2] Many animals can make the same claim—" what could one call more divine than to foreknow and foretell the future ? And this men learn from the other animals and most of all from birds ; " and if this comes from God, " so much nearer divine intercourse do they seem by nature than we, wiser and more dear to God." Thus " all things were not made for man, just as they were not made for the lion, nor the eagle, nor the dolphin, but that the universe as a work of God might be complete and perfect in every part. It is for this cause that the proportions of all things are designed, not for one another (except incidentally) but for the whole. God's care is for the whole, and this Providence never neglects. The whole does not grow worse, nor does God periodically turn it to himself. He is not angry on account of men, just as he is not angry because of monkeys or flies ; nor does he threaten the things, each of which in measure has its portion of himself."[3]

Celsus held that Christians spoke of God in a way that was neither holy nor guiltless (οὐχ ὁσίως οὐδ᾽ εὐαγῶς, iv, 10); and he hinted that they did it to astonish ignorant listeners.[4] For himself, he was impressed with the thought, which Plato has in the *Timæus*,—a sentence that sums up what many of the most serious and religious natures have felt and will always feel to be profoundly true : " The maker and father of this

---

[1] So Lucian *Icaromenippus*, 19, explicitly.

[2] iv, 88. Cf. Clem. Alex. *Pædag.* i, 7, τὸ φίλτρον ἔνδον ἐστὶν ἐν τῷ ἀνθρώπῳ τοῦθ᾽ ὅπερ ἐμφύσημα λέγεται θεοῦ.

[3] c. *Cels.* iv, 74-99. Cf. Plato, *Laws*, 903 B, ὡς τῷ τοῦ παντὸς ἐπιμελουμένῳ πρὸς τὴν σωτηρίαν καὶ ἀρετὴν τοῦ ὅλου πάντ᾽ ἐστὶ συντεταγμένα κτἑ, explicitly developing the idea of the part being for the whole. Also Cicero, *N.D.* ii, 13, 34-36.

Of. M. Aurelius, xi, 3, the criticism of the heatricality of the Christians. See p. 198.

whole fabric it is hard to find, and, when one has found him, it is impossible to speak of him to all men." [1] Like the men of his day, a true and deep instinct led him to point back to " inspired poets, wise men and philosophers," and to Plato " a more living (ἐνεργέστερον) teacher of theology " [2]—" though I should be 'surprised if you are able to follow him, seeing that you are utterly bound up in the flesh and see nothing clearly." [3] What the sages tell him of God, he proceeds to set forth.

" Being and becoming, one is intelligible, the other visible (νοητὸν, ὁρατὸν). Being is the sphere of truth ; becoming, of error. Truth is the subject of knowledge ; the other of opinion. Thought deals with the intelligible ; sight with the visible. The mind recognizes the intelligible, the eye the visible.

" What then the Sun is among things visible,—neither eye, nor sight—yet to the eye the cause of its seeing, to sight the cause of its existing (συνίστασθαι) by his means, to things visible the cause of their being seen, to all things endowed with sensation the cause of their existence (γίνεσθαι) and indeed the cause himself of himself being seen ; this HE is among things intelligible (νοητὰ), who is neither mind, nor thought, nor knowledge, but to the mind the cause of thinking, to thought of its being by his means, to knowledge of our knowing by his means, to all things intelligible, to truth itself, and to being itself, the cause that they are—out beyond all things (πάντων ἐπέκεινα ὢν), intelligible only by some unspeakable faculty.

" So have spoken men of mind ; and if *you* can understand anything of it, it is well for you. If you suppose a spirit descends from God to proclaim divine matters, it would be the spirit that proclaims this, that spirit with which men of old were filled and in consequence announced much that was good. But if you can take in nothing of it, be silent and hide your own ignorance, and do not say that those who see are blind, and those who run are lame, especially when you yourselves are utterly crippled and mutilated in soul, and live in the body —that is to say, in the dead element." [4]

Origen says that Celsus is constantly guilty of tautology, and the reiteration of this charge of ignorance and want of

---

[1] *c. Cels.* vii, 42, τὸν μὲν οὖν ποιητὴν καὶ πατέρα τοῦδε τοῦ παντὸς εὑρεῖν τε ἔργον καὶ εὑρόντα εἰς πάντας ἀδύνατον λέγειν ; *Timæus*, 28 C—often cited by Clement too.
[2] vii. 42. [3] vii, 42. [4] vii. 45.

culture is at least frequent enough. Yet if the Christian movement had been confined to people as vulgar and illiterate as he suggests, he might not have thought it worth his while to attack the new religion. His hint of the propagation of the Gospel by slaves in great houses, taken with the names of men of learning and position, whom we know to have been converted, shows the seriousness of the case. But to avoid the further charge which Origen brings against Celsus of "mixing everything up," it will be better to pursue Celsus' thoughts of God.

"I say nothing new, but what seemed true of old (πάλαι δεδογμένα). God is good, and beautiful, and happy, and is in that which is most beautiful and best. If then he 'descends to men,' it involves change for him, and change from good to bad, from beautiful to ugly, from happiness to unhappiness, from what is best to what is worst. Who would choose such a change? For mortality it is only nature to alter and be changed; but for the immortal to abide the same forever. God would not accept such a change."[1] He presents a dilemma to the Christians; "Either God really changes, as they say, to a mortal body,—and it has been shown that this is impossible; or he himself does not change, but he makes those who see suppose so, and thus deceives and cheats them. Deceit and lying are evil, taken generally, though in the single case of medicine one might use them in healing friends who are sick or mad—or against enemies in trying to escape danger. But none who is sick or mad is a friend of God's; nor is God afraid of any one, so that he should use deceit to escape danger."[2] God in fact "made nothing mortal; but God's works are such things as are immortal, and *they* have made the mortal. The soul is God's work, but the nature of the body is different, and in this respect there is no difference between the bodies of bat, worm, frog, and man. The matter is the same and the corruptible part is alike."[3]

The Christian conception of the "descent of God" is repulsive to Celsus, for it means contact with matter. "God's anger," too, is an impious idea, for anger is a passion; and

[1] iv, 14.

[2] iv, 18. See Tertullian's argument on this question of God changing, in *de Carne Christi*, 3. See Plato, *Rep.* ii, 381 B.

[3] iv, 52. See *Timæus*, 34 B ff. on God making soul.

Celsus makes havoc of the Old Testament passages where God is spoken of as having human passions (ἀνθρωποπαθής), closing with an *argumentum ad hominem*—" Is it not absurd that a man [Titus], angry with the Jews, slew all their youth and burnt their land, and so they came to nothing ; but God Almighty, as they say, angry and vexed and threatening, sends his son and endures such things as they tell?"[1] Furthermore, the Christian account of God's anger at man's sin involves a presumption that Christians really know what evil is. " Now the origin of evil is not to be easily known by one who has no philosophy. It is enough to tell the common people that evil is not from God, but is inherent in matter, and is a fellow-citizen (ἐμπολιτεύεται) of mortality. The circuit of mortal things is from beginning to end the same, and in the appointed circles the same must always of necessity have been and be and be again."[2] " Nor could the good or evil elements in mortal things become either less or greater.. God does not need to restore all things anew. God is not like a man, that, because he has faultily contrived or executed without skill, he should try to amend the world."[3] In short, " even if a thing seems to you to be bad, it is not yet clear that it is bad ; for you do not know what is of advantage to yourself, or to another, or to the whole."[4] Besides would God need to descend in order to

---

[1] iv, 73. See Clem. Alex. *Paed.* i, ch. 10, on God threatening ; and *Strom.* ii, 72 ; iv, 151 ; vii, 37, for the view that God is without anger, and for guidance as to the understanding of language in the O.T. which seems to imply the contrary. For a different view, see Tertullian, *de Testim. Animæ*, 2, *unde igitur naturalis timor animæ in deum, si deus non novit irasci?* adv. *Marc.* i, 26, 27, on the necessity for God's anger, if the moral law is to be maintained ; and adv. *Marc.* ii, 16, a further account of God's anger, while a literal interpretation of God's "eyes" and "right hand" is excluded.

[2] iv, 65.　　　　　　　　　　[3] iv, 69.

[4] iv, 70. Long before (about 500 B.C.) Heraclitus had said (fragm. 61) : " To God all things are beautiful and good and just ; but men have supposed some things to be unjust and others just." For this doctrine of the relativity of good and bad to the whole, cf. hymn of Cleanthes to Zeus :—

> ἀλλὰ σὺ καὶ τὰ περισσά τ' ἐπίστασαι ἄρτια θεῖναι,
> καὶ κοσμεῖν τἄκοσμα, καὶ οὐ φίλα σοὶ φίλα ἐστίν.
> ὧδε γὰρ εἰς ἓν πάντα συνήρμοκας ἐσθλὰ κακοῖσιν
> ὥσθ' ἕνα γίγνεσθαι πάντων λόγον αἰὲν ἐόντα.

Cf. also the teaching of Chrysippus, as given by Gellius, *N.A.* vii, 1 : *cum bona malis contraria sint, utraque necessum est opposita inter sese et quasi mutuo adverso quæque fulta nisu consistere ; nullum adeo contrarium est sine contrario altero . . . si tuleris*

learn what was going on among men?[1]   Or was he dissatisfied with the attention he received, and did he really come down "to show off like a *nouveau riche* (οἱ νεόπλουτοι)?"[2]   Then why not long before?[3]

Should Christians ask him how God is to be seen, he has his answer: "If you will be blind to sense and see with the mind, if you will turn from the flesh and waken the eyes of the soul, thus and thus only shall you see God."[4]   In words that Origen approves, he says, "from God we must never and in no way depart, neither by day nor by night, in public or in private, in every word and work perpetually, but, with these and without, let the soul ever be strained towards God."[5]   "If any man bid you, in the worship of God, either to do impiety, or to say anything base, you must never be persuaded by him. Rather endure every torture and submit to every death, than think anything unholy of God, let alone say it."[6]

Thus the fundamental conceptions of the Christians are shown to be wrong, but more remains to be done.   Let us assume for purposes of discussion that there could be a "descent of God"—would it be what the Christians say it was?   "God is great and hard to be seen," he makes the Christian say, "so he put his own spirit into a body like ours and sent it down here that we might hear and learn from it."[7]   If that is true, he says, then God's son cannot be immortal, since the nature of a spirit is not such as to be permanent; nor could Jesus have risen again in the body, "for God would not have received back the spirit which he gave when it was polluted with the nature of the body."[8]   "If he had wished to send down a spirit from himself, why did he need to breathe it into the womb of a woman?   He knew already how to

---

unum abstuleris utrumque.   See also M. Aurelius in the same Stoic vein, viii, 50; ix, 42.   On the other side see Plutarch's indignant criticism of this attribution of the responsibility for evil to God, *de comm. not. adv. Sto.* 14, 1065 D, ff.   In opposition to Marcion, Tertullian emphasizes the worth of the world; his position, as a few words will show, is not that of Celsus, but Stoic influence is not absent: *adv. Marc.* i, 13, 14; *Ergo nec mundus deo indignus: nihil etenim deus indignum se fecit, etsi mundum homini non sibi fecit, etsi omne opus inferius est suo artifice;* see p. 317

[1] iv, 3.   [2] iv, 6.   [3] iv, 7.   [4] vii, 36.   [5] viii, 63.   [6] viii, 66.

[7] vi, 69.   "Men, who count themselves wise," says Clement (*Strom.* i, 88), "count it a fairy tale that the son of God should speak through man, or that God should have a son, and he suffer."

[8] vi, 72.

make men, and he could have fashioned a body about this spirit too, and so avoided putting his own spirit into such pollution."[1] Again the body, in which the spirit was sent, ought to have had stature or beauty or terror or persuasion, whereas they say it was little, ugly and ignoble.[2]

Then, finally, " suppose that God, like Zeus in the Comedy, waking out of long sleep, determined to rescue mankind from evil, why on earth did he send this spirit (as you call it) into one particular corner? He ought to have breathed through many bodies in the same way and sent them all over the world. The comic poet, to make merriment in the theatre, describes how Zeus waked up and sent Hermes to the Athenians and Lacedæmonians; do you not think that your invention of God's son being sent to the Jews is more laughable still?"[3] The incarnation further carried with it stories of " God eating "—mutton, vinegar, gall. This revolted Celsus, and he summed it all up in one horrible word.[4]

The ignomiuy of the life of Jesus was evidence to Celsus of the falsity of his claim to be God's son. He bitterly taunts Christians with following a child of shame—" God's would not be a body like yours—nor begotten as you were begotten, Jesus!"[5] He reviles Jesus for the Passion—"unhelped by his Father and unable to help himself."[6] He goes to the Gospels ("I know the whole story," he says[7]) and he cites incident after incident. He reproaches Jesus with seeking to escape the cross,[8] he brings forward "the men who mocked him and put the purple robe on him, the crown of thorns, and

---

[1] vi, 73. Cf. the Marcionite view; cf. Tert. *adv. Marc.* iii, 11 ; iv, 21 ; v, 19, *cuius ingeniis tam longe abest veritas nostra ut* . . . *Christum ex vulva virginis natum non erubescat, ridentibus philosophis et hæreticis et ethnicis ipsis.* See also *de carne Christi,* 4, 5, where he strikes a higher note ; Christ loved man, born as man is, and descended for him.

[2] vi, 75. Cf. Tert. *de carne Christi,* 9, *adeo nec humanæ honestatis corpus fuit ; adv. Jud.* 14, *ne aspectu quidem honestus.*

[3] vi, 78. Cf. Tert. *adv. Marc.* iii, 2, *atquin nihil putem a deo subitum quia nihil a deo non dispositum.*

[4] vii, 13, σκατοφαγεῖν. Origen's reply is absurd—ἵνα γὰρ καὶ δόξῃ ὅτι ἤσθιεν, ὡς σῶμα φορῶν ὁ Ἰησοῦς ἤσθιεν. So also said Clement (*Strom.* vi, 71). Valentinus had another theory no better, *Strom.* iii. 59. Marcion, Tertullian says (*adv. Marc.* iii, 10), called the flesh *terrenam et stercoribus infusam.* They are all filled with the same contempt for matter—not Tertullian, however.

[5] i, 69.   [6] i, 54.   [7] i, 12.   [8] ii, 23, 24.

the reed in his hand ";[1] he taunts him with being unable to endure his thirst upon the cross—"which many a common man will endure."[2] As to the resurrection, "if Jesus wished really to display his divine power, he ought to have appeared to the actual men who reviled him, and to him who condemned him and to all, for, of course, he was no longer afraid of any man, seeing he was dead, and, as you say, God, and was not originally sent to elude observation."[3] Or, better still, to show his Godhead, he might have vanished from the gibbet.[4]

What befel Jesus, befals his followers. " Don't you see, my dear sir ? " Celsus says, " a man may stand and blaspheme your dæmon ; and not that only, he may forbid him land and sea, and then lay hands on *you*, who are consecrated to him like a statue, bind you, march you off and impale you ; and the dæmon, or, as you say, the son of God, does not help you."[5] " You may stand and revile the statues of the gods and laugh. But if you tried it in the actual presence of Dionysus or Herakles, you might not get off so comfortably. But your god in his own person they spread out and punished, and those who did it have suffered nothing. . . . He too who sent his son (according to you) with some message or other, looked on and saw him thus cruelly punished, so that the message perished with him, and though all this time has passed he has never heeded. What father was ever so unnatural ($\dot{a}\nu\acute{o}\sigma\iota\sigma\varsigma$)? Ah ! but perhaps he wished it, you say, and that was why he endured the insult. And perhaps our gods *wish* it too, when you blaspheme them."[6]

Celsus would seem to have heard Christian preaching, for beside deriding " Only believe " and " Thy faith will save thee," he is offended by the language they use about the cross. " Wide as the sects stand apart, and bitter as are their quarrels and mutual abuse, you will hear them all say their ' To me the world is crucified and I to the world.' "[7] In one great passage he mixes, as Origen says, the things he has mis-heard, and quotes Christian utterances about "a soul that lives, and a heaven that is slain that it may live, and earth slain with the

---

[1] ii, 34.   [2] ii, 37.

[3] ii, 66, 67. Tertullian meets this in *Apol.* 21. *Nam nec ille se in vulgus eduxit ne impii errore liberarentur, ut et fides, non mediocri praemio destinata, difficultate constaret.*

[4] ii, 68.   [5] viii, 39.   [6] viii, 41.   [7] v, 65.

sword, and ever so many people being slain to live ; and death taking a rest in the world when the sin of the world dies ; and then a narrow way down, and gates that open of themselves. And everywhere you have the tree of life and the resurrection of the flesh from the tree—I suppose, because their teacher was nailed to a cross and was a carpenter by trade. Exactly as, if he had chanced to be thrown down a precipice, or pushed into a pit, or choked in a noose, or if he had been a cobbler, or a stone-mason, or a blacksmith, there would have been above the heavens a precipice of life, or a pit of resurrection, or a rope of immortality, or a happy stone, or the iron of love, or the holy hide." [1]

The miracles of Jesus Celsus easily explains. "Through poverty he went to Egypt and worked there as a hired labourer ; and there he became acquainted with certain powers [or faculties], on which the Egyptians pride themselves, and he came back holding his head high on account of them, and because of them he announced that he was God." [2]   But, granting the miracles of healing and of raising the dead and feeding the multitudes, he maintains that ordinary quacks will do greater miracles in the streets for an obol or two, "driving devils out of men,[3] and blowing away diseases and calling up the souls of heroes, and displaying sumptuous banquets and tables and sweetmeats and dainties that are not there ;"— "must we count *them* sons of God ?" [4]   There are plenty of prophets too, "and it is quite an easy and ordinary thing for each of them to say ' I am God—or God's son—or a divine spirit. And I am come ; for already the world perisheth, and ye, oh men, are lost for your sins. But I am willing to

---

[1] vi, 34. Cf. a curious passage of Clem. Alex. *Protr.* 114, οὗτος τὴν δύσιν εἰς ἀνατολὴν μετήγαγεν καὶ τὸν θάνατον εἰς ζωὴν ἀνεσταύρωσεν ἐξαρπάσας δὲ τῆς ἀπωλείας τὸν ἄνθρωπον προσεκρέμασεν αἰθέρι, and so forth. Cf. Tert. *adv. Valent.* 20, who suggests that the Valentinians had "nut-trees in the sky "—it is a book in which he allows himself a good deal of gaiety and free quotation.

[2] i, 28.

[3] M. Aurelius, i, 6, " From Diognetus I learnt not to give credit to what was said by miracle-workers and jugglers (γοήτων) about incantations and the sending away of dæmons and such things. " Cf. Tertullian, *adv. Marc.* iii, 2-4, on inadequacy of proof from miracles alone, without that from prophecy ; also *de Anima,* 57, on these con-jurers, where he remarks, *nec magnum illi exteriores oculos circumscribere, an interiorem mentis aciem excalcare perfacile est.* See also *Apol.* 22, 23.

[4] i, 68.

save you ; and ye shall see me hereafter coming with heavenly power. Blessed is he that has worshipped me now ; but upon all the rest I will send eternal fire, and upon their cities and lands. And men who do not recognize their own guilt shall repent in vain with groans ; and them that have believed me, I will guard for ever.'"[1] Jesus was, he holds, an obvious quack and impostor. In fact, there is little to choose between worshipping Jesus and Antinous, the favourite of Hadrian, who had actually been deified in Egypt.[2]

The teaching of Jesus, to which Christians pointed, was after all a mere medley of garbled quotations from Greek literature. Thus when Jesus said that it is easier for a camel to go through a needle's eye than for a rich man to go into the kingdom of God, he was merely spoiling the Platonic saying that it is impossible for a man to be exceedingly good and exceedingly rich at the same time.[3] The kingdom of heaven itself comes from the "divinely spoken" words of Plato ; it is the "supercelestial region" of the *Phædrus*.[4] Satan is a parody of Heraclitus' conception of War.[5] The Christian resurrection comes from metempsychosis.[6] The idea that "God will descend, carrying fire (like a torturer in a law-court)" comes from some confused notion of the teaching of the Greeks upon cycles and periods and the final conflagra-tion.[7] Plato has this advantage that he never boasted and never said that God had "a son who descended and talked with me."[8] The "son of God" itself was an expression borrowed in their clumsy way by the Christians from the ancients who conceived of the universe as God's offspring.[9]

Christians lay great stress on the immortality, "but it is silly of them to suppose that when God—like a cook—brings the fire, the rest of mankind will be roasted and they themselves will alone remain, not merely the living, but even those who died long ago, rising from the earth with the identical flesh they had before. Really it is the hope of worms ! For what soul of a man would any longer wish for a body that

---

[1] vii, 9.　　　　　　　　　　　　　　　　　　　[2] iii, 36.
[3] vi, 16. Cf. Plato, *Laws*, v, 12, p. 743 A.
[4] vi, 17-19 ; *Phædrus*, 247 C.　　　　　　　　[5] vi, 42.
[6] vii, 32 ; cf. Min. Felix. 11, 9.　　[7] iv, 11.　　[8] vi, 8.
[9] vi, 47. Cf. Plato, *Timæus* (last words), 92 C, εἰς οὐρανὸς ὅδε μονογενὴς ὤν.

had rotted?"[1]   The loathsomeness of the idea, he says, cannot be expressed, and besides it is impossible.   "They have nothing to reply to this, so they fly to the absurdest refuge, and say that all is possible with God.   But God cannot do what is foul, and what is contrary to nature he will not do.   Though you in your vulgarity may wish a loathsome thing, it does not follow that God can do it, nor that you are right to believe at once that it will come to pass.   For it is not of superfluous desire and wandering disorder, but of true and just nature that God is prince ($\dot{\alpha}\rho\chi\eta\gamma\acute{\epsilon}\tau\eta\varsigma$).   He could grant immortal life of the soul ; but 'corpses,' as Heraclitus says, 'are less useful than dung.'   The flesh is full of—what it is not beautiful even to mention—and to make it immortal contrary to all reason ($\pi\alpha\rho\alpha\lambda\acute{o}\gamma\omega\varsigma$), is what God neither will nor can do.   For he is the reason of all things that are, so that he cannot do anything contrary to reason or contrary to himself."[2]   And yet, says Celsus, "you hope you will see God with the eyes of your body, and hear his voice with your ears, and touch him with the hands of sense."[3]   If they threaten the heathen with eternal punishment, the exegetes, hierophants, and mystagogues of the temples hurl back the same threat, and while words are equal, they can show proofs in dæmonic activities and oracles.[4]   " With those however who speak of the soul or the mind (whether they choose to call it spiritual, or a spirit intelligent,' holy and happy, or a living soul, or the supercelestial and incorruptible offspring of a divine and bodyless nature—or whatever they please)—with those who hope to have this eternally with God, with such I will speak.   For they are right in holding that they who have lived well will be happy and the unjust will be held in eternal woes.   From this opinion ($\delta\acute{o}\gamma\mu\alpha\tau o\varsigma$) let not them nor any one else depart."[5]

In this way Celsus surveys the main points of Christian history and teaching.   They have no real grounds beneath them.   The basis of the church is " faction ($\sigma\tau\acute{\alpha}\sigma\iota\varsigma$) and the profit it brings, and fear of those without ;—those are the things that establish the faith for them."[6]   Faction is their keynote, taken from the Jews at first ; and faction splits them up into innumerable sects beside the " great church,"[7]—" the

---

[1] v, 14.   [2] v, 14.   [3] vii, 34.   [4] viii. 48.
[5] viii, 49.   [6] iii, 14.   [7] v, 59.

one thing they have in common, if indeed they still have it, is
the name ; and this one thing they are ashamed to abandon." [1]
When they all say " ' Believe, if you wish to be saved, or
else depart ' ; what are those to do who really wish to be
saved ?   Should they throw the dice to find out to whom
to turn ? " [2]   In short, faction is their breath of life, and
" if all mankind were willing to be Christian, then they
would not." [3]

But Celsus is not content merely to refute ; he will point
out a more excellent way.   " Are not all things ruled according to the will of God ? is not all Providence from him ?
Whatever there is in the whole scheme of things, whether the
work of God, or of angels, or other dæmons, or heroes, all these
have their law from the greatest God ; and in power over each
thing is set he that has been counted fit." [4]   " Probably the
various sections are allotted to various rulers ($\epsilon\pi\acute{o}\pi\tau\alpha\iota\varsigma$) and
distributed in certain provinces, and so governed.   Thus
among the various nations things would be done rightly if done
as those rulers would have them.   It is then not holy to break
down what has been from the beginning the tradition of one
and another place." [5]   Again, the body is the prison of the soul ;
should there not then be warders of it—dæmons in fact ? [6]
Then "will not a man, who worships God, be justified in
serving him who has his power from God ? " [7]   To worship
them all cannot grieve him to whom they all belong. [8]   Over
and over Celsus maintains the duty of " living by the ancestral
usages," " each people worshipping its own traditional deities." [9]
To say with the Christians that there is one Lord, meaning
God, is to break up the kingdom of God and make factions
there ($\sigma\tau\alpha\sigma\iota\acute{a}\zeta\epsilon\iota\nu$), as if there were choices to be made, and one
were a rival of another. [10]

Ammon is no worse than the angels of the Jews ; though
here the Jews are so far right in that they hold by the ways of
their ancestors—an advantage which the Jewish proselytes have

---

[1] iii, 12.   [2] vi, 11.
[3] iii, 9.   Tertullian speaks in a somewhat similar way of heretics, especially of the
Gnostics: *de præscriptione hæret.* c. 42.
[4] vii, 68.   [5] v, 25.   [6] viii, 53, 58.
[7] vii, 68.   [8] viii, 2.   [9] Cf. v, 34, 35.
[10] viii, 11.   Cf. Tert. *adv. Prax.* 3, where it is argued that God's monarchy is not
impaired *tot angelorum numero*, nor by the οἰκονομία of the Trinity.

forfeited.[1] If the Jews pride themselves on superior knowledge
and so hold aloof from other men, Herodotus is evidence that
their supposed peculiar dogma is shared by the Persians ; and
" I think it makes no difference whether you call Zeus the
Most High, or Zeus, or Adonai, or Sabaoth, or Amûn, like the
Egyptians, or Papaios like the Scythians." [2]

The evidence for the ancillary dæmons and gods he finds in
the familiar places. " Why need I tell at length how many
things prophets and prophetesses at the oracles have foretold,
and other men and women possessed by a voice of a god
within them ? the marvels heard from shrines ? revelations from
sacrifices and victims, and other miraculous tokens ?   And some
have been face to face with visible phantoms. The whole of
life is full of these things." Cities have escaped plague and
famine through warnings from oracles, and have suffered for
neglecting them. The childless have gained children, and the
crippled have been healed, while those who have treated sacred
things with contempt have been punished in suicide and
incurable diseases.[3] Let a man go to the shrine of Trophonius
or Amphiaraus or Mopsus, and there he may see the gods in
the likeness of men, no feigned forms ($\psi\epsilon\upsilon\delta o\mu\acute{\epsilon}\nu o\upsilon\varsigma$) but clear to
see, " not slipping by them once, like him who deceived these
people [the Christians], but ever associating with those who
will." [4] " A great multitude of men, Greeks and barbarians,
testify that they have often seen and still do see Asklepios, and
not merely a phantom of him, but they see himself healing men,
and doing them good, and foretelling the future." [5]   Is it not
likely that these " satraps and ministers of air and earth " could
do you harm, if you did them despite ? [6]   Earthly rulers too
deserve worship, since they hold their positions not without
dæmonic influence.[7] Why should not the Christians worship
them, dæmons and Emperors ?   If they worshipped no other
but one God, they might have some clear argument against other
men; but, as it is, they more than worship the person who lately
appeared, and reckon that God is not wronged by the service
done to his subordinate,[8]—though in truth he is only a corpse.[9]
In any case, " if idols are nothing, what harm is there in taking
part in the festival ? but if there are dæmons, it is clear they too

[1] v, 41.   [2] v, 41.   [3] viii, 45.   [4] vii, 35.   [5] iii, 24. Cf. p. 222.
[6] viii, 35.   [7] viii, 63.   [8] viii, 12.   [9] vii, 68.

are of God, and in them we must trust, and speak them fair, according to the laws, and pray that they may be propitious."[1]

It is characteristic of the candour of Celsus that he lets slip a caution or two about the service of dæmons. Christians are as credulous, he says in one place, as "those who lightly (ἀλόγως) believe in the roaming priests of Cybele (μητραγύρταις) and wonder-seers, Mithras and Sabadios and the like—phantoms of Hecate or some other female dæmon or dæmons."[2] Again, he has a word of warning as to magic, and the danger and injury into which those fall who busy themselves with it— "One must be on one's guard, that one may not, by being occupied with these matters, become entangled in the service of them [literally ; fused with them, συντακῇ], and through love of the body and by turning away from better things be overcome by forgetfulness. For perhaps we should not disbelieve wise men, who say (as a matter of fact) that of the dæmons who pervade the earth the greater part are entangled in 'becoming' (γενέσει συντετηκός)—fused and riveted to it—and being bound to blood and smoke and chantings and other such things can do no more than heal the body and foretell future destiny to man and city ; and the limits of their knowledge and power are those of human affairs."[3]

At the last comes his great plea. Human authority is of divine ordinance. " To the Emperor all on earth is given ; and whatever you receive in life is from him."[4] "We must not disbelieve one of old, who long ago said—

Let one be king, to whom the son of wise Kronos has given it.

If you invalidate this thought (δόγμα), probably the Emperor will punish you. For if all men were to do as you do, nothing will prevent the Emperor being left alone and deserted,[5] and all things on earth falling into the power of the

---

[1] viii, 24. [2] i, 9, Μίθραις καὶ Σαβαδίοις.

[3] viii, 60. See note on ch. iii, p. 107. [4] viii, 67.

[5] Cf. Tert. *de cor. mil.* 11, if a soldier is converted, *aut deserendum statim ut a multis actum, aut*, etc. The chapter is a general discussion whether military service and Christianity are compatible. Cf. also Tert. *de idol.* 19, *Non convenit sacramento divino et humano, signo Christi et signo diaboli, castris lucis et castris tenebrarum . . . quomodo autem bellabit immo quomodo etiam in pace militabit sine gladio quem dominus abstulit? . . . . omnem postea militem dominus in Petro exarmando discinxit.* Tertullian, it may be remembered, was a soldier's son.

most lawless and barbarous savages, with the result that neither of your religion nor of the true wisdom would there be left among men so much as the name.[1]   You will hardly allege that if the Romans were persuaded by you and forsook all their usages as to gods and men, and called upon your 'Most High' or whatever you like, he would descend and fight for them and they would need no other help.   For before now that same God promised (as you say) this and much more to those who served him, and you see all the good he has done them and you.   As for them [the Jews], instead of being masters of all the earth, they have not a clod nor a hearthstone left them ; while you—if there is any of you left in hiding, search is being made for him to put him to death." [2] The Christian sentiment that it is desirable for all who inhabit the Empire, Greeks and barbarians, Asia, Europe and Libya, to agree to one law or custom, is foolish and impracticable.[3] So Celsus calls on the Christians " to come to the help of the Emperor with all their might and labour with him as right requires, fight on his behalf, take the field with him, if he call on you, and share the command of the legions with him [4]— yes, and be magistrates, if need be, and to do this for the salvation of laws and religion." [5]

It will be noted that, so far as our fragments serve us, Celsus confines himself essentially to the charges of folly, perversity, and want of national feeling.   An excessive opinion of the value of the human soul and an absurd fancy of God's interest in man are two of the chief faults he sees in Christianity.[6]   He sees well, for the love of God our Father and the infinite significance of the meanest and commonest and most depraved of men were after all the cardinal doctrines of the new faith.   There can be no compromise between the Christian conception of the Ecclesia of God and Celsus' contempt for an "ecclesia of worms in a pool"; nor between the "Abba Father" of Jesus and the aloof and philosophic God of Celsus "away   beyond   everything."   These   two

---

[1] viii, 68.   The Greeks used βασιλεύς as Emperor.

[2] viii, 69.   For this taunt against the Jews, cf. Cicero, *pro Flacco*, 28, 69.

[3] viii, 72.   [4] viii, 73.   [5] viii, 75.

[6] Cf. Clem. Alex. *Strom.* i, 55, who says that hardly any words could be to the many more absurd than the mysteries of the faith.

contrasts bring into clear relief the essentially new features of Christianity, and from the standpoint of ancient philosophy they were foolish and arbitrary fancies. That standpoint was unquestioned by Celsus.

Confident in the truth of his premisses and the conclusions that follow from them, Celsus charged the Christians with folly and dogmatism. Yet it would be difficult to maintain that they were more dogmatic than himself; they at least had ventured on the experiment of a new life, that was to bring ancient Philosophy to a new test. They were the researchers in spiritual things, and he the traditionalist. As to the charge of folly, we may at once admit a comparatively lower standard of education among the Christians; yet Lucian's book *Alexander*, with its curious story of the false prophet who classed them with the Epicureans as his natural enemies, suggests that, with all their limitations, they had an emancipation of mind not reached by all their contemporaries. If they did not accept the conclusions of Greek thinkers as final, they were still less prepared to accept sleight-of-hand and hysteria as the ultimate authority in religious truth.[1] Plutarch, we may remember, based belief in immortality on the oracles of Apollo ; and Celsus himself appeals to the evidence of shrines and miracles. If we say that pagans and Christians alike believed in the occurrence of these miracles and in dæmonic agency as their cause, it remains that the Christians put something much nearer the modern value upon them, while Celsus, who denounced the Christians as fools, tendered this contemptible evidence for the religion he advocated.

His Greek training was in some degree the cause of this. The immeasurable vanity of the Greeks did not escape the Romans. A sense of indebtedness to the race that has given us Homer, Euripides and Plato leads us to treat all Greeks kindly—with more kindness than those critics show them whose acquaintance with them has been less in literature and more in life. The great race still had gifts for mankind, but it was now mainly living upon its past. In Plutarch the pride of race is genial and pleasant ; in Celsus it takes another form—that of contempt for the barbarian and the unlettered.

---

[1] Clem. Alex. *Protr.* 56 (on idols). οὐ γάρ μοι θέμις ἐμπιστεῦσαί ποτε τοῖς ἀψύχοις τὰς τῆς ψυχῆς ἐλπίδας.

The truism may be forgiven that contempt is no pathway to understanding or to truth ; and in this case contempt cut Celsus off from any real access to the mind of the people he attacked. He read their books ; he heard them talk ; but, for all his conscious desire to inform himself, he did not penetrate into the heart of the movement—nor of the men. He missed the real motive force—the power of the life and personality of Jesus, on which depended the two cardinal doctrines which he assailed.

The extraordinary blunders, to which the very surest critics in literature are liable, may prepare us for anything. But to those who have some intimate realization of the mind of Jesus, the portrait which Celsus drew of him is an amazing caricature—the ignorant Jewish conjuror, who garbles Plato, and makes no impression on his friends, is hardly so much as a parody. It meant that Celsus did not understand the central thing in the new faith. The "godhead" of Jesus was as absurd as he said, if it was predicated of the Jesus whom he drew ; and there he let it rest. How such a dogma could have grown in such a case he did not inquire ; nor, finding it grown, did he correct his theory by the fact. Thus upon the real strength of Christianity he had nothing to say. This was not the way to convince opponents, and here the action of the Christians was sounder and braver. For they accepted the inspiration of the great men of Greece, entered into their spirit (as far as in that day it was possible), and fairly did their best to put themselves at a universal point of view.[1] They had the larger sympathies.

Yet for Celsus it may be pleaded that his object was perhaps less the reconversion of Christians to the old faith than to prevent the perversion of pagans to the new. But here too he failed, for he did not understand even the midway people with whom he was dealing. They were a large class—men and women open to religous ideas from whatever source they might come—Egypt, Judæa, or Persia, desirous of the knowledge of

---

[1] This was at all events the view of Clement, *Strom.* i, 19. οὐδὲ καταψηφίζεσθαι τῶν Ἑλλήνων οἷον τε ψιλῇ τῇ περὶ τῶν δογματισθέντων αὐτοῖς χρωμένους φράσει, μὴ συνεμβαίνοντας εἰς τὴν κατὰ μέρος ἄχρι συγγνώσεως ἐκκάλυψιν. πιστὸς γὰρ εὖ μάλα ὁ μετ᾽ ἐμπειρίας ἔλεγχος, ὅτι καὶ τελειοτάτη ἀπόδειξις εὑρίσκεται ἡ γνῶσις τῶν κατεγνωσμένων

God and of communion with God, and in many cases conscious of sin. In none of these feelings did Celsus share—his interests are all intellectual and practical. Plutarch before him, and the Neo-Platonists after him, understood the religous instincts which they endeavoured to satisfy, and for the cold, hard outlines of Celsus' hierarchy of heavenly and dæmonic beings they substituted personalities, approachable, warm and friendly (ὁ φίλος ᾿Απόλλων). Men felt the need of gods who were Saviours,—of gods with whom they might commune in sacraments—as the rise of Mithra-worship shows. They sought for salvation from sin, for holiness—the word was much on their lips—and for peace with God. To Celsus these seem hardly to have been necessities ; and whether we say that he made no effort to show that they were provided for in the old religion, or that he suggested, tacitly or explicitly, that the scheme he set forth had such a provision, the effect is the same. He really had nothing to offer.

Celsus did not bring against the Christians the charges of " Œdipodean unions and Thyestean banquets " familiar to the reader of the Apologists [1]—and to the student of the events that preceded the Boxer movement in China. While he taunted Jesus with being a bastard and a deceiver, and roundly denounced Christians generally for imposing upon the ignorance of men with false religion and false history, he did not say anything of note against ordinary Christian conduct. At least the fragments do not show anything of the kind. Later on the defenders and apologists of paganism had to own with annoyance that Christians set their fellow-citizens an example ; Maximin Daza and Julian tried vigorously to raise the tone of pagan society. Here lies an argument with which Celsus could not deal. The Fatherhood of God (in the sense which Jesus gave to the words) and the value of the individual soul, even the depraved and broken soul, are matters of argument, and on paper they may be very questionable ; but when the people, who held or (more truly) were held by these beliefs, managed somehow or other to show to the world lives transformed and endowed with the power of transforming others, the plain fact outweighed any number of *True Words*. What-

---

[1] It is regrettable that Clement should have flung one of these against the school of Carpocrates, *Strom.* iii, 10.

ever the explanation, the thing was there. Christians in the second century laid great stress on the value of paper and argument, and to-day we feel with Celsus that among them, orthodox and heretical, they talked and wrote a great deal that was foolish —"their allegories were worse than their myths"—but the sheer weight of Christian character carried off allegories and myths, bore down the school of Celsus and the more powerful school of Plutarch, Porphyry and Plotinus, and abolished the ancient world, and then captured and transformed the Northern nations.

Celsus could not foresee all that we look back upon. But it stands to his credit that he recognised the dangers which threatened the ancient civilization, dangers from German without and Christian within. He had not the religious temperament; he was more the statesman in his habit of mind, and he clearly loved his country. The appeal with which he closes is a proposal of peace—toleration, if the Christians will save the civilized world. It was not destined that his hopes should be fulfilled in the form he gave them, for it was the Christian Church that subdued the Germans and that carried over into a larger and more human civilization all that was of value in that inheritance of the past for which he pleaded. So far as his gifts carried him, he was candid ; and if sharp of tongue and a little irritable of temper, he was still an honourable adversary. He was serious, and, if he did not understand religion, he believed in the state and did his best to save it.

CHAPTER IX

CLEMENT OF ALEXANDRIA

Viderint qui Stoicum et Platonicum et dialecticum Christianismum protulerunt.—Tertullian, *de præscr. hæret.* 7.

No one can allege that the Bible has failed to win access for want of metaphysics being applied to it.—Matthew Arnold, *Literature and Dogma*, p. 121.

THOUGH Celsus had much to say upon the vulgar and servile character of the members of the Christian community, he took the trouble to write a book to refute Christianity ; and this book, as we have seen, was written from a more or less philosophical point of view. He professed himself doubtful as to whether his opponents would understand his arguments ; but that he wrote at all, and that he wrote as he did, is evidence that the new faith was making its way upward through society, and was gaining a hold upon the classes of wealth and education.

It is not hard to understand this. Though conditions of industry were not what they are to-day, it is likely that conversion was followed by the economic results with which we are familiar. The teaching of the church condemned the vices that war against thrift ; and the new life that filled the convert had its inevitable effect in quickening insight and energy. The community insisted on every man having a trade and working at it. With no such end in view, the church must have numbered among its adherents more and more people of wealth and influence in spite of all defections, just as to-day Protestantism in France has power and responsibility out of all proportions to mere numbers. The Emperor Hadrian is said to have made the observation that in Egypt, whether men worshipped Christ or Serapis, they all worshipped money.[1] The remark had probably as much truth as such sayings generally have, but we may probably infer that many Christians were punctual in

---

[1] See the letter of Hadrian quoted by Vopiscus, *Saturninus.* 8 (*Script. Hist. Aug.*)

their observance of the duty laid on them to be "not slothful in business."

The first four or five generations of Christians could not, on the whole, boast much culture—so far as their records permit us to judge. "Not many wise," said Paul, and their fewness has left an impress on the history of the church. A tendency to flightiness in speculation on the one hand, and a stolid refusal to speculate at all on the other, are the marks of second century Christianity. The early attempts made to come to terms with "human wisdom" were not happy, either at the centre or on the circumference of the body. The adjustment of the Gospel story to Old Testament prophecy was not a real triumph of the human mind, nor were the efforts at scientific theology any better. Docetism, with its phantom Christ, and Gnosticism with its antithesis of the just God and the good God, were not likely to satisfy mankind. Simple people felt that these things struck at their life, and they rejected them, and began to suspect the intellect. The century saw the growth of ecclesiastical system, episcopal order and apostolic tradition. Men began to speak of the "old church," the "original church" and the "catholic church," and to cleave to its "rule of faith" and "tradition of sound words." By 200 A.D. the church was no longer a new thing in the world; it had its own "ancient history" without going back to Judaism and the old covenant; it had its legends; and it could now speak like the Greeks of "the old faith of our fathers."

As it rose in the world, the church came into contact with new problems. As long as men were without culture, they were not troubled by the necessity of reconciling culture with faith, but the time had come when it must be done in earnest. Wealth was bringing leisure, and refinement, and new intellectual outlooks and interests. Could the church do with them? was the urgent question. Was it possible for a man to be at once a Greek gentleman of wealth and culture and a simple Christian like the humble grandfathers of his fellow-believers— or like his own slaves, the fuller and the cobbler of his household? We shall understand the problem better if we can make some acquaintance with the daily life and environment of these converts of the better classes.

In the second and third books of his *Pedagogue* Clement of

Alexandria deals with the daily round and deportment of Christians, for whom extravagance and luxury might be a real temptation. A few points, gathered here and there from the two books, will suffice. He recommends simplicity of diet with health and strength as its objects—the viands, which the Gospels suggest, fish and the honeycomb, being admirable for these purposes.[1] Wine provokes the passions—" I therefore admire those who have chosen the austere life and are fond of water, the medicine of temperance." " Boys and girls should as a general rule abstain from the [other] drug "—wine.[2] Good manners at table—no noisy gulping, no hiccupping, no spilling, no soiling of the couch, no slobbering of hand or chin —" how do you think the Lord drank, when he became man for us ? "[3] Vessels of silver and gold, furniture of rare woods inlaid with ivory, rugs of purple and rich colours, are hardly necessary for the Christian—" the Lord ate from a cheap bowl and made his disciples lie on the ground, on the grass, and he washed their feet with a towel about him—the lowly-minded God and Lord of the universe. He did not bring a silver foot-bath from heaven to carry about with him. He asked the Samaritan woman to give him to drink in a vessel of clay as she drew it up from the well,—not seeking the royal gold, but teaching us to quench thirst easily." " In general as to food, dress, furniture and all that pertains to the house, I say at once, it should all be according to the institutions of the Christian man, fitting appropriately person, age, pursuits and time."[4]

Clement passes from the table to a general discussion of manners and habits. Man is a " laughing animal," but he should not laugh all the time. Humour is recommended rather than wit ($\chi\alpha\rho\iota\epsilon\nu\tau\iota\sigma\tau\acute{\epsilon}o\nu$ $o\dot{\upsilon}$ $\gamma\epsilon\lambda\omega\tau\sigma\pi\sigma\iota\eta\tau\acute{\epsilon}o\nu$, 45, 4). " The orderly relaxation of the face which preserves its harmony " is a smile (46, 3)—giggling and excessive laughter are perversions. Care should be taken in conversation to avoid low talk, and the scoff that leads the way to insolence, and the argument for barren victory—" man is a creature of peace," as the greeting " Peace with you " shows us. Some talkers are like old shoes—only the tongue left for mischief.

---

[1] *Pædag.* ii, 2 ; 13 ; 14.   [2] *Pæd.* ii, 20, 2, 3.
[3] *Pæd.* ii, 32, 2.   [4] *Pæd.* ii, 38, 1-3.

There are many tricks unfit for a Christian gentleman—spitting, coughing, scratching and other things ; and he would do well to avoid whistling and snapping his fingers to call the servants. Fidgetting is the mark of mental levity (σύμβολον κουφότητος).[1]

In the care of one's person, oil may be used ; it is a sign of the luxury of the times that scents and unguents are so universally applied to such various purposes. The heathen crowned their heads with flowers and made it a reproach that Christians gave up the practice. But, as Tertullian said, they smelt with their noses ; and Clement urges that on the head flowers are lost to sight and smell, and chill the brain. A flower-garden in spring, with the dew upon all its colours, and all the natural scents of the open air, is another thing. The Christian too will remember—Tertullian also has this thought—that it was another crown that the Lord wore[2]— *ex spinis opinor, et tribulis.* The real objection was that the custom was associated with idol-worship.

Silk and purple and pearls are next dealt with—and earrings, " an outrage on nature "—if you pierce the ear, why not the nose too?[3] All peculiarity of dress should be avoided, and so should cosmetics—or else you may remind people of the Egyptian temple, outside all splendour, inside a priest singing a hymn to a cat or a crocodile.[4] " Temperance in drink and symmetry in food are wonderful cosmetics and quite natural." [5] Let a woman work with her hands, and health will come and bring her beauty. She should go veiled to church, like Æneas' wife leaving Troy.[6] Men may play at ball, take country walks, and try gardening and drawing water and splitting billets.[7] Finger-rings are allowed for them— gold rings, to be used as seals for security against the slaves.

---

[1] *Pæd.* ii, 45-60.

[2] *Pæd.* ii, 61-73 ; Tertullian, *de corona militis*, 5, flowers on the head are against nature, etc. ; *ib.* 10, on the paganism of the practice ; *ib.* 13 (end), a list of the heathen gods honoured if a Christian hang a crown on his door.

[3] *Pæd.* ii, 129, 3 ; iii, 56, 3 ; Tertullian ironically, *de cultu fem.* ii; 10, *scrupulosa deus et auribus vulnera intulit.*

[4] iii, 4, 2. Cf. Erman, *Handbook of Egyptian Religion*, p. 22 : " In the temple of Sobk there was a tank containing a crocodile, a cat dwelt in the temple of Bast." The simile also in Lucian, *Imag.* 11, and used by Celsus *ap.* Orig. *c. Cels.* iii, 17.

[5] iii, 64, 2.   [6] iii, 79, 5.   [7] iii, 50.

"Let our seals be a dove, or a fish, or a ship running before the wind, or a lyre, or a ship's anchor"—not an idol's face, or a sword or a cup or something worse.[1] Men should wear their hair short (unless it is curly), grow their beards and keep their moustaches trimmed with the scissors.[2] Our slaves we should treat as ourselves, for they are men as we ; "God" (as a verse, perhaps from Menander, puts it) "is the same for all, free or slave, if you think of it." [3]

All these admonitions imply an audience with some degree of wealth. The Christian artisan of Celsus had no temptation to use a silver foot-bath or to plaster himself with cosmetics. It may also be remarked that the man who gives the advice shows himself well acquainted with the ways of good society—and perhaps of society not so well gifted with taste. With all this refinement went education. The children of Christian parents were being educated, and new converts were being made among the cultured classes, and the adjustment of the new faith and the old culture was imperative. The men to make it were found in a succession of scholars, learned in all the wisdom of Greece, enthusiastic for philosophy and yet loyal to the Gospel tradition.

The first of these, whose name we know, was Pantænus ; but beyond his name there is little to be known of him. Eusebius says that he began as a Stoic philosopher and ended as a Christian missionary to India.[4] His pupil, Clement, is of far greater importance in the history of Christian thought.

Of Clement again there is little to be learnt beyond what can be gathered from his own writings. He alludes himself to the death of the Emperor Commodus as being "194 years, 1 month and 13 days" after the birth of Christ (it was in 192 A.D.); and Eusebius quotes a passage from a contemporary letter which shows that Clement was alive in 211 A.D., and another written in or about 215, which implies that he was dead.[5] We have also an indication from Eusebius that his activity as a teacher in Alexandria lasted from 180

---

[1] iii, 59, 2. [2] iii, 60, 61.
[3] iii, 92. Cf., in general, Tertullian, *de Cultu Feminarum.*
[4] Euseb. *E.H.* v, 10. [5] Euseb. *E.H.* vi, 11, 6 ; vi, 14, 8.

to 202 or 203.[1]   We may then assume that Clement was born about the middle of the century.

Epiphanius says that Clement was either an Alexandrine or an Athenian.   A phrase to be quoted below suggests that he was not an Alexandrine, and it has been held possible that he came from Athens.[2]   It also seems that he was born a pagan.[3]   Perhaps he says this himself when he writes : "rejoicing exceedingly and renouncing our old opinions we grow young again for salvation, singing with the prophecy that chants ' How good is God to Israel.' "[4]

It is obvious that he had the usual training of a Greek of his social position.   If his code of manners is lifted above other such codes by the constant suggestion of the gentle spirit of Jesus, it yet bears the mark of his race and of his period.   It is Greek and aristocratic, and it would in the main command the approval of Plutarch.   He must have been taught Rhetoric like every one else,—his style shows this as much as his protests that he does not aim at eloquence (εὐγλωττία), that he has not studied and does not practise "Greek style" (ἑλληνίζειν).[5]   He has the diffuse learning of his day—wide, second-hand and uncritical ; and, like other contemporary writers, he was a devotee of the note-book.   No age of Greek literature has left us so many works of the kind he wrote—the sheer congeries with no attempt at structure, no "beginning, middle and end,"—easy, accumulative books of fine miscellaneous feeding, with titles that playfully confess to their character.   Like other authors of this class, Clement preserves for us many and many a fragment of more interest and value than any original piece of literature could have been.   He clearly loved the poetry of Greece, and it comes spontaneously and irresistibly to his mind as he writes, and the sayings of Jesus are reinforced by those of Menander or Epicharmus.   The old words charm him, and

---

[1] Euseb. *E.H.* vi, 6 ; see de Faye, *Clément d'Alexandrie*, pp. 17 to 27, for the few facts of his life—a book I have used and shall quote with satisfaction.

[2] Epiphanius, *Haer.* I, ii, 26, p. 213 ; de Faye, *Clément d'Alexandrie*, p. 17, quoting Zahn.

[3] Euseb. *Praepar. Ev.* ii, 2, 64. Κλήμης . . . πάντων μὲν διὰ πείρας ἐλθὼν ἀνὴρ, θᾶττόν γε μὴν τῆς πλάνης ἀνανεύσας, ὡς ἂν πρὸς τοῦ σωτηρίου λόγου καὶ διὰ τῆς εὐαγγελικῆς διδασκαλίας τῶν κακῶν λελυτρωμένος.

[4] *Paed.* i, 1, 1.   [5] *Strom.* i, 48, 1 ; ii, 3, 1.

he cannot reject them. His *Stromateis* are "not like ornamental paradises laid out in rows to please the eye, but
rather resemble some shady and thickly-wooded hill, where
you may find cypress and plane, bay and ivy, and apple trees
along with olives and figs "[1]— trees with literary connotations.
Such works imply some want of the creative instinct, of
originality, and they are an index to the thinking of the age,
impressed with its great ancestry. It is to be remarked that
the writers of our period care little for the literature of the
past two or three centuries ; they quote their own teachers
and the great philosophers and poets of ancient Greece[2]   Few
of them have any new thoughts at all, and those who have
are under the necessity of clothing them in the hallowed
phrases of their predecessors. This was the training in which
Clement shared.   Later on, he emancipated himself, and
spoke contemptuously of the school—"a river of words and
a trickle of mind ";[3] but an education is not easily shaken
off.   He might quarrel with his teachers and their lessons,
but he still believed in them. It may be noted that in his
quotations of Greek literature his attention is mainly given to
the thought which he finds in the words—or attaches to them
—that he does not seem to conceive of a work of art as a
whole, nor does he concern himself with the author. He
used the words as a quotation, and it is not unlikely
that many of the passages he borrowed he knew only as
quotations.

In philosophy his training must have been much the same,
but here he had a more living interest. Philosophy touched
him more nearly, for it bore upon the two great problems of
the human soul—conduct and God. Like Seneca and Plutarch
he was not interested in Philosophy apart from these issues—
epistemology, psychology, physics and so forth were not
practical matters. The philosophers he judged by their
theology. With religious men of his day he leant to the
Stoics and "truth-loving Plato "—especially Plato, whom he

---

[1] *Strom.* vii. 111.   Such hills are described in Greek novels ; cf. Ælian, *Varia
Historia*, xiii, 1, Atalanta's bower.

[2] One may perhaps compare the admiration of the contemporary Pausanias for
earlier rather than later art ; cf. Frazer, *Pausanias and other Sketches*, p. 92.

[3] *Strom.* i, 22, 5.

seems to have read for himself—but he avows that Philosophy for him means not the system of any school or thinker, but the sum of the unquestionable dogmata of all the schools, " all that in every school has been well said, to teach righteousness with pious knowledge—this eclectic whole I call Philosophy." [1] To this Philosophy all other studies contribute—they are " the handmaidens, and she the mistress " [2]—and she herself owns the sway of Theology.

At some time of his life Clement acquired a close acquaintance with pagan mythology and its cults. It may be that he was initiated into mysteries; in his *Protrepticus* he gives an account of many of them, which is of great value to the modern student. It is probable enough that an earnest man in search of God would explore the obvious avenues to the knowledge he sought—avenues much travelled and loudly vaunted in his day. Having explored them, it is again not unlikely that a spirit so pure and gentle should be repelled by rituals and legends full of obscenity and cruelty. It is of course possible that much of his knowledge came from books, perhaps after his conversion, for one great part of Christian polemic was the simple exposure of the secret rites of paganism. Yet it remains that his language is permanently charged with technical terms proper to the mysteries, and that he loves to put Christian knowledge and experience in the old language— " Oh! mysteries truly holy! Oh! stainless light! The daduchs lead me on to be the epopt of the heavens and of God; I am initiated and become holy; the Lord is the hierophant and seals the mystês for himself, himself the photagogue." [3] It is again a little surprising to hear of " the Saviour " being " our mystagogue as in the tragedy—

He sees, we see, he gives the holy things (ὄργια);

and if thou wilt inquire

---

[1] *Strom.* i, 37, 6 ; and vi, 55, 3.

[2] *Strom.* i, 29, 10 (the phrase is Philo's) ; Truth in fact has been divided by the philosophic schools, as Pentheus was by the Mænads, *Strom.* i, 57. Cf. Milton, *Areopagitica.*

[3] *Protr.* 120, 1 ; ὦ τῶν ἀγίων ὡς ἀληθῶς μυστηρίων, ὦ φωτὸς ἀκηράτου. δᾳδουχοῦμαι τοὺς οὐρανοὺς καὶ τὸν θεὸν ἐποπτεῦσαι, ἄγιος γίνομαι μυούμενος, ἱεροφαντεῖ δὲ ὁ κύριος καὶ τὸν μύστην σφραγίζεται φωταγωγῶν. Strange as the technical terms seem to-day, yet when Clement wrote, they suggested religious emotion, and would have seemed less strange than the terms modern times have kept from the Greek—bishop, deacon, liturgy, diocese, etc.

These holy things—what form have they for thee ?

thou wilt hear in reply

Save Bacchus' own initiate, none may know."[1]

It is inconceivable that a Hebrew, or anyone but a Greek, could have written such a passage with its double series of allusions to Greek mysteries and to Euripides' *Bacchæ*. Clement is the only man who writes in this way, with an allusiveness beyond Plutarch's, and a fancy as comprehensive as his charity and his experience of literature and religion.

He had the Greek's curious interest in foreign religions, and he speaks of Chaldæans and Magians, of Indian hermits and Brahmans—" and among the Indians are those that follow the precepts of Buddha (Βούττα), whom for his exceeding holiness they have honoured as a god "—of the holy women of the Germans and the Druids of the Gauls.[2] Probably in each of these cases his knowledge was soon exhausted, but it shows the direction of his thoughts. Egypt of course furnished a richer field of inquiry to him as to Plutarch. He has passages on Egyptian symbolism,[3] and on their ceremonial,[4] which contain interesting detail. It was admitted by the Greeks—even by Celsus—that barbarians excelled in the discovery of religious dogma, though they could not equal the Greeks in the philosophic use of it. Thus Pausanias says the Chaldæans and Indian Magians first spoke of the soul's immortality, which many Greeks have accepted, " not least Plato son of Ariston." [5]

In the course of his intellectual wanderings, very possibly before he became a Christian, Clement investigated Jewish thought so far as it was accessible to him in Greek, for Greeks did not learn barbarian languages. Eusebius remarks upon his allusions to a number of Jewish historians.[6]   His debt to

---

[1] *Strom.* iv, 162, 3.

[2] *Strom.* i, 71, 4.   The Brahmans also in iii, 60.

[3] *Strom.* v, 20, 3 ; 31, 5 ; etc.   [4] *Strom.* vi, ch. iv, § 35 f.

[5] Origen, *c. Cels.* i, 2.   Celsus' words : ἱκανοὺς εὑρεῖν δόγματα τοὺς βαρβάρους, and then κρῖναι δὲ καὶ βεβαιώσασθαι καὶ ἀσκῆσαι πρὸς ἀρετὴν τὰ ὑπὸ βαρβάρων εὑρεθέντα ἀμείνονές εἰσιν Ἕλληνες. Pausanias, iv, 32, 4, ἐγὼ δὲ Χαλδαίους καὶ Ἰνδῶν τοὺς μάγους πρώτους οἶδα εἰπόντας ὡς ἀθάνατός ἐστιν ἀνθρώπου ψυχή· καὶ σφίσι καὶ Ἑλλήνων ἄλλοι τε ἐπείσθησαν καὶ οὐχ ἥκιστα Πλάτων ὁ Ἀρίστωνος.

[6] Euseb. *E.H.* vi, 13.

Philo is very great, for it was not only his allegoric method in general and some elaborate allegories that he borrowed, but the central conception in his presentment of Christianity comes originally from the Jewish thinker, though Clement was not the first Christian to use the term Logos.

Clement does not tell us that he was born of pagan parents, nor does he speak definitely of his conversion. It is an inference, and we are left to conjecture the steps by which it came, but without the help of evidence. One allusion to his Christian teachers is dropped when he justifies his writing the *Stromateis*—"memoranda treasured up for my old age, an antidote against forgetfulness, a mere semblance and shadow-picture of those bright and living discourses, those men happy and truly remarkable, whom I was counted worthy to hear." And then the reading is uncertain, but, according to Dr Stählin's text he says: "Of these, one was in Greece—the Ionian; the next (pl.) in Magna Græcia (one of whom was from Coele Syria and the other from Egypt); others in the East; and in this region one was an Assyrian, and the other in Palestine a Hebrew by descent. The last of all (in power he was the first) I met and found my rest in him, when I had caught him hidden away in Egypt. He, the true Sicilian bee, culling the flowers of the prophetic and apostolic meadow, begot pure knowledge in the souls of those who heard him. These men preserved the true tradition of the blessed teaching direct from Peter and James, John and Paul, the holy apostles, son receiving it from father ('and few be sons their fathers' peers'), and reached down by God's blessing even to us, in us to deposit those ancestral and apostolic seeds."[1] It is supposed that the Assyrian was Tatian, while the Sicilian bee hidden away in Egypt was almost certainly Pantænus.

Clement's education had been wide and superficial, his reading sympathetic but not deep, his philosophy vague and eclectic, and now from paganism with its strange and indefinite aggregation of religions based on cult and legend, he passed to a faith that rested on a tradition jealously maintained and a rule beginning to be venerable. He met men with a definite language in which they expressed a common experience—who had moreover seen a good many efforts made to mend the

---

[1] *Strom.* i, 11. The quotation is roughly from Homer, *Od.* ii, 276.

language and all of them ending in " shipwreck concerning the faith " ; who therefore held to the " form of sound words " as the one foundation for the Christian life.

It says a great deal for Clement's character—one might boldly say at once that it is an index to his personal experience —that he could sympathize with these men in the warm and generous way he did. Now and again he is guilty of directing a little irony against the louder-voiced defenders of " faith only, bare faith "[1] and " straight opinion "—" the *orthodoxasts*, as they are called."[2] (The curious word shows that the terms " orthodox " and " orthodoxy " were not yet quite developed.) But he stands firmly by the simplest Christians and their experience. If he pleads for a wider view of things—for what he calls " knowledge," it is, he maintains, the development of the common faith of all Christians. It is quite different from the wisdom that is implanted by teaching ; it comes by grace. " The foundation of knowledge is to have no doubts about God, but to believe ; Christ is both—foundation and superstructure alike ; by him is the beginning and the end. . . . These, I mean faith and love, are not matters of teaching."[3] As Jesus became perfect by baptism and was hallowed by the descent of the spirit, " so it befals us also, whose pattern is the Lord. Baptized, we are enlightened ; enlightened, we are made sons ; made sons we are perfected ; made perfect we become immortal [all these verbs and participles are in the present]. ' I,' he saith, ' said ye are gods and sons of the Most High, all of you.' This work has many names ; it is called gift [or grace, χάρισμα], enlightenment, perfection, baptism. . . . What is wanting for him who knows God ? It would be strange indeed if that were called a gift of God which was incomplete ; the Perfect will give what is perfect, one supposes. . . . Thus they that have once grasped the borders of life are already perfect ; we live already, who are separated from death. Salvation is following Christ. . . . So to believe—only to believe—and to be born again is perfection in life."[4] He praises the poet of

---

[1] *Strom.* i, 43, 1. Some who count themselves εὐφυεῖς, μόνην καὶ ψιλὴν τὴν πίστιν ἀπαιτοῦσι.

[2] *Strom.* i, 45, 6, οἱ ὀρθοδοξασταί.   [3] *Strom.* vii, 55.

[4] *Pædag.* i, 26 ; 27. Perhaps for " he saith," we should read " it saith," viz. Scripture.

Agrigentum for hymning faith, which his verses declare to be hard ; " and that is why the Apostle exhorts ' that your faith may not be in the wisdom of men '—who offer to persuade— ' but in the power of God '—which alone and without proofs can by bare faith save." [1]

It was this strong sympathy with the simplest view of the Christian faith that made the life-work of Clement possible. He was to go far outside the ordinary thoughts of the Christian community round about him—inevitably he had to do this under the compulsion of his wide experience of books and thinkers— but the centre of all his larger experience he found where his unlettered friends, " believing without letters," found their centre, and he checked his theories, original and borrowed—or he aimed at checking them—by life. " As in gardening and in medicine he is the man of real learning ($\chi\rho\eta\sigma\tau o\mu a\theta\eta s$), who has had experience of the more varied lessons . . . ; so, I say, here too, of him who brings everything to bear on the truth. . . . We praise the pilot of wide range, who ' has seen the cities of many men ' . . . so he who turns everything to the right life, fetching illustrations from things Greek and things barbarian alike, he is the much-experienced ($\pi o\lambda\upsilon\pi\epsilon\iota\rho os$) tracker of truth, the real *polymêtis* ; like the touchstone—the Lydian stone believed to distinguish between the bastard and the true-born gold, he is able to separate,—our *polyidris* and man of knowledge ($\gamma\nu\omega\sigma\tau\iota\kappa os$) as he is,—sophistic from philosophy, the cosmetic art from the true gymnastic, cookery from medicine, rhetoric from dialectic, magic and other heresies in the barbarian philosophy from the actual truth." [2]   This, in spirit and letter, is a very characteristic utterance. Beginning with the Lord as " the vine "—from which some expect to gather clusters of grapes in the twinkling of an eye—he ranges into medicine and sea-faring, from Odysseus " of many wiles, who saw the cities of many men and learnt their mind," to Plato's *Gorgias*, and brings all to bear on the Christian life. What his simple friends made of such a passage—if they were able to read at all, or had it read to them—it is not easy to guess, but contact must have shown them in the man a genuine and tender Christian as Christocentric as themselves, if in speech he

---

[1] *Strom.* v, 9.   [2] *Strom.*   43, 3—44, 2.

was oddly suited,—a gay epitome of Greek literature in every sentence.

This, then, is the man, a Greek of wide culture and open heart, who has dipped into everything that can charm the fancy and make the heart beat,—curious in literature, cult, and philosophy, and now submitted to the tradition of the church and the authority of Hebrew prophet and Christian apostle, but not as one bowing to a strange and difficult necessity. Rather, with the humblest of God's children—those "tender, simple and guileless" children on whom God lavishes all the little names which he has for his only Son, the "lamb" and the "child"[1]—he finds in Christ "thanksgiving, blessing, triumph and joy," while Christ himself bends from above, like Sarah, to smile upon their "laughter."[2] Such was the range of Clement's experience, and now, under the influence of the great change that conversion brought, he had to re-think everything and to gather it up in a new unity. Thus in one man were summed up all the elements of import in the general situation of the church of his day. He was representative alike in his susceptibility to the ancient literature and philosophy and his love of Scripture—"truth-loving Isaiah" and "St Paul"—in his loyalty to the faith, and, not less, in his determination to reach some higher ground from which the battle of the church could be fought with wider outlook, more intelligent grasp of the factors in play, and more hope of winning men for God.

Clement did not come before his time. Philosophy had begun to realize the significance of the church. The repression of the "harmful superstition" was no longer an affair of police; it was the common concern of good citizens. The model Emperor himself, the philosopher upon the throne, had openly departed from the easy policy laid down by Trajan and continued by his successors. He had witnessed, or had received reports of, executions. Writing in his diary of death, he says: "What a soul is that which is ready, if the moment has come for its separation from the body, whether it is to be extinguished, or dissolved, or to continue a whole. This readiness—see that it come from your own judgment, not in mere obstinacy, as with the Christians, but reflectively and

Pæd. i, 14, 2; 19. Cf. Blake's poem.   [2] _Pæd._ i, 22, 3.

with dignity, in a way to persuade another, with nothing of the actor in it." [1]   This sentence betrays something of the limitations of a good man—a beautiful spirit indeed, but not a little over-praised by his admirers in modern days.   Celsus at once taunts his Christian opponents with their prospects of painful death and demonstrates the absurdity of their tenets from the point of view of philosophy.   The Apologists say, too, that the philosophers lent themselves (as did also the dæmons) to inciting the mob to massacre.   But after all the dialectical weapons of Philosophy were the more dangerous, for they shook the faith of the Christian which death did not shake.

Again, the candid and inquiring temper of some notable converts and friends had led them to question the tradition of the church and to examine their Christian experience with a freedom from prejudice, at least in the evangelic direction, which had resulted in conclusions fatal, it seemed, to the Christian movement.   Their philosophy had carried them outside the thoughts of Jesus—they had abandoned the idea of the Abba Father, of the divine love, of the naturalness and instinctiveness of Christian life.   Incarnation and redemption they rejected, at least in the sense which made the conceptions of value to men.   Jesus they remodelled into one and another figure more amenable to their theories—a mere man, a demigod, a phantom, into anything but the historic personality that was and could remain the centre and inspiration of Christian life.   Of all this mischief philosophy, men said, was the cause.[2]

" I know quite well," writes Clement, " what is said over and over again by some ignorantly nervous people who insist that we should confine ourselves to the inevitable minimum, to what contains the faith, and pass over what is outside and superfluous, as it wears us out to no purpose and occupies us with what contributes nothing to our end.   Others say philosophy comes of evil and was introduced into life for the ruin of

[1] Marcus Aurelius, xi, 3.   He may have had in mind some who courted martyrdom.

[2] Euseb. *E.H.* v, 28, quotes a document dealing with men who study Euclid, Aristotle and Theophrastus, and all but worship Galen, and have " corrected " the Scriptures.   For the view of Tertullian on this, see p. 337.

men by an evil inventor."[1] They were afraid of philosophy,
as children might fear a ghost, in case it should take them away [2]
—but this, as Clement saw, was no way to meet the danger.
The Christian must not philosophize, they said—Tertullian
said it too ; but how could they know they must not philosophize unless they philosophized ? [3] Whether philosophy is
profitable or not, " you cannot condemn the Greeks on the
basis of mere statements about their opinions, without going
into it with them till point by point you discover what they
mean and understand them. It is the refutation based upon
experience that is reliable." [4]

So Clement has first of all to fight the battle of education
inside the church, to convince his friends that culture counts,
that philosophy is inevitable and of use at once for the refutation of opponents and for the achievement of the full significance of faith. Then he has to show how philosophy at its best
was the foe of superstition and the champion of God's unity
and goodness—a preparation for the Gospel. Lastly he has
to restate the Christian position in the language of philosophy
and to prove that the Gospel is reaffirming all that was best in
the philosophic schools and bringing it to a higher point, indeed
to the highest ; that the Gospel is the final philosophy of the
universe, the solution of all the problems of existence, the
revelation of the ultimate mind of God.

Clement boldly asserts the unity of all knowledge. Everything contributes, everything is concentric. " Just as every
family goes back to God the Creator, so does the teaching of
all good things go back to the Lord, the teaching that makes
men just, that takes them by the hand and brings them that
way." [5] And again :—" When many men launch a ship,
pulling together, you could not say there are many causes, but
one consisting of many—for each of them is not by himself
the cause of its being launched but only in conjunction with
others ; so philosophy, which is a search for truth, contributes
to the perception ($\kappa \alpha \tau \acute{\alpha} \lambda \eta \psi \iota s$) of truth, though it is not the

---

[1] *Strom.* i, 18, 2.   [2] *Strom.* vi, 80, 5.   [3] *Strom.* vi, 162, 5.

[4] *Strom.* i, 19, 2. $\psi \iota \lambda \hat{\eta}$ $\tau \hat{\eta}$ $\pi \epsilon \rho \grave{\iota}$ $\tau \hat{\omega} \nu$ $\delta o \gamma \mu \alpha \tau \iota \sigma \theta \acute{\epsilon} \nu \tau \omega \nu$ $\alpha \mathord{\mathring{\upsilon}} \tau o \hat{\iota} s$ $\chi \rho \omega \mu \acute{\epsilon} \nu o \upsilon s$ $\phi \rho \acute{\alpha} \sigma \epsilon \iota$, $\mu \grave{\eta}$
$\sigma \upsilon \nu \epsilon \mu \beta \alpha \acute{\iota} \nu o \nu \tau \alpha s$ $\epsilon \mathord{\mathring{\iota}} s$ $\tau \grave{\eta} \nu$ $\kappa \alpha \tau \grave{\alpha}$ $\mu \acute{\epsilon} \rho o s$ $\mathring{\alpha} \chi \rho \iota$ $\sigma \upsilon \gamma \gamma \nu \acute{\omega} \sigma \epsilon \omega s$ $\mathring{\epsilon} \kappa \kappa \acute{\alpha} \lambda \upsilon \psi \iota \nu$.

[5] *Strom.* vi, 59, 1. The exact rendering of the last clause is doubtful ; the sense
fairly clear.

cause of perception, except in conjunction and co-operation with other things. Yet perhaps even a joint-cause we might call a cause. Happiness is one, and the virtues more than one which are its causes. The causes of warmth may be the sun, the fire, the bath and the clothing. So, truth is one and many things co-operate in the search for it, but the discovery is by the Son. . . . Truth is one, but in Geometry we have geometrical truth, in Music musical ; so in Philosophy—right Philosophy—we should have Greek truth. But alone the sovereign Truth is unassailable, which we are taught by the Son of God."[1] Elsewhere, when challenged to say what use there is in knowing the causes that explain the sun's motion,[2] geometry and dialectics, when Greek philosophy is merely man's understanding, he falls back upon the mind's instinctive desire for such things, its free will (τὴν προαίρεσιν τοῦ νοῦ), and quickly marshals a series of texts from the Book of *Wisdom* on the divine source of wisdom and God's love of it, concluding with an allegory drawn from the five barley loaves and the two fishes on which the multitude were fed, the former typifying the Hebrew Law (" for barley is sooner ripe for harvest than wheat ") and the fishes Greek philosophy " born and moving amid Gentile billows." (" If you are curious, take one of the fishes as signifying ordinary education and the other the philosophy that succeeds it. . . .

A choir of voiceless fish came sweeping on,

the Tragic muse says somewhere "[3]). His appeal to the mind is a much stronger defence than any such accumulation of texts, but for the people he had in view the texts were probably more convincing.

The impulse to Philosophy is an inevitable one, native to the human mind, and he shows that it is to the Divine Reason working in all things, to Providence, that we must attribute it.

[1] *Strom.* i, 97, 1-4.

[2] Spherical astronomy. A curious passage on this at the beginning of Lucan's *Pharsalia*, vii.

[3] *Strom.* vi, 93, 94. The line comes from a play of Sophocles, fr. 695. It may be noted that Clement has a good many such fragments, and the presence of some very doubtful ones among them, which are also quoted in the same way by other Christian writers (*e.g.* in *Strom.* v, 111-113), raises the possibility of his borrowing other men's quotations to something near certainty. Probably they all used books of extracts. See Justin, *Coh. ad. Gent.* 18 : Athenagoras, *Presb.* 5, 24.

" Everything, so far as its nature permits, came into being, and does so still, advancing to what is better than itself. So that it is not out of the way that Philosophy too should have been given in Divine Providence, as a preliminary training towards the perfection that comes by Christ. . . . 'Your hairs are numbered' and your simplest movements; can Philosophy be left out of the account? [An allegory follows from Samson's hair.] Providence, it says, from above, from what is of first importance, as from the head, reaches down to all men, as 'the myrrh,' it says, 'that descends upon Aaron's beard and to the fringe of his garment'—viz.: the Great High Priest, 'by whom all things came into being, and without him nothing came'— not, that is, on to the beauty of the body; Philosophy is outside the people [possibly Israel is meant] just as raiment is. The philosophers then, who are trained by the perceptive spirit for their own perception,—when they investigate not a part of Philosophy, but Philosophy absolutely, they testify in a truth-loving way and without pride to truth by their beautiful sayings even with those who think otherwise, and they advance to under-standing (σύνεσιν), in accordance with the divine dispensation, that unspeakable goodness which universally brings the nature of all that exists onward toward the better so far as may be." [1]

Thought (φρόνησις) takes many forms, and it is diffused through all the universe and all human affairs, and in each sphere it has a separate name—Thought, Knowledge, Wisdom or Faith. In the things of sense it is called Right Opinion; in matters of handicraft, Art; in the logical discussion of the things of the mind, it is Dialectic. "Those who say that Philosophy is not from God, come very near saying that God cannot know each several thing in particular and that He is not the cause of all good things, if each of them is a particular thing. Nothing that is could have been at all without God's will; and, if with His will, then Philosophy is from God, since He willed it to be what it is for the sake of those who would not otherwise abstain from evil."

" He seeth all things and he heareth all [2]

---

[1] *Strom.* vi, 152, 3—154, 1. Cf. *Strom.* iv, 167, 4, "the soul is not sent from heaven hither for the worse, for God energizes all things for the better."—If the English in some of these passages is involved and obscure, it perhaps gives the better impression of the Greek.   [2] Cf. *Iliad*, 3, 277.

and beholds the soul naked within, and he has through all
eternity the thought (ἐπίνοια) of each several thing in particular,"
seeing all things, as men in a theatre look around and take all
in at a glance. " There are many things in life that find their
beginning in human reason, though the spark that kindles them
is from God.[1] Thus health through medicine, good condition
through training, wealth through commerce, come into being
and are amongst us, at once by Divine Providence and human
co-operation.   And from God comes understanding too.   And
the free will (προαίρεσις) of good men most of all obeys God's
will. . . . The thoughts (ἐπίνοιαι) of virtuous men come by
divine inspiration (ἐπίπνοια), the soul being disposed so and
the divine will conveyed (διαδιδομένου) to human souls, the
divine ministers taking part in such services ; for over all
nations and cities are assigned angelic governances—perhaps
even over individuals."[2]   Philosophy makes men virtuous, so
it cannot be the product of evil—that is, it is the work of God.
As it was given to the best among the Greeks, we can divine
who was the Giver.[3]

This is a favourite thought with Clement, and, as he does
with all ideas that please him, he repeats it over and over again,
in all sorts of connexions and in all variety of phrase.   When
a man is avowedly making " patchwork " books (*Stromateis*),
there is really no occasion on which we can call it irrelevant
for him to repeat himself, and this is a thought worth repeating.
" Before the advent of the Lord, Philosophy was necessary to
the Greeks for righteousness, and it is still profitable for piety,
a sort of primary instruction for those who reap faith by revelation. . . . God is the cause of all good things, of some directly,
as of the Old and New Testament, of others indirectly as of
Philosophy.   And perhaps even directly it was given in those
times to the Greeks, before the Lord called the Greeks also ;
for Philosophy too was a *paidagogos* for the Greek world, as
the Law was for the Hebrews, to bring them to Christ."[4]

---

[1] We may note his fondness for the old idea of Plato that man is an φυτὸν οὐράνιον
and has an ἔμφυτος ἀρχαία πρὸς οὐρανὸν κοινωνία. Cf. *Protr.* 25, 3 ; 100, 3.

[2] *Strom.* vi, 156, 3—157, 5.

[3] *Strom.* vi, 159. Cf. vi, 57, 58, where he asks Who was the original teacher,
and answers that it is the First-born, the Wisdom.

[4] *Strom.* i, 28, κατὰ προηγούμενον and κατ᾽ ἐπακολούθημα. See de Faye, p. 168,
169.   Note ref. to Paul, *Galat.* 3, 24.

" Generally speaking, we should not be wrong in saying that all that is necessary and profitable to life comes to us from God—and that Philosophy was more especially given to the Greeks, as a sort of covenant (διαθήκη) of their own, a step (ὑποβάθρα) toward the Philosophy according to Christ,—if Greek philosophers will not close their ears to the truths, through contempt of the barbarian speech." [1]   " God is the bestower (χορηγός) of both covenants, who also gave Philosophy to the Greeks, whereby among the Greeks the Almighty is glorified." [2]   " In those times Philosophy by itself ' justified ' the Greeks—though not to the point of perfect righteousness." [3] " As in due season the Preaching now comes, so in due season the law and the prophets were given to the barbarians and Philosophy to the Greeks, to train their ears for the Preaching." [4]

Philosophy however fell short of the Law.   Those, who were righteous by the Law, still lacked Faith ; while the others, whose righteousness was by Philosophy, not only lacked Faith but failed to break with idolatry.[5]   (This was in many quarters the capital charge against contemporary philosophy.) It was for this reason that the Saviour preached the Gospel in Hades, just as after him, according to Hermas, " the apostles and teachers, when they fell asleep in the power and faith of the Son of God, preached to those who had fallen asleep before them." [6]   It is curious that Clement not only cites Philosophy as a gift of God to the Gentiles before Faith came, that God's judgments might be just, but he also says, on the authority of the Law (quoting inaccurately and perhaps from memory), that God gave them the sun, the moon and stars to worship, which God made for the Gentiles that they might not become utterly atheistic and so utterly perish.   " It was a road given to them, that in worshipping the stars they might look up to God." [7]   That they fell into idolatry was however only too patent a fact.

---

[1] *Strom.* vi, 67, I.   [2] *Strom.* vi, 42, I   [3] *Strom.* i, 99, 3.

[4] *Strom.* vi, 44, I.   [5] *Strom.* vi, 44, 4,

[6] *Strom.* vi, 45-7 ; Cf. *Strom.* ii, 44, citing Hermas, *Sim.* ix, 16, 5-7.   A curious discussion follows (in *Strom.* vi, 45-52) on the object of the Saviour's descent into Hades, and the necessity for the Gospel to be preached in the grave to those who in life had no chance of hearing it.   " Could he have done anything else ? " (§ 51).

[7] *Strom.* vi, 110, 111 ; *Deuteronomy* 4, 19, does not bear him out--neither in Greek nor in English.

The exact means, by which the Greeks received the truths contained in their philosophy, is not certain.   A favourite explanation with Christian writers, and one to which Clement gives a good deal of thought, is that Greek thinkers borrowed at large from the Old Testament, for Moses lived some six hundred years before the deification of Dionysos, the Sibyl long before Orpheus.[1] Clement's illustrations are not very convincing.   " The idea of bringing Providence as far down as the moon came to Aristotle from this *Psalm* : ' Lord, in heaven is thy mercy and thy truth as far as (ἕως) the clouds.' "   Epicurus took his conception of Chance from "Vanity of vanities, all is vanity ; " while the Sabbath is found in several lines of Homer—unfortunately spurious.   An attempt to convict Euripides of plagiarism from Plato's *Republic* shows the worth of these suggestions, and the whole scheme wakes doubts as to the value of Clement's judgment.[2]

Another theory was angelic mediation.   God might have communicated with the Greeks by inferior angels ;[3] or those angels who fell into pleasure might have told their human wives what they knew of divine secrets, "and so the doctrine of Providence got about."[4]   Or else by happy guess or accident the Greeks found parts of the truth for themselves— or in virtue of some naturally implanted notion (ἔννοια) or common mind, and then " we know who is the author of nature."[5]

Whatever the explanation, in any case the hand of God was to be traced in it—Providence foreknew all, and so designed that the wickedness of fallen angels and men should promote righteousness and truth.[6]   So much for those who quote the text " All that ever came before me were thieves and robbers,"[7] or who say that the devil is the author of

---

[1] *Strom.* i, 105 and 108. Cf. Tert. *adv. Marc.* ii, **17**, *sed ante Lycurgos et Solonas omnes Moyses et deus* ; *de anima*, 28, *multo antiquior Moyses etiam Saturno nongentis circiter annis* ; cf. *Apol.* 19.

[2] For the Scripture parallels see *Strom.* v, 90-107.   For Euripides and other inter-Hellenic plagiarisms, *Strom.* vi, 24.

[3] *Strom.* vii, 6.

[4] *Strom.* v, 10, 2.   See an amusing page in Lecky, *European Morals*, i, 344.

[5] *Strom.* i, 94, **1** ; κατὰ περίπτωσιν ; κατὰ συντυχίαν ; φυσικὴν ἔννοιαν ; κοινὸν νοῦν.

[6] *Strom.* v, 10; i, 18 ; 86 ; **94.**   [7] *Strom.* i, 81, **1** ; *John* 10, 8.

Philosophy [1] (though we may admit Epicureanism to have been sown by the sower of tares).[2]   We might look far for a more vivid illustration of the contrast between sound instinct and absurd theory.

Thus he vindicates the right of the Christian to claim Philosophy as the manifestation of the Divine Logos, and as a fore-runner of the Gospel, and in his *Protrepticus* he shows how the Christian thus re-inforced can deal with paganism. If the *Stromateis* weary even the sympathetic reader with their want of plan, their diffuseness and repetition, and their interminable and fanciful digressions—faults inherent in all works of the kind—the *Protrepticus* makes a different impression. It is written by the same hand and shows the same tendencies, but they are under better control.   Allegories, analogies and allusions still hinder the development of his thought—like Atalanta he can never let a golden apple run past him.   He is not properly a philosopher in spite of all his love of Philosophy, and he thinks in colours, like a poet.   Yet he is not essentially a man of letters or a poet ; he is too indolent ; his style is not inevitable or compulsive.   It is too true a confession when he says that he does not aim at beauty of language.   His sentence will begin well, and then grow intricate and involved—in breaks an allusion, not always very relevant, and brings with it a quotation that has captured his fancy and paralyses his grammar—several perhaps—some accommodation is made, and the sentence straggles on, and will end somehow—with a pile of long words, for which others have been patiently waiting since before the quotation, in pendent genitives, accusatives and so forth.   But in the *Protrepticus*—in the better parts of it—something has happened to his style, for (to speak after his own manner)

> Nothing of him that doth fade,
> But doth suffer a sea-change
> Into something rich and strange.

He is no longer arguing ; he surrenders to a tide of emotion, and is borne along singing, and as he sings, he seems to gather up all the music of the ancient world ; we catch notes that come from Greek and Hebrew song, and the whole is woven together

[1] *Strom.* vi, 66 ; 159.   [2] *Strom.* vi, 67, 2.

into a hymn to "the Saviour," "my Singer," "our new
Orpheus," that for sheer beauty, for gladness and purity of
feeling is unmatched in early Christian literature. One comes
back to it after years and the old charm is there still. That
it can survive in a few translated fragments is hardly to be
expected.

He begins with the famous singers of Greek myth—
Amphion, Arion, and Eunomus with the grass-hopper. . . You
will believe empty myths, he says, but "Truth's bright face
seems to you to be false and falls under eyes of unbelief."
But Cithæron and Helicon are old. "Let us bring Truth
and shining Wisdom from heaven above to the holy mount of
God and the holy choir of the prophets. Let her, beaming
with light that spreads afar, illumine all about her them that
lie in darkness, and save men from error." "My Eunomus
sings not Terpander's strain, nor Capion's, not the Phrygian,
the Lydian or the Dorian, but the eternal strain of the new
harmony, the strain that bears the name of God, the new song,
the song of the Levite, with

> A drug infused antidote to the pains
> Of grief and anger, a most potent charm
> For ills of every name,[1]

a sweet and true cure of sorrow." Orpheus sang to enslave
men to idols, to foolish rites, to shadows. "Not such is my
singer; he has come, soon to end cruel slavery to tyrannic
dæmons; he transfers us to the gentle and kindly yoke
of piety, and calls to heaven them that were fallen to
earth."[2]

It was this new song that first made the whole cosmos a
harmony, and it is still the stay and harmony of all things.
It was this Logos of God who framed "the little cosmos, man,"
setting soul and body together by the holy spirit, and who
sings to God upon this organ of many tones—man. The
Logos himself is an organ for God, of all the harmonies, tuneful and holy.[3] What does this organ, this new song, tell us?

The Logos, that was before the Day-Star was, has appeared
among men as a teacher,—he by whom all things were made.

---

[1] *Odyssey*, iv, 221, Cowper's translation.
[2] *Protr.* 1-3. [3] *Ibid.* 5; 6.

As Demiurge he gave life ; as teacher he taught to live well ; that, as God, he may lavish upon us life forever.   Many voices and many means has the Saviour employed for the saving of men.   Lest you should disbelieve these, the Logos of God has himself become man that you might learn from man how man may become God.[1]

He casts a glance over Greek myths and mysteries— cymbals, tambourines, emblems, legends and uncleanness, the work of men who knew not the God who truly is, men "without hope and without God in the world."   "There was from of old a certain natural fellowship of men with heaven, hidden in the darkness of their ignorance, but now on a sudden it has leapt through the darkness and shines resplendent—even as that said by one of old,

> See'st thou that boundless æther there on high
> That laps earth round within its dewy arms ?

and again,

> O stay of earth, that hast thy seat on earth,
> Whoe'er thou art, beyond man's guess to see ;

and all the rest that the children of the poets sing."[2]   But wrong conceptions have turned "the heavenly plant, man," from the heavenly life and laid him low on earth, persuading him to cleave to things fashioned of earth.   So he returns to the discussion of pagan worships—"but by now your myths too seem to me to have grown old "—and he speaks of the dæmon-theory by which the pagans themselves explained their religion.   The dæmons are inhuman and haters of men ; they enjoy the slaying of men—no wonder that with such a beginning superstition is the source of cruelty and folly.   But "no! I must never entrust the hopes of the soul to things without souls."[3]   "The only refuge, it seems, for him who would come to the gates of Salvation is the Divine Wisdom."[4]

---

[1] *Protr.* 8, 4, ὁ λόγος ὁ τοῦ θεοῦ ἄνθρωπος γενόμενος ἵνα δὴ καὶ σὺ παρὰ ἀνθρώπου μάθῃς, πῇ ποτε ἄρα ἄνθρωπος γένηται θεός.

[2] *Protr.* 25, 3 ; ref. to Euripides, *fr.* 935, and *Troades*, 884.   The latter (not quite correctly quoted by Clement) is one of the poet's finest and profoundest utterances.

[3] *Protr.* 56, 6.   [4] *ibid.* 63, 5.

He now reviews the opinions of the philosophers about God. The Stoics (to omit the rest) "saying that the divine goes through all matter, even the most dishonourable, shame Philosophy."[1] "Epicurus alone I will gladly forget."[2] "Where then are we to track out God, Plato? 'The Father and maker of this whole it is hard to find, and, when one has found him, to declare him to all is impossible.' In his name why? 'For it is unspeakable.' Well said! Plato! thou hast touched the truth!"[3] "I know thy teachers," still addressing Plato, "Geometry thou dost learn from Egyptians, Astronomy from Babylonians, the charms that give health from Thracians; much have the Assyrians taught thee; but thy laws—such of them as are true—and thy thought of God, to these thou hast been helped by the Hebrews."[4] After the philosophers the poets are called upon to give evidence—Euripides in particular.[5] Finally he turns to the prophets and their message of salvation—"I could quote you ten thousand passages, of which 'not one tittle shall pass' without being fulfilled; for the mouth of the Lord, the holy spirit, spoke them."[6]

God speaks to men as to his children—"gentle as a father," as Homer says. He offers freedom, and you run away to slavery; he gives salvation, and you slip away into death. Yet he does not cease to plead—"Wake, and Christ the Lord shall lighten upon you, the sun of resurrection."[7] "What would you have covenanted to give, oh! men! if eternal salvation had been for sale? Not though one should measure out all Pactolus, the mythic river of gold, will he pay a price equal to salvation."[8] Yet "you can buy this precious salvation with your own treasure, with love and faith of life . . . that is a price God is glad to accept."[9] Men grow to the world, like seaweed to the rocks by the sea, and despise immortality "like the old Ithacan, yearning not for Truth and the fatherland

---

[1] *Protr.* 66, 3.   [2] *Ibid.* 66, 5.   [3] *Ibid.* 68, 1.

[4] *Protr.* 70, 1; in *Strom.* i, 150, 4, he quotes a description of Plato as Μωυσῆς ἀττικίζων. Cf. Tertullian, *Apol.* 47.

[5] *Protr.* 76. He quotes *Orestes*, 591 f.; *Alcestis*, 760; and concludes (anticipating Dr Verrall) that in the *Ion* γυμνῇ τῇ κεφαλῇ ἐκκυκλεῖ τῷ θεάτρῳ τοὺς θεούς, quoting *Ion*, 442-447.

[6] *Protr.* 82, 1.   [7] *Ibid.* 84, 2.

[8] *Ibid.* 85, 4.   [9] *Ibid.* 86, 1.

in heaven, and the light that truly is, but for the smoke."[1]   It
is piety that "makes us like God"—a reference to Plato's
familiar phrase.   God's function ($\xi\rho\gamma o\nu$) is man's salvation.
"The word is not hidden from any.   Light is common and
shines upon all men ; there is no Cimmerian in the reckoning.
Let us hasten to salvation, to re-birth.   Into one love to be
gathered, many in number, according to the unity of the
essence of the Monad, let us hasten.   As we are blessed,
let us pursue unity, seeking the good Monad.   And
this union of many, from a medley of voices and distrac-
tion, receives a divine harmony and becomes one symphony,
following one coryphæus ($\chi o\rho\epsilon\upsilon\tau\eta s$) and teacher, the Word,
resting upon the Truth itself, and saying ' Abba Father.' "[2]
Here indeed Philosophy and the Gospel join hands, when
the Monad and Abba Father are shown to be one and the
same.[3]

It is easy to see which of the thoughts represented by
these names means most to Clement.   " Our tender loving
Father, the Father indeed, ceases not to urge, to admonish, to
teach, to love ; for neither does he cease to save "—"only,
oh ! child ! thirst for thy Father, and God will be shown to
thee without a price."[4]   "Man's proper nature is to be at
home with God ;" as then we set each animal to its natural
task, the ox to plough and the horse to hunt, so "man, too,
who is born for the sight of heaven, a heavenly plant most
truly, we call to the knowledge of God. . . . Plough, we say, if
you are a ploughman, but know God as you plough ; sail, if
you love sea-faring, but calling on the heavenly pilot."[5]
" A noble hymn to God is an immortal man, being built
up in righteousness, in whom are engraved the oracles
of truth "[6] ; and very soon he quotes " Turn the other
cheek " as a " reasonable law to be written in the heart."[7]

---

[1] *Protr.* 86, 2.   The reference is to *Odyssey*, i, 57.   One feels that, with more
justice to Odysseus, more might have been made of his craving for a sight of the
smoke of his island home.

[2] *Protr.* 88, 2, 3.

[3] Elsewhere, he says God is beyond the Monad, *Paed.* i, 71, 1, $\epsilon\pi\epsilon\kappa\epsilon\iota\nu\alpha$ $\tau o\hat{\upsilon}$ $\epsilon\nu\delta s$
$\kappa\alpha\iota$ $\upsilon\pi\epsilon\rho$ $\alpha\upsilon\tau\eta\nu$ $\tau\eta\nu$ $\mu o\nu\alpha\delta\alpha$.   See p. 290.

[4] *Protr.* 94, 1, 2.   On God making the Christian his child, cf. Tert. *adv. Marc.*
iv, 17.

[5] *Protr.* 100, 3, 4.   [6] *Ibid.* 107, 1.   [7] *Ibid.* 108, 5.

"God's problem is always to save the flock of men. It was for that the good God sent the good Shepherd. The Logos has made truth simple and shown to men the height of salvation."[1] "Christ wishes your salvation; with one word he gives you life. And who is he? Hear in brief: the Word of truth, the Word of immortality, that gives man re-birth, bears him up to truth, the goad of salvation, who drives away destruction, who chases forth death, who built in men a temple that he might make God to dwell among men."[2]

The last chapter is a beautiful picture of the Christian life, full of wonderful language from Homer, the *Bacchæ* of Euripides, and the Mysteries, and in the centre of it—its very heart—"Come unto me, all ye that labour and are heavy-laden, and I will give you rest."

In the passages here quoted from the *Protrepticus* some of Clement's main ideas in the realm of Christian thought are clearly to be seen; and we have now to give them further and more detailed examination. We have to see what he makes of the central things in the new religion —of God, and the Saviour, and of man, and how he interprets the Gospel of Jesus in the language of Greek philosophy. It is to be noted that, whatever happened in the course of his work — and very few books are, when written, quite what the writer expected on beginning— Clement looked upon his task as interpretation. The Scriptures are his authorities—"he who has believed the divine Scriptures, with firm judgment, receives in the voice of God who gave the Scriptures a proof that cannot be spoken against."[3] Amid the prayers and hymns of the ideal Christian comes daily reading of the sacred books.[4] Clement has no formal definition of inspiration, but he loved the sacred text, and he made it the standard by which to judge all propositions. It is perhaps impossible to over-estimate the importance of this loyalty in an age, when Christian speculation was justly under suspicion on account

---

[1] *Protr.* 116, 1, ὕψος (height) is the word used in literature for "sublimity," and that may be the thought here. Cf. Tert. *de Bapt.* 2, *simplicitas divinorum operum . . . et magnificentia.* See p. 328.

[2] *Protr.* 117, 4.   [3] *Strom.* ii, 9, 6.   [4] *Ibid.* vii, 49

of the free re-modelling of the New Testament text that went with it. Clement would neither alter, nor excise, but he found all the freedom he wanted in the accepted methods of exegesis. Allegory and the absence of any vestige of historical criticism—and, not least, the inability induced by the training of the day to conceive of a work of art, or even a piece of humbler literature, as a whole—his very defects as a student secured his freedom as a philosopher. He can quote Scripture for his purpose ; the phrase will support him where the context will not ; and sometimes a defective memory will help him to the words he wants, as we have seen in the case of the worship of sun, moon and stars. To the modern mind such a use of Scripture is unwarrantable and seems to imply essential indifference to its real value, but in Clement and his contemporaries it is not inconsistent with—indeed, it is indicative of—a high sense of the value of Scripture as the *ipsissima verba* of God. And after all a mis-quotation may be as true as the most authentic text, and may help a man as effectually to insight into the thoughts of God.

We have seen that Clement quarrelled with the Stoics for involving God in matter—" even the most dishonourable." The world-soul was, in fact, repugnant to men who were impressed with the thought of Sin, and who associated Sin with matter. This feeling and a desire to keep the idea of God disentangled from every limitation led to men falling back (as we saw in the case of Plutarch) on the Platonic conception of God's transcendence. Neo-Platonism has its " golden chain " of existence descending from Real Being—God—through a vast series of beings who *are* in a less and less degree as they are further down the scale. It is not hard to sympathize with the thoughts and feelings which drew men in this direction. The best thinkers and the most religious natures in the Mediterranean world (outside the circle of Jesus, and some Stoics) found the transcendence of God inevitably attractive, and then their hearts sought means to bridge the gulf their thoughts had made. For now he was out of all knowledge, and away beyond even revelation ; for re-velation involved relation and limitation, and God must be absolute.

We have seen how Plutarch found in the existence of dæmons a possibility of intercourse between gods and men, while above the dæmons the gods, he implies, are in communication with the remote Supreme. But for some thinkers this solution was revolting. Philo, with the great record before him of the religious experience of his race, was not prepared to give up the thought " O God, thou art my God."[1] Linking the Hebrew phrase "the word of the Lord" with the Stoic Logos Spermaticos and Plato's Idea, he found in the resulting conception a divine, rational and spiritual principle immanent in man and in the universe, and he also found a divine personality, or quasi-personality, to come between the Absolute and the world. He pictures the Logos as the Son of God, the First-born, the oldest of angels, the "idea of ideas," and again as the image of God, and the ideal in whose likeness man was made. As the ambassador of God, and High Priest, the Logos is able to mediate directly between man and God, and bridges the gulf that separates us from the Absolute.[2] More than anything else, this great conception of Philo's prepared the way for fusion of Greek thought and Christianity. Clement is conspicuously a student and a follower of Philo— nor was he the first among Christian writers to feel his influence.

Clement, as already said, professed himself an eclectic in philosophy, and of such we need not expect the closest reasoning. Our plan will be to gather passages illustrative of his thoughts—we might almost say of his moods—and set side by side what he says from time to time of God. On such a subject it is perhaps impossible to hope for logic or consistency except at the cost of real aspects of the matter in hand. Something will be gained if we can realize the thoughts which most moved the man, even though their reconciliation is questionably possible. This doubt however does not seem to have occurred to himself, for he connects the dogmata of the philosophers and the teaching of the New Testament as if it were the most natural thing in the world.

[1] *Psalm* 63, 1.
[2] See Caird, *Evolution of Theology in the Greek Philosophers*, ii, pp. 183 ff: de Faye, *Clément*, pp. 231-8.

To begin with the account of God which Clement gives in philosophical language. "The Lord calls himself 'one' (ἕν)—'that they all may be one . . . as we are one; I in them, and thou in me, that they may be perfected into one.' Now God is 'one' (ἓν) and away beyond the 'one' (ἑνὸς) and above the Monad itself."[1] Again, after quoting Solon and Empedocles and "John the Apostle" ("no man hath seen God at any time"), Clement enlarges on the difficulty of speaking of God: —"How can that be expressed, which is neither genus, nor differentia, nor species, neither indivisible, nor sum, nor accident, nor susceptive of accident? Nor could one properly call him a whole (ὅλον); for whole (τὸ ὅλον) implies dimension, and he is Father of the Whole (τῶν ὅλων). Nor could one speak of his parts, for the one is indivisible and therefore limitless, not so conceived because there is no passing beyond it, but as being without dimension or limit, and therefore without form or name. And if we ever name him, calling him, though not properly, one, or the good, or mind, or absolute being, or father, or God, or demiurge, or lord, we do not so speak as putting forward his name; but, for want of his name, we use beautiful names, that the mind may not wander at large, but may rest on these. None of these names, taken singly, informs us of God; but, collectively and taken all together, they point to his almighty power. For predicates are spoken either of properties or of relation, and none of these can we assume about God. Nor is he the subject of the knowledge which amounts to demonstration; for this depends on premisses (πρότερα) and things better known (γνωριμώτερα);[2] but nothing is anterior to the unbegotten. It remains then by divine grace and by the Logos alone that is from him to perceive the unknowable."[3] Again, "God has no natural relation (φυσικὴν σχέσιν) to us, as the founders of heresies hold (not though he make us of what is not, or fashion us from matter, for *that* is not at all, and *this* is in every point different from God)—unless you venture to say that we are part of him and of one essence (ὁμοουσίους) with God; and I do not understand how anyone who

---

[1] *Pæd.* i, 71, 1; cf. Philo, *Leg. Alleg.* ii, § 1, 67 M. τάττεται οὖν ὁ θεὸς κατὰ τὸ ἓν καὶ τὴν μονάδα, μᾶλλον δὲ καὶ ἡ μονὰς κατὰ τὸν ἕνα θεόν. Cf. de Faye, p. 218.

[2] Expressions taken from Aristotle, *Anal. Post.* i, 2, p. 71 b, 20.

[3] *Strom.* v, 81, 5—82, 3.

knows God will endure to hear that said, when he casts
his eye upon our life and the evils with which we are mixed
up. For in this way (and it is a thing not fit to speak of)
God would be sinning in his parts, that is, if the parts are
parts of the whole and complete the whole—if they do not
complete it, they would not be parts. However, God, by
nature (φύσει) being rich in pity (ἔλεος), of his goodness
he cares for us who are not his members nor by nature his
children (μήτε μορίων ὄντων αὐτοῦ μήτε φύσει τέκνων). Indeed
this is the chief proof of God's goodness, that though
this is our position with regard to him, by nature utterly
'alienated' from him, he nevertheless cares for us. For the
instinct of kindness to offspring is natural (φυσική) in
animals, and so is friendship with the like-minded based
on old acquaintance, but God's pity is rich towards us
who in no respect have anything to do with him, I mean,
in our being (οὐσία) or nature or the peculiar property of
our being (δυνάμει τῇ οἰκείᾳ τῆς οὐσίας ἡμῶν), but merely by
our being the work of His will." [1] " The God of the Whole
(τῶν ὅλων), who is above every voice and every thought and
every conception, could never be set forth in writing, for his
property is to be unspeakable." [2]

It follows that the language of the Bible is not to be taken
literally when it attributes feelings to God. Clement has cited
texts which speak of "joy" and "pity" in connexion with
God, and he has to meet the objection that these are moods
of the soul and passions (τροπὰς ψυχῆς καὶ πάθη). We mistake,
when we interpret Scripture in accordance with our own
experience of the flesh and of passions, "taking the will
of the passionless God (τοῦ ἀπαθοῦς θεοῦ) on a line with our
own perturbations (κινήμασι). When we suppose that the fact
in the case of the Almighty is as we are able to hear, we err
in an atheistic way. For the divine was not to be declared as
it *is* ; but as we, fettered by flesh, were able to understand,
even so the prophets spoke to us, the Lord accommodating
himself to the weakness of men with a mind to save them

---

[1] *Strom.* ii, 74, 1—75, 2 ; cf. Plutarch, *de def. or.* 414 F, 416 F (quoted on p. 97), on
involving God in human affairs ; and also *adv. Sto.* 33, and *de Sto. repugn.* 33, 34, on
the Stoic doctrine making God responsible for human sin. Cf. further statements in
the same vein in *Strom.* ii, 6, 1 ; v 71, 5 ; vii, 2.   [2] *Strom.* v. 65, 2.

(σωτηρίως)." Thus the language of our emotions, though not properly to be employed, is used to help our weakness.[1] For God is, in fact, "without emotion, without wrath, without desire" (ἀπαθὴς, ἄθυμος, ἀνεπιθύμητος).[2] Clement repeatedly recurs with pleasure to this conception of "Apathy"; it is the mark of God, of Christ, of the Apostles, and of the ideal Christian, with whom it becomes a fixed habit (ἕξις).[3]

God is not like a man (ἀνθρωποειδὴς), nor does he need senses to hear with, nor does he depend on the sensitiveness of the air (τὸ εὐπαθὲς τοῦ ἀέρος) for his apprehensions, "but the instantaneous perception of the angels and the power of conscience touching the soul—these recognize all things, with the quickness of thought, by means of some indescribable faculty apart from sensible hearing. Even if one should say that it was impossible for the voice, rolling in this lower air, to reach to God, still the thoughts of the saints (ἁγίων) cleave, not the air alone, but the whole universe as well. And the divine power instantly penetrates the whole soul like light. Again do not our resolves also find their way to God, uttering a voice of their own? And are not some things also wafted heavenward by the conscience? . . . God is all ear and all eye, if we may make use of these expressions."[4] Thus it would seem that God is not so far from every one of us as we might have supposed from the passages previously quoted, and the contrast between the two views of God grows wider when we recall Clement's words in the *Protrepticus* about the Heavenly Father. While a Greek, the pupil of the philosophers, could never use the language of a Jew about "God our Father" with the same freedom from mental reservation, Clement undoubtedly speaks of God at times in the same spirit that we feel in the utterances of Jesus. He goes beyond what contemporary philosophers would have counted suitable or desirable, as we can see in the complaints which Celsus makes of Christian language about God, though Celsus, of course, is colder than the religious

---

[1] *Strom.* ii, 72, 1-4.   [2] *Strom.* iv, 151, 1.

[3] See *Strom.* ii, 103, 1 ; iv, 138, 1 ; vi, 71-73 ; *Pæd.* i, 4, 1.

[4] *Strom.* vii, 37, Mayor's translation. The "expressions" are said to go back to Xenophanes (cited by Sext. Empir. ix, 144) οὖλος γὰρ ὁρᾷ, οὖλος δὲ νοεῖ, οὖλος δέ τ' ἀκούει. Cf. Pliny, *N.H.* ii, 7, 14, *quisquis est deus, si modo est alius, et quacumque in parte, totus est sensus, totus visus, totus auditus, totus animæ, totus animi, totus sui.*

of his day. But the main difference between Christians and philosophers was not as to God the Father, but as to Christ.

When Clement, in his work of restatement, came to discuss Christ, he found Philo's Logos ready to his hand and he was not slow to use it. It is characteristic that, just as he unquestioningly accepted the current philosophic account of God and saw no great difficulty in equating a God best described in negations with the Abba Father of Jesus, so he adopted, not less light-heartedly, the conflate conception of the Logos. Whether its Platonic and Stoic elements would hold together; whether either of them was really germane to the Hebrew part; whether in any case any of the three sets of constituents corresponded with anything actually to be reached by observation or experience; or whether, waiving that point, the combination was equal to its task of helping man to conceive of God at once as immanent and transcendent, Clement hardly inquired. So far he followed Philo. Then came in a new factor which might well have surprised Plato, Zeno and Philo alike. Following once more, but this time another leader, Clement equates the Philonian Logos with the historic Jesus of Nazareth.

So stated, the work of Clement may well look absurd. But after all he is not the only man who has identified the leading of instinct with philosophic proof. In succession he touched the central thoughts of his various leaders, and he found them answer to cravings within him. He wanted a God beyond the contagion of earth, Supreme and Absolute; and Plato told him of such a God. Yet the world needed some divine element; it must not be outside the range and thought of God; and here the conception of divine Reason, linking man and nature with God Himself, appealed to his longing. Lastly the impossibility of thinking Jesus and his work to be accidental, of conceiving of them as anything but vitally bound up with the spiritual essence of all things, with God and with God's ultimate mind for man and eternity, was the natural outcome of entering into the thoughts of Jesus, of realizing his personality and even of observing his effect upon mankind.[1] When one remembers how in every age men have passed through one form and another of experience, and have then compacted philosophies to account for those experiences have thought their constructions final, and have recommended their theories as of more value than the facts on which, after reflection, slight or profound, but perhaps never adequate, they have based them, it will not seem strange that Clement did the same.

> Ah yet, when all is thought and said,
> The heart still overrules the head ;
> Still what we hope we must believe,
> And what is given us receive.

The old task is still to do. The old cravings are still within us ; still the imperishable impulse lives to seek some solution of the great question of the relations of God and the soul and the universe, which may give us more abiding satisfaction than Clement's can now have, and which will yet recognize those old cravings, will recognize and meet them, not some but all of them.

" Most perfect, and most holy of all," says Clement, " most sovereign, most lordly, most royal and most beneficent, is the nature of the Son, which approaches most closely to the One Almighty Being. The Son is the highest Pre-eminence, which sets in order all things according to the Father's will, and steers the universe aright, performing all things with unwearying energy, beholding the Father's secret thoughts through his working. For the Son of God never moves from his watchtower, being never divided, never dissevered, never passing from place to place, but existing everywhere at all times and free from all limitations. He is all reason, all eye, all light from the Father, seeing all things, hearing all things, knowing all things, with power searching the powers. To him is subjected the whole army of angels and of gods—to him, the Word of the Father, who has received the holy administration by reason of Him who subjected it to him ; through whom also all men belong to him, but some by way of knowledge, while others have not yet attained to this ; some as friends, some as faithful servants, others as servants merely." [2]

---

[1] Cf. *Strom.* ii, 30, 1, εἰ γὰρ ἀνθρώπινον ἦν τὸ ἐπιτήδευμα, ὡς Ἕλληνες ὑπέλαβον, κἂν ἀπέσβη. ἡ δὲ αὔξει (*sc.* ἡ πίστις). *Protr.* 110, 1, οὐ γὰρ ἂν οὕτως ἐν ὀλίγῳ χρόνῳ τοσοῦτον ἔργον ἄνευ θείας κομιδῆς ἐξήνυσεν ὁ κύριος.

[2] *Strom.* vii, 5, J. B. Mayor's translation.

The Logos is the source of Providence, the author, as already seen, of all human thought and activity, of the beauty of the human body too,[1] Saviour and Lord at once of all men —man being "his peculiar work," for into him alone of animals was a conception of God instilled at his creation. " Being the power of the Father, he easily prevails over whomsoever he will, not leaving even the smallest atom of his government uncared for."[2] " He it is in truth that devises the bridle for the horse, the yoke for the bull, the noose for the wild beast, the rod for the fish, the snare for the bird ; he governs the city and ploughs the land, rules and serves, and all things he maketh ;

> Therein he set the earth, the heaven, the sea,
> And all the stars wherewith the heaven is crowned.

O the divine creations ! O the divine commands ! This water, let it roll within itself; this fire, let it check its rage; this air, let it spread to æther ; and let earth be fixed and borne, when I will it. Man I yet wish to make ; for his material I have the elements ; I dwell with him my hands fashion. If thou know me, the fire shall be thy slave."[3]

" All[4] gaze on the supreme Administrator of the universe, as he pilots all in safety according to the Father's will, rank being subordinated to rank under different leaders till in the end the Great High Priest is reached. For on one original principle, which works in accordance with the Father's will, depend the first and second and third gradations ; and then at the extreme end of the visible world there is the blessed ordinance of angels ; and so, even down to ourselves, ranks below ranks are appointed, all saving and being saved by the initiation and through the instrumentality of One. As then the remotest particle of iron is drawn by the breath ($\pi\nu\epsilon\acute{u}\mu\alpha\tau\iota$) of the stone of Heraklea [the magnet] extending through a long series of iron rings, so also through the attraction of the holy spirit ($\pi\nu\epsilon\acute{u}\mu\alpha\tau\iota$) the virtuous are adapted to the highest

---

[1] *Pæd.* i, 6, 6, τὸ δὲ σῶμα κάλλει καὶ εὐρυθμίᾳ συνεκεράσατο.

[2] Phrases mostly from *Strom.* vii, 6-9. ἔννοιαν ἐνεστάχθαι θεοῦ. See criticism of Celsus, p. 244.

[3] *Pæd.* iii, 99, 2—100, 1. The quotation is from Homer's description of Hephaistos making the shield for Achilles, *Il.* 18, 483.

[4] All parts of the universe

mansion ; and the others in their order even to the last mansion ; but they that are wicked from weakness, having fallen into an evil habit owing to unrighteous greed, neither keep hold themselves nor are held by another, but collapse and fall to the ground, being entangled in their own passions."[1] This last clause raises questions as to evil and freewill. Clement believed in freewill ; for one thing, it was necessary if God was to be acquitted of the authorship of evil. " God made all things to be helpful for virtue, in so far as might be without hindering the freedom of man's choice, and showed them to be so, in order that he who is indeed the One Alone Almighty might, even to those who can only see darkly, be in some way revealed as a good God, a Saviour from age to age through the instrumentality of his Son, and in all ways absolutely guiltless of evil."[2]

Clement also brings in the Platonic Idea to help to express Christ. " The idea is a thought of God (ἐννόημα), which the barbarians have called God's Logos."[3] " All the activity of the Lord is referred to the Almighty, the Son being, so to speak, a certain activity (ἐνέργεια) of the Father,"[4] and a little lower he adds that the Son is " the power (δύναμις) of the Father."[5] As such he may well be " above the whole universe, or rather beyond the region of thought."[6] And yet, as we have seen, he leans to the view that the Logos is a person—the Great High Priest. In criticizing him, it is well to remember how divergent are the conceptions which he wishes to keep, and to keep in some kind of unity.

Once again, in many of Clement's utterances upon the Logos there is little that Philo, or perhaps even a pagan philosopher, could not have approved ; but through it all there is a new note which is Clement's own and which comes from another series of thoughts. For it is a distinctive mark of Clement's work that the reader rises from it impressed with the idea of " the Saviour." The *Protrepticus* is full of the thought of that divine love of men, warm and active, which

---

[1] *Strom.* vii, 9. Mayor's translation, modified to keep the double use of πνεῦμα. For the magnet see Plato, *Ion.* 533 D, E.

[2] *Strom.* vii, 12.   [3] *Strom.* v, 16, 3 (no article with Logos).

[4] *Strom.* vii, 7   [5] *Strom.* vii, 9.

[6] *Strom.* v, 38, 6, ὁ κύριος ὑπεράνω του κόσμου παντός, μᾶλλον δὲ ἐπέκεινα τοῦ νοητοῦ.

Jesus associated with "your heavenly Father," but which
Clement, under the stress of his philosophy must connect with
the Logos—"cleansing, saving and kindly; most manifest
God indeed, made equal with the ruler of the universe."[1]
He is our "only refuge" (μονὴ καταφυγή), the "sun of resurrection," the "sun of the soul."[2]   And yet one group of ideas,
familiar in this connection, receives little notice from Clement.
The Logos is indeed the Great High Priest, but the symbolism
of priest and sacrifice and sin-bearer is left rather remarkably
unemphasized.   He is "the all-availing healer of mankind,"[3]
but his function is more to educate, to quicken, and to give
knowledge than to expiate.

The great and characteristic feature of the Logos is that
"he took the mask (προσωπεῖον) of a man and moulded it for
himself in flesh and played a part in the drama of mankind's
salvation; for he was a true player (γνήσιος ἀγωνιστής), a
fellow-player with the creature; and most quickly was he
spread abroad among all men, more quickly than the sun,
when he rose from the Father's will, and proved whence he
was and who he was by what he taught and showed, he, the
bringer of the covenant, the reconciler, the Logos our Saviour,
the fountain of life and peace, shed over the whole face of the
earth, by whom (so to say) all things have become an ocean
of blessings."[4]   Though essentially and eternally free from
passion (ἀπαθής) "for our sake he took upon him our flesh
with its capacity for suffering" (τὴν παθητὴν σάρκα)[5] and
"descended to sensation (αἴσθησις)."[6]   "It is clear that none
can in his lifetime clearly apprehend God; but 'the pure in
heart shall see God' when they come to the final perfection.
Since, then, the soul was too weak for the perception of what
is (τῶν ὄντων), we needed a divine teacher.   The Saviour is
sent down to teach us how to acquire good, and to give it to
us (χορηγός)—the secret and holy knowledge of the great
Providence,"[7]—"to show God to foolish men, to end corruption,

---

[1] *Protr.* 110, 1.   [2] *Protr.* 63, 5; 84, 2; 68, 4.

[3] *Pæd.* i, 6, 2, ὅλου κήδεται τοῦ πλάσματος, καὶ σῶμα καὶ ψυχὴν ἀκεῖται αὐτοῦ ὁ
παναρκὴς τῆς ἀνθρωπότητος ἰατρός.

[4] *Protr.* 110, 2, 3.   Cf. also *Pæd.* i, 4, 1-2.

[5] *Strom.* vii, 6.   Cf. *Pæd.* i, 4, 2.   ἀπόλυτος εἰς τὸ παντελὲς ἀνθρωπίνων παθῶν.

[6] *Strom.* v, 40, 3.

[7] *Strom.* v, 7, 7-8.

to conquer death, to reconcile disobedient children to their
Father. . . . The Lord pities, educates, encourages, exhorts, saves
and guards, and as the prize of learning he promises us out of
his abundance the kingdom of heaven—this alone giving him
joy in us, that we are saved."[1]   All this was foreknown before
the foundation of the world ; the Logos was and is the
divine beginning or principle of all things, " but because he
has now taken the long-hallowed name, the name worthy of
his power, the Christ, that is why I call it the new song."[2]
And indeed he is right, for " the Epiphany, now shining among
us, of the Word that was in the beginning and before it "[3]
is new in philosophy ; and it is a new thing also that the
doctrine of a Logos should be "essentially musical."   The
Incarnation of the divine Teacher is the central fact for
Clement.

The identification of this incarnate Logos with Jesus of
Nazareth was part of Clement's inheritance, and as usual he
accepted the form which the tradition of the Church had
assumed.   But Clement's theology altered the significance of
Jesus.   For the Abba Father whom Jesus loved, he substituted
the great Unknowable, and then he had to bring in a figure
unfamiliar to the thought of Jesus—the Logos, whom he
clothed with many of the attributes of the Father of Jesus,
and then identified with Jesus himself.   Not unnaturally in
this combination the historic is outweighed by the theoretic
element, and indeed receives very little attention.   The
thought of Incarnation is to Clement much more important
than the Personality.

Jesus is "God and pedagogue," "good shepherd," and
"mystic Angel (or messenger)," "the pearl," "the great High
Priest," and so forth.[4]   In a few passages (some of them
already quoted) Clement speaks of the earthly life of Jesus—
of the crown of thorns, the common ware, and the absence of
a silver foot-bath.   But he takes care to make it clear that
Jesus was "not an ordinary man," and that was why he did
not marry and have children—this in opposition to certain

---

[1] *Protr.* 6, 1-2, τουτο μόνον ἀπολαύων ἡμῶν ὅ σωζόμεθα.
[2] *Protr.* 6, 5.   [3] *Protr.* 7, 3.
[4] The references are (in order) *Pæd.* i, 55 ; i, 53, 2 ; i, 59, 1 ; ii, 118, 5 ; *Protr*
120, 2.

vain persons who held up the Lord's example as a reason
for rejecting marriage, which "they call simple prostitution
and a practice introduced by the devil."[1] So far was Jesus
from being "an ordinary man" that Clement takes pains to
dissociate him from ordinary human experience. To the
miraculous birth he refers incidentally but in a way that
leaves no mistake possible. "Most people even now believe,
as it seems, that Mary ceased to be a virgin through the birth
of her child, though this was not really the case—for some
say she was found by the midwife to be a virgin after her
delivery."[2] This expansion of the traditional story is to be
noted as an early illustration of the influence of dogma. The
episode appears in an elaborate form in the apocryphal
Gospels.[3] But Clement goes further. "In the case of the
Saviour, to suppose that his body required, quâ body, the
necessary attentions for its continuance, would be laughable
(γέλως). For he ate—not on account of his body, which was
held together by holy power, but that it might not occur
to those who consorted with him to think otherwise of him—
as indeed later on some really supposed him to have been
manifested merely in appearance [i.e. the Docetists who
counted his body a phantom]. He himself was entirely
without passion (ἀπαθής) and into him entered no emotional
movement (κίνημα παθητικόν), neither pleasure nor pain."[4]
A fragment (in a Latin translation) of a commentary of
Clement's upon the first Epistle of John, contains a curious
statement: "It is said in the traditions that John touched the
surface of the body of Jesus, and drove his hand deep into
it, and the firmness of the flesh was no obstacle but gave way
to the hand of the disciple."[5] At the same time we read:
"It was not idly that the Lord chose to employ a body of
mean form, in order that no one, while praising his comeliness

---

[1] *Strom.* iii, 49, 1-3, οὐδὲ ἄνθρωπος ἦν κοινός.

[2] *Strom.* vii, 93.

[3] See *Protevangelium Jacobi*, 19, 20 (in Tischendorf's *Evangelia Apocrypha*, p. 36),
a work quoted in the 4th century by Gregory of Nyssa, and possibly the source of this
statement of Clement's. Tischendorf thinks it may also have been known to Justin.
See also *pseudo-Matthæi evangelium*, 13 (Tischendorf, p. 75), known to St Jerome.

[4] *Strom.* vi, 71, 2. A strange opinion of Valentinus about Jesus eating may be
compared, which Clement quotes without dissent in *Strom.* iii, 59, 3. See p. 249, n. 4.

[5] Printed in Dindorf's edition, vol. iii, p. 485.

and beauty, should depart from what he said, and in cleaving to what is left behind should be severed from the higher things of thought (τῶν νοητῶν)." [1]

It is consistent with the general scheme of Clement's thought that the cross has but a small part in his theology. "It was not by the will of his Father that the Lord suffered, nor are the persecuted so treated in accordance with his choice" ——it is rather in both cases that "such things occur, God not preventing them ; this alone saves at once the providence and goodness of God." [2] Yet "the blood of the Lord is twofold ; there is the fleshly, whereby we have been redeemed from corruption, and the spiritual, by which we have been anointed." [3] The cross is the landmark between us and our past. [4] On the whole Clement has not much to say about sin, though of course he does not ignore it. It is "eternal death" ; [5] it is "irrational" ; [6] it is not to be attributed "to the operation (energy) of dæmons," as that would be to acquit the sinner, still it makes a man "like the dæmons" (δαιμονικός). [7] God's punishments he holds to be curative in purpose. [8] He says nothing to imply the eternity of punishment, [9] and as we have seen he speaks definitely of the Gospel being preached to the dead.

The Christian religion, according to Clement, begins in faith and goes on to knowledge. The heavier emphasis with him always falls on knowledge, though he maintains in a fine chapter that faith is its foundation. [10] "The Greeks," he says, "consider faith an empty and barbarous thing," [11] but he is far from such a view. Faith must be well-founded—"if faith is such as to be destroyed by plausible talk, let it be destroyed." [12] But the word left upon the reader's mind is knowledge. A passage like the following is unmistakable. "Supposing one were to offer the Gnostic his choice, whether he would prefer

---

[1] *Strom.* vi, 151, 3. Cf. Celsus, p. 249, and Tert. *de carne Christi*, 9, *Adeo nec humanæ honestatis corpus fuit* ; Tertullian however is far from any such fancies as to Christ's body not being quite human, see p. 340.

[2] *Strom.* iv, 86, 2, 3 ; contrast Tertullian's attitude in *de Fuga in Persecutione*, etc.

[3] *Pæd.* ii, 19, 4.   [4] *Pæd.* iii, 85, 3.

[5] *Protr.* 115, 2.   [6] *Pæd.* i, ch. 13.   [7] *Strom.* vi, 98, 1.

[8] Cf. *Strom.* i, 173 ; iv, 153, 2 ; *Pæd.* i, 70, ἡ γὰρ κόλασις ἐπ᾽ ἀγαθῷ καὶ ἐπ᾽ ὠφελείᾳ τοῦ κολαζομένου.

[9] Cf. J. B. Mayor, Pref. to *Stromateis*, vii, p. xl.   [10] *Strom.* ii, ch. 4. Cf. ii, 48.

[11] *Strom.* ii, 8, 4.   [12] *Strom.* vi, 81, 1.

the knowledge of God or eternal salvation, one or the other
(though of course they are above all things an identity);
without the slightest hesitation he would choose the knowledge
of God for its own sake."[1]   The ideal Christian is habitually
spoken of in this way, as the " man of knowledge "—the true
" Gnostic," as opposed to the heretics who illegitimately claim
the title.   A very great deal of Clement's writing is devoted to
building up this Gnostic, to outlining his ideal character.   He
is essentially man as God conceived him, entering into the
divine life, and, by the grace of the Logos, even becoming
God.

This thought of man becoming God Clement repeats very
often, and it is a mark of how far Christianity has travelled
from Palestine.   It begins with the Platonic ideal of being
made like to God, and the means is the knowledge of God or
the sight of God given by the Logos.   " ' Nought say I of the
rest,'[2] glorifying God.   Only I say that those Gnostic souls
are so carried away by the magnificence of the vision ($\theta\epsilon\omega\rho\acute{\iota}a$)
that they cannot confine themselves within the lines of the
constitution by which each holy degree is assigned and in
accordance with which the blessed abodes of the gods have
been marked out and allotted ; but being counted as ' holy
among the holy,' and translated absolutely and entirely to
another sphere, they keep on always moving to better and yet
better regions, until they no longer greet the divine vision in
mirrors or by means of mirrors, but with loving souls feast for
ever on the uncloying never-ending sight, radiant in its
transparent clearness, while throughout the endless ages they
taste a never-wearying delight, and thus continue, all alike
honoured with an identity of pre-eminence.   This is the
apprehensive vision of the pure in heart.   This, then, is the
work ($\dot{\epsilon}\nu\acute{\epsilon}\rho\gamma\epsilon\iota a$) of the perfected Gnostic—to hold communion
with God through the Great High Christ being made like the
Lord as far as may be.   Yes, and in this process of becoming
like God the Gnostic creates and fashions himself anew, and
adorns those that hear him."[3]   In an interesting chapter
Clement discusses abstraction from material things as a necessary

---

[1] *Strom.* iv, 136, 5.   [2] From Æsch. *Agam.* 36.
[3] *Strom.* vii, 13. (Mayor's translation in the main).   Cf. *Protr.* 86, 2, θεοσέβεια
ἐξομοιοῦσα τῷ θεῷ ; *Pæd.* i, 99, 1 ; *Strom.* vi, 104, 2.

condition for attaining the knowledge of God ; we must " cast ourselves into the greatness of Christ and thence go forward." [1] " If a man know himself, he shall know God, and knowing God shall be made like to him. . . . The man with whom the Logos dwells . . . is made like to God . . . and that man *becomes* God, for God wishes it." [2]   " By being deified into Apathy (ἀπάθειαν) a man becomes Monadic without stain." [3] As Homer makes men poets, Crobylus cooks, and Plato philosophers ; " so he who obeys the Lord and follows the prophecy given through him, is fully perfected after the likeness of his Teacher, and thus becomes a god while still moving about in the flesh." [4]   " Dwelling with the Lord, talking with him and sharing his hearth, he will abide according to the spirit, pure in flesh, pure in heart, sanctified in word. ' The world to him,' it says, ' is crucified and he to the world.' He carries the cross of the Saviour and follows the Lord ' in his footsteps as of a god,' and is become holy of the holy." [5]

We seem to touch the world of daily life, when after all the beatific visions we see the cross again. Clement has abundance of suggestion for Christian society in Alexandria, and it is surprising how simple, natural and wise is his attitude to the daily round and common task. Men and women alike may " philosophize," for their " virtue " (in Aristotle's phrase) is the same—so may the slave, the ignorant and the child. [6]   The Christian life is not to eradicate the natural but to control it. [7] Marriage is a state of God's appointing—Clement is no Jerome. Nature made us to marry and " the childless man falls short of the perfection of Nature." [8]   Men must marry for their country's sake and for the completeness of the universe. [9]   True manhood is not proved by celibacy—the married man may " fall short of the other as regards his personal salvation, but he has

---

[1] *Strom.* v, 71, 3.   [2] *Pæd.* iii, 1, 1, and 5.   [3] *Strom.* iv, 152, 1.
[4] *Strom.* vii, 101.
[5] *Strom.* ii, 104, 2, 3, with reff. to Paul *Gal.* 6, 14 ; and *Odyssey*, 2, 406. Other passages in which the notion occurs are *Strom.* iv, 149, 8 ; vii, 56, 82. Augustine has the thought—all the Fathers, indeed, according to Harnack. See Mayor's note on *Strom.* vii, 3. It also comes in the *Theologia Germanica.*
[6] *Strom.* iv. 62, 4 ; 58, 3 ; the ἀρετή in *Pæd.* i, 10, 1.
[7] *Pæd.* ii, 46, 1.   [8] *Strom.* ii, 139, 5.
[9] *Strom.* ii, 140, 1, a very remarkable utterance.

the advantage in the conduct of life inasmuch as he really preserves a faint (ὀλίγην) image of the true Providence."[1] The heathen, it is true, may expose their own children and keep parrots, but the begetting and upbringing of children is a part of the married Christian life.[2] "Who are the two or three gathering in the name of Christ, among whom the Lord is in the midst? Does he not mean man, wife and child by the *three*, seeing woman is made to match man by God."[3]

The real fact about the Christian life is simply this, that the New Song turns wild beasts into men of God.[4] "Sail past the siren's song, it works death," says Clement, "if only thou wilt, thou hast overcome destruction ; lashed to the wood thou shalt be loosed from ruin ; the Word of God will steer thee and the holy spirit will moor thee to the havens of heaven."[5] To the early Christian "the wood" always meant the cross of Jesus. The new life is "doing good for love's sake,"[6] and "he who shows pity ought not to know that he is doing it. . . . When he does good by instinctive habit (ἐν ἕξει) then he will be imitating the nature of good."[7] God breathed into man and there has always been something charming in a man since then (φίλτρον).[8] So "the new people" are always happy, always in the full bloom of thought, always at spring-time.[9] The Church is the one thing in the world that always rejoices.[10]

Clement's theology is composite rather than organic—a structure of materials old and new, hardly fit for the open air, the wind and the rain. But his faith is another thing—it rests upon the living personality of the Saviour, the love of God and the significance of the individual soul, and it has the stamp of such faith in all the ages—joy and peace in believing. It has lasted because it lived. If Christianity had depended on the

---

[1] *Strom.* vii, 70, end.

[2] *Pæd.* ii, 83, 1, τοῖς δὲ γεγαμηκόσι σκόπος ἡ παιδοποιΐα, τέλος δὲ ἡ εὐτεκνία. Cf. Tertullian, *adv. Marc.* iv, 17, on the impropriety of God calling us children if we suppose that he *nobis filios facere non permisit auferendo connubium.* The opposite view, for purposes of argument perhaps, in *de exh. castitatis,* 12, where he ridicules the idea of producing children for the sake of the state.

[3] *Strom.* iii, 68, 1.   [4] *Protr.* 4, 3.   [5] *Protr.* 118, 4.

[6] *Strom.* iv, 135, 4.   [7] *Strom.* iv, 138, 2, 3.   [8] *Pæd.* i, 7, 2.

[9] *Pæd.* i, 20, 3, 4.

[10] *Pæd.* i, 22, 2, μόνη αὕτη εἰς τοὺς αἰῶνας μένει χαίρουσα ἀεί.

Logos, it would have followed the Logos to the limbo whither went Æon and Aporrhoia and Spermaticos Logos. But that the Logos has not perished is due to the one fact that with the Cross it has been borne through the ages on the shoulders of Jesus.

CHAPTER X

TERTULLIAN

IN his most famous chapter Gibbon speaks at one point of the affirmation of the early church that those who persisted in the worship of the dæmons " neither deserved nor could expect a pardon from the irritated justice of the Deity." Oppressed in this world by the power of the Pagans, Christians " were sometimes seduced by resentment and spiritual pride to delight in the prospect of their future triumph. ' You are fond of spectacles,' exclaims the stern Tertullian, ' expect the greatest of all spectacles, the last and eternal judgment of the universe. How shall I admire, how laugh, how rejoice, how exult, when I behold so many proud monarchs, ₍ and fancied gods, groaning in the lowest abyss of darkness ; so many magistrates, who persecuted the name of the Lord, liquefying in fiercer fires than they ever kindled against the Christians ; so many sage philosophers blushing in red-hot flames with their deluded scholars ; so many celebrated poets trembling before the tribunal, not of Minos, but of Christ ; so many tragedians more tuneful in the expression of their own sufferings ; so many dancers——' But the humanity of the reader will permit me to draw a veil over the rest of this infernal description, which the zealous African pursues in a long variety of affected and unfeeling witticisms." [1]

The passage is a magnificent example of Gibbon's style and method,—more useful, however, as an index to the mind of Gibbon than to that of Tertullian. He has abridged his translation, and in one or two clauses he has missed Tertullian's points ; finally he has drawn his veil over the rest of the infernal description exactly when he knew there was little or nothing more to be quoted that would serve his purpose. He has made no attempt to understand the man he quotes, nor the

---

[1] Gibbon, *Decline and Fall*, c. 15 (vol. ii, p. 177, Milman-Smith) ; Tertullian, *de Spectaculis*, 30.

mood in which he spoke, nor the circumstances which gave rise to that mood. Yet on the evidence of this passage and a sonnet of Matthew Arnold's, English readers pass a swift judgment on "the stern Tertullian" and his "unpitying Phrygian sect." But to the historian of human thought, and to the student of human character, there are few figures of more significance in Latin literature. Of the men who moulded Western Christendom few have stamped themselves and their ideas upon it with anything approaching the clearness and the effect of Tertullian. He first turned the currents of Christian thought in the West into channels in which they have never yet ceased to flow and will probably long continue to flow. He was the first Latin churchman, and his genius helped to shape Latin Christianity. He, too, was the first great Puritan of the West, precursor alike of Augustine and of the Reformation. The Catholic Church left him unread throughout the Middle Ages, but at the Renaissance he began once more to be studied, and simultaneously there also began the great movement for the purification of the church and the deepening of Christian life, which were the causes to which he had given himself and his genius.

Such a man may be open to criticism on many sides. He may be permanently or fitfully wrong in thought or speech or conduct ; but it is clear that an influence so great rests upon something more profound than irritability however brilliant in expression. There must be somewhere in the man something that corresponds with the enduring thoughts of mankind— something that engages the mind or that wins the friendship of men—something that is true and valid. And this, whatever it is, is the outcome of many confluent elements—of temperament, environment and experience, perhaps, in chief. The man must be seen as his personal friends saw him and as his enemies saw him ; what is more, they—both sets of them— must be seen as he saw them. The critic must himself, by dint of study and imagination, be played upon by as many of the factors of the man's experience as he can re-capture. Impressions, pleasures, doubts, hopes, convictions, friendships, inspirations—everything that goes to shape a man is relevant to that study of character without which, in the case of formative men, history itself becomes pedantry and illusion. Particularly in the case of such a man as Tertullian is it needful to repeat this caution. The impetuous dogmatism in which his mind and, quite as often, his mood express themselves, and his hard words, harder a great deal than his heart, no less than his impulsive convictions, " seem," as Gibbon put it, " to offend the reason and the humanity of the present age." On the other side, the church, which the historian in a footnote saddles with the responsibility of sharing Tertullian's most harsh beliefs, is at one with " the present age" in repudiating him on grounds of her own. Yet, questioned or condemned, Tertullian played his part, and that no little one, in the conflict of religions ; he stood for truth as he saw it, and wrote and spoke with little thought of the praise or blame of his contemporaries or of posterity—all *that* he had abandoned once for all, when he made the great choice of his life. Questioned or condemned, he is representative, and he is individual, the first man of genius of the Latin race to follow Jesus Christ, and to re-set his ideas in the language native to that race.

Tertullian was born about the middle of the second century A.D. at Carthage, or in its neighbourhood. The city at all events is the scene of his life—a great city with a great history. " Tyre in Africa" is one of his phrases for Carthage and her " sister-cities," and he quotes Virgil's description of Dido's town *studiis asperrima belli*.[1] But his Carthage was not that of Dido and Hannibal. It was the re-founded city of Julius Cæsar, now itself two hundred years old—a place with a character of its own familiar to the reader of Apuleius and of Augustine's *Confessions*,—a character confirmed by the references of Tertullian to its amusements and its daily sights. " What sea-captain is there that does not carry his mirth even to the point of shame ? Every day we see the frolics in which sailors take their pleasure." [2] Scholars have played with the fancy that they could trace in Tertullian's work the influence of some Semitic strain, as others with equal reason have found

---

[1] Both of these in *de Pallio*, 1. It may be noted that in allusions to Dido's story he prefers the non-Virgilian version, more honourable to the Queen ; *Apol.* 50 ; *ad martyras*, 4.
[2] *adv. Valentin.* 12.

traces of the Celt in Virgil and Livy. Tertullian himself has perhaps even fewer references to Punic speech and people than Apuleius, while, like Apuleius, he wrote in both Greek and Latin,[1] and it is possible that, like Apuleius, and Perpetua the martyr, he spoke both.

Jerome tells us that Tertullian was the son of a centurion.[2] He tells us himself, incidentally and by implication, that he was the child of heathen parents. " Idolatry," he says, " is the midwife that brings all men into the world ; " and he gives a very curious picture of the pagan ceremonies that went with child-birth, the fillet on the mother's womb, the cries to Lucina, the table spread for Juno, the horoscope, and finally the dedication of a hair of the child, or of all his hair together, as the rites of clan or family may require.[3] Thus from the very first the boy is dedicated to a *genius*, and to the evil he inherits through the transmission of his bodily nature is added the influence of a false dæmon—" though there still is good innate in the soul, the archetypal good, divine and germane, essentially natural ; for what comes from God is not so much extinguished as overshadowed." [4] The children of Christian parents have so far, he indicates, a better beginning ; they are holy in virtue of their stock and of their upbringing.[5] With himself it had not been so. It is curious to find the great controversialist of later days recalling nursery tales, how " amid the difficulties of sleep one heard from one's nurse about the witch's towers and the combs of the sun "—recalling too the children's witticisms about the apples that grow in the sea and the fishes that grow on the tree.[6] They come back into his mind as he thinks of the speculations of Valentinus and his followers.

His education was that of his day,—lavish rhetoric, and knowledge of that very wide character which in all his contemporaries is perhaps too suggestive of manual and

---

[1] References to his Greek treatises (all lost) may be found in *de cor. mil,* 6 ; *de bapt.* 15 ; *de virg. vel.* 1.

[2] *De viris illustribus, sub nomine.*

[3] *de anima* 39.   [4] *Ibid.* 41.   [5] *Ibid.* 39.

[6] *adv. Valent.* 3, *in infantia inter somni difficultates a nutricula audisse lamiæ turres et pectines Solis; ibid.* 20, *puerilium dicibulorum in mari poma nasci et in arbore pisces.*

cyclopædia [1]—works never so abundant in antiquity as then. But he was well taught, as a brilliant boy deserved, and his range of interests is remarkable. Nor is he overwhelmed by miscellaneous erudition, like Aulus Gellius for instance, or like Clement of Alexandria, to come to a man more on his own level. He is master of the great literature of Rome; he has read the historians and Cicero; he can quote Virgil with telling effect. *Usque adeone mori miserum est?* he asks of the Christian who hesitates to be martyred; [2] "a hint from the world" he says. Sooner or later, he read Varro's books, the armoury of every Latin Christian against polytheism.

He "looked into medicine," he tells us, and a good many passages in his treatises remind us of the fact. [3] It may help to explain an explicitness in the use of terms more usual in the physician perhaps than in the layman.

But his career lay not in medicine but in law, and he caught the spirit of his profession. It has been debated whether the Tertullian, whose treatise *de castrensi peculio* is quoted in the Digest, is the apologist or another, but no legal treatises are needed to convince the reader how thoroughly a lawyer was the author of the theological works. He has every art and every artifice of his trade. He can reason quietly and soundly, he can declaim, he can do both together. He is a master of logic, delighting in huge chains of alternatives. He can quibble and wrest the obvious meaning of a document to perfection, browbeat an opponent, argue *ad hominem*,[4] evade a clear issue, and anticipate and escape an obvious objection, as well as any lawyer that ever practised. Again and again he impresses us as a special pleader, and we feel that he is forcing us away from the evidence of our own sense and intelligence to a conclusion which he prefers on other grounds. His

---

[1] *e.g.* he alludes to a manual on flowers and garlands by Claudius Saturninus, and another on a similar subject, perhaps, by Leo Ægyptius; *de cor. mil.* 7, 12. Apart from the Christian controversy on the use of flowers, we shall find later on that he had a keener interest in them than some critics might suppose; *adv. Marc.* i, 13, 14.

[2] *de juga*, 10.

[3] *de anima*, 2; cf. *ibid.* 10, quotation of a great anatomist Herophilus who dissected "six hundred" subjects in order to find out Nature's secrets; also *ibid.* 25, a discussion of childbirth to show that the soul does not come into the child with its first breath; *ibid.* 43, a discussion of sleep. *Scorpiace*, 5, surgery.

[4] *e.g.* the end of *adv. Hermogenem*.

epigrams rival Tacitus, and there is even in his rhetoric a conviction and a passion which Cicero never reaches. The suddenness of his questions, and the amazing readiness of his jests, savage, subtle, ironic, good-natured, brilliant or common-place,[1] impress the reader again and again, however well he knows him. Yet Tertullian never loses sight of his object, whatever the flights of rhetoric or humour on which he ventures. In one case, he plainly says that his end will best be achieved by ridicule. "Put it down, reader, as a sham fight before the battle. I will show how to deal wounds, but I will not deal them. If there shall be laughter, the matter itself shall be the apology. There are many things that deserve so to be refuted; gravity would be too high a compliment. Vanity and mirth may go together. Yes, and it becomes Truth to laugh, because she is glad, to play with her rivals, because she is free from fear."[2] Then, with a caution as to becoming laughter, he launches into his most amusing book—that against the Valentinians.

Tertullian rivals Apuleius in brilliant mastery of the elaborate and artificial rhetoric of the day. He has the same tricks of rhyming clauses and balancing phrases. Thus : *attente custoditur quod tarde invenitur* ;[3] or more fully : *spiritus enim dominatur, caro famulatur ; tamen utrumque inter se communi-cant reatum, spiritus ob imperium, caro ob ministerium.*[4] Here the vanities of his pagan training subserve true thought. Elsewhere they are more playful, as when he suggests to those, who like the pagans took off their cloaks to pray, that God heard the three saints in the fiery furnace of the Babylonian king though they prayed *cum sarabaris et tiaris suis*—in turbans and trousers.[5] But when he gives us such a string of phrases as *aut Platonis honor, aut Zenonis vigor, aut Aristotelis tenor, aut Epicuri stupor, aut Heracliti moeror, aut Empedoclis furor,*[6] one feels that he is for the moment little better than one of the wicked. At the beginning of his tract on Baptism, after speaking

---

[1] Puns, *e.g.*, on *areæ, ad Scap.* 3 ; on *strophæ, de Spect.* 29 ; on *pleroma, adv. Val.* 12. See his nonsense on the tears, salt, sweet, and bituminous, of Achamoth, a Valentinian figure, *adv. Val.* 15 ; on " the Milesian tales of his Æons," *de Anima.* 23.

[2] *adv. Valent.* 6.   [3] *adv. Valent.* 1.

[4] *de baptismo,* 4.   [5] *de oratione,* 15

[6] *de anima,* 3.

of water he pulls himself up abruptly—he is afraid, he says, that the reader may fancy he is composing *laudes aquae* (in the manner of rhetorical adoxography) rather than discussing the principles of baptism.[1] His tract *de Pallio* is frankly a humorous excursion into old methods, in which the elderly Montanist, who has left off wearing the *toga*, justifies himself for his highly conservative and entirely suitable conduct in adopting the *pallium*. The " stern " Tertullian appears here in the character that his pagan friends had long ago known, and that his Christian readers might feel somewhere or other in everything that he writes. There is a good-tempered playfulness about the piece, a fund of splendid nonsense, which suggest the fellow-citizen of Apuleius rather than the presbyter.[2] But earnestness, which is not incompatible with humour, is his strong characteristic, and when it arms itself with an irony so powerful as that of Tertullian, the result is amazing. Sometimes he exceeds all bounds, as when in his *Ad Nationes* he turns that irony upon the horrible charges, which the pagans, knowing them to be false, bring against the Christians, while he, pretending for the moment that they are true, invites his antagonists to think them out to their consequences and to act upon them.[3] Or again take the speech of Christ on the judgment day, in which the Lord is pictured as saying that he had indeed entrusted the Gospel once for all to the Apostles, but had thought better of it and made some changes—as of course, Tertullian suggests, he really would have to say, if it could be supposed that the latest heretics were right after all.[4]

But, whatever be said or thought of the rhetoric, playful or earnest, it has another character than it wears in his contemporaries. For here was a far more powerful brain, strong, clear and well-trained, and a heart whose tenderness and sensibility have never had justice. In some ways he very much suggests Thomas Carlyle—he has the same passion, the same vivid imagination and keen sensibility, the same earnestness and the same loyalty to truth as he sees it regardless of conse-

---

[1] *de bapt.* 3 (end)

[2] On *de pallio* see Boissier, *La Fin du Paganisme*, bk. iii, ch. 1.

[3] *ad Natt*, i, 7 ; the charges were incest, and child-murder for purposes of magic.

[4] *de Præscriptione*, 44 (end). Similarly of resurrection, virgin-birth, etc.—*recogitavi*.

quence and compromise,—and alas ! the same " natural faculty for being in a hurry," which Carlyle deplored, and Tertullian before him—" I, poor wretch, always sick with the fever of impatience "[1]—the same fatal gift for pungent phrase, and the same burning and indignant sympathy for the victim of wrong and cruelty.[2] The beautiful feeling, which he shows in handling the parables of the lost sheep and the prodigal son, in setting forth from them the loving fatherhood of God,[3] might surprise some of his critics. Nor has every great Christian of later and more humane days been capable of writing as he wrote of victory in battle against foreigners—" Is the laurel of triumph made of leaves—or the dead bodies of men ? With ribbons is it adorned—or with graves ? Is it bedewed with unguents, or the tears of wives and mothers ?—perhaps too of some who are Christians, for even among the barbarians is Christ." [4] There are again among his books some which have an appeal and a tender charm throughout that haunt the reader—that is, if he has himself passed through any such experience as will enable him to enter into what was in Tertullian's mind and heart as he wrote. So truly and intimately does he know and with such sympathy does he express some of the deepest religious emotions.[5]

From time to time Tertullian drops a stray allusion to his earlier years. He was a pagan—*de vestris sumus*—" one of yourselves " (*Apol.* 18) ; " the kind of man I was myself once, blind and without the light of the Lord." [6] A Roman city, and Carthage perhaps in particular, offered to a gifted youth of Roman ways of thinking endless opportunities of self-indulgence. Tertullian speaks of what he had seen in the arena—the condemned criminal, dressed as some hero or god of the mythology, mutilated or burned alive, for the amusement of a shouting

---

[1] *de Patientia*, I, *miserrimus ego semper æger caloribus impatientiæ.*

[2] Cf. his tone as to the *scortum,* unexampled, so far as I know, in Latin literature, and only approached in Greek perhaps by Dio Chrysostom—the *publicæ libidinis hostiæ* (*de Spect.* 17), *publicarum libidinum victimæ* (*de cult. fem.* ii, 12). He alone of all who mention the strange annual scene on the stage, which Cato withdrew to allow, has pity for the poor women.

[3] *de Pænitentia*, 8.   [4] *de corona*, 12.

[5] I refer especially to such passages as *de Carne Christi,* 4-9, 14 ; *de Resurr. Carnis*, 7, 12, etc.

[6] *de Pænit.*, I, *hoc genus hominum quod et ipsi retro fuimus, cæci, sine domini lumine.*

audience,[1] "exulting in human blood."[2] "We have laughed, amid the mocking cruelties of noonday, at Mercury as he examined the bodies of the dead with his burning iron ; we have seen Jove's brother too, with his mallet, hauling out the corpses of gladiators."[3] In later days when he speaks of such things, he shudders and leaves the subject rather than remember what he has seen—*malo non implere quam meminisse.*[4] He knew the theatre of the Roman city—"the consistory of all uncleanness" he calls it. "Why should it be lawful (for a Christian)," he asked, "to see what it is sin to do? Why should the things, which ' coming out of the mouth defile a man,' seem not to defile a man when he takes them in through eyes and ears ?"[5] He speaks of Tragedies and Comedies, teaching guilt and lust, bloody and wanton ; and the reader of the *Golden Ass* can recall from fiction cases wonderfully illuminative of what could have been seen in fact. When he apostrophizes the sinner, he speaks of himself. "You," he cries, "you, the sinner, like me—no! less sinner than I, for I recognize my own pre-eminence in guilt."[6] He is, he says, "a sinner of every brand, born for nothing but repentance."[7] To say, with Professor Hort, on the evidence of such passages that Tertullian was "apparently a man of vicious life" might involve a similar condemnation of Bunyan and St Paul ; while to find the charge "painfully" confirmed by " the foulness which ever afterwards infested his mind" is to exaggerate absurdly in the first place, and in the second to forget such parallels as Swift and Carlyle, who both carried explicit speech to a point beyond ordinary men, while neither is open to such a suggestion as that brought against Tertullian. With such cases as Apuleius, Hadrian or even Julius Cæsar before us, it is im-possible to maintain that Tertullian's early life must have been spotless, but it is possible to fancy more wrong than there was. The excesses of a man of genius are generally touched by the

---

[1] *Apol.* 15, cf. *ad Natt.* i, 10, another draft of the same matter.
[2] *de Spect.* 19, *eamus in amphitheatrum . . . delectemur sanguine humano* (ironically).
[3] *Apol.* 15. The burning-iron was to see whether any life were left in the fallen.
[4] *de Spect.* 19 (end). [5] *de Spectaculis*, 17.
[6] *de Pænit.* 4.
[7] *de Pænit.* 12, *peccator omnium notarum, nec ulli rei nisi pænitentiæ natus.*

imagination, and therein lies at once their peculiar danger, and also something redemptive that promises another future.

Tertullian at any rate married—when, we cannot say ; but, as a Christian and a Montanist, he addressed a book to his wife, and in his *De Anima* he twice alludes to the ways of small infants in a manner which suggests personal knowledge. In the one he speaks with curious observation of the sense-perception of very young babies ; in the other he appeals to their movements in sleep, their tremors and smiles, as evidence that they also have dreams. Such passages if met in Augustine's pages would not so much surprise us. They suggest that the depth and tenderness of Tertullian's nature have not been fully understood.[1]

Meanwhile, whatever his amusements, the young lawyer had his serious interests. If he was already acquiring the arts of a successful pleader, the more real aspects of Law were making their impression upon him. The great and ordered conceptions of principle and harmony, which fill the minds of reflective students of law in all ages, were then reinforced by the Stoic teaching of the unity of Nature in the indwelling of the Spermaticos Logos with its universal scope and power. Law and Stoicism, in this union, formed the mind and character of Tertullian. In later days, under the stress of controversy (which he always enjoyed) he could find points in which to criticize his Stoic teachers ; but the contrast between the language he uses of Plato and his friendliness (for instance) for *Seneca sæpe noster*[2] is suggestive. But that is not all. A Roman lawyer could hardly speculate except in the terms of Stoicism—it was his natural and predestined language. Above all, the constant citation of Nature by Tertullian shows who had taught him in the first instance to think.

When, years after, in 212 A.D., he told Scapula that "it is a fundamental human right, a privilege of Nature, that any and every man should worship what he thinks right," he had sub-consciously gone back to the great Stoic *Jus Naturæ*.[3]

---

[1] *de anima*, 19 and 49. Add his words on the wife taken away by death, *cui etiam religiosiorem reservas affectionem*, etc., *de exh. cast.* 11.

[2] *de anima*, 20. Cf. *ibid.* 17, on the moderation of the Stoics, as compared with Plato, in their treatment of the fidelity of the senses.

[3] *ad Scap.* 2. *Tamen humani iuris et naturalis potestatis est unicuique quod putaverit colere.*

Nature is the original authority—side by side, he would say
in his later years, with the inspired word of God,—yet even so
"it was not the pen of Moses that initiated the knowledge of
the Creator. . . . The vast majority of mankind, though they
have never heard the name of Moses—to say nothing of his
book—know the God of Moses none the less."[1]   One of his
favourite arguments rests on what he calls the *testimonium
animæ naturaliter Christianæ* — the testimony of the soul
which in its ultimate and true nature is essentially Christian ;
and this argument rests on his general conception of Nature.
Let a man " reflect on the majesty of Nature, for it is from
Nature that the authority of the soul comes.   What you give
to the teacher, you must allow to the pupil.   Nature is the
teacher, the soul the pupil.   And whatever the one has taught
or the other learnt, comes from God, who is the teacher of the
teacher (*i.e.* Nature)" ;[2] and neither God nor Nature can lie.[3]
An extension of this is to be found in his remark, in a much
more homely connexion, that if the "common consciousness"
(*conscientia communis*) be consulted, we shall find "Nature
itself" teaching us that mind and soul are livelier and more
intelligent when the stomach is not heavily loaded.[4]   The
appeal to the *consensus* of men, as the expression of the
universal and the natural, and therefore as evidence to truth, is
essentially Stoic.

Over and over he lays stress upon natural law.   "All
things are fixed in the truth of God,"[5] he says, and "our God
is the God of Nature."[6]   He identifies the natural and the
rational—"all the properties of God must be rational just as
they are natural," that is a clear principle (*regula*);[7] "the
rational element must be counted natural because it is native
to the soul from the beginning—coming as it does from a
rational author (*auctore*)."[8]   He objects to Marcion that
everything is so "sudden"—so spasmodic—in his scheme of
things.[9]   For himself, he holds with Paul ("doth not Nature
teach you?") that "law is natural and Nature legal," that

---

[1] *adv. Marc.* i, 10, *major popularitas generis humani.*

[2] *de testim. animæ,* 5.   [3] *de test. an.* 6.

[4] *de jejunio,* 6.   [5] *de spectaculis,* 20.

[6] *de cor. mil.* 5,   *Naturæ deus noster est.*

[7] *adv. Marc.* i, 23.   [8] *de anima,* 16.   [9] *adv. Marc.* iii, 2 ; iv, 11.

God's law is published in the universe, and written on the natural tables of the heart.[1]

This clear and strong conception of Nature gives him a sure ground for dealing with antagonists. There were those who denied the reality of Christ's body, and declaimed upon the ugly and polluting features in child-birth—could the incarnation of God have been subjected to this?[2] But Nature needs no blush—*Natura veneranda est non erubescenda*; there is nothing shameful in birth or procreation, unless there is lust.[3] On the contrary, the travailing woman should be honoured for her peril, and counted holy as Nature suggests.[4] Here once more we have an instance of Tertullian's sympathy and tenderness for woman, whom he perhaps never includes in his most sweeping attacks and condemnations. Similarly, he is not carried away by the extreme asceticism of the religions of his day into contempt for the flesh. It is the setting in which God has placed "the shadow of his own soul, the breath of his own spirit"—can it really be so vile? Yet is the soul *set*, or not rather blended and mingled with the flesh, " so that it may be questioned whether the flesh carries the soul or the soul the flesh, whether the flesh serves the soul, or the soul serves the flesh. . . . What use of Nature, what enjoyment of the universe, what savour of the elements, does the soul not enjoy by the agency of the flesh?" Think, he says, of the services rendered to the soul by the senses, by speech, by all the arts, interests and ingenuities dependent on the flesh ; think of what the flesh does by living and dying.[5] The Jove of Phidias is not the world's great deity because the ivory is so much, but because Phidias is so great ; and did God give less of hand and thought, of providence and love, to the matter of which he made man? Whatever shape the clay took, Christ was in his mind as the future man.[6]

Some of these passages come from works of Tertullian's later years, when he was evidently leaning more than of old to ascetic theory. They are therefore the more significant.

---

[1] *de cor. mil.* 6, *et legem naturalem suggerit et naturam legalem.*

[2] Cf. *de carne Christi*, 4.   [3] *de anima*, 27.

[4] *de carne Christi*, 4, *ipsum mulieris enitentis pudorem vel pro periculo honorandum vel pro natura religiosum.*

[5] *de Resurr. Carnis*, 7.   [6] *Ibid.* 6.

If he wrote as a pagan at all, what he wrote is lost; but it is not pushing conjecture too far to suggest that his interest in Stoicism precedes his Christian period, when such an interest is so clearly more akin to the bent of the Roman lawyer than the Christian of the second century.

The rationality and the order of the Universe are commonplaces of Stoic teachers, and, in measure, its beauty. Of this last Tertullian shows in a remarkable passage how sensible he was. Marcion condemns the God who created this world. But, says Tertullian, " one flower of the hedge-row by itself, I think—I do not say a flower of the meadows; one shell of any sea you like,—I do not say the Red Sea; one feather of a moor-fowl—to say nothing of a peacock,—will they speak to you of a mean Creator? " " Copy if you can the buildings of the bee, the barns of the ant, the webs of the spider." What of sky, earth and sea ? " If I offer you a rose, you will not scorn its Creator! " [1] It is surely possible to feel more than the controversialist here. " It was Goodness that spoke the word; Goodness that formed man from the clay into this consistency of flesh, furnished out of one material with so many qualities; Goodness that breathed into him a soul, not dead, but alive; Goodness that set him over all things, to enjoy them, to rule them, even to give them their names; Goodness, too, that went further and added delight to man . . . and provided a help-meet for him." [2]

Of his conceptions of law something will be said at a later point. It should be clear however that a man with such interests in a profession, in speculation, in the beauty and the law of Nature, could hardly at any time be a careless hedonist, even if, like most men converted in mid-life, he knows regret and repentance.

On the side of religion, little perhaps can be said. He had laughed at the gods burlesqued in the arena. To Mithras perhaps he gave more attention. In discussing the soldier's crown he is able to quote an analogy from the rites of Mithras, in which a crown was rejected, and in which one grade of

---

[1] adv. Marcion. i, 13, 14. Compare the beautiful picture at the end of de Oratione, of the little birds flying up, "spreading out the cross of their wings instead of hands, and saying something that seems to be prayer."

[2] adv. Marc. ii, 4.

initiates were known as " soldiers." [1]   Elsewhere he speaks of the
oblation of bread and the symbol of resurrection in those rites,
" and, if I still remember, Mithras there seals his soldiers on
the brow." [2]   *Si memini* is a colloquialism, which should not be
pressed, but the *adhuc* inserted may make it a more real and
personal record.

To Christian ideas he gave little attention.   There were
Christians round about him, no doubt in numbers, but they did
not greatly interest him.   He seems, however, to have looked
somewhat carelessly into their teaching, but he laughed at
resurrection, at judgment and retribution in an eternal life.[3]
He was far from studying the Scriptures—" nobody," he said
later on, " comes to them unless he is already a Christian." [4]
Justin devoted about a half of his *Apology* to prove the fulfilment of Old Testament prophecy in the life of Jesus—an
Apology addressed to a pagan Emperor.   Tertullian, in his
Apology, gives four chapters to the subject, and one of these
seems to be an alternative draft.   The difference is explained
by Justin's narrative of his conversion, in which he tells us how
it was by the path of the Scriptures and Judaism that he, like
Tatian and Theophilus, came to the church.   Tertullian's story
is different, and, not expecting pagans to pay attention to a
work in such deplorable style [5] as the Latin Bible, which he had
himself ignored, he used other arguments, the weight of which
he knew from experience.   In his *de Pallio*, addressed to a
pagan audience, as we have seen, he alludes to Adam and the
fig-leaves, but he does not mention Adam's name and rapidly
passes on—"But this is esoteric—nor is it everybody's to know
it." [6]

Tertullian is never autobiographical except by accident,
yet it is possible to gather from his allusions how he became a
Christian.   In his address to Scapula [7] he says that the first
governor to draw the sword on the Christians of Africa was
Vigellius Saturninus.   Dr Armitage Robinson's discovery of
the original Latin text of the *Acts of the Scillitan Martyrs*, who

[1] *de cor. mil.* 15.   [2] *de præscr.* 40, *et si adhuc memini, Mithra signat*, etc.

[3] *Apol.* 18.   *Hæc et nos risimus aliquando.   De vestris sumus.*

[4] *de test. animæ*, 1.

[5] So Arnobius (i, 58, 59) and Augustine felt.   Tertullian does not complain of the
style himself, but it was a real hindrance to many.

[6] *de Pallio*, 3, *Sed arcana ista nec omnium nosse.*   [7] *ad Scap.* 3.

suffered under Saturninus, has enabled us to put a date to the event, for we read that it took place in the Consulship of Præsens (his second term) and of Claudianus—that is in 180 A.D., the year of the death of Marcus Aurelius. These *Acts* are of the briefest and most perfunctory character. One after another, a batch of quite obscure Christians in the fewest possible words confess their faith, are condemned, say *Deo Gratias*, and then—" so all of them were crowned together in martyrdom and reign with the Father and the Son and the Holy Spirit for ever and ever. Amen." That is all. They were men and women, some of them perhaps of Punic extraction— Nartzalus and Cittinus have not a Roman sound. After this, it would seem that in Africa, as elsewhere, persecution recurred intermittently ; it might be the governor who began it, or the chance cry of an unknown person in a mob, and then the people, wild and sudden as the Gadarene swine and for the same reason (Christians said),[1] would fling themselves into unspeakable orgies of bloodshed and destruction. What was more, no one could foretell the hour—it might be years before it happened again ; it might be now. And the Christians were surprisingly ready, whenever it came.

Sometimes they argued a little, sometimes they said hardly anything. *Christiana sum*, was all that one of the Scillitan women said. But one thing struck everybody—their firmness, *obstinatio*.[2] Some, like the philosophic Emperor, might call it perversity ; he, as we have seen, found it thin and theatrical, and contrasted it with " the readiness " that " proceeded from inward conviction, of a temper rational and grave "[3]—an interesting judgment from the most self-conscious and virtuous of men. On other men it made a very different impression—on men, that is, more open than the Cæsar of the passionless face[4] to impression, men of a more sensitive and imaginative make, quicker in penetrating the feeling of others.

Tertullian, in two short passages, written at different dates, shows how the martyrs—perhaps these very Scillitan martyrs

---

[1] " The devils entered into the swine." Cf. p. 164.

[2] Pliny to Trajan, 96, 3, *pertinaciam et inflexibilem obstinationem*.

[3] Marcus Aurelius, xi, 3. Cf. Aristides, *Or.* 46, who attributes αὐθάδεια to οἱ ἐν τῇ Παλαιστίνῃ δυσσεβεῖς.

[4] *Hist. August. M. Anton.* 16, *Erat enim ipse tantæ tranquillitatis ut vultum nunquam mutaverit mærore vel gaudio.*

—moved him. "That very obstinacy with which you taunt us, is your teacher. For who is not stirred up by the contemplation of it to find out what there is in the thing within? who, when he has found out, does not draw near? and then, when he has drawn near, desire to suffer, that he may gain the whole grace of God, that he may receive all forgiveness from him in exchange for his blood?"[1] So he wrote in 197-8 A.D., and fourteen years later his last words to Scapula were in the same tenor—"None the less this school (*secta*) will never fail—no! you must learn that then it is built up the more, when it seems to be cut down. Every man, who witnesses this great endurance, is struck with some misgiving and is set on fire to look into it, to find what is its cause; and when he has learnt the truth, he instantly follows it himself as well."[2] It would be hard to put into a sentence so much history and so much character. *Et ipse statim sequitur.*

The martyrs made him uneasy (*scrupulo*). There must be more behind than he had fancied from the little he had seen and heard of their teaching. "No one would have wished to be killed unless in possession of the truth," he says.[3] In spite of his laughter at resurrection and judgment, he was not sure about them. When he speaks in later life of the *naturalis timor animæ in deum*[4]—that instinctive fear of God which Nature has set in the soul—he is probably not himself without consciousness of sharing here too the common experience of men; and this is amply confirmed by the frequency and earnestness with which he speaks of things to come after death. Here however were men who had not this fear. Their obstinacy was his teacher. He looked for the reason, he learned the truth and he followed it at once. That energy is his character—to be read in all he does. Like Carlyle's his writings have "the signature of the writer in every word."

---

[1] *Apol.* 50, *Illa ipsa obstinatio quam exprobratis magistra est. Quis enim non contemplatione eius concutitur ad requirendum quid intus in re sit? quis non ubi requisivit accedit? ubi accessit pati exoptat,* etc.

[2] *ad. Scap.* 5. *Quisque enim tantam tolerantiam spectans, ut aliquo scrupulo percussus, et inquirere accenditur, quid sit in causa, et ubi cognoverit veritatem et ipse statim sequitur.*

[3] *Scorpiace,* 8 (end).

[4] *de testim. animæ,* 2. Cf. *de cult. fem.* ii, 2, *Timor fundamentum salutis est.*

' It is the idlest thing in the world," he says, " for a man to say, ' I wished it and yet I did not do it.' You ought to carry it through (*perficere*) because you wish it, or else not to wish it at all because you do not carry it through."[1] And again : " Why debate ? God commands."[2] Tertullian obeyed, and ever after he felt that men had only to look into the matter, to learn and to obey. " All who like you were ignorant in time past, and like you hated,—as soon as it falls to their lot to know, they cease to hate who cease to be ignorant."[3]

Tertullian's tract *On Idolatry* illustrates his mind upon this decisive change. There he deals with Christians who earn their living by making idols—statuaries, painters, gilders, and the like ; and when the plea is suggested that they *must* live and have no other way of living, he indignantly retorts that they should have thought this out before. *Vivere ergo habes ?*[4] *Must* you live? he asks. Elsewhere he says "there are no *musts* where faith is concerned."[5] The man who claims to be *condicionalis*,[6] to serve God on terms, Tertullian cannot tolerate. " Christ our Master called himself Truth — not Convention."[7] Every form of idolatry must be renounced, and idolatry took many forms. The schoolmaster and the *professor litterarum* were almost bound to be disloyal to Christ ; all their holidays were heathen festivals, and their very fees in part due to Minerva ; while their business was to instruct the youth in the literature and the scandals of Olympus. But might not one study pagan literature? and, if so, why not teach it ? Because, in teaching it, a man is bound, by his position, to drive heathenism deep into the minds of the young ; in personal study he deals with no one but himself, and can judge and omit as he sees fit.[8] The dilemma of choosing between literature and Christ was a painful thing for men of letters for centuries after this.[9] So Tertullian lays down the law for others ; what for himself?

---

[1] *de Pænitentia*, 3.   [2] *de Pænit.* 4. *Quid revolvis ? Deus præcipit.*

[3] *ad Natt.* i, 1.   [4] *de Idol.* 5.

[5] *de cor. mil.* 11, *non admittit status fidei necessitates.*   [6] *de Idol.* 12.

[7] *de virg. vel.* 1, *Dominus noster Christus veritatem se non consuetudinem cognominavit.*

[8] *de Idol.* 10.   [9] See the correspondence of Ausonius and Paulinus.

Under the Empire there were two ways to eminence, the bar and the camp, and Tertullian had chosen the former. His rhetoric, his wit, his force of mind, and his strong grasp of legal principles in general and the issue of the moment in particular, might have carried him far. He might have risen as high as a civilian could. It was a tempting prospect,—the kingdoms of the world and the glory of them—and he renounced it ; and never once in all the books that have come down to us, does he give any hint of looking back, never so much as suggests that he had given up anything. Official life was full of religious usage, full too of minor duties of ritual which a Christian might not discharge. Tertullian was not the first to see this. A century earlier Flavius Clemens, the cousin of Domitian, seems to have been a Christian—Dio Cassius speaks of his atheism and Jewish practices, and Suetonius remarks upon his " contemptible inertia," though he was consul.[1] In other words, the Emperor's cousin found that public life meant compromise at every step. This is Tertullian's decision of the case—it has the note of his profession about it. " Let us grant that it is possible for a man successfully to manage that, whatever office it be, he bears merely the title of that office ; that he does not sacrifice, nor lend his authority to sacrifices, nor make contracts as to victims, nor delegate the charge of temples, nor look after their tributes ; that he does not give shows (*spectacula*) at his own or the public cost, nor preside over them when being given ; that he makes no proclamation or edict dealing with a festival ; that he takes no oath ; that—and these are the duties of a magistrate—he does not sit in judgment on any man's life or honour (for you might bear with his judging in matters of money) ; that he pronounces no sentence of condemnation nor any [as legislator] that should tend to condemnation ; that he binds no man, imprisons no man, tortures[2] no man "—if all this can be managed, a Christian may be a magistrate.[3] Tertullian made his renunciation and held no magistracy. It may be said that, as he held none, it was easy to renounce it ; but hopes are often harder to renounce than realities. So Tertullian left the law and the Stoics, to study

---

[1] Dio Cassius, 67, 14 ; Suetonius, *Domit.* 15 ; Eusebius, *E.H.* iii, 18. See E. G. Hardy, *Studies in Roman History*, ch. v., pp. 66, 67.

[2] To obtain evidence—legal in the case of slaves.   [3] *de Idol.* 17.

the Scriptures, Justin and Irenæus [1]—the Bible and the *regula fidei* his new code, and the others his commentators. The Christian is "a stranger in this world, a citizen of the city above, of Jerusalem"; his ranks, his magistracies, his senate are the Church of Christ; his purple the blood of his Lord, his *laticlave* in His cross.[2]

But Tertullian could speak, on occasion, of what he had done. "We have no fear or terror of what we may suffer from those who do not know," he wrote to Scapula, "for we have joined this school (*sectam*) fully accepting the terms of our agreement; so that we come into these conflicts with no further right to our own souls." [3]   The contest was, as he says elsewhere, "against the institutions of our ancestors, the authority of usage, the laws of rulers, the arguments of the wise; against antiquity, custom, necessity; against precedents, prodigies and miracles," [4] and he did not need Celsus to remind him what form the resistance of the enemy might take. He knew, for he had seen, and that was why he stood where he did. But it is worth our while to understand how vividly he realized the possibilities before him.

There were the private risks of informers and blackmailers, Jews [5] and soldiers, to which the Christians were exposed.[6] They were always liable to be trapped in their meetings— "every day we are besieged; every day we are betrayed; most of all in our actual gatherings and congregations are we surprised." [7]   How are we to meet at all, asks the anxious Christian, unless we buy off the soldiers? By night, says Tertullian, "or let three be your church." [8]   Then came the appearance before the magistrate, where everything turned on the character or the mood of the official. Tertullian quotes to Scapula several instances of kindness on the bench, rough and ready, or high-principled.[9]   Anything might happen—

---

[1] Cf. *adv. Valentin.* 5.

[2] *de cor. mil.* 13, *clavus latus in cruce ipsius.* There is a suggestion of a play upon words.

[3] *ad Scap.* i, opening sentence of the tract.   [4] *ad Nat.* ii, 1.

[5] *Apol.* 7.   Cf. *Scorp.* 10, *synagogas Judæorum fontes persecutionum.*

[6] Cf. *de fuga,* 12; *ad Scap.* 5.   [7] *Apol.* 7.

[8] *de fuga,* 14, *sit tibi et in tribus ecclesia.*

[9] *ad Scap.* 4.

"then," wrote Perpetua, " he had all our names recited together
and condemned us to the beasts." [1]

What followed in the arena may be read in various Acts
of Martyrdom—in the story of Perpetua herself, as told in
tense and quiet language by Tertullian. He, it is generally
agreed, edited her visions, preserving what she wrote as she
left it, and adding in a postscript what happened when she
had laid down her pen for ever. The scene with the beasts
is not easy to abridge, and though not long in itself it is too
long to quote here; but no one who has read it will forget
the episode of Saturus drenched in his own blood from the
leopard's bite, amid the yells of the spectators, *Salvum lotum !
salvum lotum !* nor that of Perpetua and Felicitas, mothers
both, one a month or so, the other three days, stripped naked
to be tossed by a wild cow. And here comes a curious
touch ; the mob, with a superficial delicacy, suggested clothing ; rough cloths were put over the women, and the cow
was let loose ; they were tossed, and then all were put to the
sword.

"At this present moment," writes Tertullian, "it is the
very middle of the heat, the very dog-days of persecution—
as you would expect, from the dog-headed himself, of course.
Some Christians have been tested by the fire, some by the
sword, some by the beasts ; some, lashed and torn with hooks
have just tasted martyrdom, and lie hungering for it in
prison." [2] Cross, hook, and beasts [3]—the circus, the prison,
the rack [4]—the *vivicomburium,* [5] burning alive—and meanwhile the renegade Jew is there with his placard of the "god
of the Christians," an ugly caricature with the ears and one
hoof of an ass, clad in a toga, book in hand [6]—the Gnostic
and the nervous Christian are asking whether the text " flee
ye to the next " may not be God's present counsel—and
meantime " faith glows and the church is burning like the
bush." [7] Yet, says Tertullian to the heathen, " we say, and
we say it openly,—while you are torturing us, torn and bleed-
ing, we cry aloud ' We worship God through Christ.' " [8]   To

---

[1] *Passio Perpetuæ,* 6. [2] *Scorpiace,* 1. [3] *Apol.* 30. [4] *Scorp.* 10.
[5] *de anima,* 1. [6] *Apol.* 16 ; *ad Natt.* i, 14.
[7] *Scorpiace,* 1 ; the reference is to Moses' bush, *nec tamen consumebatur.*
[8] *Apol.* 21.

the Christian he says : " The command is given to me to
name no other God, whether by act of hand, or word of
tongue . . . save the One alone, whom I am bidden to fear,
lest he forsake me ; whom I am bidden to love with all my
being, so as to die for him.   I am his soldier, sworn to his
service, and the enemy challenge me.   I am as they are, if
I surrender to them.   In defence of my allegiance I fight it
out to the end in the battle-line, I am wounded, I fall, I am
killed.   Who wished this end for his soldier—who but he
who sealed him with such an oath of enlistment ?   There you
have the will of my God." [1]   " And therefore the Paraclete is
needed, to guide into all truth, to animate for all endurance.
Those, who receive him, know not to flee persecution, nor to
buy themselves off ; they have him who will be with us, to
speak for us when we are questioned, to help us when we
suffer." [2]   " He who fears to suffer cannot be his who
suffered." [2]   The tracts *On Flight in Persecution* and *The
Antidote for the Scorpion* are among his most impressive
pieces.   They must have been read by his friends with a
strange stirring of the blood.   Even to-day they bring back
the situation—living as only genius can make it live.

But what of the man of genius who wrote them ?   At
what cost were they written ?   " Picture the martyr," he
writes, " with his head under the sword already poised, picture
him on the gibbet his body just outspread, picture him tied
to the stake when the lion has just been granted, on the
wheel with the faggots piled about him " [3]—and no doubt
Tertullian saw these things often enough, with that close
realization of each detail of shame and pain which is only
possible to so vivid and sensitive an imagination.   He saw
himself tied to the stàke—heard the governor in response to
the cry *Christiano leonem* [4] concede the lion—and then had to
wait, how long ?   How long would it take to bring and to
let loose the lion ?   How long would it seem ?   Through all
this he went, in his mind, not once, nor twice.   And meanwhile, what was the audience doing, while he stood there tied,

---

[1] *Scorpiace*, 4 (end).   [2] *de fuga*, 14 (both passages).
[3] *de pudicitia*, 22.
[4] For this cry in various forms see *Apol.* 40 ; *de res. carn.* 22 ; *de exh. castit.*
12 ; *de spect.* 27, *conveniens et catus . . . illic quotidiani in nos leones expostulantur.*

waiting interminably for the lion? He knew what they would be doing, for he had seen it, and in the passage at the end of *de Spectaculis*, which Gibbon quotes, every item of the description of the spectator is taken in irony from the actual circus. No man, trained, as the public speaker or pleader must be, to respond intimately and at once to the feelings and thoughts, expressed or unexpressed, of the audience, could escape realizing in heightened tension every possibility of anguish in such a crowd of hostile faces, full of frantic hatred,[1] cruelty and noise. To this Tertullian looked forward, as we have seen, and went onward—as another did who "steadfastly set his face for Jerusalem." The test of emotion is what it has survived, and Tertullian's faith in Christ and his peace of mind survived this martyrdom through the imagination. Whatever criticism has to be passed upon his work and spirit, to some of his critics he might reply "*Ye* have not yet resisted unto blood, striving against sin."

So much did martyrdom mean to the individual, yet it was not merely a personal affair. It was God's chosen way to propagate his church—so it had been foretold, and so it was fulfilled. "Nothing whatever is achieved," says Tertullian to the heathen, "by each more exquisite cruelty you invent;[2] on the contrary, it wins men for our school. We are made more as often as you mow us down ; the blood of Christians is seed."[3]

Sixteen centuries or so later, Thoreau in his *Plea for Captain John Brown*, a work not unlike Tertullian's own in its force, its surprises, its desperate energy and high conviction, wrote similarly of the opponents of another great movement. "Such do not know that like the seed is the fruit, and that in the moral world, when good seed is planted, good fruit is inevitable, and does not depend on our watering and cultivating ; that when you plant, or bury, a hero in his field, a crop of heroes is sure to spring up. This is a seed of such

---

[1] *Scorpiace*, 11, *ecce autem et odio habemur ab omnibus hominibus nominis causa ; de anima*, 1, *non unius urbis sed universi orbis iniquam sententiam sustinens pro nomine veritatis.*

[2] Cf. *de anima*, 1, *de patibulo et vivicomburio per omne ingenium crudelitatis exhauriat.*

[3] *Apol.* 50, *semen est sanguis Christianorum.*

force and vitality, that it does not ask our leave to germinate."

There were yet other possibilities in martyrdom. It was believed by Christians that in baptism the sins of the earlier life were washed away ; but what of sins after baptism ? They involved a terrible risk—"the world is destined to fire like the man who after baptism renews his sins"[1]—and it was often felt safer to defer baptism to the last moment in consequence. Constantine was baptized on his death-bed. "The postponement of baptism is more serviceable especially in the case of children ; " says Tertullian, "let them become Christians when they shall be able to know Christ. Why should the innocent age hasten to the remission of sins?"[2] As to sins committed after baptism, different views were held. In general, as the church grew larger and more comprehensive, it took a lighter view of sin, but Tertullian and his Montanist friends did not, and for this they have been well abused, in their own day and since. They held that adultery and apostasy were not venial matters, to be forgiven by a bishop issuing an "edict," like a *Pontifex Maximus*, in the legal style, "I forgive the sins of adultery and fornication to such as have done penance, *pœnitentia functis.*"[3] The Montanist alternative was not so easy ; God, they held, permitted a second baptism, which should be final—a baptism of blood. "God had foreseen the weaknesses of humanity, the stratagems of the enemy, the deceitfulness of affairs, the snares of the world—that faith even after baptism would be imperilled, that many would be lost again after being saved—who should soil the wedding dress, and provide no oil for their lamps, who should yet have to be sought over mountain and forest, and carried home on the shoulders. He therefore appointed a second consolation, a last resource, the fight of martyrdom and the baptism of blood, thereafter secure."[4] This view may not appeal to us to-day ; it did not appeal to Gnostic, time-server and coward. The philosophy of sin involved is hardly deep enough, but

---

[1] *de Bapt.* 8. [2] *Ibid.* 18.

[3] Ironic chapter in *de pudicitia*, 1. The *edict* is a technical term of the state, and the *Pontifex Maximus* was the Emperor, till Gratian refused the title in 375 A.D.

[4] *Scorpiace*, 6 ; cf. *de Bapt.* 16.

this doctrine of the second baptism cannot be said to lack virility.

But Tertullian himself did not receive the first baptism with any idea of looking for a second. Like men who are baptized of their own motion and understanding, he was greatly impressed by baptism. "There is nothing," he says, "which more hardens the minds of men than the simplicity of God's works, which appears in the doing, and the magnificence, which is promised in the effect. Here too, because, with such simplicity, without pomp, without any novel apparatus, and without cost, a man is sent down into the water and baptized, while but a few words are spoken, and rises again little or nothing cleaner, on that account his attainment of eternity is thought incredible."[1] It must be felt that the illustration declines from the principle. It may also be remarked that this is a more magical view of baptism than would have appealed to Seneca or to his contemporaries in the Christian movement, and that, as it is developed, it becomes even stranger.

Tertullian's description of baptism is of interest in the history of the rite. The candidate prepares himself with prayer, watching and the confession of sin.[2] "The waters receive the mystery (*sacramentum*) of sanctification, when God has been called upon. The Spirit comes at once from heaven and is upon the waters, sanctifying them from himself, and so sanctified they receive (*combibunt*) the power of sanctifying."[3] This is due to what to-day we should call physical causes. The underlying matter, he says, must of necessity absorb the quality of the overlying, especially when the latter is spiritual, and therefore by the subtlety of its substance more penetrative.[4] We may compare "the enthusiastic spirit," which, Plutarch tells us, came up as a gas from the chasm at Delphi,[5] and further the general teaching of Tertullian (Stoic in origin) of the corporeity of the soul and of similar spiritual beings. He illustrates the influence of the Spirit in thus affecting the waters of baptism by the analogy of the unclean spirits that haunt streams and fountains, natural and artificial, and similarly affect men, though for evil—"lest any should think it a hard thing that God's holy angel should be present to temper

---

[1] *de Bapt.* 2.   [2] *Ibid.* 20.   [3] *Ibid.* 4.
[4] *Ibid.* 4.   [5] Cf. p. 102.

waters for man's salvation."[1]   Thus when the candidate has solemnly " renounced the devil, his pomp and his angels,"[2] he is thrice plunged,[3] his spirit is washed corporeally by the waters " medicated " and his flesh spiritually is purified.[4]   " It is not that in the waters we receive the Holy Spirit, but purified in water under the angel, we are prepared for the Holy Spirit. . . . The angel, that is arbiter of baptism, prepares the way for the Spirit that shall come."[5]   On leaving the water the Christian is anointed (*signaculum*).   The hand of blessing is laid upon him, and in response to prayer the Holy Spirit descends with joy from the Father to rest upon the purified and blest.[6]

Tertullian never forgot the baptismal pledge in which he renounced the devil, his pomp and his angels ; and, for his part, he never showed any tendency to make compromise with them—when he recognized them, for sometimes he seems not to have penetrated their disguises.   Again and again his pledge comes back to him.   What has the Christian to do with circus or theatre, who has renounced the devil, his pomp and his angels, when both places are specially consecrated to these, when there, above all, wickedness, lust and cruelty reign without reserve ?[7]   How can the maker of idols, the temple-painter, etc., be said to have renounced the devil and his angels, if they make their living by them ?[8]   We have seen the difficulty of the schoolmaster here.   The general question of trade troubles Tertullian—its cupidity, the lie that ministers to cupidity, to say nothing of perjury.[9]   Of astrologers, he would have thought, nothing needed to be said—but that he had " within these few days " heard some one claim the right to continue in the profession.   He reminds him of the source of his magical information—the fallen angels.[10]   One must not even name them —to say *Medius fidius* is idolatry, for it is a prayer ; but to say " I live in the street of Isis " is not sin—it is sense.[11]   Many inventions were attributed by pagans to their gods.   If every implement of life is set down to some god, " yet I still must recognize Christ lying on a couch—or when he brings a basin

---

[1] *de Bapt.* 5.   [2] *de Spectac.* 4 ; *de cor. mil.* 3.
[3] *de cor. mil.* 3, *ter mergitamur.*   [4] *de Bapt.* 4.   [5] *Ibid.* 6.
[6] *de Bapt.* 8.   For other minor details as to food and bathing see *de cor. mil.* 3.
[7] *de Spectac.* 4.   [8] *de Idol.* 6.
[9] *de Idol.* 11.   Cf. Hermas, *Mandate*, 3, on lying in business.
[10] *de Idol.* 9.   [11] *Ibid.* 20.

to his disciples feet, or pours water from the jug, and is girded with linen—Osiris' own peculiar garb."[1] In fact, common utility, and the service of ordinary needs and comforts, may lead us to look upon things (to whomsoever attributed) as really due to the inspiration of God himself "who foresees, instructs and gives pleasure to man, who is after all His own."[2] Thus common sense and his doctrine of Nature come to his aid. "So amid rocks and bays, amid the shoals and breakers of idolatry, faith steers her course, her sails filled by the Spirit of God."[3]

Tertullian had been a lawyer and a pleader, as we are reminded in many a page, where the man of letters is over-ridden by the man of codes and arguments ; and a lawyer he remained. The Gospel, for instance, bade that, if any man take the tunic, he should be allowed to take the cloak also. Yes, says Tertullian, if he asks—"if he threatens, I will ask for the tunic back."[4] A man, with such habits of mind, will not take violent measures to repel injustice, but he may be counted upon to defend himself in his own way. Tertullian, accordingly, when persecution broke out in the autumn of 197 in Carthage, addressed to the governor of the province an Apology for the Christians. It is one of his greatest works. It was translated into Greek, and Eusebius quotes the trans-lation in several places. It is a most brilliant book. All his wit and warmth, his pungency and directness, his knowledge and his solid sense come into play. As a piece of rhetoric, as a lawyer's speech, it is inimitable. But it is more than that, for it is as full of his finest qualities as of his other gifts of dexterity and humour. It shows the full grown and developed man, every faculty at its highest and all consecrated, and the book glows with the passion of a dedicated spirit.

He begins with the ironical suggestion that, if the governors of provinces are not permitted in their judicial capacity to examine in public the case of the Christians, if this type of action alone their authority is afraid—or blushes—to investigate in the interests of justice, he yet hopes that Truth by the

---

[1] de cor. mil. 8.   [2] Ibid. 8.

[3] de Idol. 24, inter hos scopulos et sinus, inter hac vada et freta idololatriæ, velificata spiritu dei fides navigat.

[4] de fuga, 13.

silent path of letters may reach their ears. Truth makes no excuse—she knows she is a stranger here, while her race, home, hope, grace and dignity are in heaven. All her eagerness is not to be condemned unheard. Condemnation without trial is invidious, it suggests injustice and wakes suspicion. It is in the interests of Christianity, too, that it should be examined— that is how the numbers of the Christians have grown to such a height. They are not ashamed—unless it be of having become Christians so late. The natural characteristics of evil are fear, shame, tergiversation, regret; yet the Christian criminal is glad to be accused, prays to be condemned and is happy to suffer. You cannot call it madness, when you are shown to be ignorant of what it is.

Christians are condemned for the name's sake, though such condemnation, irrespective of the proving of guilt or innocence, is outrage. Others are tortured to confess their guilt, Christians to deny it. Trajan's famous letter to Pliny, he tears to shreds ; Christians are not to be hunted down—that is, they are innocent ; but they are to be punished—that is, they are guilty. If the one, why not hunt them down? If the other, why punish? Of course Trajan's plan was a compromise, and Tertullian is not a man of compromises. If a founder's name is guilt for a school, look around! Schools of philosophers and schools of cooks bear their founders' names with impunity. But about the Founder of the Christian school curiosity ceases to be inquisitive. But the " authority of laws " is invoked against truth—*non licet esse vos !* is the cry. What if laws do forbid Christians to be? " If your law has made a mistake, well, I suppose, it was a human brain that conceived it ; for it did not come down from heaven." Laws are always being changed, and have been. " Are you not yourselves every day, as experiment illumines the darkness of antiquity, engaged in felling and cutting the whole of that ancient and ugly forest of laws with the new axes of imperial rescripts and edicts ? "[1] Roman laws once forbade extravagance, theatres, divorce—they forbade the religions of Bacchus, Serapis and Isis. Where are those laws now? " You are always praising antiquity, and you improvise your life from day to day."[2]

In passing, one remark may be made in view of what is

[1] *Apol.* 4.   [2] *Apol.* 6.

said sometimes of Tertullian and his conception of religion.
" To Tertullian the revelation through the Christ is no more
than a law." [1]   There is truth in this criticism, of course ; but
unless it is clearly understood that Tertullian drew the distinction, which this passage of the *Apology* and others suggest,
between Natural law, as conceived by the Stoics, and civil law
as regarded by a Propraetor, he is likely to be misjudged.
He constantly slips into the lawyer's way of handling law,
for like all lawyers he is apt to think in terms of paper and
parchment ; but he draws a great distinction, not so familiar
to judges and lawyers—as English daily papers abundantly
reveal—between the laws of God or Nature and the laws of
human convention or human legislatures.   The weak spot was
his belief in the text of the Scriptures as the ultimate
and irrefragable word and will of God, though even here,
in his happier hours, when he is not under stress of
argument, he will interpret the divine and infallible code, not
by the letter, but by the general principles to be observed at
once in Nature and the book.   *Legis injustæ honor nullus est* [2]
is not the ordinary language of a lawyer.

The odious charges brought by the vulgar against the
Christians then, as now in China, and used for their own
purposes by men who really knew better, he shows to be
incredible.   No one has the least evidence of any kind for
them, and yet Christian meetings are constantly surprised.
What a triumph would await the spy or the traitor who
could prove them !   But they are not believed, or men
would harry the Christians from the face of the earth
(c. 8).   As to the·idea that Christians eat children to gain
eternal life—who would think it worth the price ?   No ! if
such things *are* done, by whom are they done ?   He reminds
his fellow-countrymen that in the reign of Tiberius priests of
Saturn were crucified in Africa on the sacred trees around
their temple—for the sacrifice of children.   And then who
are those who practise abortion ? " how many of those who
crowd around and gape for Christian blood ? "   And the
gladiatorial shows ? is it the Christians who frequent them ?

Atheism and treason were more serious charges.   " You do

---

[1] Gwatkin, *The Knowledge of God* (Gifford Lectures) ii, p. 163.
[2] *ad Natt.* i, 5.

not worship the gods." What gods? He cannot mention them all—" new, old, barbarian, Greek, Roman, foreign, captive, adoptive, special, common, male, female, rustic, urban, nautical and military "—but Saturn at any rate was a man, as the historians know. But they were made gods after they died. Now, that implies " a God more sublime, true owner (*mancipem*), so to speak, of divinity," who made them into gods, for they could not of course have done it themselves ; and meanwhile you abolish the only one who could have. But why should he ? —"unless the great God needed their ministry and aid in his divine tasks "—dead men's aid ! (c. 11). No, the whole universe is the work of Reason ; nothing was left for Saturn to do, or his family. It rained from the beginning, stars shone, thunders roared, and "Jove himself shuddered at the living bolts which you put in his hand." Ask the spiders what they think of your gods and their webs tell you (c. 12). To-day a god, to-morrow a pan, as domestic necessity melts and casts the metal. And the gods are carried round and alms begged for them—*religio mendicans*—"hold out your hand, Jupiter, if you want me to give you anything ! " [1] Does Homer's poetry do honour to the gods (c. 14)—do the actors on the stage (c. 15)?

Christians are not atheists. They worship one God, Creator, true, great, whose very greatness makes him known of men and unknown.[2] Who he is, and that he is one, the human soul knows full well—*O testimonium animæ naturaliter Christianæ!* But God has other evidence—*instrumentum litteraturæ.* He sent into the world men " inundated with the divine spirit " to proclaim the one God, who framed all things, who made man, who one day will raise man from the dead for eternal judgment. These writings of the prophets are not secret books. Anyone can read them in the Greek version, which was made by the seventy elders for Ptolemy Philadelphus. To this book he appeals,—to the majesty of Scripture, to the fulfilment of prophecy.

Zeno called the Logos the maker of all things—and named him Fate, God, mind of Jove, Necessity. Cleanthes described him as permeating all things. This the Christians also hold to

---

[1] Cf. pp. 20-22.

[2] *Apol.* 17, *ita eum vis magnitudinis et notum hominibus obicit et ignotum.*

be God's Word, Reason and Power—and his Son, one with him in being, Spirit as He is Spirit. This was born of a Virgin, became man, was crucified and rose again. Even the Cæsars would have believed on Christ, if Cæsars were not needful to the world, or if there could be Christian Cæsars.[1] As for the pagan gods, they are dæmons, daily exorcised into the confession of Christ.

But the charge of Atheism may be retorted. Are not the pagans guilty of Atheism, at once in not worshipping the true God and in persecuting those who do? As a rule they conceive, with Plato, of a great Jove in heaven surrounded by a hierarchy of gods and dæmons.[2] But, as in the Roman Empire, with its Emperor and its procurators and prefects, it is a capital offence to turn from the supreme ruler to the subordinate, so " may it not involve a charge of irreligion to take away freedom of religion, to forbid free choice of divinity, that I may not worship whom I will?" Every one else may; but " we are not counted Romans, who do not worship the god of the Romans. It is well that God is God of all, whose we are, whether we will or no. But with you it is lawful to worship anything whatever—except the true God."

But the gods raised Rome to be what she is. Which gods? Sterculus? Larentina? Did Jove forget Crete for Rome's sake—Crete, where he was born, where he lies buried?[3] No, look to it lest God prove to be the dispenser of kingdoms, to whom belong both the world that is ruled and the man who rules. Some are surprised that Christians prefer " obstinacy to deliverance "—but Christians know from whom *that* suggestion comes, and they know the malevolence of the dæmon ranks, who are now beginning to despair since " they recognize they are not a match for us " (c. 27).

For the Emperor Christians invoke God, the eternal, the true, the living. They look up, with hands outspread, heads bared, and from their hearts, without a form of words, they pray for long life for the Emperor, an Empire free from alarms, a safe home, brave armies, a faithful senate, an honest people and a quiet world (c. 30). They do this, for the Empire stands

[1] *Apol.* 21.

[2] Chapters 22 to 24 give a good summary of his views on dæmons.

[3] Celsus refers to Christian discussion of this ; Origen, *adv. Cels.* iii 43.

between them and the world's end. (It was a common thought that the world and Rome would end together.) Christians however honour Cæsar as God's vice-gerent; he is theirs more than any one's, for he is set up by the Christians' God. They make no plots and have no recourse to magic to inquire into his "health" (c. 35).[1] In fact "we are the same to the Emperors as to our next-door neighbours. We are equally forbidden to wish evil, to do evil, to speak evil, to think evil of anyone." So much for being enemies of the state (c. 36).

Christians do not retaliate on the mob for its violence, though, if they did, their numbers would be serious. " We are but of yesterday, and we have filled everything, cities, islands, camps, palace, forum," etc. ; "all we have left you is the temples." But "far be it that a divine school should vindicate itself with human fire, or grieve to suffer that wherein it is proved " (c. 37). Christians make no disturbances and aspire to no offices. They are content to follow their religion and look after the poor, the shipwrecked, and men in mines and prisons. " See how they love each other ! " say the heathen.[2] They are not, as alleged, the cause of public disasters ; though if the Nile do not overflow, or if the Tiber do, it is at once *Christianos ad leonem !* But they are "unprofitable in business ! " Yes, to pimps, poisoners and mathematicians ; still they are not Brahmans or solitaries of the woods, exiles from life, and they refuse no gift of God. " We sail with you, take the field with you, share your country life, and know all the intercourse of arts and business " (cc. 42, 43). They are innocent, for they fear God and not the proconsul. If they were a philosophic school, they would have toleration—" who compels a philosopher to sacrifice, to renounce, or to set out lamps at midday to no purpose ? " Yet the philosophers openly destroy your gods and your superstitions in their books, and win your applause for it—and they " bark at your princes." He then points out how much there is in common to Christians and philosophers, and yet (in a burst of temper) how unlike they are. No, " where is the likeness between the philosopher and the Christian ? the disciple of Greece and of heaven ? the trafficker in fame and in life ? the friend and the foe of error ? " (c. 46).

---

[1] Cf. *ad. Scap.* 2, with argument from end of world.
[2] c. 39 *vide, inquiunt, ut invicem se diligant.*

The Christian artisan knows God better than Plato did.   And yet what is knowledge and genius in philosopher and poet, is "presumption" in a Christian!   "Say the things are false that protect you—mere presumption! yet necessary.   Silly! yet useful.   For those who believe them are compelled to become better men, for fear of eternal punishment and hope of eternal refreshment.   So it is inexpedient to call that false or count that silly, which it is expedient should be presumed true.   On no plea can you condemn what does good " (c. 49).

Yet, whatever their treatment, Christians would rather be condemned than fall from God.   Their death is their victory ; their " obstinacy " educates the world ; and while men condemn them, God acquits them.   That is his last word—*a deo absolvimur* (c. 50).

Such, in rough outline, is the great Apology—not quite the work of the fuller or baker at whom Celsus sneered.   Yet it has not the accent of the conventional Greek or Latin gentleman, nor that of the philosophic Greek Christian.   The style is unlike anything of the age.   Everything in it is individual ; there is hardly a quotation in the piece.   Everything again is centripetal ; Tertullian is too much in earnest to lose himself in the endless periods of the rhetorician, or in the charming fancies dear to the eclectic and especially to contemporary Platonists.   Indeed his tone toward literature and philosophy is startlingly contemptuous, not least so when contrasted with that of Clement.

For this there are several reasons.   First of all, like Carlyle, Tertullian has " to write with his nerves in a kind of blaze," and, like Carlyle, he says things strongly and sweepingly.   It is partly temperament, partly the ingrown habit of the pleader.   Something must be allowed to the man of moods, whose way it is to utter strongly what he feels for the moment.   Such men do a service for which they have little thanks.   Many moods go in them to the making of the mind, moods not peculiar to themselves.   In most men feelings rarely find full and living expression, and something is gained when they are so expressed, even at the cost of apparent exaggeration.   The sweeping half-truth at once suggests its complement to the man who utters it, and may stir very wholesome processes of thought in the milder person who hears it.

In the next place the philosophers may have deserved the criticism. Fine talk and idle talk, in philosophic terms, had disgusted Epictetus;[1] and for few has Lucian more mockery than for the philosophers of his day—Tertullian's day—with their platitudes and their beards, their flunkeyism and love of gain. Clement of Alexandria, who loved philosophy, had occasional hard words for the vanity of its professors.[2] For a man of Tertullian's earnestness they were too little serious. *Gloriæ animal*[3] is one of his phrases—a creature of vainglory was not likely to appeal to a man who lived in full view of the lion and the circus. He had made a root and branch cleavage with idolatry, because no men could die like the Christians unless they had the truth. The philosophers—to say nothing of their part now and then in stirring the people against the Christians— had made terms with polytheism, beast-worship, magic, all that was worst and falsest in paganism, " lovers of wisdom " and seekers after truth as they professed themselves to be. Ancient Philosophy suggests to the modern student the name of Heraclitus or Plato ; but Tertullian lived in the same streets with Apuleius, philosopher and Platonist, humorist and *gloriæ animal*. But even Plato vexed Tertullian.[4] The " cock to be offered to Æsculapius " was too available a quotation in a world where the miracles of the great Healer were everywhere famous. The triflers and the dogmatists of the day used Plato's myths to confute the Christian doctrine of the resurrection. And of course Plato and Tertullian are in temperament so far apart, that an antipathy provoked by such causes was hardly to be overcome.

Again, Tertullian remarks frequently that heresy has the closest connexion with philosophy. Both handle the same questions : " Whence is evil, and why ? and whence is man and how ? and whence is God ? "[5] Marcion, for instance, is " sick (like so many nowadays and, most of all, the heretics) with the question of evil, whence is evil?"[6] and turns to dualism. Or else " the heretics begin with questions of the resurrection, for the resurrection of the flesh they find harder to believe than the unity of the Godhead."[7] What Celsus, a typical product of

---

[1] Epictetus, *D.* iii, 23.   [2] Clement, *Strom.* vi, 56, φιλαυτία.   [3] *de anima*, I.
[4] Cf. *de anima*, 6, 17, 18, 23, etc.   [5] *de Præscr.* 7.
[6] *adv. Marc.* i, 2.   [7] *de res. carnis*, 2.

contemporary philosophy, thought of the resurrection of the flesh we have seen—a " hope of worms ! " Lastly, there was a strong tendency in the church at large for re-statement of the gospel in the terms of philosophy ; and in such endeavours, as we know, there is always the danger of supposing the terms and the philosophy of the day to be more permanent and more valid than the experience which they are supposed to express. In Tertullian's century there seemed some prospect that every characteristic feature of the gospel would be so " re-stated " as to leave the gospel entirely indistinguishable from any other eclectic system of the moment.　Jesus became a phantom, or an æon ; his body, sidereal substance, which offered, Clement himself said, no material resistance to the touch of St John's hand.　God divided, heaven gone, no hope or faith left possible in a non-real Christ even in this life—Christians would be indeed of all men most miserable, and morality would have no longer any basis nor any motive.　What in all this could tempt a man to face the lions ?　It was not for this that Christians shed their blood—no, the Gnostics recommended flight in persecution. It is easy to understand the sweeping *Viderint*—Tertullian's usual phrase for dismissing people and ideas on whom no more is to be said —" Let them look to it who have produced a Stoic and Platonic and dialectic Christianity.　We need no curiosity who have Jesus Christ, no inquiry who have the gospel."[1]

It was natural for Clement and his school to try to bring the gospel and philosophy to a common basis—a natural impulse, which all must share who speculate.　The mistake has been that the church took their conclusions so readily and has continued to believe them.　For Tertullian is, on his side, right, and we know in fact a great deal more about Jesus than we can know about the Logos.

Accordingly a large part of Tertullian's work, as a Christian, was the writing of treatises against heresy.　He has in one book—*de Præscriptionibus Hæreticorum*—dealt with all heretics together.　The *Regula Fidei*, which is a short creed,[2] was instituted, he says, by Christ, and is held among Christians without questions, " save those which heretics raise and which make heretics."　On that *Regula* rests the Christian faith.　To know nothing against it, is to know everything.　But appeal is

[1] *de Præscr.* 7.　　　　　　[2] *de Præscr.* 13.

made to Scripture. We must then see who has the title to Scripture (*possessio*),[1] and whence it comes. Jesus Christ while on earth taught the twelve, and they went into the world and promulgated "the same doctrine of the same faith," founding churches in every city, from which other churches have taken faith and doctrine—he uses the metaphors of seed and of layers (*tradux*) from plants. Every day churches are so formed and duly counted Apostolic. Thus the immense numbers of churches may be reckoned equivalent to the one first church. No other than the Apostles are to be received, as no others were taught by Christ. "Thus it is established that every doctrine which agrees with those Apostolic mother-churches, the originals of the faith, is to be set down to truth, as in accordance with what the churches have received from the apostles, the apostles from Christ, and Christ from God." [2] But have the churches been faithful in the transmission of this body of doctrine? Suppose them all to have gone wrong, suppose the Holy Spirit to have been so negligent—is it likely that so vast a number should have wandered away into *one* faith? Again let Marcion and others show the history of their churches. Let their doctrines be compared with the Apostolic, and their varieties and contradictions will show they are not Apostolic. If then Truth be adjudged to those who walk by the *Regula*, duly transmitted through the church, the Apostles and Christ from God, then heretics have no right of appeal to the Scriptures which are not theirs. If they are heretics, they cannot be Christians; if they are not Christians, they have no right (*ius*) to Christian literature. "With what right (*iure*) Marcion, do you cut down my wood? By what licence, Valentinus, do you divert my springs? . . . This is my estate; I have long held it; I am first in occupation; I trace my sure descent from the founders to whom the thing belonged. I am the heir of the Apostles." [3]

In this, as in most human arguments, there are strands of different value. The legal analogy gave a name to the book —*præscriptio* was the barring of a claim—but it is not

---

[1] *de Præscr.* 15.   [2] *de Præscr.* 21.

[3] *de Præscr.* 37, *Mea est possessio.* Cf. definition which says *possessiones appellantur agri . . . qui non mancipatione sed usu tenebantur et ut quisque occupaverat possidebat.* Tertullian improves this title as ne goes on.

the strongest line. Law rarely is. But Tertullian was not content to rule his opponents out of court. He used legal methods and manners too freely, but he knew well enough that these settled nothing. As a rule he had much stronger grounds for his attack. He wrote five books against Marcion to maintain the unity of the Godhead and the identity of the Father of Jesus, the God of the Old Testament and the God of Nature. His book against the Valentinians has a large element of humour in it—perhaps the best rejoinder to the framers of a cosmogony of so many æons, none demonstrable, all fanciful,—the thirty of them suggest to him the famous Latin sow of the *Æneid.*[1] Against Hermogenes he maintains the doctrine of the creation of the world from nothing. The hypothesis that God used pre-existing matter, makes matter antecedent and more or less equal to God. And then, in legal vein, he asks a question. How did God come to use matter? " These are the three ways in which another's property may be taken,—by right, by benefit, by assault, that is by title, by request, by violence." Hermogenes denies God's title in this case ; which then of the other means does he prefer?[2]

His best work in the controversial field is in his treatises, *On the Flesh of Christ, On the Resurrection of the Flesh,* and *On the Soul.* The first of these, above all, will appeal to any reader to whom the historic Jesus is significant. Much has changed in outlook and preconceptions since Tertullian wrote, but his language on the reality of Jesus, as an actual human being and no sidereal or celestial semblance of a man, on the incarnation, and the love of God, still glows and still finds a response. " Away," he pictures Marcion saying, " Away with those census-rolls of Cæsar, always tiresome, away with the cramped inns, the soiled rags, the hard stall. Let the angelic host look to it ! "[3] And then he rejoins, Do you think nativity impossible—or unsuitable—for God? Declaim as you like on the ugliness of the circumstances ; yet Christ *did* love men (born, if you like, just as you say) ; for man he descended, for man he preached, for man he lowered himself with every humiliation down to death, and the death of the cross. Yes,

[1] This gibe is in *adv. Marc.* i, 5 ; there are plenty without it in *adv. Val.*

[2] *adv. Hermog.* 9, *iure, beneficio, impetu, id est dominio precario vi.*

[3] *de carne Christi,* 2.

he loved him whom he redeemed at so high a price. And with man he loved man's nativity, even his flesh. The conversion of men to the worship of the true God, the rejection of error, the discipline of justice, of purity, of pity, of patience, of all innocence—these are not folly, and they are bound up with the truth of the Gospel. Is it unworthy of God? "Spare the one hope of all the world, thou, who wouldst do away with the disgrace of faith. Whatever is unworthy of God is all to my good." [1] The Son of God also died—"It is credible because it is foolish. He was buried and rose again; it is certain because it is impossible." And how could all this be, if his body were not true? "You bisect Christ with a lie. The *whole* of him was Truth." [2] The gospel narrative from beginning to end implies that Christ's body was like ours—"he hungered under the devil, thirsted under the Samaritan woman, shed tears over Lazarus, was troubled [3] at death (for, the flesh, he said, is weak), last of all he shed his blood." How could men have spat in a face radiant with "celestial grandeur"? Wait! Christ has not yet subdued his enemies that he may triumph with his friends.

Jesus is to come again, as he was, as he is, sitting at the Father's right hand, God and man, flesh and blood, the same in essence and form as when he ascended; so he shall come.[4] And men will be raised in the flesh to receive judgment. A storm overhangs the world.[5] What the treasure-house of eternal fire will be, may be guessed from the petty vents men see in Etna and elsewhere.[6] There will be white robes for martyrs; for the timid a little portion in the lake of fire and sulphur.[7] All that Gibbon thought would "offend the reason and humanity of the present age" in the last chapter of the *de Spectaculis* may recur to the reader. But, continues Tertullian in that passage, my gaze will be upon those who let loose their fury on the Lord himself—"'This,' I shall say, 'is he, the son of the carpenter or the harlot, Sabbath-breaker, Samaritan, demoniac. This is he whom you bought from

---

[1] *de carne Christi*, 5, *Quodcunque deo indignum est mihi expedit.*

[2] *de carne Christi*, 5, *prorsus credibile est quia ineptum est, . . . certum est quia impossibile. . . . Quid dimidias mendacio Christum? Totus veritas fuit.*

[3] *de carne Christi*, 9, *trepidat* perhaps represents the ἀγωνία of Luke.

[4] *de res. carnis*, 51.   [5] *de pœnit.* 1.   [6] *de pœnit.* 12.   [7] *Scorpiace*, 12

Judas, this is he, whom you beat with the reed and the palms of your hands, whom you disfigured with your spittle, to whom you gave gall and vinegar. This is he whom his disciples stole away, that it might be said he had risen,—or the gardener took him away, that his lettuces might not be trodden by the crowds that came.'" "A long variety of affected and unfeeling witticisms," is Gibbon's judgment.

A mind less intent on polemic will judge otherwise of Tertullian and his controversies. There is, first of all, much more of the philosophic temper than is commonly supposed. He does not, like Clement and other Greeks, revel in cosmological speculations as to the Logos, nor does he loosely adopt the abstract methods of later Greek philosophy. But in his treatment of the Soul, of moral order and disorder, and of responsibility, he shows no mean powers of mind. He argues from experience, and from the two sources, from which he could best hope to learn most directly the mind of God, Nature and the Scriptures. The infallibility of the Scriptures is of course a limitation to freedom of speculation, but it was an axiom of the early church, and a man of experience might accept it, bound up as it was with sound results in the martyr-death and the changed life. Tertullian will get back to the facts, if he can ; and if he judges too swiftly of Nature and too swiftly accepts the literal truth of Scripture,—while these are drawbacks to our acceptance of his conclusions, there is still to be seen in him more independence of mind than in those Greek Fathers for whom Greek philosophy had spoken the last word in metaphysics. It is psychology that interests Tertullian more, and moral questions, and these he handles more deeply than the Stoics. He stands in line with Augustine and Calvin, his spiritual descendants.

If he speaks more of hell than certain Greeks do, it is not unnatural. The man, who saw such deaths in the amphitheatre as he describes in the *Passion of Perpetua*, who remembered the expressions he had then seen on the faces of the spectators, who knew too well the cruelty that went with Roman lust, could hardly help believing in hell. What was the origin of evil ? asked philosopher and heretic. What is its destiny ? and what are you to do with it now ? asked Tertullian ; and, in all seriousness, the answer to the former question is more likely to be found when the answers of the latter are reached. At any rate the latter are more practical, and that adjective, with what it suggests of drawback and of gain, belongs to Tertullian.

His application of the test of utility to belief is obviously open to criticism. " It is expedient," said Varro, " for men to be deceived in religion." No, Tertullian would have said, it is more expedient for them to know the truth ; and he backed his conviction by his appeal to Nature, on the one hand, Nature, rational through and through, and ever loyal to law, to fixity of principle, and on the other hand by reference to the verification of his position yielded by experience—once more the martyr-death and the transformed character. These fundamental ideas he may have misused in particulars, if not in matters more essential ; but, if he is wrong from the beginning in/ holding them, human knowledge, progress and conduct become fortuitous and desultory at once. Nature and verification from life are substantially all we have. To these of course Tertullian added revelation in a sense distinct.

From the question of conduct we pass naturally to the great cleavage of Tertullian with the church. A change had come in church practice and government since the days when the *Teaching of the Apostles* represented actual present fact,— perhaps even since the *Apology of Aristides*. The church had grown larger, it had developed its organization, and it was relying more on the practical men with a turn for administration, who always appear when a movement, begun by idealists, seems to show signs of success. The situation creates them, and they cannot be avoided. They have their place, but they do not care for ideas. Thus in the church the ministry of the Spirit, the ministry of gifts, was succeeded by the ministry of office, with its lower ideals of the practical and the expedient. The numbers of the church swelled, and a theory began to spread, which Cyprian took up later on, and which was almost inevitable on his principles, that the church was an ark, with beasts clean and beasts unclean within it. This theory answered to the actual facts, hardly to the ideal, and Tertullian rejected it.[1] Conduct at once suggested the theory,

---

[1] *de Idol.* 24 (end), *Vidcrimus enim si secundum arcæ typum et corvus et milvus et lupus et canis et serpens in ecclesia erit.*

and responded to it.   Christians fell into adultery and apostasy,
and while at first this meant "delivery to Satan," restoration
became   progressively   easy.   The   *Shepherd*   of   Hermas
extended second chances, till Tertullian fiercely spoke of
"that apocryphal shepherd of adulterers.[1]"

From Phrygia came the suggestion of reformation.   Our
evidence as to the history of Montanism in its native land is
derived from hostile sources, and the value of it must partly
depend on the truth of the witnesses and partly on their intelligence, and of neither have we any guarantee at all.   That
they are clearly hostile is plain from the fragments in Eusebius.
That they understood the inner meaning of what they condemned, we have no indication.   Montanus, however, asserted
Christ's promise of the Paraclete—his enemies allege that he
identified himself with the Paraclete, a statement which might
be used to show how quotation may lead to *suggestio falsi.*
But the coming of the Paraclete was not in fact a synonym for
fanaticism and the collection of money, as the enemies of
Montanus hinted.   It meant the bracing of Christian life and
character, and the restoration of prophecy, new revelation of
truth, power and progress.   It appealed to the Christian world,
and the movement spread—probably with modifications as it
spread.   The oracles of Montanus and of two women, Prisca
and Maximilla, became widely known, and they inculcated a
stern insistence on conduct, which was really needed, while they
showed how reformation was to be reached.   To use language
of more modern times, involves risk of misconception ; but if
it may be done with caution, we may roughly say that the
Montanists stood for what the Friends call the Inner Light, and
for progressive revelation—or, at any rate, for something in
this direction.   The indwelling of God was not consistent with
low living ; and earnest souls, all over the world, were invested
with greater power and courage to battle with the growing
lightness in the church and to meet the never-ceasing hostility
of the world—the lion and the cruel faces of the amphitheatre.

Yet Montanism failed for want of a clear conception of
the real character of primitive Christianity.   Aiming at morals,
Montanists conceived of life and the human mind and God in a

[1] *de Pud.* 20.

way very far from that of Jesus. They laid a stress, which is not his, on asceticism and on penance, and they cultivated ecstasy —in both regions renouncing the essentially spiritual conception of religion, and turning to a non-Christian view of matter. They thus aimed at obtaining or keeping the indwelling spirit of Jesus, known so well in the early church, but by mechanical means ; and this, though the later church in this particular followed them for generations, is not to be done. Still, whatever their methods and their expedients, they stood for righteousness, and here lay the fascination of Montanism for Tertullian.

Throughout his later life Tertullian, then, was a Montanist, though the change was not so great as might be expected. Some of his works, such as that *On Monogamy*, bear the stamp of Montanism, for re-marriage was condemned by the Montanists. Elsewhere his citation of the oracles of Prisca suggests that a book belongs to the Montanist period ; or we deduce it from such a passage as that in the work *On the Soul* where he describes a vision. The passage is short and it is suggestive.

" We have to-day among us a sister who has received gifts (*charismata*) of the nature of revelations, which she undergoes (*patitur*) in spirit in the church amid the rites of the Lord's day falling into ecstasy (*per ecstasin*). She converses with angels, sometimes even with the Lord, and sees and hears mysteries, and reads the hearts of certain persons, and brings healings to those who ask. According to what Scriptures are read, or psalms sung, or addresses made, or prayers offered up, the matter of her visions is supplied. It happened that we had spoken something of the soul, when this sister was in the spirit. When all was over, and the people had gone, she—for it is her practice to report what she has seen, and it is most carefully examined that it may be proved—'amongst other things,' she said, 'a soul was shown to me in bodily form and it seemed to be a spirit, but not empty, nor a thing of vacuity ; on the contrary, it seemed as if it might be touched, soft, lucid, of the colour of air, and of human form in every detail."[1]

Such a story explains itself. The corporeity of the soul

[1] *de anima*, 9.

was a tenet of Stoicism, essential to Tertullian, for without it he could not conceive of what was to follow the resurrection. He spoke of it and we can imagine how. It would hardly take a vision to see anything of which he spoke. The sister however was, what in modern phrase is called, psychopathic, and the vision occurred, controlled by the suggestion that preceded it.

It must be admitted that there is in some of his Montanist treatises, particularly where he is handling matters of less importance, such as re-marriage, fasting, and the like, a bitterness of tone which is not pleasant. As long as his humour and his strong sense control his irony, it is no bad adjunct of his style, it is a great resource. But it declines into sarcasm, and "sarcasm," as Teufelsdröckh put it, "is the language of the devil"; and we find Tertullian, pleading for God and righteousness, in a tone and a temper little likely to win men. But the main ideas that dominate him still prevail—conduct, obedience, God's law in Nature and in the book, the value of the martyr-death.

Little is to be got by dwelling on his outbursts of ill temper; they hardly do more than illustrate what we knew already, his intensity, his sensibility, his passion. They form the negative side of the great positive qualities. Let me gather up a few scattered thoughts which come from his heart and are better and truer illustrations of the man, and with them let chapter and book have an end.

Conduct is the test of creed (*de Præscr. Hær.* 43). To lie about God is in a sense idolatry (*de Præscr.* 40). Security in sin means love of it (*de Pudic.* 9). Whatever darkness you pile above your deeds, God is light (*de Pænit.* 6). What we are forbidden to do, the soul pictures to itself at its peril (*de Pænit.* 3). Truth persuades by teaching, it does not teach by making things plausible (*adv. Valent.* 1). Faith is patience with its lamp lit—*illuminata* (*de Pat.* 6). Patience is the very nature of God. The recognition of God understands well enough the duty laid upon it. Let wrong-doing be wearied by your patience (*de Pat.* 3, 4, 8). There is no greater incitement to despise money than that the Lord himself had no wealth (*de Pat.* 7). Love is the supreme mystery (*sacramentum*) of faith (*de Pat.* 12). Faith fears no famine (*de Idol.* 12). Prayer is the wall of faith (*de Or.* 29). Every day, every moment, prayer is necessary to men. . . . Prayer comes from conscience. If conscience blush, prayer blushes (*de exh. cast.* 10). Good things scandalize none but the bad mind (*de virg. vel.* 3). Give to Cæsar what is Cæsar's—his image on the coin ; give to God what is God's—his image in man, yourself (*de Idol.* 15).

But to this there is no end, and an end there must be. By his expression of Christian ideas in the natural language of Roman thought, by his insistence on the reality of the historic Jesus and on the inevitable consequences of human conduct, by his reference of all matters of life and controversy to the will of God manifested in Nature, in inspiration and in experience, Tertullian laid Western Christendom under a great debt, never very generously acknowledged. For us it may be as profitable to go behind the writings till we find the man, and to think of the manhood, with every power and every endowment, sensibility, imagination, energy, flung with passionate enthusiasm on the side of purity and righteousness, of God and Truth ; to think of the silent self-sacrifice freely and generously made for a despised cause, of a life-long readiness for martyrdom, of a spirit, unable to compromise, unable in its love of Christ to see His work undone by cowardice, indulgence and unfaith, and of a nature in all its fulness surrendered. That the Gospel could capture such a man as Tertullian, and, with all his faults of mind and temper, make of him what it did, was a measure of its power to transform the old world and a prophecy of its power to hold the modern world, too, and to make more of it as the ideas of Jesus find fuller realization and verification in every generation of Christian character and experience.

TABLE OF DATES

THE dates of birth and death of many men of note in antiquity may be guessed within a few years. In the case of men of letters it is safer to indicate roughly their period of literary activity. In the case of single books the problem of date is often bitterly controversial. As a framework, the names of the earlier Emperors and their years of accession are picked out in capitals below.

B.C.	
59	Consulship of Cæsar.
49	Cæsar crosses the Rubicon.
44	Murder of Cæsar.
42	Murder of Cicero.
	Battle of Philippi.
31	Battle of Actium and victory of Octavian (Augustus).
	AUGUSTUS in sole power from now onwards.
19	Death of Virgil.

A.D.	
14	TIBERIUS.
37	GAIUS (CALIGULA).
41	CLAUDIUS.
	Banishment of Seneca.
49	Recall of Seneca.
c. 50	Birth of Plutarch.
54	NERO.
	Seneca minister.
55	Murder of Britannicus.
59	Seneca retires.
65	Death of Seneca.
66	Nero on tour in Greece.
69	Year of revolts. Five Emperors.
	VESPASIAN.
70	Destruction of Jerusalem.
79	TITUS.
c. 80–117	Literary activity of Tacitus.
81	DOMITIAN.
c. 90	Epictetus at Nicopolis.
c. 95	*Epistle* of Clement of Rome (Lightfoot).
c. 97–109	*Letters* of Pliny.
96	NERVA.

A.D.	
98	TRAJAN.
c. 100–120	Literary activity of Juvenal.
later than 105	Death of Plutarch.
c. 110	Martyrdom of Ignatius.
117	HADRIAN.
c. 120	Birth of Irenæus.
c. 125	Birth of Lucian.
c. 130	Birth of Galen.
138	ANTONINUS PIUS.
c. 138	*Apology* of Aristides.
c. 148	*Apology* of Justin.
c. 150	*Shepherd* of Hermas.
c. 150–180	Literary activity of Pausanias.
c. 155 (?)	Birth of Tertullian.
c. 155–6	Martyrdom of Polycarp.
161	MARCUS AURELIUS.
c. 163–165	Martyrdom of Justin.
c. 173	*Apologia* of Apuleius.
c. 175	Literary activity of Tatian.
178	*The True Word* of Celsus.
c. 180 (*or later*)	Death of Lucian.
180	COMMODUS.
	Martyrdom of the Scillitan Martyrs.
c. 190–203	Clement of Alexandria in charge of the School of Alexandria.
c. 197–217	Literary activity of Tertullian.
197	*Apology* of Tertullian.
c. 200	Death of Irenæus.
202	Passion of Perpetua and Felicitas.
313	Edict of Milan.
325	Council of Nicæa.

INDEX

GREEK INDEX